WANTED

SECRETS OF A MAFIA WHISTLE-BLOWER

PAUL BLANCHARD

WANTED: SECRETS OF A MAFIA WHISTLE-BLOWER

Published by Whitevilla Publishing Limited
8 Peel Close, Heslington, York, YO10 5EN

www.secretsofamafiawhistle-blower.com
First published in 2021

ISBN: 978-0-9576391-2-6 (Paperback)
ISBN: 978-0-9576391-9-5 (Hardback)
ISBN: 978-0-9576391-3-3 (eBook)

© Paul Blanchard 2021
All rights reserved

The right of Paul Blanchard to be identified as the author of this work has been asserted by him in accordance with the Copyright, Designs and Patents Act 1988

A catalogue record for this book is available from the British Library

This book is a memoir. It reflects the author's recollections of experiences over time. Some names and characteristics have been changed to protect identities but, where applicable, those characters have been clearly indicated. Dialogue transcribed from recorded conversations is accurate. Other dialogue has been recreated as closely as possible but may not be verbatim.

Photo Credits

PA Images: John Palmer. Boris Berezovsky. Vladimir Putin. Tavistock Square Bus Explosion. Osma Bin Laden. Baltasar Garzon. Scot Young. Kings Cross Explosion. Madrid Bomb Explosion. Kenneth Noye. Jawad Akbar. Omar Khyam. Salahuddin Amin. Anthony Garcia. Waheed Mahhood. Kamal Zougam.
Metropolitan Police: Hasib Hussain. Germaine Lindsay. Mohammad Sidique Khan. Shehzad Tanweer.
Getty Images: Mohamed Atta.
Reach Publishing Services Limited: Darren Steadman.

Design & Typesetting by SWATT Books.
Printed by Clays Limited, Popson Street, Bungay, NR 35 1ED

For Gill, Sarah and Paul Jnr

Special thanks

To my son Paul Jnr, my daughter Sarah and my wife Gillian. To Sam Pearce of SWATT Books, Prof. Jaime Campaner, my Spanish lawyer Vidal Merchan, Sarah Hill, Keith Wood, solicitor at Lewis Nedas Law, George Hepburn Scott, barrister at Church Court Chambers and Mark Summers QC from Matrix Chambers. To Sam Stein QC, Richard Ferguson QC, Simon Eldritch, Barrister Yimi Yangye, solicitor Jim Nichol, Diana Ellis QC, Helen Lynch, Mr Justice Douglas Brown, Alex Wade at Reviewed & Cleared, Nick Earnshaw, Nick Peckham, David Rose, Jon Austin, Mike Laycock.

Contents

Foreword 7

Chapter One:	Madrid	9
Chapter Two:	Bird	13
Chapter Three:	Family	39
Chapter Four:	Tenerife	52
Chapter Five:	Clients	61
Chapter Six:	Offshore	72
Chapter Seven:	Bread	87
Chapter Eight:	Guayota	96
Chapter Nine:	Assets	120
Chapter Ten:	Isabella	140
Chapter Eleven:	Terror	162
Chapter Twelve:	Heat	180
Chapter Thirteen:	Cleanskins	202
Chapter Fourteen:	Betrayal	205
Chapter Fifteen:	Fightback	226
Chapter Sixteen:	'Fugitive'	244
Chapter Seventeen:	Trial & Error	264
Chapter Eighteen:	D-Day	282

Related Websites 299

Foreword

Over the past forty years, I've been told by family and friends that I have a unique story to tell about the shady side of business and the justice system – the internecine relationships between legitimate finance, 'dark' money, policing, petty crooks, mafias, terrorism and intelligence.

I always replied by saying that when I could tell the whole story, unencumbered by legal constraints, it would not be sanitised. It would be glamorous and grotesque, admiring and admonishing, uncomfortable and unflinching. Because that is the true story of my life.

So, what follows is a warts-and-all account. From my beginnings as a music-obsessed teenager from a humble Yorkshire village, via vermin-infested prisons, to the success of a millionaire offshore business expert and, eventually, a betrayal by supposed friends within Spain's police and intelligence community.

When I reflect on the past forty years, I realise that many problems were of my own making – whether through impulsiveness, recklessness, greed or a failure to think things through. This is not a legal *mea culpa*. I categorically deny any suggestion of guilt over what happened on Tenerife and what followed. But there is no doubt that I made some poor decisions. We're all human. We all make mistakes.

Regardless, my story should disturb anybody who still has unquestioning faith in the judicial process and the rule of law. I was no more a drug dealer than most pub landlords, no more a mafia member than most bankers, no more a fraudster than some intelligence officers.

I've battled for decades with police, solicitors, barristers, judges and intelligence agents – only to take regular steps back in my attempts to prove the truth. The only reason I can now tell this story is that, along the way, I recorded crucial conversations and retained essential documents. Without such firm and largely unchallenged evidence, presented to UK courts from 2019, I would still be labelled a fantasist by those who sought to discredit or prosecute me.

In the media, I've been described as a playboy, conman, fraudster and drug dealer. My family has endured slurs aimed at destroying my credibility ever since I was prosecuted for trading while insolvent. I cannot measure the hurt that has caused my loved ones over decades.

Without the support and love of my wife Gill, my children Sarah and Paul Jnr and loyal friends, I would not have had the strength to continue fighting the gangsters, bureaucrats and corrupt officials who, until as recently as June 2021, wanted to put me back in prison.

In the following pages, you will read about my experiences with legitimate offshore businessmen and some of the world's wealthiest people. But you will also learn about my dealings with Lebanese and Russian mafias and the new breed of international oligarchs dominating global business. You will read about money launderers, drug dealers, fraudsters and a myriad of global intelligence agents so confused about their role in the twenty-first century that it's sometimes hard to know whether they are on the side of right or wrong. Perhaps, as with most of us, they now stand somewhere between those pure extremes.

And then there are the terror networks. Those who help to fund and supply terror, and those actively plotting and carrying out attacks. The money men and practitioners behind some of the most devastating, deadly and sickening murders in recent years.

From alleged Irish republicans behind major frauds and Al-Qaeda cells exploiting the 'blood diamond' market in war-torn Sierra Leone, through to the evil ideologues behind mass murders in Madrid and London: I've had the misfortune to encounter many of these men and women. With others, notably some now-infamous gangsters and terrorists, I spotted the threat they posed and tried to report them, only for the authorities to turn on me.

This brings me neatly to Mohamed Derbah – a one-time friend who allegedly battled his way to the top of Europe's underworld.

On Tenerife, locals refer to a malignant deity that lived atop Mount Teide, the awe-inspiring volcano which dominates the island's skyline. Tenerife's original god-fearing inhabitants named this dark force *Guayota*. They described his home as the gateway to hell or the underworld.

When I discovered the truth about Mohamed, I couldn't help but draw parallels with *Guayota*. But readers should make up their own minds.

My reward for risking everything to fight gangsters, mafias and terrorism was a prison sentence in 2007 and a recent extradition request from Spain, a demand which could have led to a further fifteen years behind bars.

It is now 2021, and I write this in the warm afterglow of a Court of Appeal victory against Spain which, while not definitive, was a major step in an eighteen-year battle to prove my innocence. Along the way, I faced the longest-running Proceeds of Crime Act (POCA) case in British history.

My legal team over the past three years have been masters of their trade. I would especially like to thank Keith Wood, solicitor at Lewis Nedas Law, George Hepburn Scott, barrister at Church Court Chambers, and Mark Summers QC from Matrix Chambers: three elite-level professionals who restored some of my faith in the UK's creaking and underfunded legal system.

I'm exhausted but elated. The following pages will explain why.

Paul Blanchard
October 2021

CHAPTER ONE
Madrid

Spain was warned. But Madrid did not know what was coming.

During three horror-filled minutes from 7.37am on 11 March 2004, Spain – the dazzling, sun-drenched state which had been my second home for six years – suffered the worst terrorist attack in its history.

Ten bombs exploded inside four packed commuter trains travelling to Atocha station, south of Madrid's city centre.

Once the smoke had cleared – amid the twisted and bloodied wreck of seats, body parts and unexploded devices – emergency services personnel recovered the bodies of 191 innocent victims. Another 2,000 people were injured, many physically and mentally scarred for life.

It was Europe's worst terrorist atrocity since the bombing of Pan Am Flight 103 over Lockerbie, Scotland in 1988.

What became known as The Madrid Bombings, or '11-M' to appalled Spaniards, was an attack of such ferocity that the limbs of unsuspecting victims heading to work that bright Thursday morning were blown straight through train windows and into nearby buildings.

The senseless and indiscriminate violence reflected Pablo Picasso's brutal masterpiece, *Guernica*, hanging two hundred metres away from Atocha Station inside the Museo Reina Sofia.

For many, the bombing of the Basque town of Guernica during the Spanish Civil War signalled the start of Franco's strategy of targeting local populations. More than seventy years later, terrorists had done the same under the shadow cast by Picasso's dark reminder of man's capacity for brutality.

The powerful Goma-2 explosives used in the Madrid bombs had been bought illegally from a retired miner in northern Spain by a drug dealer linked to the Moroccan Islamic Combatant Group (GMIC), a Salafi jihadist outfit affiliated with Al-Qaeda.

The timing of the Madrid attacks may not have been a coincidence. The bombs exploded 911 days after the epoch-defining 11 September 2001, or 9/11, attacks on New York's World Trade Centre and the Pentagon building in Virginia.

More specifically, the Madrid bombings took place three days before a Spanish general election, at which prime minister Jose Maria Aznar, who led the country into the unpopular 2003 Iraq War, hoped to win another term for the Falangist conservatives of the Partido Popular (PP).

In the immediate and confusing aftermath of 11-M, opinion was divided over who was responsible for the atrocities.

Many correctly feared that Islamic extremists had hijacked the general election to highlight Aznar's support for the Iraq War.

There was some justification for this instinctive belief. In October 2003, Osama Bin Laden – Al-Qaeda's notorious figurehead – had released a video in which he warned Western states with soldiers in Iraq of reprisal attacks.

With Spain's election result in the balance, the bombings had the potential to unseat Aznar. He already faced stiff competition from the Spanish Socialist Workers' Party (PSOE), led by Jose Luiz Rodriguez Zapatero, committed to withdrawing troops from Iraq.

Possibly in response to this threat, Aznar and his officials initially dismissed the idea that 11-M was the work of Islamic extremists. Instead, his team suggested the Basque separatists of the Euskadi Ta Askatasuna, commonly known as ETA, were to blame.

Aznar had some success in tackling ETA before 11-M, and it seems likely that forces within his party believed voters would support their hard-line approach if people thought the bombings were the work of Basque terrorists.

There was just one problem: most evidence linked to 11-M did not point towards ETA. Days before the general election, Spanish citizens took to the streets to demand that Aznar's government revealed what it really knew about the Madrid attacks.

Perceived self-interest by the PP after the bombings proved to be Aznar's undoing, and the socialists won the election. To this day, and despite overwhelming evidence, many PP supporters refuse to accept the bombings were the work of Al-Qaeda-inspired extremists.

But while the political disputes over responsibility for the bombings raged, Spain's police and intelligence agencies leapt into action.

In the days after 11-M, officers located key members of the terror cell behind the attacks. When armed police surrounded the group's hideout in the Madrid suburb of Leganes, several suspects blew up the apartment – killing themselves and a police officer.

But the uncomfortable truth is that Europe's police and intelligence agencies, particularly those in Spain, had known about Al-Qaeda operating locally years before 11-M.

Mohamed Atta, the Egyptian-born leader of the 9/11 hijackers, travelled to Spain in July 2001 to meet with senior Al-Qaeda contacts. This was just two months before Atta crashed American Airlines Flight 11 into the north tower of the World Trade Centre.

Later that summer, Atta flew into Madrid from Florida, where he had undertaken his pilot's training, via Switzerland, where he purchased two Swiss Army knives. The blades were possibly used to overpower cabin crew on the hijacked American Airlines jet weeks later.

After landing in Spain, Atta travelled east to Tarragona, a coastal town near Barcelona. En route, he picked up Yemeni national Ramzi bin al-Shibh, one of Bin Laden's right-hand men in Europe, who had landed at Reus

Airport. After staying for one night at a Tarragona hotel, the two men disappeared under the radar – most likely into a local Al-Qaeda safe house.

Atta and bin al-Shibh had been close allies since their days together in Hamburg, Germany. From their hideout in Tarragona, US intelligence services believe the two men planned the final phase of 9/11.

According to interviews conducted with Ramzi bin al-Shibh after his arrest following 9/11, it was while in Tarragona that he informed Atta about Bin Laden's preferred list of targets: the World Trade Centre, the Pentagon and the Capitol Building in Washington. The last of these was a likely target of the Lebanese pilot who hijacked United Airlines Flight 93, which crashed in a Pennsylvania field after passengers attempted to seize back control of the jet.

Ramzi bin al-Shibh also claims that Bin Laden expressly forbade an attack on US nuclear facilities, indicating that Al-Qaeda operatives considered something far worse than what took place on 9/11.

But it was not just the terrorists behind attacks on America who frequented Spain. The country's lax fiscal, banking and (former) extradition rules had long made it a hub for international money laundering operations.

British readers will know that, from the 1960s, this attracted the strangely celebrated criminals of London's underworld to Spain's shores – including members of the gang which carried out the Great Train Robbery. Rubbing shoulders with these criminals in Spain's resorts would be the usual suspects you'd find in the drunk tank on a Friday night: career fraudsters, confidence tricksters, low-level drug dealers, smugglers and dodgy traders.

In recent years, Spain has also attracted a new generation of highly organised, ruthlessly violent and globally connected international crime syndicates:

'McMafias'.

At least, that's what we now call these organisations, thanks to Misha Glenny's superb 2008 book of that name, which explained how powerful and mega-rich criminal networks operate.

McMafias do not sell weekend 'party bags' of cocaine or marijuana. They move cargo containers full of drugs sourced directly from Afghanistan, Lebanon or Peru.

They don't dabble in property fraud. They own entire villages of holiday homes that act as bases for industrial-scale timeshare scams.

McMafias don't just secure the odd gun for wannabe train robbers or stick-up merchants. They shift entire shipments of rifles, rocket launchers and explosives. Enough weaponry to start wars. That is precisely what some do for clients willing to pay them enough, including national governments, rebel troops and terror networks.

But mafias, their middlemen and supply chain clients all needed some way of banking their ill-gotten gains, which run into tens of billions of dollars annually.

And that's where I enter this story. I moved money around the world, legitimately, on behalf of hundreds of offshore clients.

Before 11-M, Spain knew how alleged mafias and suspected Al-Qaeda financiers operated. The country's top investigative judges, police and intelligence agents knew how global criminal networks laundered cash to fund terror directly under the noses of authorities in Madrid.

Spain knew about Al-Qaeda's links with the alleged Lebanese mafia and its vast network of criminal and legitimate associates who exploit the tax benefits and financial secrecy offered by the country's 'offshore' centres on the Canary Islands.

How do I know?

Because I told Spain's intelligence services.

I was Spain's 'offshore asset'.

CHAPTER TWO

Bird

England, October 1992.

The heavy, metallic clang of the cell door and rustle of keys would be accompanied by a scream from the latest crack junkie going 'cold turkey' along the corridor – hollering desperate pleas for a fresh hit while guards pinned him down.

Amid such cacophonies of noise, I awoke with a start each morning before shooting bolt upright. Momentarily disoriented, I'd glance over excitedly, hoping to meet Gill's eyes.

Nothing.

Except, perhaps, for the startled stare of a shameless cell mate squatting over the bucket that doubled as our cell toilet.

Welcome to Her Majesty's Prison (HMP) Durham in north-east England: a sprawling complex of buildings close to the River Wear, east of the elevated castle that dominates the city's skyline.

Twenty-eight years ago, UK retailer WH Smith withdrew vinyl records from sale because compact discs had stolen the market. That same year, computer geeks created the first popular Internet browser, IBM produced a prototype smartphone with touch-screen technology, and the world's first text message was sent. NASA's Ulysses space probe skimmed past Jupiter, six hundred million kilometres from Earth, on its way to the sun. The rate of human progress was mind-boggling.

But at HMP Durham in 1992, inmates still had to shit in a bucket.

The original prison, some of which is still in use today, was built in 1819 – the year Queen Victoria was born. I did not expect luxury at 'Her Majesty's Pleasure'. But to say that conditions were appalling when I began my sentence would be an understatement. Romans had access to indoor toilets two thousand years before cellmates at Durham.

Still, it was home. And we were the lucky ones: at least our bucket had an ill-fitting lid.

Once the crack addicts screams died down, the inmates' day would grind into action and the ever-present background din of prison life intensified. As well as the clanging metal doors and rattling keys, regular alarms battled for your attention with the echoes of hundreds of simultaneous conversations bouncing from walls and ceilings.

Prison discussions often occur at ear-bursting volume because many inmates – usually the younger, testosterone-laden wannabe gangsters – cannot express themselves without anger. If you're not shouting or being shouted at, you are forced to talk loudly over the furore created by others. For this reason, most inmates have little chance of hearing anything spoken more than three cells away. So, you hear everything, and yet nothing, in prison. Background chatter is an indiscernible constant. Once the morning roll call starts, the noise doesn't stop until lights-out signals the end of another day inside. You get used to it.

What you never get used to, however, is the smell.

Each prison has a unique aroma yet, as with most perfumes, each stink consists of the same key ingredients. In Durham in 1992, it was three parts industrial detergent or bleach, two parts sweat and body odour, two parts shit, two parts urine and at least three parts smoke.

In some parts of the prison, this *Parfum de Durham* was thick enough to induce dizziness. For most inmates, though, while the odour hung heavy in the air, it was tolerable. It merely left some of Britain's toughest men permanently pulling faces like they'd been sucking lemons.

There were areas of the prison unaffected by the smell, including the kitchen, laundry and showers. But wherever you were permitted to wander, fresh air was at a premium. Unless you enjoyed the forty-five minutes of daily exercise in the yard. In which case, Durham's regulation grey skies, biting winds and incessant drizzle awaited.

As with many prisons in Britain, almost every wall inside HMP Durham was a mind-numbing tint of magnolia. In 1992, only intermittent streaks of nicotine yellow generated by the relentless smoke exhalation broke the visual assault. The peeling doors, flaking skirting boards and window frames in the remand wing were, somewhat mockingly, a shade of blue that resembled police uniforms.

Everything in HMP Durham looked and felt worn. Every mop was threadbare, every dishcloth discoloured to black, every prisoner's uniform smelt of sweat or must. The food trays were often so dented and out of shape you couldn't help but wonder which poor sod had taken one full in the face during the many violent assaults which punctuated the day.

HMP Durham was merely a reflection of the broader penal regime. Twenty-eight years ago, Britain's prison system didn't work because it was an under-funded and broken patchwork of crowded pre-Victorian estates populated by lunatics, egos and wannabe dictators. And that was just the staff.

Not much has changed.

* * *

They say in prison, 'don't do the crime if you can't do the time'. I couldn't agree more.

But what if you did not do the crime?

Heaven knows how many inmates claim they are innocent, even those caught with their fingers in a shop till. But some are innocent and, in 1992, I was among that number.

Prison is among the toughest of physical and psychological challenges under any set of circumstances. But dealing with incarceration when you shouldn't even be inside, a loss of liberty and dignity so absolute that you find yourself squatting over that steel bucket in full view of violent sex offenders, takes a level of determination most folk do not possess. Those men break down in jail. Some get aggressive and commit further crimes. Others go nuts. Some do both.

* * *

So how did an innocent man end up behind bars?

On 29 October 1992, I was found guilty of conspiracy to supply 'ecstasy' – the party drug of choice across Europe's hedonistic club and illegal rave scene. As I saw it, there was just one sticking point: I had never supplied, or conspired to supply, drugs in my life. Unless you counted paracetamol or Milk of Magnesia which, I confess, I gave to my kids when they were unwell.

I was forty-seven-years-old and my partying days were long behind me. While I'd heard of ecstasy, I barely knew what it was.

Yet on a cold, crisp January morning in 1992, shortly after dropping off my children Sarah and Paul Jnr at school, I watched two cars screech to a halt outside my home in Yorkshire, northern England. A group of heavily built men leapt from the vehicles, trampled through my front garden and, within milliseconds, I heard a series of shuddering knocks at the door.

I thought I was about to be burgled. Anxiously, I flipped open the letterbox and questioned the men through the slot.

One of them bellowed: "We're police officers. Please open the door, Mr Blanchard. We have a warrant to search the premises."

When I swung the door open, the unfamiliar man standing before me was smiling and clutching a search warrant. He looked as smug as a dog that had just discovered it could lick its testicles.

DC Kenneth Wilkes from the Regional Crime Squad in the north-east of England introduced himself.

Before I could speak, I was told I was being arrested on suspicion of conspiracy to supply drugs. After a cursory wave of Wilkes' warrant, several plain-clothed officers stormed past me and began rifling through my home.

When the detectives had finished their search, my house looked like a flash-mob of drunken, disoriented burglars wearing blindfolds and muddy boots had paid a visit. Two officers seized reams of business files from the ground-floor office.

I was taken to a police station in South Shields, Tyneside, and allowed to phone my solicitor Jim Nichol. He arranged for a local lawyer to be present during my police interview and advised me to say "no comment" to all questions. I also called my long-term partner, Gill, so that she could be at my home when Sarah and Paul Jnr arrived back from school. They would be devastated.

My first thought was that the raid was a terrible mistake that would quickly become obvious to competent detectives. That was until somebody mentioned the name Richard Henson.

* * *

I had known Richard Henson since 1984, when he'd been head of security at a rock festival I promoted. He was an ex-con determined to go straight.

Tall and heavily built, Richard looked like he could tear a man's head off with his bare hands. But he was polite and respectful. That combination made him an ideal head of security. He'd had his problems, I later learned, including a prison sentence in the late 1980s. But we'd stayed in touch, even after he split from his girlfriend and returned to his native north-east from Yorkshire.

When Richard was jobless in 1991, I'd loaned him a BMW car in return for picking up my Tenerife-based business partner Carlos Giacometti, and other clients, from airports. He acted as my company's chauffer and, in return, used the car, had a mobile phone and a monthly wage.

Once back home in the north-east, Henson met widower Alison Kay through his new girlfriend, Pearl Ritchie. Kay's husband had been a police officer whose untimely death had left her financially secure. Richard helped Kay, doing small jobs around her house and Henson introduced me to Alison when she needed financial advice. Kay and I discussed her options, but no business materialised.

One evening, shortly after leaving Kay's home, Richard was stopped by police in South Shields. Officers found twenty-six ecstasy tablets in the car Henson was driving, which was my BMW. Worse followed when officers later searched Kay's home and discovered a stash of 1,000 ecstasy pills in the garage.

It transpired that the police had Henson under surveillance for some time. He and Kay were arrested. Kay was released without charge after denying any knowledge of the drugs. Her release and apparent exoneration all happened suspiciously quickly.

Henson was interviewed and initially admitted to detectives that he'd acted alone. He told officers that, as far as he was aware, Kay did not know the pills were stored in her garage.

Shortly after this, Henson's girlfriend, Pearl, called to ask whether I would visit Richard while he was on remand. She also provided me with the name of the detective in charge of the case, DC Wilkes, so that I could arrange the return of my BMW.

Big mistake. An honest mistake, but a mistake nonetheless. I should have made the arrangements through my solicitor. Suddenly, I was directly linked to Richard's arrest. And I had a previous criminal record, albeit for the business-related crime of trading while insolvent.

I kept my promise to Pearl and visited Henson at HMP Durham.

Richard apologised for the embarrassment caused by his arrest, but he was surprisingly open about dealing ecstasy. I was gobsmacked and couldn't understand why he had risked so much – his freedom and his relationship with Pearl – for what sounded like a piffling amount of money.

By the time I made a second visit, I'd made up my mind. I wished Richard well, but decided to sever contact with him. I didn't need any hassle from the police and could not afford the reputational damage of being associated with a drug dealer. I was a single parent with a criminal history, and my first loyalty was to Gill and my children. After that, my commitment was to my business and Carlos.

I thought I was making a mature and responsible decision – being the grown-up I'd not been when I received my first conviction. But on reflection, I could have handled the situation more delicately. Henson was angry that I'd ended our friendship when he'd reached a low point. He wanted to lash out and was desperate to save his skin.

I should have seen the subsequent development, the raid on my home, coming. But I was naïve and thinking of protecting my family. I knew nothing about the murky world in which Henson operated.

* * *

After being held in custody on Tyneside for two days, I was taken to South Shields Magistrates Court and charged with conspiracy to supply drugs.

I'd followed Jim Nichol's advice and said little during my interview. Instead, I'd wanted to discover what led the police to believe I was dealing drugs.

At court, prosecutors claimed they had evidence of my involvement in supplying ecstasy. They had also identified twenty-two different bank accounts linked to me. For that reason, the prosecution team argued, I had the means to flee. So, they urged the magistrate to keep me in custody, without bail, until the case was committed to crown court. To my astonishment, the magistrate agreed. I was remanded in custody and sent to join Henson at HMP Durham.

'Evidence of involvement in supplying ecstasy'?

'Means to abscond'?

I was a forty-seven-year-old single-parent with a settled home life, children whom I loved and drove to school each day, a girlfriend I adored and an addiction to little more than coffee and work. I couldn't tell the difference between ecstasy pills and Smarties. What exactly, Jim Nichol and I wondered, was the 'evidence' of my involvement with the drugs trade?

Oh, and of course there were multiple bank accounts linked to me: I owned or co-owned several businesses. Most of my firms had combinations of client accounts and deposit accounts. In the business world, that is often done to separate or ring-fence cash for legal reasons and to protect clients. I also had several personal bank accounts. The police and prosecutors seemed to think this was somehow suspicious – indicating they knew little, if anything, about legitimate business.

Jim quickly discovered that the key evidence against me was a dubious-sounding confession made by Henson long after he was arrested. It turned out that Henson's official account of his involvement had changed significantly from when he was first collared. Shortly after I'd severed ties with him, Henson had implicated me in his drugs scam. The timing could not have been more obvious.

Henson belatedly told Wilkes that I was the Mr Big behind his planned sale of ecstasy.

Other evidence was gleaned from Alison Kay, who, it first appeared, supported Henson's account.

The prosecution case was that absurd. But Jim Nichol had a hunch that, even after Henson's change of story, something else had influenced the police's actions.

Despite feeling anxious and upset about the allegations against me, I was confident the case would collapse when Henson's lies were carefully unpicked by well-trained detectives interested in a forensic pursuit of truth.

The problem was, there would be no Hercule Poirot investigating these issues. Instead, my case seemed to be handled by a police unit that resembled the Keystone Cops.

So it was that I joined the list of people to be incarcerated at HMP Durham. Notable former inmates include the child-killers Ian Brady and Myra Hindley, as well as gangsters such as the Kray twins, John McVicar and 'Mad' Frankie Fraser.

* * *

Seated in the cramped, locked cell on the prison van to HMP Durham, I heard someone shout.

"Hey, you! Are you Blanchard? The bloke from York who Henson's grassed-up?"

Somewhat taken aback to hear my name spoken aloud, I stumbled over a reply.

"Er…yes…that's me," I said tentatively.

"I'll talk to you in the reception, mate," the faceless voice said. "Henson's a fucking cunt."

Upon arrival at HMP Durham, those of us inside the van were taken to a holding area. There, I was intercepted by a man unphased by his surroundings who moved with purpose.

"I'm David. We spoke on the meat wagon," a tall, lanky Geordie with long hair said while offering a handshake. David's appearance did not fit his voice. I'd expected a squat, bald-headed thug. But he seemed friendly enough.

I nodded and extended my right hand. "I'm Paul. Don't take this the wrong way, David, but you look like you know your way around. You're the only one here with a sense of direction," I smiled.

"Been on remand here for six months. Today was just another court visit. It gets me out of the house," my new friend joked. "We've heard all about how you got stitched up by 'Supergrass' Henson."

Vital information was coming at me quickly. The cramped and uncomfortable journey had disoriented me. But I was trying to figure out how my case was already familiar to inmates and what that meant for me inside.

I was a well-educated country boy, about as middle-class as you get in prison, and I'd been charged with supplying drugs. Naively, I wondered whether some of my new housemates would take offence at the mere sight of me. I nodded again to David.

After an awkward few seconds, I joked: "Fuck me! The prison grapevine works quickly."

David beamed, almost proudly. "Ay, so it does, Paul. We're like the intelligence services in here, man.

"We're inside every court in the region, every day. Everybody knows everybody else's business around here. Especially when snitches are involved," he added.

"That's good news for you. But that fucker Henson? He's on a hiding to nothing. Every time he opens his mouth, someone's going to want to fill it with their fist."

I breathed a sigh of relief. My first appearance inside couldn't have gone any better, yet I'd barely said a word. It seemed that was the secret to doing 'bird'.

* * *

British justice at its weakest is a joke. But losing my liberty when I knew I was innocent? That was no laughing matter.

I've seen men so eaten up by prison that they hanged themselves, cut their wrists to ribbons or opened other veins out of desperation to escape the hell of doing time. While many were as guilty as sin – and some crimes are simply unforgivable acts for which there are no excuses – I know that at least some were either innocent or received a custodial sentence when an alternative punishment would have been appropriate.

Most of the men I met inside were probably guilty and had made terrible mistakes, some with extreme consequences. Many had committed the sort of crimes that heaped misery on innocent victims and their families. But prisoners are still human beings—men with wives, children, families and futures.

In the 1990s, the squalid conditions in which British prisoners served their sentences were not conducive to rehabilitation and, for many, punished men disproportionately for their crimes.

Mistakes get made by the authorities, too. And each error within the criminal justice system effectively steals a life because it doesn't matter how mentally or physically tough you are – and I've been cellmates with some of the toughest men in Britain – injustice eats away at you from the inside. By the time others can see it, part of you is lost forever.

Those first few nights inside HMP Durham's remand wing, amid the echoing sound of clanging doors, bust-ups between inmates and cries for help, were among the darkest of my life. I'd be a liar if I said I wasn't scared. Mentally, I'm a tough character. But I was shit scared.

I'd lie awake at night panicking about getting targeted by thugs, or what Gill thought of this ludicrous situation. My mind would wander but always came back to the same concerns. I'd fret over whether the kids would be OK, and how my family and friends viewed what had happened. Mentally, I beat myself up over how I'd handled Henson. I couldn't help but think that if I'd eased away from him, rather than abruptly severed contact, then perhaps he would not have turned on me.

I was still confident that I'd be cleared because the Crown's evidence was flimsy. But the mere fact that I was already inside and facing trial scared me senseless. Internally, of course. Externally, I forced myself to develop a hardened persona. You can't show weakness in prison.

* * *

You get used to bird. You have to, or you will go mad. It is hard, physically and mentally, because it's so mind-numbingly repetitive. Harder when you're ill. Harder still when you have lost heart because your appeal against a ludicrous conviction has been dismissed. That's when a burning sense of injustice can turn into a rage that becomes a hindrance. An innocent man in prison walks an emotional tightrope, torn between fury and cooperation for the sake of his sanity.

The banality of prison life threatens you more than other inmates.

Don't get me wrong, though: trouble is never far away if that's what you're looking for. Pumped-up warriors looking for fights: all muscle, sinew and smuggled-in 'roid rage. You watch them carefully.

On most days, the combination of goodfellas, quiet hard men and outright lunatics on each wing keep the peace. The simmering undercurrent of violence, while never far from the surface, is usually subordinate to an understanding that 'mutually assured destruction' applies in prison even more appropriately than in a Cold War context.

If you start a fight inside, you'd best end it quickly or there will be a dozen other inmates – friends of the aggrieved – who will finish you. That's generally what keeps the peace. That and the decent screws. Only some of them are cunts.

I'm not a fighter. I'll stand my ground, of course, because I'm nobody's whipping boy. But I don't throw punches unless I have no choice. If you fight in prison, you can get seriously hurt. I've seen it happen too many times: the biggest of men brought to their knees by the fury of a mob. The crack of bone and the crunch of cartilage and gristle. A pack of hyenas feeding on a single lion.

There are exceptions to this rule, of course. Genuine prison hardmen – those who could fight three big men at once, knock each of them to the floor and walk away with little more than a bloody lip and a vengeful smile. There are only a handful of such inmates in any prison, even though many will tell you they belong in that category.

In my experience, the genuine tough inmates tended to be quietly confident types: those who exert authority without the need to shout and scream. So, whenever a prisoner claimed they were 'king of the wing', I knew they were probably talking nonsense. Instead, I would observe prisoner interaction from a distance to work out who the real powerbrokers were – and avoid them or befriend them.

No, violence was not my biggest enemy in prison. That title went to the monotony of passing thousands of hours, many with just your thoughts for company. That can drive you insane.

* * *

David, the beanpole Geordie I'd met upon arrival, was proven right.

I quickly befriended several of HMP Durham's toughest prisoners simply because of how my court case unfolded. My co-accused, Henson, had turned Queen's Evidence to try to mitigate his sentence.

Big mistake.

To turn Queen's Evidence means that as both a participant in, and witness to, an alleged crime, you are prepared to assist the prosecution's case by ratting on your co-accused. While this may convince a judge to be lenient towards a compliant witness, the act is considered an unforgivable violation of the prisoners' unwritten code: never become a grass.

In prison, if you 'turn QE' then other inmates consider you on a par with wife-beaters or child molesters. Not only are grasses targeted, but the person against whom they give evidence is often singled out for additional support.

By the time I arrived at HMP Durham, David had ensured that key inmates knew Henson, who had been placed on the same wing as me, had turned QE.

To my surprise and relief, I found that other prisoners were sympathetic despite me never having been a career criminal and sharing few experiences with my new peers. In contrast, Henson had a tough time. While I was secretly pleased, it also made me nervous that my giant former head of security might seek revenge.

My nervousness intensified after I was attacked in my cell shortly after arriving at Durham. The incident had nothing to do with Henson, but it was a sharp reminder of my vulnerability in prison.

A younger inmate had taken offence to the fact that I looked and sounded different from most prisoners: "all educated and shit", to use his words. One day, the lad entered my cell and rushed at me with a broom handle. Thankfully I managed to deflect the blow and landed a couple of quick punches in return. The youngster fled, presumably still angry about the fact that I could conjugate verbs.

I should have been pleased. I'd fought off a thug and could have milked the situation. But the whole event made me feel exposed. I was still new inside, had no idea how long I would be there, did not fully understand my fellow inmates and was potentially vulnerable to those who posed a genuine threat.

After just a day or two on remand, David approached me to provide some moral support. It turned out he was quite the fixer, and he'd been impressively busy.

"Listen, mate," he began. "I know Henson's a big feller, but you'll have no problems with him in this prison. All the lads will look after you. If there's anything you need, just ask."

It was reassuring. But being the new boy inside, I wondered how true it would prove to be. I didn't have to wait long to find out.

Within a day or two, Henson and I bumped into each other in the prison exercise yard. The *Parfum de Durham* ensured I was always eager to get some fresh air but, initially, I knew few inmates and exercised alone.

One bitterly cold morning, Henson approached and asked if we could talk. I said nothing. My heart was beating faster than usual – Richard loomed large.

Seemingly out of nowhere, a familiar voice broke the silence.

"Leave him alone, you fucking grass!" David bellowed from across the yard. "We're watching and waiting, Henson!" My Guardian Angel had been walking with several friends and was, as always, keeping one eye on developments.

"I just want to talk," Henson shouted back, looking around at several large men now staring back at him. Richard looked back towards David and then me, as though he had to go through my minder.

I indicated to David that it was OK and nodded to Henson to continue talking. I'd still not said a word. Inadvertently, that was becoming quite a habit.

Richard was full of remorse and said he would talk to his solicitor about retracting the police statement in which he'd implicated me. I nodded.

Lord knows where my silent, brooding Clint Eastwood-like veneer had developed. It was a natural defensive reaction, but it worked well enough. More importantly, though, David's intervention and the fact that several huge inmates were demonstrably on hand to intervene, proved that I was a protected man.

Several friendships that developed in jail reinforced the point.

* * *

Tommy Hindmarch was a feared, but widely respected, man inside HMP Durham.

At first glance, he looked like the archetypal con people would go out of their way to avoid. Barrel-chested, Popeye-sized arms and heavily tattooed, Tommy spoke with a heavy Sunderland accent and was proudly blue-collar. He was on remand for armed robbery, was universally regarded as a genuine hardman and knew many of northern England's most prominent villains. I saw first-hand how inmates were intimidated by him.

Yet Tommy also had an innately friendly side and a dry, wicked sense of humour. We gelled from the moment we met. It probably helped that, physically, I did not present as a threat. I stood just under six feet tall and was sinewy. I could look after myself, but people would not cling to the side of corridors when I walked past – as they did with Tommy and his pals. To that extent, I was a disarming figure.

Hindmarch was a cleaner on my wing. Perhaps counter-intuitively, everybody wanted to be a cleaner in prison. For a start, it was a paid role – and that meant extra cash, which gave cleaners spending power within the sizable black market for prison contraband.

But more pertinently, cleaners had more freedom than other inmates. Their cell doors would be unlocked for most of the day so that they could perform their tasks of mopping floors, dishing out meals in the servery, washing up and keeping the all-important wing toilets in usable order: a role of near-heroic proportions if you recall that the alternative was *that* bucket.

The physical freedom afforded by having your cell door unlocked was a considerable benefit. Cleaners exercised more than most inmates and the activity helped with the most essential thing inside prison: passing the time.

But the psychological benefit of being a cleaner outweighed even the physical bonus. Cleaners could move around and enjoy a sense of freedom, even within the relentless magnolia-splashed walls of HMP Durham. They also had more opportunities to escape the terrible *Parfum*.

After Tommy and I had been friends for a while, he helped me secure a cleaning role. We also became cellmates, which gave me greater credibility on the remand wing.

Cleaning HMP Durham was hard work, but the days passed quicker than when I had to sit around for long periods with nothing but my regrets with which to keep busy. We made sure the wing was as spotless as it could be. Believe it or not, most prisoners took pride in keeping the wing tidy – though some disgusting blokes happily lived like pigs in shit.

Our cleaning detail also used the extra freedom to have some fun.

Meals would be dished up from the servery, but there was no canteen like you see in Hollywood films about prisons. Instead, inmates would attend the servery to collect their food and eat it back in their cell.

The food itself would be wheeled in from the kitchen on giant metal serving trays. It was generally boiled meat, tasteless mash or scrawny-looking chips, and vegetables so old and stewed that they appeared to have lost any nutritional value before Hitler invaded Poland.

However, there were days when the prison kitchen staff would surpass themselves and produce a dish which, if you squinted and pinched your nose, almost passed as home cooking. It was generally a curry or chicken casserole.

On such occasions, the cleaners designated to serve food would ensure that hefty portions were set aside for our group. We'd simply remove the best-looking chicken legs or cuts of meat and place the extra pieces in a concealed tray below the serving counter. Towards the end of dinner, we'd dish out the best food to ourselves while the inmates who were late to join the queue made do with the dregs. Which usually meant eating the unpopular vegetarian option – these were northern men in the 1990s, remember!

You'd be surprised how many fights would break out in the servery. Often, a jack-the-lad inmate would demand a second or bigger serving, but without Oliver Twist's faultless manners. With the screws looking on, those serving were careful not to cave in to such demands, or they faced being stripped of their coveted role. But that didn't stop some inmates from kicking-off when their demand for more was refused. I dodged a few flying metal trays and fists.

During one dinner period, a muscular and loudmouth newbie made the mistake of ordering Tommy to serve him extra chips. Tommy knew that he couldn't and nonchalantly refused. The affronted youngster flew into a rage. Still seething, he later made the mistake of door-stepping Tommy in our cell. I kept guard outside while the matter was settled.

It didn't take long.

To say that Tommy gave the egotistical kid a pasting would be an understatement: the lad was hurled around the room like a ragdoll. Seconds later, the youngster stumbled past me on the way out – his face a bloodied mess.

To his credit, the chastised newbie never complained to the screws. And he never bothered Tommy again.

For his part, Tommy had tried to avoid the confrontation. But being able to look after yourself is in the Hindmarch DNA. All these years later, Tommy's son is a successful Mixed Martial Arts fighter. The big fella himself, now a far calmer figure than the pre-prison armed robber, still works out regularly – often performing hundreds of press-ups on camera. Tommy and I remain firm friends, and I still wouldn't get on the wrong side of him.

★ ★ ★

Tommy Hindmarch introduced me to another fearsome inmate who became a good friend.

Willy Hunter was well-connected across the north-east's underworld. When I met him, this man-mountain from North Shields was on remand for murder. One night while out drinking, Hunter had got involved in a fight with a group of rugby players from Sheffield. It was the sort of alcohol-fuelled brawl that often ends in bruised egos, a few cuts and little more. But one of Willy's punches caught his victim in a vulnerable spot on the temple and inadvertently caused death.

There is no excusing what Willy Hunter did, and he was the first to admit that when I met him. Hunter wreaked indescribable devastation on the victim and the victim's family. I write that not to dramatise the incident, but to acknowledge the real tragedy and terror unleashed by violence. The victim was somebody's son and would most likely have become a husband and father. Willy took that away – however drunken, intimidating and confused the circumstances were.

I've heard thousands of prison tales about fighting, feuds and revenge. But once you scratch below the surface of most anecdotes, the fights led to more violence, bloodshed and tragedy.

Despite this, I am a firm believer in the rehabilitative function of prison and giving everybody a second chance to break cycles of violence, offending behaviour and addiction. Prison isn't, and should never be, just about punishment – even if most jails can barely afford to support rehabilitation programmes.

Willy did not intend to kill anybody that night on Tyneside. When I heard Hunter had been charged with murder, we discussed how his lawyers should push for a lesser charge because it was not a pre-meditated or cold-blooded act.

Of course, Willy's solicitor was already working on that: a decision that would succeed and give Hunter a second chance in life.

★ ★ ★

Being friends with Tommy and Willy meant that other inmates rarely targeted me. For my part, I helped both men, and other members of our tight-knit group, prepare for court hearings by assisting with the seemingly endless paperwork.

I also dished out some business advice while I worked on my case.

***

On Tuesday 21 January 1992, Richard Henson appeared outside my prison cell and shouted: "Get Nichol up here to see me – alright?"

Later that day, a sealed envelope was slipped under the cell door. It was marked: 'Statement to Mr Paul Blanchard by Richard Henson.' Inside was Richard's revised account for me and, more importantly, my solicitor Jim Nichol.

The letter revealed that Henson had made a false statement to DC Wilkes at South Shields Police Station on Christmas Eve in 1991, that I had nothing to do with supplying drugs and that Richard made his false claims to get bail and a reduced sentence.

My heart jumped and I felt an adrenaline rush. I was euphoric: "At last," I thought. "Henson's told the truth – I'm getting out!"

How naïve.

Within weeks, Henson was refused the bail that he believed his original police confession would secure. Worse was to follow. Richard was on remand for alleged offences relating to the possession of drugs. However, he was told he would be charged with conspiracy to supply drugs – the same, more serious charge I faced.

At a committal hearing on 27 March 1992, Henson and I pleaded not guilty to all charges. But it soon dawned on Richard that he was locked into giving QE. He was advised by his lawyers that he should not withdraw his earlier statement and was instead expected to be called by the prosecution in their case against me.

Shortly after our hearing, Henson sought protection under 'Rule 43', which allows prisoners to be segregated for their safety. It is often used by sex offenders, especially paedophiles, to avoid being attacked by other inmates. Still recognised as a grass by others, Henson was moved from our wing.

For my part, the seriousness of the situation suddenly dawned on me. Until this point, I'd been labouring under the view that the charges against me would be easily disproved.

While I put on a brave face inside HMP Durham, I'd gone from a state of euphoria upon opening Henson's letter, to one of despair in just a few weeks. I began to fret that I faced a lengthy custodial sentence, despite having one of the best solicitors in the country. My morale plummeted and, during private discussions with friends, I expressed concerns that I would not see Gill and the kids in a typical environment for years.

It's easy to lose it in those moments: to rapidly bounce between anger, frustration and despair. But if you lose it in prison, whatever hell you're going through will get a lot worse because of the unforgiving environment – not to mention those prisoners who revel in Schadenfreude.

My remand had already impacted negatively on Sarah and Paul Jnr. Initially, the kids went to stay with Gill. But after a few weeks, they returned to live with their mother, Dawn. After *The York Press* published a story stating that I'd been remanded in custody and charged with conspiracy to supply drugs, the city was alive with gossip – not least the myths peddled by pupils at Paul and Sarah's school.

Paul Jnr was just sixteen years old, yet quickly developed a firm grasp of the legal issues. I sensed that my son genuinely believed I would be acquitted. In the ordinary course of events, his hopes would have been justified. But nothing about my case was typical.

Tommy, Willy Hunter and other pals inside HMP Durham helped me stay focused after I was charged. They made sure I always had company, laughed and joked as best they could in the circumstances and forced me to stick to a daily routine – knowing that personal discipline and a busy schedule would help prevent depression. To the outside world, Tommy and Willy were brutal thugs and a danger to society. But to me, inside HMP Durham, they became real friends who supported me when I was at one of my lowest points. I will never forget how much they helped. It is why, to this day, I find it hard to tolerate criticism of either man.

Prison creates situations and interactions most humans could never imagine, and you develop strong bonds with the most unexpected of friends. It also reminds you that most people, even those on remand for murder, are not simplistically black or white, good or evil.

**

I've always been fascinated by money flows, business and trade – irrespective of locality.

In the early 1990s, the UK's Conservative government introduced an 'internal market' within the National Health Service: a system of decentralised funding under which hospital departments traded their services. This new commercial approach was alien to a previously centralised health service, and the project failed miserably. The internal market was later described by *The Spectator*, a respected British political magazine, as an 'expensive catastrophe' because there had been no culture of competition within the UK's health system.

Ministers would have been well-advised to study the intricate economics of prison contraband to understand how an internal market could have operated. Inmates certainly know a thing or two about creating trade where markets don't exist!

Given the challenge of accessing goods from the outside world, you would imagine that a prison economy suffers from excess demand and supply-side problems? Not so.

Today, we often read about prisoners' friends or fellow gang members flying drug-laden drones into exercise yards, or through cell windows, to keep inmates stocked with contraband. But back in the 1990s, more rustic methods were often employed to smuggle tradeable goods. Inevitably, this included mules wrapping drugs, money and even mobile phones in clingfilm and shoving the items up their backsides before a prison visit. There seems to be an unhealthy media infatuation with this method but, in the absence of fail-safe alternatives, I'm told it was reliably successful.

But it wasn't the only tactic used. You'd be surprised how easy it was for family and friends to abuse visitors' rules. One classic method was for wives or girlfriends to place cannabis, heroin or cocaine wraps inside hairbands or scrunchies. The success of this tactic often relied on a corrupt screw turning a blind eye during family visits, or sheer incompetence on the part of officers. It worked regularly.

I'm also aware of prisoners who established a mail-order service involving family and friends, through which 'acid' stamps – the psychedelic drug LSD on blotting paper – were hidden inside magazines posted to inmates. Incredibly, the stamps often made it through the prison's mail vetting system. I'm not into drugs, but my guess is that was one heck of a way to enliven copies of *National Geographic*!

Separate from these innovations, a corrupt prison guard or contractor was always willing to walk through the gates with contraband. But you had to manage relationships with such screws with as much care, and attention to detail, as a surgeon.

★ ★ ★

As my trial neared, Jim Nichol was busy investigating the circumstances through which Richard Henson changed his story after his arrest, leading Richard to belatedly accuse me of being the Mr Big behind an ecstasy empire that didn't exist.

Through dogged determination, Nichol eventually discovered that Henson took almost six weeks to change his story. On 18 December 1991, six weeks after his initial arrest, Richard made a bail appearance at court. His application was declined, but he was told that bail would be reconsidered if he assisted the police investigation.

Henson wasted no time. On 19 December, DC Wilkes met Henson and his solicitor at HMP Durham.

Richard was formally re-interviewed the following day and – hey presto! – his account of the events leading up to his arrest had changed.

Potential bail and a more comfortable pre-trial life, the alluring incentive that the court had offered, had been all that was required for a spectacular *volte-face*. But Henson was again denied bail at his next substantial court hearing, this time overseen by Judge MacDonald.

Instead, the judge took the unusual step of directing Henson's barrister to visit his client in prison and explain that Richard's assistance could be advantageous at any later sentencing. In my view, what the judge was saying to Richard was: "Help convict Paul Blanchard and you could get a shorter sentence."

To my legal team, this smacked of a stitch-up. Yet most legal professionals will try to tell you that British justice is clean.

★ ★ ★

In April 1992, the prosecution papers were served and my trial was listed for 12 October.

Within the bundle of documents was a copy of Henson's interview on 20 December 1991. It was just thirteen pages long. More suspiciously, the transcript as it appeared on the documents ended without any warning from the interviewing officer: DC Wilkes.

Jim Nichol was suspicious and had a hunch. He quickly obtained a defence copy of the same document, which turned out to be thirty pages long. Somebody within the police or prosecution team had withheld the full transcript from my legal team and, in doing so, had conveniently masked the inducements offered to Henson to implicate me.

In the same early interview, Henson implicated Alison Kay – claiming she had agreed to buy two hundred ecstasy tablets from the stash in her garage. Other witness statements also showed that the official story behind the drugs deal had changed throughout the police investigation. These included three statements from Kay.

In her first statement, Alison made no mention of me whatsoever. Her second, provided later, bizarrely claimed that two men had visited her home on 23 December 1991 and threatened her son.

By the time Kay made her final statement, dated 20 February 1992, her story had changed again. I was suddenly in the frame. The whole thing was a diabolical mess. Kay now recalled, in great detail, accounts of my alleged actions that were entirely false. Yet, I had not even featured in her initial statement.

Kay's revised accounts included a wonderfully prosaic description of how I'd sent an un-named man in a distinctive purple tracksuit to her home one lunchtime, carrying a gun that was clearly visible to Kay. This hoodlum allegedly warned Kay to pay all of the money from drug deals – which, of course, she claimed to have nothing to do with – directly to me. Apparently, this life-threatening encounter happened outside Kay's home as she put out her rubbish.

Now, I'm not a drug dealer. But if I were, I'd have the foresight to recommend to my 'heavies' that they *conceal* any illegal firearms they carried: particularly in residential neighbourhoods during daylight hours. I might also have suggested that heavies should not refer to me by name when issuing criminal threats, and avoid wearing easily identifiable purple tracksuits. Not only because potential witnesses could remember such clothes, but also because they constitute an actual crime: against fashion.

Kay also claimed that she was so upset by her experience with the gun-toting, obscenely dressed, hoodlum that she tried to contact me that evening – and that she later drove down to York, with Pearl Ritchie, to meet me. Of course, having a friendly face-to-face with an alleged gangster is what you would do when the aforementioned person has just sent a gunman to threaten you. Isn't it?

Alison Kay's fast-changing story deserved ridicule. In one police interview, Kay stated that she had called me from a public telephone box on the day she was threatened. But I could prove that the call was made from her home phone.

Nowhere in the prosecution bundle was it explained which steps, if any, detectives took to challenge Kay's illogical and inaccurate account. The documents also failed to explain why her story changed so dramatically.

But despite what Jim Nichol described as "flaky" evidence from Henson and Kay, the fact that a trial date had been set left me with a deep sense of foreboding. I felt vital witnesses were framing me under the noses of authorities which were, at best, ludicrously credulous.

My sense of foreboding intensified when another of Jim's hunches turned out to be correct. Among the telephone records disclosed as court evidence, Jim noticed that Kay had called a mobile number immediately after Henson had left her home with ecstasy tablets on the day he was arrested. By cross-referencing the numbers on Kay's disclosed phone logs, we ruled out all obvious candidates for the unknown number.

Jim suspected that it would turn out to be a police mobile and that Kay was an informant.

Bingo!

Jim issued a witness summons against the relevant mobile phone company, and the number was indeed traced back to the police. Specifically, the north-east's Regional Crime Squad. Within seconds of Henson leaving Kay's home with the ecstasy, she had contacted an officer.

The problem now was that the prosecution knew about Jim's witness summons and knew that Kay's role as an informant had been compromised. It would give prosecution lawyers time to adjust their court strategy. Nonetheless, as the trial loomed, I felt a little more confident that truth would prevail.

Paul Jnr and Sarah visited me in prison on the weekend before my trial and said they wanted to attend court. Dawn also sent a 'good luck' message and offered to come to court on the final day.

The kids were exceptionally supportive – full of warmth, love and dark humour which helped everybody relax despite our understandable nerves. As they left, I remember thinking that, somehow, Dawn and I had raised children who were intelligent and mature beyond their years. I was proud to be their dad. In my confident state of mind, I did not dissuade them from attending the trial.

I should have.

★ ★ ★

At 12.48 pm on Thursday, 29 October 1992, after a fourteen-day trial, I was found guilty of conspiracy to supply drugs and sentenced to six years in prison.

I was devastated and disgusted.

★ ★ ★

As the jury foreman confirmed the verdict, I felt like I'd been hit by a shotgun blast to the chest.

I almost passed out with shock. To this day, I can still hear the foreman's matter-of-fact utterance of the word "guilty". It was not his fault, of course: the decision was reached by twelve jury members based on information that Judge MacDonald had allowed them to hear. At every turn, the judge denied my barrister what, in my view, were valid opportunities to cross-examine key witnesses.

On the first day of the trial, Henson threw his weight behind the prosecution and changed his plea to guilty. He then provided a new statement identifying me as the drugs kingpin. My legal team had insufficient time to restructure our case based on Henson's latest account, but the judge seemed inured by my co-defendant's late U-turn.

Day two of the trial saw Judge MacDonald reject my barrister Diana Ellis's request to have Henson's evidence against me thrown out because Richard had been offered a significant inducement: a potential reduction to his sentence.

Diana's follow-up request for the judge to stand down specifically from oversight of Henson's evidence was also rejected – by Judge MacDonald. Diana argued that the judge should withdraw from that part of the proceedings due to a conflict of interest: he had offered Henson the incentive of a reduced sentence.

In summing up the situation, Diana warned that court proceedings would otherwise be overseen by a "judge in his own cause".

But Judge MacDonald refused and reassured the court of his independence. "If my actions are open to misconstruction, or are said to be possibly open to misconstruction, let me take it on my own shoulders to disabuse the witness of that at the onset," he said.

In my view, there was a deeply troubling and inherent bias in Judge MacDonald's actions. He had affirmed himself as the sole arbiter of his contentious decision to encourage Henson to change his story and plea.

Things went from bad to worse for my team when Diana lost her battle to call Alison Kay as a witness and identify her as a police informant. Instead, Judge MacDonald permitted mere sequential facts about Kay's interaction with officers to be presented in court. It was for the jury to make up their minds about Kay's role, the judge ruled.

I couldn't believe what I was hearing!

Their hands tied, confidence gradually seeped away from my legal team. Unable to cross-examine Kay about her interaction with detectives, and with so little time to unpick Henson's revised evidence, we did not stand a chance. The rest of the trial passed by in a haze. This included pointless days spent pouring over my financial affairs, during which I could see jury members looking confused and bored.

The prosecution asserted that my businesses had hit financial difficulties and that I'd borrowed £5,000 from a friend, Nigel Mead, so that Henson could buy ecstasy tablets in Amsterdam to be sold for a profit in England.

That was far removed from reality.

I did borrow money from Nigel Mead: to supply water purification units as part of a deal with a Spanish firm called Sandeos Del Norte. DC Wilkes, the police officer in charge of the case, gave evidence claiming he knew nothing about Fileder Filter Systems and claimed there was no evidence the £5,000 was used to buy purification units.

Nigel Mead provided reliable and truthful evidence to support my account. He was a true friend and, even from the dock, I could sense that he felt awful about the situation. But it meant little inside the courtroom. At the end of his evidence, Nigel looked drained.

By the third and final week of the trial, my legal team was brow-beaten and dispirited. It felt like they'd been handed a plastic knife at a gunfight.

All of this played out before my teenage children. I could see the hurt it caused Paul Jnr and Sarah. On one occasion, the three of us exchanged glances from across the courtroom and I saw pure fear staring straight back at me. As a parent, you spend your life putting a comforting arm around your children when they are worried and helpless. Yet, in those extreme circumstances, I couldn't even reassure them.

After the jury delivered their verdict, the judge asked me to stand to receive my sentence. I was described as a 'respectable businessman' who had fallen on hard times and chosen the wrong response. But, to me, most of the judge's words were empty and hollow. The only two that mattered were "six years".

* * *

I was taken from the dock before Henson was sentenced, but later learned that he got just twenty-seven months. He'd already served a fair chunk of that time while on remand and would soon be released on license. Judge MacDonald had delivered on his offer of clemency, in my view skewing the trial outcome.

That is British justice for you. But you rarely read about *that* in the textbooks.

* * *

After being found guilty, I returned to HMP Durham and was moved from the remand wing to the prison's notorious A-Wing.

Other inmates were aware of my cellmates while on remand, so bullying was not a problem. Besides, a third hard-nut I'd befriended while on remand, Chris Curry, had also been convicted and was my new neighbour.

Chris once fought off two inmates who attacked him with socks filled with tinned beans. While we all admired the innovation of the wannabe hitmen, the makeshift weapons didn't help. Despite being bloodied and bruised by the hefty tins, Chris overpowered both attackers and dished-out a severe, bloody beating. He wasn't bothered again.

I wrote earlier that violence is rarely justified. On this occasion, it probably was. Chris was outnumbered, unarmed and attacked in his cell. In my opinion, his response was a likely case of what philosophers refer to as *jus ad bellum*, or 'just war'.

Henson remained on HMP Durham's segregation wing for his own safety after his conviction. But he could not resist the temptation to brag about how he'd betrayed me. I would soon take advantage of his loose tongue.

* * *

Chris Curry had contacts throughout HMP Durham, including bent screws, and could arrange for almost anything to be smuggled into the site.

Shortly after I was moved to A-Wing, a small Dictaphone was smuggled inside the prison. Ken Williams, a friendly cleaner to whom Henson had bragged about stitching me up, agreed to conceal the device while chatting to Richard. The trap was set.

***

I played the tape back in my cell. We'd hit the jackpot!

The ingenious Ken Williams had recorded Henson's confession in full. How Richard concocted an elaborate story to avoid a lengthy sentence, how he felt committed to his account even after discovering that Kay was a police informant, and how he claimed his court team was part of the same legal "clique" as the judge and prosecutor.

The recording remains in my possession to this day.

It was tough to hear. Henson gloated throughout that his plan to make me the fall guy worked perfectly. I'd known this, but hearing Richard's deceit in his own words left me feeling embarrassed, foolish and furious.

My friends inside prison took it almost as personally. Some offered to harm Henson. These were not empty offers, either. As a known grass, Richard had hundreds of enemies who would gladly have hurt him.

But any attack on Richard would only lead the screws to my door. Moreover, I'm not a man of violence. So, I declined all offers from Durham's 'dogs of war', however well-meaning, and settled on mere hatred of the coward. That and a rational, legal commitment to clearing my name.

Chris Curry arranged for the recording of Henson's braggadocio to be delivered to Paul Jnr, who produced a transcript. Ken Williams offered to make a formal statement supporting me. The fightback had begun.

***

In mid-November 1992, I was transferred to Thorp Arch Prison in West Yorkshire, a Category C facility next to the former Rudgate Open Prison. Travelling down on the secure bus from Durham, I was handcuffed to Willy Hunter, who moved to HMP Leeds ahead of his murder trial in Sheffield.

Willy and I talked about old times and agreed to stay in contact. Several weeks later, he was found not guilty of murder – and guilty of manslaughter. I felt sure it was the correct verdict. I also felt confident that Willy would serve his time, continue to show heartfelt remorse and grab any second chance that came his way. I raised a smile for my friend, even in those difficult and complicated circumstances.

***

It never rains, it pours.

In early 1993, I discovered that my building society had repossessed my home. With me behind bars, and my bank accounts frozen, I was unable to pay the mortgage. The house where I'd lived with Paul Jnr and Sarah was gone forever.

My Spanish investment companies also ceased trading and all properties and assets relating to them were seized. Carlos could not continue our business while I was inside, but he stayed on Tenerife. I felt awful for my Argentinean friend. He had sacrificed a considerable amount of time and energy on our businesses and done nothing wrong. He was confused by what had taken place in Britain. More than anybody, Carlos knew how legitimate my operations were and he deserved better.

In all, I lost almost a million pounds in assets while I was imprisoned. It left me with almost nothing. But the courts remained convinced that I'd put my entire life and standard of living at risk for a few ecstasy pills.

The public rightly doesn't spend much time thinking about what happens to prisoners' broader life prospects and finances. It's not something that elicits sympathy, and I don't want any. But there is a level of secondary punishment involved, which requires careful consideration if the UK wants to develop an effective penal policy.

When your bank accounts are frozen, you tend to lose your home. When you lose your home, your bank or building society also seeks to sell other assets, such as furniture, to retrieve debts. Bills go unpaid, so you get angry letters from the local council and utility companies. They cut off your gas and electricity, which means that bailiffs also visit your property to retrieve unsold assets. Your credit cards go unpaid, so lenders rack up enormous debts or close your accounts. That affects your credit rating. Many prisoners tend to be people on lower incomes, so that pushes them into a spiral of debt and financial distress. All because of a short stint in prison.

All of these issues, I'm pretty sure, are among the many complicated factors which contribute to high reoffending rates among ex-prisoners. I'm not making excuses for criminality, but this complex interaction of events is something that progressive governments should consider if they genuinely want the rehabilitative function of prison, and not just punishment, to work effectively.

Public policy lecture over.

* * *

Diana Ellis appealed against my drugs conviction in November 1992. It focused on four points: that the judge failed to disqualify himself from adjudication on the admissibility of Henson's evidence; wrongful admittance of Henson's evidence; refusal to admit Kay as a witness; and refusal to refer to Kay as an alleged police informer.

In January 1993, Paul Jnr also took it upon himself to write directly to Judge MacDonald, expressing his disgust at the handling of the court case. I felt proud of Paul Jnr: he pulled no punches in his letter, but he also avoided abusing the judge personally. Instead, my teenage son opted for a forensic assessment of Judge MacDonald's contentious oversight of Henson's bail application.

Paul Jnr also asked why my lawyers were blocked from describing Alison Kay as a police informant. Finally, he challenged MacDonald to explain why Henson claimed his legal team was part of the same professional "clique" as the judge. Paul Jnr demanded to know whether they were all Freemasons: not something which had been central to our thinking.

Paul Jnr's letter was firm, but measured, and reflected my family's legitimate anger at the way the judge, in our view, bulldozed the case through the court. Paul Jnr also copied the letter to my lawyers, so that his interaction with MacDonald was transparent. This was a loving son fighting from his dad's corner.

Judge MacDonald did not reply to Paul Jnr's initial letter. So in mid-February 1993, Paul Jnr wrote again – urging the judge to respond to earlier correspondence – and sent it by recorded delivery.

Within days, my seventeen-year-old son experienced just how the British establishment looks after its own.

* * *

Early one morning, there was a loud knock at Dawn's door in York. Paul Jnr answered and two detectives from Northumbria Police introduced themselves. One explained that officers were investigating a complaint from Judge MacDonald that he had received correspondence from a Mr Paul Blanchard. The detectives advised Paul Jnr not to write to the judge again.

Two weeks later, the detectives returned. During this second discussion, there was some confusion over whether Judge MacDonald had received the second copy of Paul's letter – the version which accompanied a new cover letter, sent by recorded delivery.

But what was clear from the police's account, was that the judge appeared to have received the cover letter Paul Jnr had placed inside the second letter. The explanation provided by the police did not make sense. They seemed to be saying that Judge MacDonald got the cover letter, but not the copy of the original substantive letter from Paul Jnr, which was in the same envelope.

It was rather convenient, therefore, that the police did not have to ask questions about the content of the original letter, in which Paul Jnr raised questions about Judge MacDonald's handling of my case. Those issues were not on the officers' radar because, they inferred, they had not seen the letter. The whole thing stank to high heaven.

Instead, the police opted to repeatedly grill a seventeen-year-old who had asked legitimate questions of a senior public official.

In my honestly held opinion, Northumbria Police gave the impression of representing the judge's interests and put at risk their reputation as independent investigators of fact.

* * *

On 17 February 1993, Mr Justice Blofeld refused my appeal application. So, I renewed the application to the full court, where three judges would hear it. But that appeal was quickly put on hold pending the outcome of a separate complaint I had made to the Police Complaints Authority (PCA) about the conduct of DC Wilkes and others during Northumbria Police's drugs investigation.

The PCA case was investigated by a senior officer from Cumbria Police, Superintendent Steven Reed.

But my legal team was denied access to Reed's final report. It was excluded as part of a Public Interest Immunity argument. However, we did get to see the accompanying documentation – including new witness statements made by DC Wilkes and Alison Kay.

Reed had indeed been thorough and had put difficult questions to both interviewees. The witnesses came across as defensive and critical questions over the evidence used to prosecute me went unanswered.

Reed visited Thorp Arch on 27 September 1993 to update me on his investigation. I'd asked that Paul Jnr also attend the meeting. By then, my son had got to know the prison staff so well that he was able to walk a small tape recorder through security. Reed had discovered that the prosecution withheld a tape-recorded police interview made three months before the trial. The content of the police interview demonstrated that DC Wilkes had known about Fileder Filter Systems during his investigation – something the detective had denied in court. Therefore, DC Wilkes had every reason to know that the £5,000 I'd borrowed from Nigel Mead was used to buy water purification units and not ecstasy.

A copy of the cheque payable to Fileder Filter Systems was later obtained, proving it was a legitimate transaction. Court transcripts of his interview with Reed show that Wilkes belatedly recalled knowing about Fileder during his investigation. On my audio recording, Reed also states he supported my defence team's idea of trying to "destroy" Alison Kay's evidence. Six weeks later, on 7 November 1993, a journalist contact, David Rose at *The Observer* newspaper, published a story suggesting Wilkes may have committed perjury.

I wrote to the PCA, asking them to contact Reed to see whether he would confirm the statements we had recorded him making. But almost a year after Reed's prison visit, the PCA reported back: "Mr Reed denies making any personal observations in respect of the witness Alison Kay and I am sorry that the Authority is therefore unable to assist you."

It was left to the Director of Public Prosecutions (DPP), Barbara Mills, to decide whether to act against Northumbria Police officers or court witnesses. But within months, I learned that Mills would take no further action.

* * *

Throughout this period, Paul Jnr effectively acted as my 'McKenzie Friend' – somebody who provides administrative and advisory help to litigants in person or complainants. The role allowed him to visit me at Thorp Arch regularly.

Paul Jnr had grown in confidence during his late-teens and cut an impressive, educated and humorous figure. His help in drafting documents and knocking my disjointed and dyslexic prose into shape was invaluable. My son was an outgoing and energetic character and quickly befriended many prison staff, to the point where they stopped searching him. But the most significant advantage of seeing Paul Jnr regularly was that we could chat over a cup of coffee and catch up on family gossip. There were times when it almost felt like life on the outside.

* * *

David Rose refused to drop his interest in my case.

When the police had raided my home that cold January morning in 1992, an officer found an article by Paul Foot, the campaigning journalist from

Private Eye. I'd kept the article because it covered a 1978 court case in which I had been accused of fraudulent trading. It later emerged that, during the case, my barrister John Barry Mortimer QC failed to declare a vital conflict of interest – and that is what Paul Foot had reported.

Upon finding the article in my office in 1992, one police officer remarked: "Oh, this is the judge you're going against!"

The policeman's remarks and how Judge MacDonald conducted my drugs trial triggered my suspicions of a fit-up. So, on my behalf, Nigel Mead employed an enquiry agent to delve a little further.

On my application for leave to appeal, the case reference number was listed as 92/6687/W3. But to assist the judge, there was also a reference to a second number which read "see89/6687/W3". Enquiries made at the appeal court office revealed that the second number related to an earlier appeal against my fraud conviction.

It was unusual for the judge considering my drugs case appeal to be directed to previous appeal files that had nothing to do with the contemporary application. Further investigation by the enquiry agent revealed that John Barry Mortimer QC knew Judge MacDonald QC. The same inquiries also revealed that Mortimer and Judge Blofeld, who had refused my appeal application, had once shared chambers. I smelled a rat.

With my first home leave scheduled for January 1994, Nigel Mead made arrangements for me to meet the enquiry agent in the car park of the Plough Inn pub in Fulford, York. We sat in the agent's car while I was shown photocopied documents, including telephone records relating to Judge MacDonald and Judge Blofeld, revealing direct contact between the three judges during my drugs trial.

I asked if I could keep the records, but the agent knew they had a higher value than the £2,500 already paid by Nigel. I could have copies, he said, but they would cost a further £5,000. He also sought a guarantee that I would never reveal his identity, which I promised to uphold. I told the agent I would try to find the money he wanted and asked if I could jot down relevant dates from the telephone records. He agreed and, minutes later, I left the car park.

The information within the telephone records had far-reaching consequences. Never had three judges been accused of potentially corrupt collusion, so obtaining a copy of the documents became a priority, so that I could establish compelling grounds for my appeal.

Meanwhile, Diana lodged at the Court of Appeal a 'further advice on appeal against conviction'. The document set out the history of my two convictions and reiterated that my defence to the earlier charges of fraudulent trading was that I had been owed £100,000 from a former business partner. The Court of Appeal document also listed the calls between judges, and I signed an affidavit revealing I'd seen the phone records. But we needed the court to grant a witness summons to obtain official copies of the phone records.

David Rose was sent a copy of my affidavit and legal documents. Five days later, *The Observer* published David's story on their front page under the headline 'Judges Named in Bias Appeal.' The judicial establishment was rocked to its foundation. Legal sources contacted for comment by

The Observer said the case was unprecedented. One added: "We are in uncharted waters."

The next directions hearing was on 15 August 1994, during which the presiding judge, Lord Justice Russell, said no application for a witness summons would be considered unless I named the enquiry agent. The hearing was adjourned, pending a second affidavit from me confirming the agent's identity, but I had no intention of revealing the information. My source had risked a lot to get the documents, and I had a duty to protect him.

I knew that without the phone records, we could not prove the "improper motives" of the judges cited in my appeal documents. But I couldn't ask Nigel Mead for another £5,000 to obtain the telephone records from the agent, so we were stuck.

Lord Justice Russell dismissed my legal team's request for the telephone records at the following directions hearing, effectively killing our collusion argument.

Jim and Diana continued with the remaining grounds of appeal, which were then listed to be heard on 20 December 1994. In the meantime, David Rose convinced *The Observer* to pay £5,000 for the telephone records and sent them to Jim Nichol on 6 December 1994.

In later correspondence to me, Jim wrote: "It is obvious that this new evidence is of vital importance to your case. We must take great care in presenting the new evidence to the Court of Appeal."

However, with only two weeks to reconstruct my application, and the 'collusion' grounds of appeal dismissed, Lord Justice Russell was almost certain to reject attempts to exhibit the records.

I needed more time to process the evidence. So, reluctantly, I decided to dismiss Jim and Diana as my lawyers on the day of the hearing – to force an adjournment and allow time for me to instruct a new legal team. It was a purely tactical decision and not one which reflected my attitude towards Jim and Diana. They had fought hard for me.

Lord Russell was unhappy, but there was little he could do. He ordered a rescheduled hearing for 14 July 1995.

Back at Thorp Arch, my insistence that I was innocent put my future parole application at risk. Inmates always stand a better chance of being granted parole if they accept guilt and show remorse. At my pre-parole interview, one of my case officers asked whether I admitted guilt. In disgust, I replied with one word: "No."

The poor officer, a large and sweaty young man who would not have looked out of place at a local Weightwatchers meeting, was only doing his job. He tried his best to get me to change my statement. But I told him I'd rather do another year inside than admit to something I didn't do.

I could have lied. I could have come up with some bullshit about how I'd done wrong, accepted the court's ruling, learned my lesson and was determined to go straight. But that would have betrayed every principle I ever stood for – and every person who had supported me throughout the previous three years. So I insisted that I was innocent.

As the meeting ended, the officer pointed out that, if successful, I was due parole in early January. That was just weeks away.

I'd spent almost two years at Thorp Arch and met many inmates from the Leeds, Bradford and Liverpool areas. Three, in particular, would feature in my later life: Nicholas Evans from North Wales and Sonny Fletcher and Ray Daniels from Bradford. All three men approached me for business advice while behind bars, and I agreed to assist them once they were released.

* * *

Early one morning, with Christmas almost upon us, I was called to the Governor's office. As I entered, the Governor looked stern and unemotional. This was not a planned appointment, so I had no idea what it was about. Initially, I wondered who had made a complaint about me so serious that it was referred to the Governor.

I chose to stand before the Governor, who was sat scribbling behind his impeccably neat desk. Suddenly, he looked up from the letter he was drafting.

"Congratulations, Blanchard," the Governor said. He affected an efficient, token smile and handed me an envelope. "You have been granted parole."

I ripped open the letter. In seventeen days, on 6 January 1995, I would be a free man. And I was not going to miss the prison *Parfum* or those rattling keys!

CHAPTER THREE
Family

I'm no angel.

As a young man, long before my drugs conviction, I'd been found guilty of trading while insolvent. I had been naïve, desperate to do well in business and a little gullible.

It's hard to explain to people that you are a convicted criminal. Many folks meet ex-cons and think that we must all be lifelong ne'er-do-wells, constantly on the lookout for the next cold-blooded criminal act the moment a police officer turns their back.

Life isn't like that. It's not binary, or black and white. Neither am I.

Despite having been to prison three times, I consider myself a primarily law-abiding and decent human being. There were mitigating factors involved in my first offence and, as you will read, I dispute all my convictions. But I accept that in law – based on the liquidator's statement of affairs, which did not consider those mitigating factors – my companies were insolvent, and I had therefore committed a criminal offence. I had not acted with malice or criminal intent, and it followed a meteoric rise through the business world.

I was born in January 1945, the dog days of the Second World War, in the lush and undulating countryside of Yorkshire, northern England.

Picturesque Yorkshire is colloquially referred to as 'God's Own County'. Economically powerful cities and an energy-rich landscape made my home county the engine room of Britain's epoch-defining industrial revolution. Consequently, Yorkshire is home to a fiercely proud, stubborn, refreshingly blunt and hard-working population – people who often identify more strongly with the county than their nation. I'm a Yorkshireman to my bones.

I was raised by an extraordinary and loving mother, Barbara Tune, whose warmth, humour and uncannily accurate observations about life still guide me to this day. Mum came from a large and traditional northern family. She was the second youngest of nine siblings and her religious and royalist beliefs shaped her conservative morals.

But mum was far from staid or uptight. She had a deep, visceral love for her children, liked to have fun and was not beyond parodying herself. She once won our village's coveted 'best legs' competition and we never heard the end of it!

Mum could be as plain-speaking Yorkshire as Geoffrey Boycott. But she was hardy, cool-headed and rational – a typical wartime mother. Little, if anything, phased Barbara Tune. It was a good job, too, because I was a curious and accident-prone child.

At the age of four, I decapitated the end of a finger on my left hand in a caravan door during a summer holiday. As I screamed in agony, mum swung into action. She matter-of-factly popped the loose digit into her pocket, told me to keep the noise down and whisked me off to the hospital, where the fingertip was stitched back on.

The whole event passed without so much as a raised heartbeat from my mother. After that, I realised that hysteria was not going to be an option while growing up.

Ours was a tight-knit family of characterful aunts, uncles and grandparents. My happy childhood was initially spent at the family home, White Villa, in the quiet village of Osgodby to the south of York.

White Villa was a beautiful, detached home set in picturesque grounds with an orchard full of apple, cherry and pear trees. My grandfather, a master housebuilder, had left the property in trust to my grandma when he died. The financial arrangement, which protected other family members, fascinated me and would be something I turned to in later life.

But one person was missing from my family home.

I never met my father. In fact, for many years while growing up, I had assumed 'dad' was somebody else altogether.

While the Second World War raged across Europe in 1940, mum had married Don Blanchard, whose dad owned a carpentry business in nearby Barlby.

Don had fathered my older sister, Mary. He returned home from his wartime role as a welder at the naval docks in Southampton on several occasions but showed little interest in his beautiful daughter and his loyal wife.

When Don returned permanently once the war had ended in 1945, he had another woman in tow. In quiet Osgodby, it was a local scandal when the lovers moved into a house near White Villa.

Don had little to do with my family after that, and he and mum eventually divorced. I don't recall ever setting eyes on him. He lived close by, but, as far as I was concerned, 'dad' might as well have been living on the other side of the world.

After they separated, mum said little about Don Blanchard. For decades she never bad-mouthed him, choosing instead to keep a dignified silence. Some family members found that puzzling, considering how badly 'dad' had treated her. But mum's love and unswerving dedication to her children more than made up for our absent father.

Besides, I had mum's brothers – Fred and Paul – to look up to. They helped my grandparents raise Mary and me after mum landed a job at the sugar beet factory in Selby.

Uncle Paul, a plumber, would often take me fishing. He'd put me on the handlebars of his bike and pedal to the banks of the gently flowing River Ouse. When he had a bite on his line, Uncle Paul would let me reel in the fish. In my mind, I became the best fisherman in the village – yet I rarely made a catch of my own!

Uncle Fred had the same way of making Mary and I feel important. He couldn't serve or work during the war due to a disability and instead drew an income from the family trust. That meant he frequented White Villa and was available for child-minding duties. Fred was full of fun and made the days pass quickly.

As well as my uncles, I had a close circle of friends to play with. Mum's best friend was a woman named Ethel, whose son, John, was my age. We became close pals.

Back in the pre-gadget era, most families in Osgodby did not have a television or telephone. Instead, John and I spent seemingly endless summer months playing cowboys and Indians, conkers and marbles. Sometimes we'd fish for sticklebacks or newts in nearby dykes, or walk two miles to the woodlands on Skipton Common to spot deer.

We'd also go bird spotting and spent a vast, but enjoyably fruitless, amount of time trying to find the nests and eggs of the elusive Goldcrest – Britain's smallest bird. This beautiful creature, notable for its punk-style mohawk of 'hair', was sometimes seen at Skipton Common. But try as we might, we could never track one down. Despite never having seen a Goldcrest in the wild, it remains my favourite bird. But you'll find that out soon enough.

Whenever spring arrived, the village would be fresh with the smell of grass, heather and wildflowers. The aroma filled the damp air after rainfall. At that time of year, frogs and toads would emerge from hibernation and migrate to the breeding ponds on Skipton Common. John and I used to catch them for our homemade pond back at White Villa.

The third member of our gang was my faithful golden Labrador, Butch. We were inseparable. He even slept at my bedside.

These were blissful, carefree days and 'dad' was just a distant thought during my childhood.

It wasn't until many years later that mum revealed that Don Blanchard was not my father at all.

My real dad, it transpired, was a man by the name of Aubrey, and he was indeed living on the other side of the world. He was a French-Canadian fighter pilot whose family had emigrated to Australia. During the war, 'Aub' was stationed at nearby Riccall Airfield and flew Lancaster Bombers over Germany.

To my relief, I learned that mum had met Aubrey after Don Blanchard told the family about his new love in Southampton. Don had assured mum that he would not insist on custody of Mary after their divorce, and they had parted as amicably as possible in the circumstances.

Two years later, mum met Aubrey on a night out with friends at The Wadkin Arms pub in our village. Mum was swept off her feet by the dashing, uniformed young airman and they fell in love. In July 1944, mum told Aubrey she was pregnant and I was born six months later.

My real dad visited several times after I was born. I'm told that I have his features. But when the war ended in May 1945, Aubrey and mum were forced by circumstances to go their separate ways. Neither of us would ever see or hear from him again. It was a common occurrence in the immediate post-war period.

So, there you have it. I wasn't a 'war child' – that moniker is reserved for the children of occupying soldiers. I was instead the child of a dashing, globe-trotting airman who put his life in danger every time he did his job, tens of thousands of miles from where he lived. One day, I hope to learn more about my father.

Mum's decision to tell me about Aubrey in later life also helped clear up a family mystery.

When Aubrey returned to Australia, Don Blanchard was made aware of the unenviable position in which my mother found herself. He offered to put his name on my birth certificate so that mum could avoid cruel local gossip about illegitimate children. This was still conservative and God-fearing Britain in the 1940s, after all.

It was a selfless and gentlemanly act by Don in the circumstances, irrespective of his other failings. And that is why my mother did not bad-mouth Mary's father even after their divorce.

* * *

Uncle Paul bought me a guitar and a music book in my early teens and introduced me to the joy of playing live music. I was immediately hooked on skiffle and, later, rock 'n' roll. I practised relentlessly, initially playing along to Lonnie Donegan and Tommy Steele tracks.

As a teenager, I even flirted with a rock 'n' roll career – playing lead guitar alongside my good friend Alex Bladen-Hill in a moderately successful band called *The Cheavours*.

I'd met Alex at the age of seventeen. He was the son of mum's good friend and nursing colleague, Marjory, but had a father who beat him. In characteristically caring fashion, mum let Alex come and live with us while his parents went through a divorce – to keep him out of harm's way.

Ordinarily, putting two teenage boys who barely knew each other in the same house would be the cause of tension. But Alex and I hit it off immediately due to our shared love of music. And, boy, could Alex sing!

We regularly practised – me on guitar and Alex belting out amazing vocals – and soon put together a band. The Cheavours' line-up was completed by local lads Don Gargett on rhythm guitar, Dave Crabtree on drums and Pete Allen on bass.

We were pretty good, too.

Within months of forming in 1963, the band performed well in a talent contest at the Mecca Casino in York. We also built a dedicated local fan base and secured a regular slot at the city's hottest nightspot, The Boulevard. There, we supported Lulu while *Shout* was at number one in the UK charts.

Suddenly, we were the talk of the town. We even recorded a few tracks professionally and enjoyed a local hit with a cover version of the Chuck Berry song *Bye Bye Johnny*.

It was the 'Swinging 60s', and my family had long moved from White Villa after my grandmother passed away. Mum had taken us to York, where she worked as an auxiliary nurse at Bootham Park mental health hospital. She eventually remarried, too: tying the knot with her long-term beau, Neville Cousans.

The Cheavours were a handsome bunch, even if I say so myself, and we were a surprising hit with young women – something our parents, siblings and friends found hilarious and we initially found nerve-wracking!

Britain was finally escaping from post-war austerity and nights out, music, sex and fast living were what young adults sought. I learned a lot about women during those head-spinning teenage days, and I'd be a liar if I said that the casual sex – in hotel rooms or uncomfortable car seats – was over-rated. Instead, it was a delightful awakening for a young lad from a small village in Yorkshire, even when it wasn't always glamorous.

But as with many bands, The Cheavours' momentum stalled amid the harsh realities of life.

Gigging was enjoyable, but a grind. Especially when we started to secure bookings as far afield as Durham and the Midlands. We all had day jobs, and holding down regular work while driving through the night on the way back from gigs was physically demanding.

Alex had also started a relationship and his girlfriend, Sue, did not like him being in a band that spent nights on the road.

Eventually, in 1965, The Cheavours went their separate ways – albeit on good terms. Alex and I remained lifelong friends.

I still miss the thrill of playing live music. But being in the band, and the lifelong friendships which developed from it, made me grow up fast. It sounds like a terrible cliché, but it is true: we started the group as teenagers and disbanded it as men.

Not long after The Cheavours split up, I was out with some friends in a coffee house when I noticed a beautiful, slim brunette. As luck would have it, one of our group knew the mystery woman and introduced us. Her name was Anne Passmore, and she worked as a beautician for Elizabeth Arden in a York department store.

Anne and I became an item and swiftly fell in love. I found being in a settled relationship enhanced my desire for financial success. I no longer had to think about going on lad's nights out, leaving me to focus on making money. And I discovered that I liked having money.

From my early twenties, I ran an interior design and furnishing business in York.

Initially, I'd been an apprentice upholsterer at a firm called Hunter and Smallpage, starting my career straight from school on a wage of two pounds, sixteen shillings and ten pence: the equivalent of three Euros in today's money!

Hunter and Smallpage was one of the oldest and most respected firms in the country, with a string of wealthy clients, and the gentlemanly staff welcomed me from day one.

I would accompany more experienced employees to stately homes and castles owned by the firm's biggest clients to help drape curtains and dress four-poster beds with pelmets, festoons, or swags and tails. And it was certainly an eye-opener when, as a teenager, I saw how wealthy landowners in Britain lived.

One memorable visit was to Castle Howard, the magnificent seventeenth-century Baroque stately home later used as the setting for screen adaptations of *Brideshead Revisited*. One of the architects to assist in the design of Castle Howard was Nicholas Hawksmoor, a former protege of Sir Christopher Wren who, like his mentor, went on to design some of the most spectacular churches in London. The first time I set eyes on Castle Howard, I thought I was on a film set. I have never seen anything like it to this day.

But my favourite stately home was Hovingham Hall, which stood on the edge of the forested Howardian Hills on the North Yorkshire Moors.

The beautiful Palladian-style home was built in the eighteenth century and the site has been the seat of the Worsley family for even longer. The house itself stands among breath-taking ornamental gardens on the edge of a quiet village.

At the time, the Worsley Baronetcy had passed to the fourth Baron, Sir William Arthington Worsley, and his wife Lady Joyce.

On my first visit to Hovingham Hall, I had the good fortune to meet Lady Worsley and her daughter Katherine – who later became Her Royal Highness the Duchess of Kent following her marriage to Prince Edward, the Queen's cousin, in 1961.

I learnt a vast amount about the furnishings industry, and the hard graft required in the world of work, from exceptional mentors at Hunter and Smallpage. But being a naturally energetic and entrepreneurial type, I harboured ambitions to strike out on my own – and did just that at the age of twenty-one.

Going it alone at such an early age led mum to provide me with one of her many insightful-but-serious lectures. I remember the conversation like it was yesterday.

She said: "Always do what is right and honourable in business, and don't be irresponsible with money. If you want to end up like your grandfather, you will only achieve that through hard work.

"But it's also about who you know and associate with. If you do become successful, you'll get lots of superficial friends – hangers-on.

"Mix with the Lady Worsleys of this world. It's just as easy to aim high as it is to aim low. I know you are serious about Anne and will marry one day. But before you do, get money behind you and own your own home. And don't, whatever you do, get married and be unfaithful – because the most important thing of all is a man's good name and reputation."

The lecture, and the look on mum's face during it, was as pure Yorkshire as was imaginable. But it was also the kind of pep talk loving parents should give to their children: frank, full of accumulated wisdom and sensible advice which hinted at mistakes made by previous generations.

I wish I'd taken note.

* * *

Initially, my firm enjoyed success. I drew heavily on my experience at Hunter and Smallpage and gradually attracted wealthy clients of my own.

Before long, I employed a team of expert upholsters, carpet fitters and seamstresses.

I also learned to play the contacts game that underpinned successful regional businesses during the 1960s and 70s. Through informal meetings of the local Conservative Party, often in the pub, I'd be introduced to like-minded entrepreneurs seeking to strike deals.

I wasn't really 'party' political. But back then, I could most accurately be described as aligned to the One Nation wing of the Conservative Party: a supporter of market economies underpinned by rational welfare designed to benefit the common man. It was a tradition later developed by Michael Heseltine and Ken Clarke, and it differed significantly from the less restrained monetarist policies that morphed first into Reaganomics and, later, Thatcherism.

Local political meetings were merely a forum through which I could gain access to influential businesspeople across Yorkshire. Back in the 1960s and 70s, *who* you knew was often as important as *what* you knew.

I would find out later, on more than one occasion, that there are limits to this theory.

Nonetheless, the model of globalisation based on free trade that we associate with the digital age, and its rapid cross-border capital flows, was still decades away. In the late 1960s and early 70s, vast amounts of business in Britain was still conducted through informal networks: pubs, bars, members clubs and masonic halls were central to economic growth. It was necessary to 'work' them – and I had the energy, drive and determination to work any room. I also had a knack for spotting an excellent opportunity. For example, I thought nothing of handing my business card to the England and Yorkshire cricketer Freddie Truman when I bumped into him at a plush bash.

The Paul Blanchard group of companies expanded quickly over the next few years, and I began to make serious money. In 1968, Anne and I bought a luxurious home in a modern development in the village of Haxby, north of York. I was settling down and, in January 1969, Anne and I married.

Anne looked beautiful as she walked down the aisle in St Oswald's Church, Fulford. She wore an Empire line grosgrain dress and tulle lace veil – and drew admiring gasps of breath from guests.

Little did Anne know that 'best man' Alex and I were forced to stop for a quick drink on the way. Initially unflustered at the thought of delivering a speech, Alex was overcome with nerves and needed some Dutch courage. It worked! He later gave a charming, warm and humorous speech that reflected our strong bond.

The day after the wedding, local papers ran articles about the event under headlines such as 'Furnishing Chief Weds'.

By the early 1970s, Anne and I were living a more-than-comfortable life. But I was hungry for greater success and, in November 1972, made a bold decision to sell my interior design business. The furnishings market was crowded and beginning to slow down, and I'd become interested in Britain's expanding property and financial services sectors. I started several small businesses investing in property, shares and other financial tools.

I was introduced to two local Conservative bigwigs through my business network: Alderman Wilfred Ward and his multi-millionaire partner, Wilson Pulleyn. The two men effectively became sleeping partners for my new businesses, introducing land and property deals which returned large profits split three ways. My change of career towards professional services all happened rather quickly, and mum was not best pleased. She even warned that my new partners would use me when it suited them and then ditch me. I felt she was over-reacting, and the prospect of making money blinded me.

One of my first investments was to purchase from Wilf Ward a substantial detached house in Derwent Road, Fulford. I planned to renovate the property then sell it at a vast profit. However, economies are fragile and vulnerable to the folly of political egos – and nobody envisaged quite what was coming.

In 1973, Arab oil-producing countries imposed an embargo on states perceived to have supported Israel during the Yom Kippur War – including the USA, Britain and Japan. This led to the decade's first oil crisis and several recessions that would define the era.

In Britain, the effect of the oil crisis was exacerbated by rising inflation, which led to strikes by coal miners. That, in turn, led the Conservative government to declare the 'three-day week': restrictions on industrial practices designed to save energy.

The boom years were over. Money was suddenly scarce, and Britain's economy slid into a crisis. Millions of people, and thousands of firms, felt the pinch. My group of companies was no exception.

I kept telling myself that I'd turn the situation around. But the crash happened at a point in my life when I was particularly vulnerable. After several years of enjoyable marriage with Anne, we quarrelled over when to start a family. I wanted to have children quickly, but Anne preferred to wait.

Around this time, I made a foolish move. I began an affair with Angela Burton, an attractive barmaid from the local pub. Looking back, I did what many cowardly men do. I invented reasons for being unfaithful to my wife to justify my foolish actions when, in reality, there was no excuse for my behaviour.

By mid-1973, Anne was aware of my affair and I had moved out of the marital home and into the house on Derwent Road. Things became more complicated, however, when we discovered that Anne was pregnant.

During emotional and tearful discussions, Anne said she wanted to give our marriage another chance. She was admirably prepared to forgive my adultery and try to move on. But shortly afterwards, I discovered through a friend that Anne had also been having an affair.

We'd both been stupid, but now there was a bigger problem. The period of Anne's affair overlapped with when she had conceived, raising the inevitable and awkward question: who was the father? There was no DNA testing in 1973, so we had few options. Anne was adamant that the baby was mine, so I agreed to be named as the father on the child's birth certificate.

I told Anne that my affair with Angela had been a mere fling and that I was not serious about my lover. But the fact that we had both been unfaithful would always be at the back of our minds if we tried to continue our relationship and, we both knew, it would ever come between us. I didn't blame Anne for having an affair: I'd been unfaithful and had no excuses for how I behaved. But there was no future in our marriage.

As painful as our split was, Anne and I separated as amicably as possible. Supporting our baby was never in doubt. I reassured everybody that I would not be an absent father, and Anne agreed to stay in touch with my family after the birth. It seemed we'd reached an arrangement that would be fair and workable. But just a month before Anne was due to give birth, a bigger bombshell dropped.

Angela announced that she was also pregnant.

What a mess I'd made! It was the fault of neither woman: I had dug a hole so deep that I could have buried myself after a quick chat with Satan.

Mum hit the roof when she found out. Once she'd bounced back down, what followed was the kind of red-faced lecture about life that you could hear from the end of the street. I was a full-grown man, but stayed quiet and let my mother say what she needed to.

"Haven't you heard of protection?"

"You're being reckless."

"And now *this*!"

* * *

Anne gave birth to our son, Michael, in July 1973. She stayed faithful to her word and brought my son round for regular visits. We shot some footage of the three of us playing in the garden and, occasionally, I would dig out the film and wonder what might have been.

Five months after Michael was born, Angela gave birth to my second son, Christian. I was now father to two boys by different mothers: one I was divorcing, the other I knew would be nothing more than a lover. I felt for Angela – this was not the motherhood she had envisaged, and the emotional strain was evident. I'd created a mess but vowed to support everybody.

I threw myself back into work and had little intention of starting another long-term relationship. I decided to live in the house I'd bought from Wilf Ward and turned it into a classic bachelor pad, including a games room large enough for a full-sized snooker table.

On one occasion, Alex 'Hurricane' Higgins, the heavy-drinking world snooker champion from Northern Ireland, came to stay at my home and gave me and some friends a few lessons. The Hurricane played a few frames, posed for photographs, smoked incessantly and, of course, sank a few drinks and told lewd tales!

I was twenty-eight years old, single and owned a beautiful home. I also had a collection of cars on the drive, including an E-type Jaguar, a Jaguar XJ6, a Jensen Healey convertible and, my prized possession, a Jensen Interceptor. I was the proverbial 'man about town' and even had a steady stream of girlfriends. Wealthy people do indeed get laid more often.

My singleton days lasted another eighteen months before a close working relationship with my assistant, Dawn, became something else.

After another party at my house, we ended up in bed together – a move that later had significant ramifications.

Later, we would have two children together: Paul Jnr, born in May 1975, and Sarah, born in July 1976. After Dawn and I went our separate ways, we agreed that I would have sole custody of our children from July 1989.

In the meantime, mum was proved right about my business partners.

Wilson Pulleyn and Wilf Ward turned out to be unreliable. The sort of unreliable that bordered on corrupt.

Ward was an alderman and held high-profile positions locally, including chair of the North Yorkshire Police committee. He was also a powerful Freemason who had milked his town hall contacts to secure consistent revenues for his housing and development firms. Ward had been Lord Mayor of York in 1960. Like all good hustlers, he looked smart in a suit, talked an awful lot and could charm you with his insider knowledge of local and national politics.

Ward had seen me as an opportunity to make him more money. He'd acted as my business mentor, introducing me to his influential circle of friends. But there had always been money in it for him. I'd be a liar if I said I did not take full advantage of the opportunities. I diversified my businesses and branched out into housing development, too. But despite having Ward in my corner, there was always an edge to him. Like he could turn against me at any moment. Initially, I was blinded to that fact by the money which rolled in.

Wilson Pulleyn was a similar beast. He was what I would describe as 'soft corrupt': consistently in the background when deals were struck, always slightly at arm's-length of events and intelligent enough to avoid being dragged into any scandal. Pulleyn was a former Sheriff of York – a ceremonial town hall role that involved cutting ribbons and eating many free dinners – and he came from a well-respected Yorkshire family.

Pulleyn and Ward promised me the Earth. Ultimately, though, they delivered dirt. I should have seen them coming, but when the financial crises of the 1970s overwhelmed Britain, my two mentors left me high and dry.

When the banks began to restrict access to credit, Wilf proposed a rescue package for my business group that involved me transferring properties to him at knock-down prices. In return, Pulleyn said, he would advance me £100,000 to keep various firms afloat. In theory, it was fine. But there was a major snag: Pulleyn had no intention of repaying the profit he would make on the sale of the properties.

As the recession deepened, I consulted Desmond Simpson – a solicitor and partner at the law firm R. C. Moorehouse & Co based in Leeds.

I told Simpson the facts, warts and all, and this meticulous and intelligent man mulled it over for some time.

Breaking the silence, Simpson finally asked: "Excluding the assets transferred to Wilfred Ward and Pulleyn, are the companies' solvent or insolvent?"

"Insolvent," I replied honestly.

"And with the assets returned to the group?"

"Solvent."

In that case, the solicitor said, my companies should be placed in voluntary liquidation immediately. I was taken aback, but Simpson explained the harsh legal reality. He then insisted I make a statement setting out my relationship with Ward and Pulleyn and state which assets were transferred to them so that the liquidator could recover them for the benefit of any creditors.

On 26 September 1974, I placed all of my companies into voluntary liquidation.

Word spread like wildfire across York as creditors received notice of a creditors' meeting to be held in Sheffield later that month. The liquidator, John Priestley, told creditors the statement of affairs showed a group-wide financial shortfall of £66,632 – meaning that they would receive no payments. But, the liquidator added, debts owed to my group amounted to £100,000, which he would seek to recover. Pulleyn owed the debt.

As the years ticked by, Priestley repeatedly failed to recover the debts owed by Pulleyn and Ward – and I was eventually arrested for fraudulent trading. Technically speaking, the City of London's fraud squad argued, I was bankrupt and should not have continued trading. I explained that I was not insolvent because Pulleyn owed me £100,000, which could be recovered.

My trial started on 6 March 1978. In conference before the proceedings, I told my defence barrister, John Barry Mortimer QC, about the deals I'd done – including the fact that Pulleyn owed me £100,000.

Mortimer replied: "I have read the brief and am fully conversant with all aspects of your case. I understand the significance of the deals you did with Alderman Ward and Wilson Pulleyn and it is my advice that you plead not guilty to all charges."

But, unbeknown to me at the time, Mortimer was conflicted from the moment he agreed to represent me. His interest in my case breached the professional code of ethics that applies to lawyers, barristers and judges in criminal trials.

He'd certainly considered Alderman Ward and Wilson Pulleyn's involvement in the case. As he reviewed the case papers, fountain pen in hand, my barrister crossed out the section of my police interview that confirmed my statement to a solicitor in Leeds setting out the Blanchard Group's dealings with other York-based businesses.

It was an odd move.

During the trial, Mortimer never mentioned the deals I'd undertaken with Ward and Pulleyn or the £100,000 I was owed. As a result, I was found guilty of fraudulent trading.

As I stood waiting to be sentenced, Judge Bennett said: "I accept this is not one of those cases of fraud in which the person concerned has managed to line his own pockets at the expense of his firms or creditors.

"I accept you have not, in the end, made anything out of this. But I have to bear in mind that while these frauds were being operated, you were doing well in a number of ways out of the activities being carried on. You have enjoyed certain benefits in kind which must have made life very agreeable. I bear in mind the lapse of time that these matters have been hanging over you and that you are of previous good character. You will go to prison for twelve months – take him down."

To my absolute astonishment, I was going to jail.

My conviction was devastating. It was only due to the strength of my family and friends that I got through it.

After eight months, I was released on parole. Two weeks before I came out, I was told something that would affect the course of my life for the next forty years. John Barry Mortimer QC was the nephew and godson of Wilson Pulleyn: the very man who owed my companies £100,000.

Mortimer, my barrister, had not mentioned it once.

* * *

After I learned of Mortimer's failure to inform me of his relationship with Pulleyn, I embarked on a search for a solicitor who would be prepared to challenge my conviction but, locally at least, such lawyers were hard to find. Mortimer was a highly regarded silk, and Pulleyn and his family were well-connected. Few legal eagles were prepared to take on my case. But I was determined, and for a good reason.

After I was convicted, my mother entered a period of mild depression. Mum had first worried herself into a frenzy about my then-impending court case. But when I discovered that Mortimer was related to Pulleyn and had not declared as much, she lost a considerable amount of faith in the judicial and political system: pillars of democracy in which she had invested so much trust. Mum was a religious and selfless woman, and innately conservative. For somebody who had sacrificed so much for her family, she struggled with the idea that anybody could be ultimately motivated by selfishness or personal gain.

My conviction and incarceration, swiftly followed by the revelation that my barrister had been less than fully transparent, hit her hard. Around the same time, perhaps because of the shock, her health began to deteriorate. I promised mum that I would fight to clear my name and, in her twilight, Barbara Tune held firm her belief that her son was innocent. A faithful and loving mother to the end.

Mum died of emphysema on 27 February 1984. To this day, I find it hard to articulate the loss my family felt. My mother was a family Titan who had endured the ravages of war, failed marriage and family crises stoically and emerged from it all with only love in her heart. I miss her dearly and was proud to be her son. Even in my mid-70s, I can still hear mum's life lectures. They are always delivered with unflinching love.

Barbara Tune believed in the afterlife. She believed our souls outlive their time on Earth. I was sceptical. But if she was right, then I hope mum's in Heaven now – giving admirably patient Gods some sage Yorkshire advice, dealing with crises without so much as a raised heartbeat and laughing about her Best Legs in the Village title. May her beautiful spirit live on for eternity.

* * *

I was still recovering from mum's passing when, one evening in May 1984, I met the woman I would spend the rest of my life with.

A business colleague had persuaded me to go out for a drink, and we bumped into Gill and one of her girlfriends inside the Cock and Bottle pub in Skeldergate, York. Gill was a stunning woman: slim and with long, lustrous dark hair and beautiful brown eyes. Men did not forget her in a hurry! We had actually met many years before, at Gill's twenty-first birthday party. She had been at school with Angela, the barmaid with whom I had an affair and a child as a younger man, and the former classmates had remained firm friends. For years afterwards, Gill and I swapped friendly "hellos" whenever we bumped into each other in town. She was a mother of two and had recently split up with her husband.

In the pub that that evening, we joked about how we were suddenly both single again. Having been friends with Angela, Gill already knew much of my history. She knew that I'd been to prison, that I'd been an unfaithful husband, that I had two children with Dawn, and that I'd abandoned Angela when she was pregnant with Christian. Likewise, I knew about Gill's previous relationship. It meant that neither of us had to pretend to be somebody we were not – a surprisingly liberating experience.

There was an indefinable spark between us that night and, even though I had been down about my mother's passing, I felt entirely at ease in Gill's company. As the evening wore on, I plucked up the courage to ask the beautiful woman sitting opposite me out for a date. Initially, neither of us was looking for a permanent relationship. Yet, we have been inseparable ever since.

CHAPTER FOUR
Tenerife

Readers would be forgiven for thinking that I was overwhelmed with emotion upon release from prison in January 1995.

Not so.

The stereotypical Hollywood image of release day is of an ex-con standing behind giant doors, shaking with excitement or fear at the thought of re-entering mainstream society. In these dramatic depictions, the ex-con is often smothered by a long-suffering partner – or friends clutching bottles of champagne – after the gates open, whereupon he throws his arms in the air, and a cigar into his mouth, to celebrate.

But as I stood outside the prison gates on that cold, grey morning in January 1995, clutching a holdall containing my belongings, my heart was not racing. Neither was I smiling or celebrating wildly. I was waiting patiently in silence. Reflecting.

Sure, I could feel the fresh air on my face. I could walk, unchallenged, for great distances and in whichever direction I wanted without somebody carrying a rattling set of keys behind me. There were no muscle-bound prison weightlifters with 'roid rage getting in my way while I strolled. It was just me and the relentlessly depressing weather. I was free.

But it did not even feel unusual.

By the time I was released, I had already been granted several periods of leave – including permission to visit my solicitors and the Court of Appeal. I had slept in our comfortable bed at Gill's home, eaten homemade food and spent entire days at the seaside. All on the proviso that I reported back to Thorp Arch.

The reality of prison release is that the authorities ease you back into home life, as best as they can, before the end of your custody period. So, by the time Paul Jnr and Sarah came to collect me at Thorp Arch, there was a sense of relief and familiarity in the air – rather than wild celebration or trepidation. I hugged my children tightly, of course. My ordeal inside was finally over, and they had helped me through it. But we had already planned for my release.

There was something reassuringly normal about the whole day. Sorry, Hollywood: that's how it is.

* * *

Within twenty minutes of Paul Jnr and Sarah picking me up, we had arrived at my new home – Gill's house in Fulford, which she shared with her sons Carl and Chris.

Even Gill's parents were delighted to see me. Lord only knows what they thought of my incarceration. Most parents wouldn't want their daughter anywhere near an ex-con, but Doreen and Arthur had been supportive throughout. They love Gill dearly and had witnessed her pain for three years. They were delighted for her, as much as me.

Gill did not look a day older either, despite the stress she had endured.

My wife-to-be had been an emotional giant from the day that the police knocked on my door. Yet Gill is also the softest, most gentle and loving woman – and I was so proud of her. I'm mentally tough, but my first embrace with Gill after release from prison was as close as we got to that Hollywood stereotype. I almost shed a tear and didn't want to put her down. We had company, though, so at some point I must have done!

★ ★ ★

Prison changes people, and I knew that adjusting back to life on 'civvy street' would take time. But there was a more pressing issue: what was I going to do for money while waiting for my appeal?

I had no job, no business and no assets. I was a skint, fifty-year-old, unemployed ex-millionaire with few prospects in Britain.

The UK was still suffering during the dog days of John Major's fragile government, which had been hindered by a small Parliamentary majority and torn apart by sex and corruption scandals. Major's Conservative Party, which I had left by this point, was running out of ideas and support. Millions of Brits were unemployed, Barings Bank was about to collapse and the economy had stalled. The dynamic young leader of the opposition Labour Party, Tony Blair, was still two years away from his epoch-defining 1997 election victory that would reinvigorate the country.

In early 1995, even the non-economic news was terrible. The UK was still in shock at the discovery of serial killer Fred West's crimes, and those seeking escapism through sport witnessed one of the Premier League's superstars, Manchester United's Eric Cantona, Kung-Fu kick a fan after being sent off.

Like John Major himself, Britain looked cold, grey and troubled. Especially to a man recently released from prison.

Personally, I knew that there would be some considerable hurdles to jump if I tried to rebuild my business empire solely in Yorkshire.

The local media had widely reported my stint in prison, so I was known to many residents and potential customers as a convicted drug dealer. That is not a good profile for any new business. So, I considered a new business venture further afield.

In the meantime, I instructed solicitor Mark Foley and barrister Tim Owen QC to represent me during my appeal before Lord Russell. At the hearing in London that July, it took mere seconds for me to tell what the result was going to be: I could see rejection written all over the judge's face.

Sat high in his chair, Lord Russell prattled on about the grounds of appeal for little more than fifteen minutes, in what felt like a tokenistic manner, before turning towards my legal team.

"The application for leave to appeal is refused," he said, a wry smile breaking across his face.

I was frustrated but not at all surprised: the judge had already dismissed my previous legal attempts to submit evidence of improper contact between judges – meaning it did not form part of his thinking about the appeal.

Lord Russell dismissed Tim's protests about his final decision, but added: "As you know, that matter was investigated to the extent that it could be before this court. It was contended that not only the trial judge, but the single judge, and judge [Mortimer] of the Supreme Court in Hong Kong had been in improper communication with each other relating to Blanchard's case.

"It was about as serious an allegation against any single judge, let alone three, as one could imagine and, if untrue, the allegation was outrageous.

"It seems to us that the time has now arrived when the registrar of this court should prepare a file containing all relevant material on this part of the case and he should forward it to the Director of Public Prosecutions for such further investigation and action as she is advised."

And with that, my appeal was buried. The judges had won.

For now.

* * *

Paul Jnr had devoted three years of his young life to helping me fight my arrest, lobby for release from prison and put together my appeal. Yet, he'd already acted as my Mackenzie Friend and typed hundreds of documents, petitions, and letters to support my cause. More than that, he had been a tower of strength and a loving son.

But this all came at a cost. Paul Jnr had sacrificed his studies and now needed to earn a living. So, in 1995, he started in business as a computer software consultant.

I don't recall having any doubts about my son's commercial acumen. But if I did, then they were quickly laid to rest. Upon starting his new venture, Paul Jnr bombarded the Clifton Moor Retail Park, on the outskirts of York, with promotional literature. Within weeks he was inundated with work.

Paul Jnr supported me while I was out on license, at least until I could pay my way. Yet again, my son had gone above and beyond the call of duty. I love him dearly: he's a fine human being, and without his help, my financial recovery would have taken far longer.

* * *

The solution had been staring me in the face.

Tenerife.

I needed to re-build my business away from Britain. My pre-arrest partnership with Carlos had been both enjoyable and profitable. He had survived my downfall without reputational damage and was working hard on the Canary Islands. I would re-join him.

Having holidayed there several times, I knew Tenerife and I was not a tainted brand there. I loved the year-round warmth – the climate had done wonders for my asthma – and the thought of regular sunshine compared favourably with dreary Britain.

Moreover, Tenerife's economy was growing fast. Developers had seized opportunities to build holiday rental and timeshare properties across the Canaries. In many areas, what for centuries had been small fishing villages had grown into bustling towns.

Hundreds of thousands of European holidaymakers annually were flocking to Tenerife, Lanzarote, Fuerteventura and the other Canary Islands searching for sun, sea, sand and sex. Each visitor clutched a wad of cash. And while Tenerife in the 1980s had been crammed with oiled-up Brits and Germans flying in for cheap, all-inclusive holidays or two-week timeshare deals, the 1990s had seen a new clientele arrive on the island.

These new arrivals were a wealthier breed. Sure, they were also sun-seekers and, yes, they were often holidaymakers who arrived with excited children in tow. But they wanted a very different experience to the Costa del Sol's kiss-me-quick crowd. They demanded luxury, which meant better properties to rent, excellent restaurants, high-end entertainment, top-of-the-range cars to rent, yachts to hire, and more.

By definition, a lot more money followed the newbies.

In addition to this middle-class invasion, there was a growing number of older northern European couples or families seeking to retire to Tenerife's warmer climate. These silver-haired explorers were quitting the grey skies of Scotland, Stuttgart or Stockholm for a calmer life by the sea or in hill-top villages. Such people worked hard, nine-to-five, throughout their adult lives. They wanted to spend their golden years floating around in the warm surf off the coast of north-west Africa, and their evenings drinking a glass of fine wine on a terrace overlooking a small bay.

This second influx to Tenerife intended on being near-permanent residents of the island. Which meant they were not just bringing a wallet full of cash with them – they were seeking to move critical assets abroad.

As if that was not enough, there was also a third group of new arrivals to the Canaries whose wealth, assets and spending power dwarfed the kiss-me-quicks and the aspiring middle-classes. These were high net-worth individuals, also known as HNWIs or 'hin-wees'.

Some of these men and women were a new breed within the global elite. Mega-wealthy business figures; the international jet-set, the first wave of oligarchs emerging from eastern Europe after the break-up of the Soviet Union; and sons and daughters of families so wealthy that they'd never have to do a day's work in their life.

What they needed locally was somebody who could provide bespoke, high-quality, and dependable advice on moving or managing their vast wealth.

All of this sounded extremely promising to a man seeking fresh opportunities to re-build his life and recover a lost fortune.

I soon discovered that I did not need to re-train or qualify as an offshore financial consultant if I operated from Tenerife. While such professions were heavily regulated in the UK and mainland Europe, back in the 1990s, you did not need professional qualifications to offer offshore consultancy services. This was partly because consultants could provide access to services in a vast range of 'offshore' jurisdictions – making it impossible for any single country, continent or regulator to produce a set of generally accepted standards or oversee the industry.

In addition, and I have never hidden away from this fact, part of the offshore world revelled in its slightly lawless reputation. I knew that when I entered the business. But rather than seek to join this group, I wanted to take them on: to earn a reputation as a reliable, professional and thorough operator who would present as an alternative to nefarious operators. I sought to bring greater professional discipline to the sector, not ride roughshod over people or laws to make a quick buck. I figured that was the way to secure sustained, well-paid work.

The sector's cowboys did not worry me. I was more concerned about other professional, well-established firms that would not take kindly to new competition. But I figured there would be enough new business for everybody and committed to doing everything by the book.

Many years later, I'm pleased I took that commitment literally. It would be my detailed accounts and documentation that would save me.

* * *

Carlos and I had identified the business potential of the world's vast network of offshore financial centres. But I couldn't just up and leave York. Gill, the kids and my friends were in the UK, and I had no intention of abandoning those I loved.

Instead, I opted to use York as a base for UK business and separately offer international consultancy services from Tenerife. That set-up provided the best of both worlds. Besides, I had little more than a basic grasp of Spanish at the time. While many people on Tenerife spoke some English, I did not want to live permanently somewhere I did not speak the local language. I would instead relish the challenge of improving my Spanish.

Having thought it all through, the change of profession made a lot of sense. Sure, it was a significant departure from my previous work. It involved a lot of planning and reading to master the myriad of tax and financial laws that operated across Europe, the Caribbean and the South Pacific. But it was also a growth sector, offered the prospect of regular and well-paid work and the promise of a fresh start. Like any new venture, it was risky. But it was a risk worth taking.

I was also attracted to it because I had long been fascinated by financial planning, ever since I learnt that my grandfather left White Villa to my grandmother in trust.

In Britain, there has long been a culture of residents legitimately staying one step ahead of the taxman: protecting their family's assets and minimising tax liabilities through legal means. Before the 1980s, this had been mainly the preserve of the wealthy and landed classes: those who could afford to employ talented accountants and consultants, while the rest of Britain coughed up vast sums in annual tax payments. But, like my grandfather, I saw no reason why those of us on middle, or even lower, incomes could not make use of the same practices, and bend the same laws – without breaking them – for our benefit.

Why should only toffee-nosed, wealthy types enjoy the benefits of what were, in the 1990s, very flexible national and global tax policies?

It was time to bring tax-efficient financial planning to all people, regardless of their background.

* * *

I needed a UK base to work from and found a small apartment in the village of Heslington, close to York University, for sale at £32,000. I borrowed £2,000 from Paul Jnr and arranged a mortgage for the balance. Paul helped with furnishings and, suddenly, I was up and running. In September 1995, I incorporated Goldcrest Finance Corporation Limited (Goldcrest) as the vehicle for my UK activities.

Perhaps more importantly than anything else, though, I managed to convince Carlos to front a Tenerife office as soon as my finances permitted. In the meantime, I got my head down and started to secure some UK-based work.

* * *

On his release from prison, Willy Hunter founded Protector Security Services (PSS) in North Shields, east of Newcastle at the mouth of the River Tyne. The business was a rapid success and turnover soon exceeded £500,000 annually. Willy and his team landed a significant contract with North Tyneside Council, under which the firm guarded property on the infamous Meadow Well estate. To give you some idea of how rough the Meadow Well estate was before Willy's firm arrived, it was the kind of low-income social housing 'sink' estate where even the police feared to tread. And that was before riots in 1991 triggered by the deaths of two joyriders killed after the car they had stolen crashed during a police chase. When coppers and firefighters attended the riots at Meadow Well, they were pelted with bricks and bottles. Fifty people were arrested. Friendly place!

But despite PSS's swift success in restoring order on the estate, a local newspaper, *The Journal,* was soon tipped-off about Willy's history as a convicted killer. Around this time, the UK government planned legislation preventing people with serious convictions from running security-related businesses. So, Willy and his friend, John Harvey, hatched a plan to circumvent the problem.

In 1994, Hunter effectively sold the business to Harvey. But behind the scenes, Willy and his brother Jimmy retained control of the firm. The presentational change gave the business respectability because Harvey had served as a Royal Marine in Ulster and Iraq. Willy and his partner, Sharon, were officially mere employees.

Things should have worked smoothly. Willy was going straight and had a good business up and running. He successfully walked a fine line, too: balancing old friendships with underworld contacts with his new legitimate role as a security expert. But Willy believed that Northumbria Police, led by chief constable John Stevens, were out to get him after his murder charge had been reduced to manslaughter.

Willy's underworld contacts soon tipped him off that a northeast-based detective was conspiring with a police informant to plant a gun and drugs inside a gym which Willy ran underneath Protector Security Services' office. The informant had the good sense not to cross Willy. Instead, he handed over a tape recording of the detective allegedly discussing plans to frame Hunter. With this evidence, Willy and John Harvey asked me to prepare a dossier of complaints for submission to the Police Complaints Authority (PCA). This was not really what I had in mind for my new business, but Willy had been impressed with the work I'd done inside prison to help get his murder charge downgraded. There was a lot of specialist work involved in the new proposal, so I agreed to do the job for £100,000. The two men accepted my terms and, suddenly, I had some money again.

Partially because of my work, the detective appeared before a disciplinary panel. To the best of my knowledge, the investigator pleaded guilty but received only a fine.

* * *

I barely had time to celebrate my modest financial success. At 6.30am on 8 May 1996, there was a loud knock on the front door of our home. I immediately knew that it was the police – they had a particular way of saying hello. I opened the door and was greeted with a question: "Mr Paul Blanchard?"

"Yes," I replied.

"I'm Detective Sergeant Trevor Wells of the Metropolitan Police. I am arresting you for perverting the course of justice and attempted deception."

DS Wells produced his warrant card and cautioned me before his officers barged past. After their search, I was taken to York Police Station and interviewed. The whole event was so ridiculous that I didn't feel the need to ask for my solicitor.

I answered all of DS Wells' questions. The police argued that I had made up my story about the judges calling each other during my case. I knew that was utter nonsense, but this was the British establishment doing what it does best: looking after itself.

Later released on unconditional bail, I would not hear about my alleged perjury for a further three and a half years.

* * *

I was back in business, and quickly committed to open the Goldcrest office in Spain. Throughout 1997, I visited Tenerife regularly to see Carlos and to talk through our plans.

The two of us had always seen eye-to-eye on business. We dovetailed and our meetings produced plenty of ideas which we would, through more robust analysis, narrow down to projects which could realistically be delivered. I respected Carlos's opinion, and he respected mine. He had an infectious enthusiasm, an eye for detail, excellent business acumen and he was a good judge of character. To his eternal credit, Carlos accepted my explanation of what led to my jail term – although he grilled me first, as part of his own due diligence. I don't blame him: whether I liked it or not, I was an ex-con.

In February 1998, I incorporated Goldcrest Finance Corporation Hispania: the Spanish trading arm of my new empire. I leased large premises, which we converted into a business centre in the heart of Los Cristianos. The complex consisted of seven other office suites, which I rented to accountants, tax advisers and book-keepers. Carlos placed adverts in local newspapers, urging Tenerife's business community to take high-quality advice on how to minimise their tax liabilities and safeguard assets.

We were all set. It felt like old times.

* * *

Neither of us predicted what happened next.

Demand for Goldcrest's services was intense from day one. Somehow, we had stumbled upon a magic formula, striking the right balance between high levels of professionalism and discretion, and a friendly local service that put clients at ease when discussing their financial affairs.

Customers poured into the office, and we often had a queue of people waiting to talk. It was pretty insane. There were times when Carlos and I exchanged "I can't quite believe this" glances as wealthy clients left the office smiling. But we also spared the time for many small local business owners and lower-income ex-pats.

Within months, we had taken on a full-time receptionist, a secretary and an office junior. Demand for offshore services was so high and varied that I had little choice but to become an expert in tax and business laws as far afield as Barbados, the Cayman Islands, Belize and the Cook Islands.

The work was exhilarating and exhausting. Each new client's needs required a lot of research and many staff hours to meticulously move monies in compliance with all relevant laws. But Carlos and I saw it as a challenge. We took pride in always finding ways to help clients keep a larger share of their assets. Consequently, word of our expertise and discretion spread.

I found myself travelling to Tenerife every week, only having time to plan new business while sitting on planes moving between Britain's grey, overcast skies and the cloudless blue above the volcanic Canaries. It was hectic but profitable.

* * *

My UK business also grew steadily, boosted by two clients I'd met in prison: Sonny Fletcher and Nicholas Evans.

Sonny had been inside HMP Thorpe Arch after copping a burglary charge. Upon release, he was determined to go straight and wanted a legal structure for his used-car business. I agreed to act as his business adviser. But I made it clear that I could not provide advice on investments – a carefully regulated and professional activity in the UK, for which I was not qualified.

I knew Sonny well. He had always treated me with respect inside. So while I was wary about adopting him as a client – he was a convicted criminal, after all – I soon relented. Sonny explained exactly which services he wanted. Thankfully, they were standard and the whole arrangement was surprisingly straightforward. Besides, who was I to make sweeping judgements about ex-cons? If I wasn't prepared to help a man trying to go straight, then who would be?

Another former HMP Thorpe Arch inmate soon made his way onto my books. Nicholas Evans was originally from Wales but moved to York after he was released and started several businesses. He'd always been an affable and intelligent inmate.

* * *

In early 1999, to my utter delight, Gill agreed to marry me. Life with my fiancé had been wonderful since my release. I was in love – still am! – and knew that Gill was the woman with whom I wanted to spend the rest of my life.

Both of us had both been married before, so we knew what it would entail. But that did not mean we'd settle for a mundane future sitting on the sofa watching television. I could not have asked for more. Gill got on incredibly well with my children and family, and we'd developed into a tight-knit and inseparable unit.

Our wedding day was set for 15 May, exactly fifteen years since our first date.

Life had become remarkably enjoyable again. But it wasn't to last.

CHAPTER FIVE

Clients

Occasionally, you meet someone you know will have a significant impact on your life.

It could be a friend, teacher, lover, business partner, politician or an enemy. Sometimes they are a combination of these things.

When you first meet such people, you are not entirely sure how they will impact you. But you know there will be an impact. If you exercise good judgement, you can weed out those who will cast a dark shadow over you and focus only on those who bring light into your world.

But that is not always easy. We all exercise lousy judgement. It happens. It's how you deal with the aftermath that counts.

* * *

Stocky, brooding and muscular, if a little overweight in his middle age, Mohamed Jamil Derbah looked like a retired middleweight boxer freed from the tyranny of dietary controls.

Mohamed was olive-skinned, sported a carefully trimmed moustache and wiry dark hair slicked back along his scalp and flecked with grey. A strong jawline framed his square face, and he was always immaculately dressed in smart trousers, polished shoes and a cuff-linked shirt – usually with the top two or three buttons undone, exposing a gold neck chain. The Lebanese-born businessman reminded me of the high-spending Middle-Eastern 'playboys' who frequented Marble Arch and Mayfair in London.

But despite his imposing appearance, Mohamed oozed charm and a gentle, disarming warmth.

It was 7 April 1999, and I was sat in the air-conditioned main reception at Mohamed's headquarters in Los Cristianos, Tenerife. An earlier-than-usual summer heatwave had sent locals into a discomforted tailspin. Drivers argued with each other on the narrow, busy streets as I made my way to Derbah's lair, competing timeshare touts snarled abuse at rivals and even the area's stray dogs sought solace from the blazing morning sun.

Upon arrival, what I observed was akin to a queue of visitors waiting for an audience with Don Corleone.

Five huge bodyguards blocked the entrance to Mohamed's personal office. One muscular giant managed the queue, showing would-be clients to a smaller waiting area from where Mohamed's glamorous personal assistant would usher visitors through to the man himself. Several people anxiously awaited their turn to see a businessman who, I had already been briefed, was a big name on Tenerife.

One Englishman who entered Derbah's office shortly before me was having difficulty obtaining a licence for a local bar he'd purchased. After a quick meeting with Mohamed, the Brit emerged wearing the broadest of smiles. When I asked the outcome, he simply said: "Mr Derbah has taken care of everything."

I had no idea what that meant in practice. It was too easy to jump to conclusions.

* * *

A few days before my inaugural meeting with Derbah, a member of his entourage had contacted Goldcrest in Tenerife.

Carlos immediately expressed concern. He knew Derbah's reputation and repeated what others on the island had told him. Mohamed, Carlos explained, had been the right-hand man and head of security for the British gangster John Palmer before a fall-out between the two men allegedly kick-started a bloody turf war between their rival gangs. During this period, the police investigated several murders and vicious assaults on the island – but there was no firm evidence linking the deaths and attacks to either gang.

Carlos acknowledged he had no proof to support the most severe claims made about Derbah and his associates. The gossip, Carlos said, was just that: largely unevidenced chatter, which I knew from personal experience could be wildly inaccurate. I decided Goldcrest had nothing to lose by hearing what Derbah had to say.

I'd heard little about Derbah before I met him. But I was very familiar with the name John Palmer. A semi-literate and self-made businessman then in his late forties, Palmer was one of Europe's biggest gangsters and was on bail in the UK accused of running a colossal timeshare fraud on Tenerife. Palmer and some of his associates had defrauded as many as seventeen thousand people. The case, and Palmer's colourful past, had been widely covered by the media.

Somewhat surprisingly, Palmer's UK bail conditions allowed him to visit Tenerife to oversee his businesses while he awaited trial. But as the twentieth century came to an end, sizable chunks of Europe's lucrative timeshare market had been seized by other criminal gangs desperate to expand into new territory – as well as some legitimate operators. Even Palmer, with all of his cash and a gang of hoodlums behind him, feared for his safety once he was no longer a permanent presence on Tenerife. He kept a low profile, creating a criminal vacuum on the island.

Tabloid journalists had given Palmer the nickname 'Goldfinger' after his involvement in the theft of £26m worth of gold bullion from a Brinks Mat security depot near Heathrow Airport in November 1983. Palmer, who owned a jewellery business, admitted to smelting some of the bullion following the heist. But he claimed he did not plan, or participate in, the robbery. Nonetheless, Palmer's name became synonymous with the Brinks Mat heist.

Detectives raided the businessman's home following the robbery, but were too late: he had been tipped-off about police interest in him and fled Britain for Tenerife, avoiding arrest by mere minutes. Detective Tony Curtis from the Metropolitan Police Service, who worked on the Brinks Mat investigation, said that when Scotland Yard's officers raided Palmer's home, they discovered two gold bars still warm from being melted down in a smelter on Palmer's land.

When Palmer went on the run, there was no extradition treaty between Spain and Britain. That meant parts of Spain, usually the sun-drenched 'Costas', or coasts, were home to scores of British fugitives.

When Spain and the UK finally agreed to an extradition treaty, Palmer fled to Brazil but was caught because his passport had expired. He was deported to London and, in 1987, stood trial at the Old Bailey – Britain's highest criminal court – for his role in the Brinks Mat robbery.

Incredibly, Palmer was acquitted. He told the court that while he did melt down gold from the heist, he did not know where the bullion had come from. After leaving the Old Bailey a free man, Palmer returned to Tenerife and his timeshare businesses at Island Village in Playa de las Americas.

Over the next decade, John Palmer amassed a fortune – squirrelled away in more than one hundred offshore bank accounts as far afield as Madeira and the British Virgin Islands. By the time I arrived on Tenerife in 1997, Palmer was estimated to be worth £350m.

He was later ranked 105th on *The Sunday Times*' annual Rich List of the UK's wealthiest people – a position he shared with Queen Elizabeth II. Palmer owned a private jet, a yacht, helicopters and several luxury properties. The Brinks Mat case had made him a regular fixture in British tabloids, and he appeared to enjoy his notoriety.

But European police forces had long suspected Palmer of accumulating his post-Brinks Mat wealth through fraud, racketeering, money laundering and other criminal activities. And if his role in the heist had made Palmer a cult figure, it also brought with it an unprecedented amount of scrutiny.

After Palmer was murdered in the back garden of his £3m home near Brentwood, Essex, in 2015 – shot six times in the chest by an unknown gunman – it was revealed that he had been under surveillance by Britain's intelligence services from 1999. The top-secret operation had been managed from a military base in Cumbria, northern England, because intelligence officers feared corrupt senior police officers in London protected Palmer.

Palmer was something of a legendary local figure when I landed on Tenerife. His 115-foot luxury yacht, *Brave Goose of Essex*, was moored in the harbour at the island's bustling capital, Santa Cruz, and he was often the focus of local gossip.

Everybody appeared to have a story about John Palmer. They ranged from how he was a misunderstood and 'loveable rogue' who wouldn't hurt the proverbial fly, to how he ran a violent global mafia that could 'disappear' those who dared to cross him.

Somewhere between those two extremes sat scores of tales. How Palmer's frauds worked; women he screwed; cash he made; corrupt officials he paid; drug-taking; celebrity friends; and where he hid his wealth.

But many of these local legends began as the sort of inflated, drunken gossip you'd pick up in bars. I didn't doubt that the timeshare scams were real, or that Palmer was involved in other illegal acts. But beyond that, you never knew exactly who, or what, to believe when it came to John Palmer. Like so many of Britain's legendary gangsters – the Krays, the Richardsons or Kenneth Noye –inflated mythology had grown around them, and it was difficult to unpick truths from falsehoods.

Britain's scandal-obsessed tabloid media had long been fascinated by these underworld figures. Consequently, they were simultaneously deplored and revered by the public, as well as the cheap hacks who pandered to their reputations. But many of the stories about these 'loved his mum-killed his enemy' figures were patently nonsense. It did not take an investigative journalist to figure that out.

As luck would have it, though, a dogged journalist – Britain's Roger Cook – eventually exposed Palmer. Cook famously door-stepped the gangster on camera and was allegedly placed on a hit-list afterwards. British police informed Cook about Palmer's plan to target him, so I'll assume that particular story has some basis in fact.

I was nobody's fool and had been on the lookout for the likes of John Palmer when I established Goldcrest's Tenerife office. He was on my list of people to avoid.

Mohamed Derbah was not.

* * *

It was 7 April 1999.

"Paul! Welcome to my office, my friend! Welcome. It is a pleasure to meet you."

Mohamed Derbah stretched out a chunky forearm arm and gave my hand a firm shake.

He had a way of disarming visitors with a huge grin, a friendly slap on the back and his infectious enthusiasm. Like all good hustlers, Derbah could make you feel like you were the only person in the room. This was ironic, because several of his pumped-up bodyguards had followed me into his personal office and were watching my every move.

One giant stared intensely at my briefcase for minutes after I placed it on the floor. I'm not sure what he thought might be in the leather case, but my diary, notebooks, pens, calculator and business cards were unlikely to pose a threat. For now, at least.

"I'm sorry to make you wait, Paul. As you can see, I am a popular man here on Tenerife. People come to me for many things. But today, I wish to see you. Can I offer you some fresh mint tea? Water, perhaps?"

Mohamed's English was good, if a little stilted. He spoke deliberately and surprisingly softly. He also moved his hands a lot.

"It's a pleasure to meet you, Mr Derbah. Tea would be great, please. And you do not need to apologise – I can see that you are busy," I replied.

"Likewise, Paul. Likewise. Please, call me Mohamed," he said, placing the palm of his hand on his chest. As he did that, his shirt sleeve slipped above his wrist, exposing a large gold Rolex watch.

When he finished speaking, Mohamed flashed a broad smile. He nodded towards his assistant, Veronica, a glamorous French woman, who left to fetch the tea.

Mohamed sat back in a luxurious leather chair behind a vast wooden desk at one end of his office. Elsewhere in the room, comfortable, low-slung single seats were placed around a rectangle rug on which stood a coffee table strewn with newspapers and magazines.

The office was immaculate, organised. Pictures of Mohamed, his family and various celebrities adorned the walls – including a photograph of Derbah with the British-Yemeni featherweight world champion boxer, 'Prince' Naseem Hamed.

I recognised Hamed immediately. The Prince was a fellow Yorkshireman, born in Sheffield to Yemeni parents, and his unconventional southpaw boxing skills and remarkable punching power made him a global star.

"My friend, The Prince," Mohamed smiled. "He is from Britain, like you. And like you, Paul, he visits Tenerife. We are proud of him in the Middle East. A great champion," he said, leaning back in his chair.

At this point, I noticed that Mohamed held a string of *misbaha* prayer beads in his left hand. I was familiar with similar rosary beads often clasped by Catholics. Being a Muslim, of course, Derbah's beads were not attached to a cross pendant. He began to move them back and forth between his hands. Not out of nervousness, more obviously out of habit.

The beads were the only visible sign of Mohamed's religion, but he never glanced at them – preferring instead to maintain eye contact.

My every response was being carefully watched. Assessed.

"I hear that you are doing well on Tenerife, Paul. People speak positively about you. About Goldcrest. Many people on Tenerife need your services," Mohamed said, suddenly leaning forward while maintaining eye contact.

"We've done very well so far, Mohamed," I replied. "Business here is excellent, although I still run a company from England, too."

Mohamed tilted his head slightly, intrigued. "You are a man who does business in many countries?"

"Oh, yes," I smiled. "As much business in as many countries as I can!"

"You have family in England?"

"Yes," I replied coyly. I didn't want to reveal that I had a partner and children until I knew more about Mohamed. I may have been prepared to give Derbah the benefit of the doubt following Carlos's warning. But I knew to divulge little about my personal life.

Besides, in business, few clients care about your family life. They mostly pay lip service to it out of politeness. It's small talk, a lubricant that allows people to chat before getting down to real business.

Mohamed continued: "Why don't you move your family to Tenerife? The weather is better, no?"

"Yes, there's little doubt about that! Maybe one day," I replied. "Goldcrest Tenerife is still establishing itself locally. But we pride ourselves on having good clients already."

"I know this," Mohamed said, nodding gently. His face broke into a knowing smile which told me, without any doubt, that he had already undertaken his due diligence on my company.

"You have some *very* good clients already, Paul. People tell me that you are a man of discretion. Privacy! I want to discuss with you, in private, how you might help me?"

"Everything we discuss today will be private, Mohamed. You have my word on that. People want discretion when it comes to their finances. Goldcrest is client-focused, so that is what we deliver for our clients."

Mohamed leaned forward in his chair. "Thank you. That is perfect for me and my business, Paul. You see, many people on Tenerife think of me only as a business partner of John Palmer. You know John Palmer?"

I smiled. "Yes. Well, I know *of* John Palmer. I can't say I've ever met him."

"Hahaha! *Everybody* in England knows about John Palmer. He is famous, no? Brinks Mat gold! And now, of course, he is under arrest in England. They say he committed fraud. People here tell me that John did not pay money back to his timeshare customers. I don't know if this is true. I know John, but...he was a private businessman."

Mohamed's face tightened upon mention of Palmer's crimes. He stared straight into my eyes and began to run his prayer beads through his hands again.

"John Palmer's way of doing business is not my way of doing business, Paul. We are very different. I am a legitimate businessman. I want to make money, sure. But I have many lawyers, accountants and advisers..."

Mohamed clutched his prayer beads in his left hand and waved his right arm several times as he spoke.

"They are professional people. I pay them to be professional for me. Business reputation is important."

"Of course," I said. "To be successful over the long-term, you have to act professionally at all times."

"Yes. You are right, Paul. But there are many ways to act professionally and legally. Yes?"

"Absolutely, Mohamed. When it comes to finances, you have a wide range of options as to how to structure your businesses, manage your wealth... that sort of thing."

I dragged the chat back to how Goldcrest could help Derbah.

"Exactly!" Mohamed exclaimed. "That is what I tell my people, Paul."

He leaned forward again, extended an arm, and pointed towards the door to his reception.

"You see, my lawyers and advisers are good people," he said. "But they are trained in the old ways. I am a modern businessman. I do business all over the world. One day, Tenerife. The next day, Lebanon. Maybe some business in Spain, maybe some in France. Africa. It's globalisation, yes?"

Mohamed shrugged and held out his hands. His powerful, broad shoulders raised to his neck.

"I need my businesses to be flexible, just like I must be flexible. You see?"

"Absolutely, Mohamed," I replied. "This is not a unique requirement for the modern international businessman. You need your assets to be liquid and accessible. Presumably, you're also seeking to minimise your corporate and personal tax bills?"

"Precisely! You know this already because you are a clever businessman, Paul. But I am an honest man. I know important people on Tenerife and in Madrid: politicians, lawyers, policemen, businessmen. Powerful people."

He nodded several times. I nodded back. Judging by the size of Mohamed's entourage, and the queue of people I'd seen in his office that morning, I didn't doubt him.

"These people are my friends. So, I must be careful and legal. John Palmer was not careful."

Fleetingly, Derbah's tone changed. I could have sworn I glimpsed delight on his face when he mentioned his rival's demise.

"So, I need good business advice from somebody who knows globalisation, Paul," he nodded gently. "Somebody who knows modern business. I don't want to pay taxes in Tenerife when I don't need to pay taxes in Tenerife. You understand? Somebody who can make sure that my business and my money is very safe. And legal. That is very important to me."

"I understand entirely, Mohamed. And, rest assured, Goldcrest Tenerife will always seek to comply with all relevant jurisdictional and tax laws. We would not be in business for long if we did not."

Then I delivered the line I had been mulling over since before I arrived. "We undertake full due diligence checks on all of our clients. Our checks mirror those undertaken by international banks, so Goldcrest will need to see all relevant paperwork from you before setting up any new business or accounts. But before we get into that, let me talk you through what sort of services Goldcrest offer..."

* * *

Mohamed Derbah struck me as professional and diligent – certainly a lot more business-like than I had expected. But throughout our discussion, he also exhibited warmth and humour.

Mohamed was switched on. He was intelligent, talked the language of business and used financial terms accurately. I later learned that he spoke several languages. And he always paused politely while others talked.

He was also street-smart. I had multi-millionaire clients who knew less about the world than Mohamed.

Derbah wanted to create a small number of offshore companies to help minimise his taxes. To get things rolling, he prioritised an off-the-shelf firm with an HSBC bank account on the Isle of Man. It was a particular requirement, he acknowledged, but it would help him to attract more clients from the lucrative British and European timeshare and 'holiday pack' market.

Tenerife was a key market for those selling both products, and most operators on the island were legitimate. Mohamed already offered holiday packs, under the banner of the Millennium Club Card, through a firm called Libano Sur SL.

In Britain, we tend to gloss over how the rest of the world views our banking system. Mohamed's demand for an HSBC account was a reminder that, rightly or wrongly, British banking carries an international seal of approval or credibility. Britain's banks are generally considered secure and discreet, and clients must pass vigorous due-diligence checks: even at offshore branches. I was already an approved HSBC agent and knew that I could deliver Mohamed's request for an account.

I made several calls to agents during that first meeting and, before I even left the building, Mohamed had purchased a company called Fleet Securities Limited registered in the Turks and Caicos Islands.

What remained was for Goldcrest to perform its due diligence on Mohamed Jamil Derbah. I'd be a liar if I said that I had absolutely no reservations about taking him on as a client after Carlos's warning and John Palmer's timeshare-related troubles. But that first meeting with Mohamed was disarming, and his professionalism put me at ease.

Goldcrest's standard due diligence procedures included taking references from a lawyer and an accountant and having the client's passport notarised. But in Mohamed's case, the latter stage did not happen. Mohamed instead had his passport authenticated by Jose Antonio Martin Fernandez, a senior police officer within Tenerife's Guardia Civil.

In these unique circumstances, other references were not required. The bank manager who established the accounts even remarked on the credibility of Mohamed's application when reviewing it. In all his years in banking, the manager said, he'd never seen an endorsement from a senior policeman. The bank had no hesitation in opening the account.

My fee for this basic work was just £2,000, or 486,000 pesetas. It was a small sum, but it was lucrative enough for what amounted to a morning's work and some necessary follow-up administration. Besides, in return for me acting as his offshore corporate consultant, Mohamed said he would introduce me to his business associates and open some doors for me on Tenerife.

Mohamed and I promptly shook hands and went about our separate business. Little did I know that I had just become a corporate adviser to one of the world's biggest, wealthiest and, allegedly, most violent mafias.

* * * #

Carlos was not happy when I updated him on Goldcrest's new client. He warned that any arrangement with Derbah could end in tears. Or worse.

I respected my business colleague enormously, but we sometimes held different views. Carlos sometimes expressed reservations about clients that turned out to be misplaced. His warning about Mohamed was not unique. On occasion, I had taken warnings from Carlos on board, and we had lost out on good business. Likewise, there had been times when I ignored his advice and it led to minor problems such as fee disputes.

But I had a business to run, one in which all of Goldcrest's staff and advisors were invested because it paid their bills. Mohamed Derbah promised not just lucrative work from him, but also his influential contacts. He had coasted through the due diligence checks performed by Goldcrest and an independent bank. One of the most senior police officers in Spain supported his applications, and no concerns had been flagged. I respected Carlos' opinion but could not see an immediate problem.

I saw pound signs, and one of the reasons I wanted to get Goldcrest Tenerife onto a solid footing was because I had a wedding in England. Married life with Gill to plan. The big day was just weeks away.

* * *

Glorious weather greeted us as we awoke on 15 May 1999, and the day still lives long in my memory. Gill and I married at York Registry Office, an event attended only by our tight-knit families. The marriage ceremony was followed by a 100-guest reception onboard a luxury boat, which cruised along the beautiful River Ouse until midnight.

Friends old and new attended the relaxed, slightly alcohol-soaked, reception. Much to my delight, my former prison cell-mate Tommy Hindmarch and his wife Julie came along. Carlos, of course, delighted everybody by flying in from Tenerife. A wonderful evening passed too quickly amid food, music, singing and dancing.

The only person missing was my pal from The Cheavours, Alex. I'd lost touch with our former singer after he and Sue separated and his son, also called Paul, died tragically in a road accident. Alex had moved to London, and I could not trace him. There was no Facebook or Twitter in 1999. It would be many years before we'd see each other again.

Of course, the wedding day itself belonged to my beautiful bride – Gill. She looked incredible and the smile on her face throughout the day brought me more pleasure than I could have wished for. Secretly, I was a little relieved when she uttered those immortal words: "I do"! You can be the most confident of men, and I was, but there is always just that little moment when you think...well, it's not worth thinking about!

Gill and I had been through some tough times together. To see her so happy that evening, chatting with friends and family, warmed the heart of this hard-bitten Yorkshireman. I wanted nothing but the best for my new wife, our marriage, families and friends.

The day after our wedding, we flew to Cyprus for a relaxing honeymoon.

* * *

The first client Mohamed Derbah introduced me to was a Belgian businessman, Wim De Groote. When I attended Mohamed's office on 7 July 1999, Wim was sitting behind Mohamed's desk. It struck me as unusual that a man of Derbah's stature would allow somebody else to look like the kingpin in his office. But I went along with it.

Also present was another Belgian, Thierry Boinnard, who later became my client.

Introductions over, Wim De Groote explained that, like Mohamed, he wanted an offshore company with banking facilities at the HSBC Isle of Man. The idea was to duplicate Derbah's company structures because Wim also had a Tenerife-based company, Sowi Holidays SL, which made the initial sale of holiday packs for the Millennium Club Card to holidaymakers via his onshore firm. As the four of us talked, I realised that many companies selling holiday packs on the Canary Islands and the Costa del Sol were selling membership of Mohamed's Millennium Club. Derbah would later inform me that he was 'moving in' on the gap in the market created by John Palmer's demise. The difference, he assured me, was that his business was legitimate.

Membership of the Millennium Club came with a long list of benefits: discounted accommodation throughout Europe; cheap flights; discounted car hire, more affordable excursions and travel insurance. Costs varied according to the terms of each membership with no official fees in place – allowing local marketing teams to decide how much to charge customers after calculating their income. Incredibly, prices ranged from £2,000 to a whopping £25,000 for a three to five-year membership – for the same product.

The pricing system seemed hawkish, but who was I to judge? These were not my companies and, I figured, if customers were prepared to pay higher prices, then all power to the sales teams. Somebody was earning a good commission.

A quick mental calculation told me that the holiday pack sales could generate tens of millions of pounds in profits – and Mohamed and Wim wanted the majority of their funds diverted, legally, to offshore jurisdictions and out of reach from Europe's revenue authorities.

At the end of the meeting, Wim asked what fees I charged. Mohamed swiftly interjected. Two million Pesetas, around £8,000, he told the Belgian. I was going to ask for £3,000, so I held my breath.

"It's a done deal," Wim said without blinking, leaning forward to shake my hand. I completed the client application form for a company called Goldguard Investments Limited, and Wim paid the full fee in cash before he and Thierry departed. It all went rather smoothly.

After the two Belgians left, I sat back in my chair, clutching two million pesetas and glanced across the room. Mohamed saw the slightly puzzled look on my face and broke the silence. "Every deal I introduce to you, Paul, we will split fifty-fifty and your cut will always be at least twice what you would normally charge me," he said. "I know my associates. They will pay good fees for your expertise."

Secretly, I was a little taken aback. It was not in my nature to let somebody else set my fees, but Mohamed had just secured for me £1,000 more than I was going to ask from Wim. He'd also helped himself to £4,000 of the Belgian's money. But a quick re-assessment of what had just happened reminded me that Goldcrest had made £4,000 for one hour's work, and Mohamed had promised more of the same from other associates. I paused.

"Sounds good to me," I said after a few seconds of reflection. Mohamed's face turned into the broadest of grins, and he laughed as we divided up the money.

* * *

In the first week of October 1999, two uniformed police officers knocked at the front door of my home. I was getting used to this.

One officer explained that he was serving a summons on me to attend Bow Street Magistrates Court in London on 18 October. The police investigation into my claims against the three judges had concluded and, incredibly, I was now going to be charged with two counts of perjury.

It was ludicrous beyond words.

At the hearing, Mark George, a barrister acting on my behalf, accepted there was a *prima facia* case against me and agreed to the case being committed for trial at the Central Criminal Court at the Old Bailey. At home later that evening, my entire family was in a state of disbelief. *The Observer* newspaper had obtained identical sets of telephone records revealing that the judges had been in contact with each other, yet here was the legal establishment trying to discredit my claims.

Regardless, I could do nothing until the Crown's case was served and a trial date set.

CHAPTER SIX
Offshore

Moving money offshore is easy. But successful practitioners make it look complicated. That is the art – and that is hard work.

It takes time, organisation, energy, a little creativity and relentless attention to detail to move money legally on behalf of a client. But at its heart, it is a simple process.

* * *

When I set up as an international corporate consultant in 1997, many UK newspaper readers falsely believed the purpose of the 'offshore' world to be a way of masking illegally earned money from the prying eyes of the taxman and law enforcement agencies. Following twenty-five years of 'The Troubles', people often associated offshore banks with the Irish Republican Army (IRA) and loyalist paramilitary groups, which used offshore banks to hide cash that funded terrorist activities.

A succession of scandals involving offshore banks reinforced this view. In 1994, for example, a former Iranian diplomat claimed that Tehran's government gifted the IRA £4m paid into a Jersey bank account.

For decades, the UK public had also been fed sensationalist media stories about London's underworld figures using offshore banks to hide their ill-gotten gains.

The network of criminals alleged to have laundered the £26m proceeds from the 1983 Brinks Mat depot gold bullion robbery, including notorious south London gangster Kenneth Noye, are believed by detectives to have used a complex chain of offshore banks and companies to attempt to hide the cash.

New information on this came to light in 2016 following a massive leak of data from a Panama-based law firm that specialised in offshore services – Mossack Fonseca. What became known as 'The Panama Papers' show that, as early as 1986, one of Mossack Fonseca's co-founders, Jurgen Mossack, acted as a nominee corporate director for an offshore company linked to the Brinks Mat gang.

It is common for international lawyers or consultants at firms offering offshore incorporation services to act as directors when establishing companies. I have done it hundreds of times on behalf of my clients. It is perfectly legal, providing you follow the strict requirements of the jurisdiction in which you incorporate the firm, providing that you are unaware that the money is from the proceeds of crime – and providing that you undertake all necessary due diligence checks on clients.

As Mossack's internal memos reveal, his firm had done nothing illegal. But there were suspicions that a company incorporated by Mossack Fonseca was linked to Gordon Parry, the man alleged to have laundered cash from Brinks Mat gold bullion sales.

According to detectives who followed the Brinks Mat money trail, the gang created a network of offshore structures on the Isle of Man, in Switzerland and Liechtenstein. Money linked to the heist was also discovered in the British Virgin Islands, Channel Islands, Bahamas and Spain. Approximately one-quarter of proceeds from the heist was used to invest in the UK's booming property market – netting the gang sizable profits.

Kenneth Noye was among those prosecuted for handling the Brinks Mat robbery proceeds and was sentenced to fourteen years in prison. He served eight. In 1995, while on release from prison on licence, Noye stabbed Stephen Cameron to death during a 'road rage' incident. The gangster claimed he acted in self-defence, but a jury found him guilty of murder. Noye spent a further twenty-four years in jail.

Detectives at Scotland Yard, the nickname for London's Metropolitan Police Service (MPS), also believe that the Clerkenwell Crime Syndicate, commonly known as 'The Adams Family', stashed up to £200m in offshore accounts during its violent reign.

In sentencing the syndicate's alleged leader, Terry Adams, for money laundering in 2007, a UK judge told the gangster: "You have a fertile, cunning and imaginative mind capable of sophisticated, complex and dishonest financial manipulation."

After he was released from prison in 2010, Terry Adams was subject to a Proceeds of Crime Act (POCA) case, under which he was ordered to repay £700,000 directly linked to his criminality. Despite pleading poverty, Adams produced the money.

Given the many high-profile examples of criminals using the offshore world to mask their illegal activity, it is no surprise that the sector enjoys something of a tainted reputation. The association of at least some criminal activity with the offshore world will always linger – despite a significant tightening of offshore business rules by most governments since the 9/11 terror attacks. There's little point disputing this when the evidence from data leaks such as the Panama Papers revealed considerable tax evasion and fraud.

But believe it or not, the primary purpose of using an offshore financial vehicle is to minimise tax liabilities legally. Or, to put it another way, to facilitate tax avoidance.

You see, tax *evasion* is illegal. Tax *avoidance* is not.

Let that sink in before you read on because, to this day, that statement remains an often unpopular fact.

There is a fine line between *avoidance* and *evasion* – a line constantly re-drawn to keep pace with regulatory changes across hundreds of jurisdictions. But most offshore activity falls within the legal category of tax avoidance. As a practitioner, I would often describe tax avoidance to my clients as tax *minimisation*, because that was the original purpose of the offshore world.

* * *

The term 'offshore banking' was first used in Europe during the late nineteenth century. However, the industry's origins date back further.

During the Napoleonic-era wars of the early nineteenth century, amid political turmoil in Europe and high taxes used to fund bloody military battles, the continent's wealthiest families sought safe, low-tax havens for their money. In response, jurisdictions such as Austria, the Channel Islands and Switzerland offered wealthy elites the opportunity to securely squirrel away their money at much lower tax rates – far from the prying eyes of cash-hungry and warring governments.

In those early days, offshore services consisted mainly of basic private bank accounts. But such was the demand from Europe's royal families and wealthy industrialists that these pioneering low-tax states prospered. Vast chunks of Europe's wealth made their way to new banking centres, which also protected clients' identities.

Other jurisdictions adapted this model around the turn of the twentieth century. These included many smaller island nations devoid of alternative industries, for whom private banking offered the prospect of economic growth.

The relaxation of business incorporation rules boosted demand for banking services in these second-generation offshore centres – and what became known as the 'tax haven' was born.

But as the British journalist Oliver Bullough explains in *Moneyland*, his excellent book about offshore finance and dark money, it took frustrated bankers' response to Europe's post-Second World War malaise to kick-start the real offshore finance revolution.

The 1939-45 war left Europe's economies devastated and reinforced the United States' position as the world's capitalist superpower. Through the Bretton Woods system, agreed during the dog days of the conflict, the US tied the global value of gold to the dollar – and introduced a system of fixed exchange rates for other major currencies, also linked to the dollar. These actions focused even more financial services on the US economy, including huge loans and bonds issued to states or companies seeking to rebuild Europe.

To the dismay of the Bank of England, the financial services market in the City of London became a casualty of the Bretton Woods regime. That is, until the 1960s.

Then, London-based bankers designed a way to challenge New York's financial services dominance by offering customers more significant incentives than powerful US banks.

How? After a meticulous study of financial services laws across scores of jurisdictions, London's bankers spotted legal loopholes which, when combined, allowed them to develop a new product that would avoid the tight financial controls imposed by the Bretton Woods rules.

UK banks, they discovered, could legally offer bonds that were officially listed in the City of London, but which were physically issued in Holland: thereby avoiding taxes on UK-registered investments. Moreover, the same bonds could be designed so that they paid lucrative tax-free interest in Luxembourg.

Clients who bought these bonds did not even need to be in Holland or Luxembourg to reap the benefits. Legally, the bonds were physically present (listed) in London, yet all the key benefits accrued 'offshore' – at arm's length of the UK taxman. These tax-efficient bonds meant that London's banks could offer financial products that guaranteed higher interest rates than those provided by their US competitors.

The lucrative Eurobond market, the first-born child of the offshore industry, had arrived. And London once again challenged New York as the world's premier financial centre.

Furthermore, there was no obligation to record who owned Eurobonds. Whoever had them in their possession could redeem them. This is what is known as a 'bearer' bond – a product that would go on to play a crucial role in the history of offshore jurisdictions, in part because they became the preferred choice of organised criminal gangs.

This all makes for uncomfortable reading for some British lawmakers, so allow me to reiterate the critical point: the City of London was the first modern 'offshore' jurisdiction.

London was the mother of offshore. Most major offshore activities which followed the development of these early products, good and bad, can be traced back to the innovation of London's bankers.

So next time you hear a British MP lament how the offshore world has taken vital tax funding away from the National Health Service, schools or policing – remember that, while it is true, it has happened legally. And the system which facilitated it was designed under the noses of the 'Mother of Parliaments'.

MPs in Westminster tacitly encouraged the creation of the offshore behemoth because it brought vital jobs and growth to London when the city was still suffering from the aftermath of war. So, there is an element of pious virtue signalling which runs through modern criticism of the offshore world by the very political parties which, at the time, welcomed the new market.

Of course, other jurisdictions quickly followed London's lead. Soon there were scores of offshore products and services registered across the world – ranging from basic banking and investment funds to complex offshore trusts. Even US banks responded by setting up rival offshore operations on Caribbean islands, where they were out of reach of Washington's government.

This is where the modern stereotype of the offshore centre as a tiny desert island offering 'brass plate' services comes from.

Much of my sneering towards past coverage of offshore issues can be attributed to the fact that media often reported on offshore financial centres as though they were an indistinct, homogenous mass – like each jurisdiction provided identical services from islands with different average temperatures.

This couldn't be further from the truth. As the potted history above shows, offshore centres developed in competition with each other. It was and remains a marketplace like any other.

Consequently, each offshore centre has developed different rules around tax, trust status, financial deposits, business incorporation and money transfers – leading to a complex web of international legislation and, for some clients, a confusing choice of where to safely place their cash or business.

Some centres quickly cornered critical parts of the market and became synonymous with specific activities. London had its popular bonds, of course, while Switzerland has stayed true to its private banking roots. The British Virgin Islands specialises in company incorporations and, for many consultants, has been the go-to jurisdiction for purchasing off-the-shelf firms for clients.

The Cook Islands, an archipelago in the South Pacific that is among the most secretive of offshore centres, specialises in trusts which are so impenetrable to outsiders – including the world's most powerful governments and law enforcement agencies – that it is almost impossible to access information on them. Of course, operators on the Cook Islands charge vast sums for such secrecy.

Customers' choice of offshore centre has often reflected geography or history. So initially, British families or firms tended to place their money in the Channel Islands or one of the many Caribbean islands with historical links to the British empire – such as the BVI or Caymans. The Bahamas developed as a jurisdiction of choice for US offshoring while, in more recent years, Cyprus has become the preferred option for clients from the former Soviet Union or Eastern Europe.

I'm not going to pretend that all money and trade running through these offshore centres is legitimate, or that these locations have not been targeted by organised criminals. Another factor to consider when assessing jurisdictions has always been the level of due diligence – authentication checks, to use layman's language – that must be undertaken on those seeking to place money or business offshore. Are these people who they say they are? Has their cash come from illegitimate sources or activities?

Of course, some people seeking to use offshore centres only want to do so because they have dodgy cash they want to keep away from the taxman or law enforcement agencies – or to launder such ill-gotten gains.

But in most jurisdictions, laws quickly emerged which were designed to ensure that banks, lawyers, consultants and intermediaries facilitating offshore business knew their clients and where their money and business came from.

Today, up to half of the world's capital is estimated to flow through offshore financial centres. These jurisdictions account for just 1.2% of the world's population, yet they hold approximately 26% of its wealth. In 2012, a study commissioned by the UK-based pressure group Tax Justice Network estimated that between £13 trillion and £20 trillion – the combined size of US and Japanese economic activity annually – was held offshore. That figure is likely to have increased significantly since, buoyed by increasingly borderless and frictionless global trade.

This is a purposefully over-simplified history of the 'offshore' world, and I have stripped away heavy moral judgements wherever possible – so that readers can understand the system before deciding whether it is right or wrong. For a more detailed, humorous and genuinely illuminating assessment, I recommend Oliver Bullough's book *Moneyland*. As a practitioner, I may not agree with every word of Bullough's award-nominated prose (I think he'd prefer that my consultancy role never existed), but there is little doubt that he understands the subject.

* * *

So most offshore financial activity is legal. It was designed to be.

Those cynical about my consultancy work might sneer at such a claim. Yet over a decade or so, I created hundreds of companies, trusts, foundations and beneficial tax structures for my clients. I can confidently say that almost all of them were legitimate businesses or activities that passed strict due diligence tests and adhered to all applicable registration and reporting requirements. All to legally reduce tax liabilities and facilitate trade.

As you will read later, the few companies I created for clients that allegedly involved illegal activities were those set up to shift money in circumstances where I was unaware of the origins of the cash. Generally, however, I was extremely diligent and thorough. I only did business with individuals I believed were trustworthy, transparent and robust.

And if you don't believe me, just ask one of Britain's most high-profile judges: His Honour Judge Behrens, who sat in the Crown Court at Leeds. When I was slapped with a Proceeds of Crime Act (POCA) claim in 2008 – meaning Britain attempted to claw back monies that, the state argued, I earned following illegal activity – UK police employed forensic accountants to assess my offshore business in microscopic detail.

Most companies I'd set up were assessed, every transaction analysed and every invoice logged. It must have been quite a chore! But once completed, the results were described in open court by the judge.

His Honour Judge Behrens observed: "The creation of offshore companies was very much part of Paul Blanchard's legitimate business activities. There were over seventy companies and it is not suggested that they formed part of the offending behaviour."

Sceptics may well ask: if most offshore companies are legitimate, then why the secrecy surrounding the sector?

Well, there are many legitimate reasons why a company or individual may want to operate with a higher degree of secrecy than in other states. I've already touched upon one example: to avoid being clobbered for huge rates of tax by undemocratic governments. While this was often a rationale for using offshore entities during the Napoleonic period, some modern states still disproportionately target successful individuals to fund military activity, silence opposition or sustain power.

One of my wealthiest offshore clients was a legitimate businessman from a state with a penchant for targeting, often aggressively, successful individuals critical of the government. He lived in an offshore jurisdiction, where he paid a low rate of tax. He also did a lot of business from that same offshore jurisdiction. I once asked my client whether he missed his home country. He replied: "Not one bit. If I went back there, Paul, the government would seize my wealth and find a way to stop me operating, simply because I do not support that government."

He wasn't kidding. In the preceding few months, the same government had been accused of murdering dissidents, imprisoning critics and illegally seizing assets. Also, criminal gangs in the same state tended to kidnap wealthy businessmen and demand ransoms. So personal safety was vital to my client.

That was probably the most extreme example of a client's need for offshore anonymity that I encountered, but it cut to the heart of the matter. Why should my client be forced to live and pay tax in an authoritarian state, which presented a risk to his life, simply because he was born there? He wasn't a threat to that government. As far as I could tell, he had never harmed anybody. All my client wanted to do was run an international business that employed supportive staff on good salaries: something he did well.

Other reasons for operating offshore include complying with legal requirements. In this era of fluid capital, where businesses gravitate towards low-cost jurisdictions, it is sometimes necessary to establish an offshore company purely so that you can operate in a particular state. In some countries, for example, you cannot buy property if you do not have a corporate presence locally. Some jurisdictions insist that if you are a foreign national and want to buy a factory in their area, for example, you must incorporate a subsidiary company in that jurisdiction. That subsidiary will effectively be an offshore company.

As former UK prime minister David Cameron's father showed, using legal investment funds in tax neutral locations is another reason to use the offshore world.

The US's Securities Exchange Commission (SEC), which regulates the securities industry in America, is rightly or wrongly perceived by many investment managers as over-zealous when it comes to rule-making. Other jurisdictions, such as the Cayman Islands, offer more relaxed rules for investment funds – meaning they can often invest in a broader range of activities or companies.

Again, there is a lot of moralising about whether tax havens should offer more relaxed investment rules than the likes of the US. I don't have a firm view. I'm not an investment fund manager and won't pretend to be an expert in that field. But specific laws allow offshore investment funds to exist, providing the money invested or paid out is not dirty and the funds or beneficiaries pay whichever taxes are stipulated.

The problem, reputationally, for the offshore world is created by the smaller number of cases in which the same secrecy, tax structures and bank accounts are exploited to move or launder dirty money.

The same flexibilities afforded to those seeking to legitimately minimise tax liabilities are hijacked by criminal enterprises seeking to hide billions earned from fraud, extortion, fake goods, non-existent services, protection rackets, corruption, drugs, arms trading, the sex trade, people smuggling and outright tax evasion.

But these dramatic activities are the exceptions and not the norm: a paradoxically fetishised world in which gangsterdom is valued and thrives. While we may disapprove of such activities, we are all fascinated by this aspect of the offshore world. Just look at the success of investigative journalist Misha Glenny's superb book exposing these increasingly globalised criminal enterprises, *McMafia*.

Glenny presents a warts-and-all assessment of the global connectivity of organised crime and its use of offshore structures. But while his extraordinary work provided fresh insight into the complexities of dark money flows, I have little doubt that at least part of *McMafia's* success was due to the public's pre-existing fascination with the additional themes of violence, revenge and power.

This has long been the case. Observe how the tone of UK tabloid newspaper coverage in the late twentieth century turned violent fraudsters or thieves such as John 'Goldfinger' Palmer or Ronnie Biggs, into mere rogues whose luxury gangster lifestyles were to be admired.

Whether by default or design, some media coverage turned these men – they're almost always men – into working-class heroes who gave the taxman and police a bloody nose.

What the coverage sometimes ignored were the thousands of hard-up victims of Palmer's timeshare frauds – such as the vulnerable retired couples who invested their life savings in non-existent property. Similarly, it is too easy now to find accounts of the Great Train Robbery which fail to mention the gang's violent assault on the train carriage guard.

Most offshore clients are not like these strangely fetishised gangsters. My clients were reassuringly mundane, suit-wearing types focused on using their business acumen to become more tax-efficient – or to establish networks of companies allowing them to conduct business in multiple jurisdictions.

As trade has become increasingly globalised, shrewd enterprises want business and tax structures that reflect that new reality. They will pay tax. But they will do what they can to pay as little tax as possible within the law. That makes their businesses more efficient and profitable. But it means moving money and staying one step ahead of regular legal changes and jurisdictional developments.

That is where I come in. That's my job, and I'm pretty damn good at it.

* * *

So how does a typical offshoring arrangement work?

One standard method is known as 'transfer pricing'. You may be familiar with this term because of recent media coverage of, and political rows over, the UK tax liabilities of multinationals such as Google, Amazon and Starbucks.

In short, transfer pricing refers to the rules governing business transactions between companies or entities within the same group. I'm not an academic or economist, I'm a practitioner. So please forgive any oversimplification.

The significance of transfer pricing is how it can be utilised to legitimately move business income or costs from a high-tax jurisdiction to low-tax areas.

Let's say Joanne Bloggs has a business called 'JoCo' registered in the UK, where the firm is subject to a 2021 corporation tax rate of nineteen per cent on profits. She may do business around the world, often with capital and resources flowing back and forth across borders.

Joanne may want to consider setting up a sister company, under a parent company, providing unrelated services in a second jurisdiction – let's say the Isle of Man, where the corporation tax rate is five per cent. We'll call this new firm 'InterBloggs'.

JoCo sells coffee in the UK and makes a profit of £10 million a year.

InterBloggs supplies coffee beans to retailers and wholesalers.

If Joanne wants to move her taxable profits to the lower-tax jurisdiction, international rules allow her to, providing a transaction within her group of companies meets specific criteria.

In the circumstances outlined above, JoCo could buy all of its coffee beans from InterBloggs.

InterBloggs could, therefore, charge JoCo for its coffee beans.

If InterBloggs charges JoCo £9m a year for its coffee beans, JoCo's taxable profit in the UK will be reduced from £10m a year to £1m. At the same time, InterBloggs now has £9m of potentially taxable income sitting in an account in the lower-tax jurisdiction (the Isle of Man).

While JoCo operates in the UK and would make £10m of profit there, it is charged supply costs by InterBloggs.

HMRC, the UK taxman, would be hostile to such arrangements. It would have just £1m of annual profits in the UK on which a levy of 19 per cent corporation tax would apply: giving the state £190,000 that year.

If JoCo had declared £10m of taxable profit in the UK, its annual tax bill would have been £1.9m. Ten times higher than its eventual tax bill.

Instinctively, such arrangements seem grossly unfair. Some even argue that they are illegal.

I can assure you that while they may be morally unfair, the likelihood is that – providing both firms have complied with stated rules on transfer pricing – this arrangement is not illegal.

That, in vastly oversimplified terms, is how one key method of moving money offshore works.

Of course, the day-to-day reality is far more complicated. In the example above, I have over-simplified for effect. Tax authorities rightly insist that transfer pricing deals must involve appropriate charges between companies that form part of the same group – and that the percentage of profit retained by each company is not diluted to a ridiculous amount. In the example above, it is unlikely that InterBloggs would be allowed to charge £9m for the sale of coffee beans to JoCo if the market price of coffee beans was significantly lower. But what constitutes an 'appropriate' charge varies according to the jurisdictions involved. Explaining all of those variables would get complicated.

Many multinational organisations and medium-sized enterprises are now made up of complex chains of businesses operating under the same ownership – often selling or exchanging a vast range of goods, services, and other taxable activities both internally and externally. Once the parent group has established its offshore chain, the result is often a tangled web of global transactions, loans, lease-back deals and credit arrangements. But the core structures and methods employed to facilitate this web of activity are pretty simple.

Many companies now employ small armies of accountants, tax consultants, analysts and economists to advise on and undertake legal tax-minimisation activities within the arrangements described above – all to pay as little tax as possible.

I've seen complex corporate structures begin in the UK and end in the British Virgin Islands – via entities based in mainland Europe, the Middle East, Oceania and Central America. For critics of this form of enterprise, the uncomfortable truth is that these chains are often legal.

Like it or not, that is the nature of globalisation.

In the case of Mohamed Derbah, I created a series of legal transfer pricing arrangements between his Spanish onshore companies and offshore entities.

The downside, critics point out, is that vital tax income from the economic activity in one state is lost to lower-tax, or zero-tax, jurisdictions. That is what lay behind the UK media's well-observed criticism of global giants such as Starbucks, Google or Amazon paying relatively small tax sums to HMRC despite doing a considerable amount of business through the UK.

I have some sympathy for these criticisms. But it is a simple fact that, if these corporations have followed increasingly tight rules correctly, these 'loopholes' – as the media likes to call them – are not illegal.

I'm seventy-six years old as I write this book: a cynical, experienced man who, as you will read, has been through rather a lot. It is not that I'm immoral when it comes to global finance and the use of offshore centres. Instead, I've learned that wherever any state or organisation sets legal boundaries when developing terms on which domestic or international business can be conducted, people or companies naturally gravitate towards those boundaries – and stretch those laws as far as they can without breaking them. That ensures profitability is maximised.

Therefore, if you have a situation whereby one European country taxes corporate profits at twenty per cent, why is anybody surprised when businesses use every legal method at their disposal to move profits to a state which taxes profits at fifteen per cent?

Moreover, should anybody be surprised when that same second country, which taxes profits at fifteen per cent, then sees its potential taxable profits find their way to an offshore centre which taxes profits at five per cent?

One obvious solution to all of this – some sort of agreement over baseline tax levels between international governments, and how they treat genuine 'offshore' centres – is nigh-on impossible in the current political climate.

How, for example, would any global agreement accommodate both Sweden's tradition of 'high-tax, high-welfare standards' and the United States' cultural desire to roll back the frontiers of the state and keep taxes low? Both are valid cultural standpoints. But they necessitate largely incompatible taxation systems.

And would a co-ordinated global tax regime elicit the support of corrupt states which actively engage in illegal financial activity? Or the myriad of tiny offshore centres – each with distinct business cultures – offering low-tax regimes to improve their otherwise-moribund economies?

International taxation laws are a flawed, some would say a broken system. But they are a harsh and uncomfortable reality. They are also manipulated and abused by those with outright illegal agendas. And that fact brings us to money laundering.

* * *

I won't linger on technical definitions and examples of offshore money flows for too long. But one key issue which merits attention, if any lay reader wants to fully understand the offshore world and how it is hijacked by criminals, is the term 'money laundering'.

It is one of the most widely misunderstood and misused terms I have come across in my professional career – and not just among those who rarely encounter offshore finance or business. Even experienced people in my industry, police officers, tax authorities and national governments misuse the term repeatedly.

Money laundering is commonly misunderstood for one key reason: for an activity to be defined as 'money laundering', it generally involves the purposeful concealment of *illegally* obtained money or assets – by converting it into legitimate funds. This disguising of cash obtained unlawfully (let's say, the proceeds of drug dealing) as legitimate money (for example, a legal offshore company account) constitutes laundering. In short, 'washing' dirty funds to give them the appearance of being clean.

It does not mean the movement of general monies or assets from one jurisdiction or bank to another. This may seem like an obvious point, given that all money laundering is illegal. But you would be surprised at the number of people from the finance, investment, legal, media or law enforcement communities who fall into the trap of describing legal offshore cash flows designed to minimise tax as 'laundering'.

Even within the range of criminal behaviours associated with finance, money laundering is often misdiagnosed. You may feel like I'm pernickety here but, as you read on, I hope that you will understand why I am making these essential points.

A more humorous myth linked to money laundering centres on the origin of the term. It has often been reported that the term derives from the period of Prohibition in the USA (1920 to 1933), during which gangsters such as Al Capone used laundromat businesses – launderettes, to Europeans

– as fronts through which they would disguise the financial proceeds of gangland activities.

While it is true that Capone did own several laundromats, references to 'money laundering' existed long before Capone and Prohibition. It is more likely that the term derives from the figurative idea that dirty money is washed clean or 'laundered'.

* * *

Most experts agree that there are three stages involved in money laundering.

Firstly, it involves the *placement* of dirty cash: putting the money into activities that appear legitimate. In the offshore world, this is most often done when illegal funds are placed into bank accounts, registered corporations or trusts.

Most experts also agree that this first phase is where criminals are most vulnerable to detection because they are introducing significant new wealth into the financial system.

The second phase is the *layering* of dirty money. This generally involves using multiple transactions to create further distance from the illegal origins of the cash. In simple cases, this might include a drug dealer buying physical assets – luxury cars, properties and artworks – which increase in value over time and can quickly be turned back into clean cash.

Alternatively, criminal gangs often establish legitimate-looking and cash-based businesses through which to wash their money. For example, Walter White, the protagonist in the American TV series *Breaking Bad*, purchases a carwash business through which his wife layers cash from illegal drug sales.

Historically, one well-known layering ruse favoured by money launderers was to take wads of cash to a casino, exchange the money for playing chips, and then participate in multiple high-stakes games. Win or lose, the gambling itself didn't matter: the real aim was to ensure that, at the end of the night, the value of the launderer's remaining chips was received as a cheque from the casino. That way, the dirty cash was handed to the casino and the launderer walked away with a new payment from a legitimate business. As you might imagine, the world's governments, not to mention casinos themselves, quickly got wise to this method.

In the superb Netflix dark comedy series *Ozark,* in which the financial adviser protagonist is forced to launder hundreds of millions for a Mexican drug cartel, most classic tactics are deployed: he buys a bar, expands it into a hotel, invests in land, helps to build a church and uses other common methods to layer cash.

A slightly more advanced layering technique involves stock markets. 'Mirror trading' means that illegally obtained money is used to purchase shares in a company. Through a separate trade the same shares, worth broadly the same value, would quickly be sold abroad. There is often no profit made on the shares (indeed, it usually costs the launderer to undertake share trades) – but the dirty cash is washed clean.

In the offshore world, layering often involves criminals either washing money through numerous banks in multiple jurisdictions – potentially mixing the cash with other sources of income at each stage – or through a string of transfer-pricing deals between anonymous offshore companies around the world. Each time the money is moved to another jurisdiction, regulators or law enforcement agencies have another layer of secrecy they must unpick to uncover the true origins of the cash.

The final stage of most money laundering scams is to *integrate* the funds back into the legitimate economy. This generally involves spending the newly-washed money – on cars, houses, artwork and other investments that can easily be turned back into hard cash if required.

Placement. Layering. Integration.

PLI.

Once again, I have over-simplified for effect. But that is typically how criminal gangs launder money. The whole point is to make it difficult for authorities to trace dirty money back to the launderer.

One additional and common method employed by criminal gangs at the placing or layering stage of a money laundering process is the use of 'smurfing'. This involves breaking up the initial lump sum of dirty money and using various associates, known as 'smurfs', to layer the money – often through several small bank deposits, buying gold or precious gems.

This practice became common among gangs and mafias in the 1980s after the US government introduced rules requiring banks to report cash deposits worth $10,000 or more. By dividing dirty money into smaller sums, launderers were able to stay under the radar. Of course, this required an army of lower-level criminals to do the legwork – wandering from bank to bank depositing cash in multiple accounts. In the 1980s, *The Smurfs* was a popular TV cartoon series based on the tiny Belgian comic characters – hence smaller criminals working for bigger gangsters were referred to as 'smurfs'. Finance experts often prefer to use the term 'structuring' to describe smurfing.

Terrorist networks make extensive use of smurfing to move money, gems or precious commodities from one country to another.

* * *

That is a beginner's guide to money laundering.

There are, of course, many other methods used – including the use of crypto-currencies in the modern era. But these are too numerous to list in any single book without boring readers senseless. The critical thing to remember is that, while money laundering is unquestionably an unfortunate part of the offshore financial services landscape, it by no means represents the majority of offshore business. The idea that it does is a media myth, regularly exploited by politicians or law enforcement agencies who use the sector as a convenient whipping boy and should know better.

One of the many reasons politicians should know better is that they often come from families that have benefited from offshore financial arrangements. Former UK prime minister David Cameron, for example, inherited £300,000 from his late father's estate in 2010. Ian Cameron was a stockbroker who increased his wealth by using offshore investment funds in Jersey, Panama City, and Geneva.

Cameron and his wife, Samantha, even invested in one of his father's offshore funds. But they paid UK taxes on £19,000 of profit made through the transaction, thereby avoiding the ire of HMRC. Nonetheless, Cameron was the beneficiary of legitimate offshore business – and I strongly suspect he is not alone among recent politicians!

Offshore financial consultants, bankers, lawyers and other agents know about money laundering not because they engage in it (although some nefarious professionals do). Instead, we know about it because the core methods employed to launder dirty money offshore – using banks, trusts, investment funds, corporations and other tools – usually involve the use of generally legitimate vehicles. It is the illegal *origins* of the money, and the failure of individuals to declare their cash for lawful tax purposes that distinguishes money laundering from legal incorporation, offshore business or trust services.

Offshore professionals know about money laundering because we are supposed to be on the lookout for it – and have a duty to report it when we see it. In most jurisdictions, laws usually exist requiring bankers, advisers, asset managers and wealth management firms to adhere to report suspected money laundering.

But there is an earlier phase of conducting offshore business that is more important than retrospectively performing your professional duty and reporting suspected money laundering.

Due diligence.

Also referred to as 'know your client' information.

* * *

Due diligence essentially means taking reasonable steps to avoid committing a breach of rules or offence. In the financial services industry, it means taking the time to check your customer's background and take reasonable steps to check that their money or assets have not been obtained illegally.

It may surprise some readers to learn that some tight due diligence requirements have existed in the offshore world for decades. But perhaps the most significant push towards global due diligence requirements followed the establishment of the Organisation for Economic Co-Operation and Development (OECD) in 1961.

The OECD is an inter-governmental organisation designed to stimulate economic progress and world trade. Historians are quick to remind us that it was another of the organisations and initiatives which grew out of the United States' position of global dominance following the Second World War. The OECD's predecessor, the Organisation for European Economic Co-Operation, was established to oversee the US-led Marshall Plan to rebuild Europe. So, it won't surprise readers to discover that the US remains the OECD's driving force, even though its headquarters are in Paris.

Today, the OECD has 36 member countries responsible for approximately 62 per cent of the world's GDP. As well as the US, membership now includes most of the democratic world's biggest economies – including Japan,

Germany, France and the UK. In 1989, amid concerns that organised criminal networks had hijacked the global banking system and were able to move dirty cash around the world at will, the OECD created the Financial Action Task Force (FATF) on Money Laundering.

In 1990, the FATF published forty recommendations to tackle money laundering – including thorough due diligence standards. The recommendations were updated in 1996, and it was these revised standards that effectively governed most international banking and offshore practices when I began working as an offshore consultant. All OECD member states were assumed to have implemented FATF recommendations.

But that wasn't the only way that the OECD put pressure on the financial services sector, and other countries, to tackle money laundering. In 2000, the FATF also published a 'blacklist' of countries that ignored its standards. Blacklisted countries faced a barrage of international criticism and political pressure designed to force them to adopt FATF recommendations – including threats to limit future borrowing from the International Monetary Fund, credit rating downgrades and blocks on wire transfers.

So, even before the overhaul of the offshore finance sector following the terror attacks of 9/11, which led to the targeting of terrorist funding, you generally had to know your client when conducting offshore business.

And that's how it was when I met Mohamed Derbah.

CHAPTER SEVEN

Bread

After accepting Mohamed Derbah as a client, I made a point of staying close to him. After all, Mohamed had passed Goldcrest's due diligence checks and, true to his word, he introduced Goldcrest to other businessmen seeking offshore corporate services.

In those early months, I accompanied Derbah on successful trips to Marbella and Malaga on Spain's southern coast, Amsterdam, Paris and Madrid. Mohamed even jokingly referred to me as his 'legal adviser', because it helped puzzled clients to understand what the quiet British man with the funny accent was doing by his side.

I was never employed by Mohamed and was instead a freelance corporate consultant: I owned and ran Goldcrest Hispania, a service company, and was paid by Mohamed on a piecemeal basis. But Mohamed's throw-away and informal description did not bother me while it secured my firm new business.

Derbah worked hard. He would be at his office early on most days and had an insatiable desire to make money by chasing hard after new business opportunities. He ran timeshare-related companies, import and export firms, a restaurant and had interests in several security operations. In meetings he would be charming, but direct. He did not waste words. In that respect, Derbah reminded me of a straight-talking Yorkshireman.

But what impressed me most about Mohamed in those early days was that he and his entourage knew everything that happened on Tenerife. *Everything.* The constant flow of politicians, police officers, customs officials, doctors, public bureaucrats, bar owners, businessmen, travel agents and lawyers through his office saw to that. Even dignitaries from Africa and the Middle East dropped by to visit him when they were in town. Everybody wanted to see Mohamed, and they all liked to gossip.

At an early stage, I was introduced to Jose Antonio Martin Fernandez, the senior officer at the Guardia Civil who had endorsed Derbah's passport. Fernandez attended barbeques at Mohamed's villa, where I also met other national and secret police officers.

Because of his vast network of contacts, you could barely fart on Tenerife without Mohamed and his henchmen knowing. He knew who was doing business with who, where and when. He knew who was fucking who, where and when. And he knew which criminal gangs were warring with who, where and when. Such information, he knew, provided him with leverage on the island – and significant business opportunities.

I soon realised just how easy it had been for Mohamed to undertake his due diligence on Goldcrest before meeting me. His contacts extended to every part of the island, and he had many associates within the police and private security sector.

Mohamed's reach was not limited to the Canaries, either, and his regular trips to the European mainland and Beirut helped him to secure further business for us both.

The wealthy city of Marbella, situated between Malaga and Gibraltar on Spain's southern coast, became one of his favourite places to meet clients – primarily due to his penchant for the high-life once his working day was complete. Appointments invariably took place at exclusive hotels and would be followed by visits to 'Milady's'.

Mohamed liked to party, but his favourite venue left a lot to be desired. For those unfamiliar with the Milady Palace nightclub, probably the best way to describe its former incarnation would be as Marbella's 'infamous super-brothel for the super-rich'.

Housed in a converted million-dollar villa on a leafy street one block from the seafront in the millionaires' suburb of Puerto Banus, Milady Palace looks like a discreet-yet-classy restaurant from the outside. But once past the hedgerows, through the front gate and under the roof, the site opened up into a mega-construction that stretched half the length and the entire width of the block. And it didn't matter where you walked inside – be it one of the many plush-looking bars or perfumed dancefloors – the venue was full, wall-to-wall, with obscenely wealthy men relaxing in the company of women.

Including women for hire.

But, if you'll forgive me for being un-PC for a moment, we're not talking about the pasty-skinned, emaciated and crack-addicted prostitutes forced to give blowjobs to punters in back-allies to keep their abusive pimps in drug money. We're talking about some of the most beautiful, exotic and glamourous young women men could dream of.

By the late 1990s, Marbella enjoyed a reputation as the hedonistic capital of the Costa del Sol. But unlike neighbouring Fuengirola and Torremolinos – which had attracted the budget 'kiss me quick' tourism during Spain's package holiday boom – Marbella had promoted itself as a destination for the rich and famous since Ricardo Soriano, the Marquis of Ivanrey, bought land there in 1943. By the 1950s, Soriano's wealthy friends and relatives had arrived and so had the luxury hotels and spa-style resorts that lined the city's golden beaches. By the 1960s, Marbella was firmly established as a chic party destination for European royalty, aristocrats, film stars and other members of the international jet-set.

While some of that exclusivity had worn off by the 1990s, Marbella remained a playground for the wealthy. Its well-kept marinas were crammed with luxury yachts and its streets lined with designer shops.

But wherever there is substantial wealth in Europe, organised crime follows. It is true of London, Paris, Monaco and Milan. And it was true of Marbella.

The wealthy playboys who colonised the tiny fishing villages of the Costas in the 1940s and 1950s brought with them illegal excess.

By the 1970s, Marbella had a prostitution problem. By the 1980s, the area had been described as a "den of bohemian iniquity". By the 1990s, the city had an estimated 10,000 working girls operating locally. Young, attractive women would be trafficked from all over the world to service the customers of organised crime and legitimate wealthy spenders. Other young women actively chose sex work because they could make more money in one week in Marbella than they would get in a year back in Colombia, rural Russia or South Africa.

I'm told that the women at Milady's had chosen their profession and were well paid. They were also heavily protected and monitored. But, regardless, I was – and still am – no fan of prostitution because somewhere in the sex-trade loop, there is always a degree of exploitation. And that's at the classier establishments. Marbella was also awash with street-level thugs and criminals, some of whom treated women with barely concealed disdain.

No thanks.

* * *

The first time Mohamed invited me to the Milady Palace, I knew a little about what to expect.

In 1990, Carlos and I were busy establishing a new business and met Don Enrique Sanchez, owner of Spain's largest water distributor, Sandeos Del Norte, based in the northern port of La Coruna. Sanchez was interested in buying water purification units we could import.

Sandeos Del Norte was the company I'd paid the £5,000 which Northumberland Police mistakenly believed I'd given to Richard Henson to buy ecstasy.

By January 1991, Sanchez agreed to purchase 1,300 purification units for around $50,000 and signed a contract to receive them in September. The deal, completed on my birthday, gave Sanchez exclusive rights to sell our units in Spain. It was quite a present!

After finalising the deal, Sanchez said it was customary for the host to invite his guests to dinner, followed by a visit to a local bar or nightclub. Carlos nodded along and said he was familiar with the custom. So later that evening, I was enthusiastically guided into a local nightspot. Except that, within minutes, I clocked that it was no ordinary club – it was packed full of women wearing very little and behaving accordingly.

A brothel.

Sanchez spoke little English, so Carlos explained that, at the end of the evening, I would be expected to choose one of the women and take her back to my hotel.

My face dropped. "No way, I'm not interested," I replied. "Hey, listen. Each to their own, my friend – but that's not really my thing!"

"Look, Paul, if you don't, then you will offend Enrique – and it is his treat," Carlos protested, nodding towards Sanchez.

After a good-natured stand-off, Carlos and I arrived at a compromise: we would each take a woman back to the hotel, to keep Sanchez happy, but Carlos would spend the night with them both. Funny enough, Carlos did not need much convincing.

The next morning there was a gentle knock at my hotel room door. When I answered, Carlos was stood in the hallway with a brassy woman on each arm, looking a little the worse for wear but smiling like a Cheshire Cat. He hadn't slept a wink.

"These wonderful ladies told me that I'm the best lover they've ever had, Paul," my friend said without any sense of irony. Carlos swayed gently as he spoke.

"Really, pal?" I looked at Carlos, nodded along for fun and then smiled at both of the women. "And you don't think they've used that line before?"

The two women giggled. Carlos laughed louder.

* * *

So, in 1999, it was expected that Mohamed and his entourage would visit Milady's at least once during visits to Marbella. It would have been considered rude of me not to attend. Besides, Mohamed effectively compelled everybody to go by arranging to talk business for the first hour at the club. So I tolerated the place.

I should also point out that not everybody inside Miladys was a sex worker or their client. The venue also doubled as a genuine nightclub. You could, should you choose to, spend a costly evening there drinking hugely over-priced beer, bubbles and cocktails, ogling the scantily clad dancers in the back room, or innocently dancing the night away. Many men and women did just that.

Mohamed's approach to Milady's contrasted sharply with mine. Within minutes of entering, he would have a tall, elegant, beautifully attired and expensively thirsty woman on each arm. Mohamed would throw cash around all night, ordering bottles of champagne even though, as a Muslim, he did not drink alcohol. Each visit was like a scene out of a James Bond movie – leggy, pouting women wearing alluring perfumes and tight dresses, casually draped over expensively-suited men wearing nostril-burning aftershave. Like Carlos seven years earlier, a regular flow of excited-looking men would then leave with their 'dates' on their arms.

On occasions, I would be sat at a table, people-watching, and spot the same stunning woman leave the bar and return from several visits to upstairs rooms in a few hours. They had money, those international playboys, but they seemed to lack stamina!

* * *

On my travels with Mohamed, I was introduced to scores of clients who wanted to create sales and marketing teams and sell variants of Derbah's Millennium Club Card. Each client also wanted their own offshore company with banking facilities, which Goldcrest created.

Mohamed and I would split the profits from these deals: he would take half as his finder's fee, but Goldcrest still made good money. Within weeks of meeting Derbah, I noticed that any associate wanting to do business on the Canary Islands, or mainland Spain, effectively sought his permission before they began trading. I came to realise just how powerful Mohamed was because he controlled every aspect of the process that led to the sale of his holiday-related products – including a sizable chunk of Tenerife's timeshare market. There was a Machiavellian shrewdness about how he positioned himself at the centre of so many financial deals. Initially, I was impressed: Mohamed was a money-making machine.

★ ★ ★

It's hard to overstate just how big the timeshare and holiday club market was in the Canaries. The islands had vast plots of land available for development – and edge-of-town holiday apartment complexes were springing up everywhere.

Timeshares are properties with a divided form of ownership. Typically, customers bought a share in an apartment or condo and were entitled to use that property for a specified number of weeks each year. Once a property had been purchased, many owners were also able to trade or swap their entitlements. In 1999, a timeshare in a decent Tenerife apartment would have set you back around £6,000 for one week's use each year.

I'd arrived on the island following the John Palmer timeshare scandal, but not all timeshare or holiday pack offerings were illegal. Many established holiday companies ran legitimate schemes, with offerings often enhanced by discounted flights, excursions and meals. The widespread availability of timeshares, combined with the advent of budget and chartered airline routes to the islands, reduced prices significantly during the 1980s and 1990s – allowing individuals or families on lower incomes to invest. Many timeshare deals also provided steady returns as property prices soared.

But as the John Palmer case showed, the lucrative timeshare market also attracted less reputable operators. The problem for customers was that, contrary to popular opinion, it wasn't always easy to tell the difference between reputable operators and sharks.

By the late 1990s, the market was crowded and most firms were using similar high-pressure techniques to sell their packages. It was what happened after deals were signed which separated reputable providers from dodgy traders or fraudsters. I knew of several timeshare firms on Tenerife that had been accused of being 'Del Boy'-style operators, but which always delivered what their customers paid for. The sector had become synonymous with barrow-boy types, but most were legitimate – they just wanted to make money. That's why, initially, I made a point of not judging Derbah or his associates.

The success of any company selling timeshare or holiday pack deals depended on Outside Personal Contacts (OPCs), more commonly known as timeshare 'touts'. This was the army of young adults who worked the streets of resorts, generally by stopping passers-by and using whatever sweet-talking, tricks, sob story or genuine sales techniques they knew to get holidaymakers to attend high-pressure sales presentations.

One classic method employed by OPCs was to offer holidaymakers a potential prize from a free scratch-card. Of course, the cards were fixed so that almost all participants 'won' a prize, usually a cheap bottle of sparkling wine, but were forced to attend a sales presentation to collect their winnings. If the prospect of a warm glass of fizz wasn't enticing enough, though, potential timeshare or holiday-pack customers were also told that they could win a free holiday – if they attended the sales presentation. Unsuspecting couples were not immediately informed that they would have to pay, expensively, for the flights.

Of course, not every customer fell for these obvious tout techniques – particularly the prospect of a bottle of a sickly sweet sparkly that anybody could pick up at a local supermarket for a few Euros. But the OPCs only needed one in ten people to relent to ensure that tens of thousands of potential customers attended sales presentations linked to Mohamed's products.

Once inside the sales presentation, however, things would become decidedly more abrupt and forceful. Gone were the smiling young street touts. Instead, well-drilled, hawkish and more experienced salespeople would subject holidaymakers to high-pressure techniques designed to get them to sign-up, that day, to a timeshare or holiday pack deal via their credit card. Sales staff were ferocious in pursuit of their commission. Tactics included watching undecided customers from behind a two-way mirror and taking it in turns to join their colleagues in the presentation room with hot-off-the-press news that fresh discounts were suddenly being offered – if customers signed up there and then.

Another trick saw sales staff play fast and loose with potential customers' finances. They would somehow calculate that the couple in front of them could spend up to £40,000 on holidays over the next ten years, yet would pay just £15,000 for a two-week guaranteed timeshare in a luxury resort over the same period. Of course, all of the timeshare packages would be costed at the bare minimum in front of potential customers. Additional costs such as cleaning fees, maintenance and local taxes would be tucked away in the small print of the contracts which followed.

The whole point was to spend an hour or two convincing cash-rich retirees, families with disposable income and even lower-income earners to part with their hard-earned money. For Mohamed and his associates, this meant convincing customers to buy the Millennium Cub Card.

Some presentations would last four or five hours, after which couples often emerged visibly shaken and several thousands of pounds lighter.

I was no fool and could see that Derbah's firms used high-pressure techniques to sell holiday packs. But in that respect, they were little different from other operators who were household names.

There is nothing untoward or criminal in the marketing and sale of 'holiday packs' provided that funds are set aside in a client account for future disbursements – such as the cost of providing customers with the benefits and services stated in the sales literature and contracts. Mohamed assured me that he was accounting for all disbursements by transferring funds to his master company, Worldwide Investments, based in Lebanon and administered by a separate team of accountants and bankers. Through

Mohamed's accounts, I could certainly see huge sums being paid into Lebanese-based banks. So, his initial story stacked up.

* * *

Business with Mohamed Derbah was going so well that I felt comfortable introducing some of my acquaintances to him.

In early 2000, Nicholas Evans, another former HMP Thorp Arch inmate, had flown out to Tenerife for a holiday. I'd got on well with Nick in prison even though he was what some would describe as an 'oddball'. Evans, who was bisexual, had gone off the rails shortly after his wife's death from cancer in 1990. He was convicted for blackmail and false imprisonment in 1993 and received an eight-year sentence. It's worth noting that Nicholas blamed his conviction on a Freemason-led conspiracy. Yes, *that* kind of oddball. However, he was harmless, friendly and always treated me well.

After release from prison, Evans changed his identity so that he could start life afresh. He settled on the name Jeremy Sinclair. He was also diagnosed with the early signs of Parkinson's Disease but refused to let the condition rule his life. He retired from nine-to-five work, drew a generous private pension, made extra money through a company called Gay Club International and started to relax.

That brought him to Tenerife.

I introduced Jeremy to Mohamed, not expecting the two men to get on. How wrong I was. They clicked and, by March 2000, Mohamed asked Sinclair to manage a business for him in return for a share of the profits. The new venture was a 'cash-back' service offered to Derbah's Millennium Club Card members.

I had no reason to suspect Mohamed's cash-back firm was dodgy, but two similar services belonging to Derbah's rivals, known as Hyprafund and Reclaim, had recently been accused of scam-like practices. I wasn't sure that Jeremy wanted the hassle of entering a sector with a chequered reputation.

Nonetheless, my fellow ex-prisoner accepted the role and carried out his work with gusto. Jeremy was an excellent salesman and, within months, the new venture was turning over millions of pounds – boosted by customers desperate to avoid rival firms whose cash-back schemes had been the subject of media criticism. Jeremy was so successful that he rented a luxurious apartment in Los Cristianos.

Initially, Mohamed asked me to incorporate the offshore company that would sell the cash-back product to holidaymakers. But I declared a potential conflict of interest, which forced Derbah to use a Gibraltar-based corporate services provider. It meant that Goldcrest had nothing to do with Belmar Investments Ltd, the Belize-registered company eventually bought to provide the cash-back regime. For marketing purposes, Belmar Investment Ltd traded as Sovereign Gold Trust.

The Belize-registered firm opened two bank accounts: one at the Royal Bank of Scotland in Gibraltar and another at the Banque Senegalo-Tunisienne in Dakar, Senegal. Mohamed had many contacts in west Africa – a legacy of his time spent sniffing around the diamond mining market in Sierra Leone, which is where he met John Palmer.

* * *

Shortly after I was introduced to Mohamed, I noticed that several rival firms offering alternatives to the Millennium Club Card had been shut down at short notice. At first, this news was received by Derbah's entourage with jokes about how rival sales teams "weren't up to it" and made heavy losses. After a few months, the claim was that rival firms "couldn't compete".

Quite literally, as it turned out.

It transpired that some rival companies were effectively closed down by the island's police following tip-offs from anonymous sources. Sometimes, offices were raided and paperwork seized – but usually, the police just stopped rival firms' street touts from operating by arresting them. In contrast, touts working for firms that punted the Millennium Club Card were often left alone.

I soon noticed that some policemen I'd seen at Mohamed's office had been involved in closing down Derbah's rivals. As my relationship with Derbah solidified throughout those early months, he became almost blasé about what was going on. Mohamed never verbally confirmed it, but he seemed aware that police officers worked to shut down rivals and simultaneously turn a blind eye to Millennium Club Card touts. I knew it – and Mohamed knew that I knew it. But he didn't care because the whole issue went unspoken between us. Whenever the matter was mentioned by others, Derbah's team claimed that the firms being closed down were those operating unlawfully.

In return for their increasing monopoly, Mohamed received an additional monthly payment from firms run by his close associates – on top of the payments they already made to sell the Millennium Club Card. I had no idea whether Mohamed was bribing police officers – something he was later accused of. But there seemed little doubt that, at the very least, his firms were viewed positively.

Through Carlos, I knew about Spain's corruption culture – such as the fact that foreign investors sometimes only paid fifty per cent of the price of an apartment or villa, in front of a public notary, when signing the deeds for the property. Often, the other fifty per cent was 'black' money paid in cash and tax-free for the developer at the expense of Spain's revenue department.

When I told Carlos about my suspicions that Mohamed enjoyed a close relationship with local police on Tenerife, he simply shrugged his shoulders. He said: "I've heard these allegations. But even if it is true, that sort of thing happens all over this island. Welcome to Tenerife, Paul. Be careful with these people. You know my thoughts."

* * *

Separately from my business with Derbah, in late 1999, I met with an American businessman in York who claimed to be on the lookout for investment in high-end projects.

Eric Reiner was a brash and straight-talking man who acted like he was in a Martin Scorsese film. I'd met several people like him in Tenerife, everything about him was "big", and most of them were legitimate businessmen. If a little uncouth.

During a meeting at my office in York, Reiner explained that he wanted to raise significant capital for three or four projects worth around $450m – and he wanted my help in trying to identify potential investors. Eric wondered whether any of my clients would be interested and, if so, what sort of investment return they would seek.

I can't say that I smelled a rat immediately, but I was not convinced by Eric Reiner. Nonetheless, I kept his details and stayed in touch, just in case he was a genuine deal-maker.

* * *

Around the turn of the Millennium, the legitimate timeshare and holiday pack market on Tenerife was so popular, and lucrative, that I decided to get in on the action. Unlike the sharkish operators, I had no intention of misleading or pressurising customers such as retirees. I also knew I could not compete with the likes of Derbah and his Millennium Club Card associates, so I decided to experiment in a small corner of the market.

The new venture would not be my primary business, more of a side-project, but it promised decent returns if I could get even a tiny foothold in the sector. I figured I would need a full-time book-keeper capable of operating between the UK and Tenerife to stay on top of all legal and accounting requirements. To my surprise and joy, my daughter Sarah volunteered for the role.

In January 2000, I incorporated a UK company called 'WeLoveTenerife.Com Ltd'. I also obtained Air Travel Organisers' License (ATOL) and Association of British Travel Agents (ABTA) approval, which gave the company the legal respectability I hoped would distinguish us from hawkish operators. Whilst the registration fees were minimal, I had to block £200,000 in a bank account as a guarantee to support the licences. The new company's head office was in central York, and I opened a sister firm in Tenerife. 'WeLoveTenerife SL' traded from Goldcrest House in Los Cristianos and dealt with the Spanish side of my new venture.

With several business interests all profitable, I was cash-rich again. The building blocks of what I hoped would be the revitalised Blanchard corporate empire were in place. After some hard graft and no shortage of commitment, flying back and forth across Europe regularly, I finally felt that the dark years of imprisonment and scandal were behind me.

How little I knew.

CHAPTER EIGHT
Guayota

The Canary Islands sit 62 miles north-west of Morocco and this beautiful, if now over-developed, volcanic archipelago is one of Spain's nineteen autonomous cities or regions.

While the Canaries have never been 'offshore' jurisdictions in the classic sense of the term, they enjoy a special status as a low-tax region within Europe. In Spain, the islands' official status is the Zona Especial Canarias (ZEC) and the current corporation tax rate is just four per cent. Hence, you can understand why 'offshore' specialists flocked to the islands.

Contrary to popular opinion, the islands do not take their name from the famous canary bird. Instead, the name comes from the Latin word for dog, or *canariae*. King Juba II, Berber monarch of Numidia between 30-25 B.C., is often credited with giving the islands their name after noting that they were home to packs of wild dogs.

Other historians claim the name derives from the more general practice of dog worship among locals thousands of years ago. Either way, the original reference is almost certainly to canines. Hence, *Canariae Insulae* – or 'Island of Dogs'. Even in the modern era, the Canary Islands' coat-of-arms still depicts two hounds.

Tenerife is the largest and most populous of the Canaries and home to 900,000 people. But three thousand years ago, the island's original inhabitants were the Guanches people – whom scientists have linked through DNA to Berbers from North Africa.

The Gaunches were a god-fearing folk who believed in the existence of a supreme deity, known as *Achamán*, which translates as 'the skies'. According to Guanche legend, *Achamán* was the creator of all civilisation. He lived in the heavens but had an adversary on Tenerife:

Guayota.

The devil, or evil spirit.

It is said *Guayota* once kidnapped the sun god and locked him inside Mount Teide – the world's third-largest volcano that dominates Tenerife's skyline – plunging humanity into darkness. When Guanche people prayed to *Achamán* to bring them light, the supreme god freed the sun and punished *Guayota* by trapping him inside Mount Teide.

To those who follow Guanche legend, therefore, Mount Tiede remains the gateway to hell or the underworld and is home to Guayota – often depicted as a giant black dog – and his fellow demons, known as *Tibicenas*. Together, they represent the dark side of Tenerife.

* * *

It had been ten months since Wim De Groote – an affable, if slightly slippery, Belgian – had started Goldguard Investments and business had exceeded expectations. During meetings at Derbah's office, Wim would often sit in Mohamed's chair while the Lebanese calculated his cut from the millions which flowed from holiday pack sales.

But I began to suspect that letting Wim take his chair was part of Derbah's calculated plan. Ostensibly, it was a show of generosity by Mohamed – indicating that Wim was an equal partner in the broader business, somebody Derbah trusted. That could not be further from the truth.

Privately, Mohamed had become jealous of Wim because Goldguard was outselling other holiday pack companies on Tenerife. I'd first detected Derbah's jealousy during casual chats with him, but initially dismissed it as little more than professional rivalry. After all, Mohamed was making a lot of money from Wim because the Belgian was selling an enhanced version of the Millennium Club Card. Wim was an impressive and energetic salesman – and had a knack of recruiting high-quality staff. But as De Groote's success snowballed, Mohamed began to resent losing what he considered *his* market to Goldguard. Resentment then developed into a grudge against Wim. In private, at least.

When the two men were together, Mohamed was a picture of charm and philanthropy. The three of us sometimes dined at Mohamed's restaurant in Playa de las Americas. Neither Wim nor I were big drinkers which, for teetotal Mohamed and his brothers, made spending an evening with us a lot more tolerable than a night out with the drunken 'Brits abroad' crowd. Instead of alcohol, laughter became our drug. We'd take it in turns to tell stories of past capers and make jokes at the expense of pompous, self-important local bureaucrats we'd all encountered.

Wim was dating Anne Ritserveldt, a friendly and outgoing Belgian woman, who sometimes accompanied him to meetings or social events.

De Groote always had a tale to tell. He had a market trader's mentality, including the all-important 'gift of the gab'. But underneath the humorous stories about run-ins with authority, there was a shrewdness and a work ethic about Wim that marked him out from most of his competitors. Of course, he wasn't all sweetness and light. At some point, Wim got himself caught up in a credit card fraud or scam. I knew few details but didn't doubt that he could be a slippery character. Yet he paid my fees on time, treated me with respect and was no threat to Goldcrest.

Derbah, on the other hand, increasingly treated Wim as a threat.

While he was sat eating and sharing jokes with the Belgian at his restaurant, Mohamed would be quietly calculating how to get one over on his business partner. As resentment turned to hatred, and a desire to seize Wim's share of the holiday pack market, I saw another side to Derbah. Once Wim was not around, Mohamed would fly into a rage about how much money he was "losing" to Goldguard – even though he received a cut the sales Wim made. The transformation would be sudden, verbally violent and aimed at both Wim and Goldguard's other staff.

"Wim is fucking me over, Paul, I tell you...Goldguard is taking more of my money and this is not good for my reputation on Tenerife...Wim is selling me short...He is up to no good...and that mouthy fucking personal assistant of his is in on it."

Over the next few weeks, I became aware that Mohamed attended many meetings with senior police, council and business contacts on Tenerife. Something was brewing.

* * *

On 22 March 2000, I received an early morning phone call from Derbah, urgently requesting that I meet him at his office. When I asked why, he replied with one word: "Wim."

The day's events would indicate just who the real Mohamed Derbah was, and the lengths he was prepared to go to in pursuit of money and power.

I had been preparing for a busy morning at Goldcrest, dealing with matters which had nothing to do with Derbah, so the urgent face-to-face was an inconvenience. Nonetheless, Mohamed was a key client. In the service and consultancy sector, if a key client wants to meet you urgently, you make every effort to see them. I arrived at Mohamed's headquarters within twenty minutes. Unusually, the office was empty except for the two of us. I don't mind saying that when I clocked that nobody else was around, I became a little nervous. After all, Mohamed had become a little erratic whenever Wim's name was mentioned.

Derbah dispensed with the niceties the moment we sat down. He wasn't angry, certainly not with me, but he wore the expression of a concerned man. If it was an act, it was a good one.

Derbah explained that he'd made a 12.30 pm appointment at the police station in Las Americas that day, at which he wanted me to file a deposition against Wim De Groote for alleged fraud linked to Goldguard.

* * *

As I understood it, Wim had allegedly used the credit card terminal of other merchants when taking deposits from some people who purchased his holiday packs. The suspicion was that Visa had stopped accepting credit card payments made to Goldguard, amid concerns that disgruntled holiday pack customers had asked for their money back when they did not receive their benefits. There had been several complaints made to HSBC Bank on the Isle of Man, where I had arranged Wim's account. The credit card company would have shut down Goldguard's service if it feared that Wim's firm would not pay its outstanding bills – forcing Wim to use other firm's merchant services to receive customer payments. But if that was what Wim was doing, it was potentially illegal.

Mohamed proceeded to show me evidence that Wim *may* have been doing just that. I can't say it was definitive. But if there had been complaints that customers hadn't received their Millennium Club Card membership, well, in my view that was equally an issue for Derbah and his team. As the Card supplier, Mohamed's firm was partially responsible for ensuring customers received the benefits. At the time, I had no way of knowing whether Derbah, Wim or an honest mistake was the reason customers may not have received services they had been promised.

* * *

Mohamed sipped a mint tea and looked directly into my eyes as he spoke.

"I finish Wim on this Island. Maybe get him put in prison."

"What?" I nearly spat out my tea when I replied. I couldn't believe what I was hearing.

Derbah sat back in his office chair – the same chair he offered to Wim during meetings – and outlined a plan that would stop De Groote, Goldguard and its high-performing staff. Mohamed justified his action by explaining more about Wim's alleged fraud. Derbah also advised me to "back away" from De Groote because he would be "damaged goods" if prosecuted. Finally, he urged me to accompany him to the police station later that day – so that he could be present while I made a statement explaining what I understood about alleged frauds.

Mohamed just assumed I would help him. But although I tried not to show it, I was torn.

Sure, I was aware of independent claims that De Groote was up to no good. And for that reason, I understood why any supplier to Goldguard, such as Derbah, might want to sever ties with Wim's firm. I owed a degree of loyalty to Mohamed, as the man who had introduced me to so much business on Tenerife. Besides, the whole island stood to lose out if Wim was committing fraud: it was still suffering reputational damage following the John Palmer timeshare scandal.

But I suspected that Mohamed could be trying to frame Wim.

I had to think. Fast.

Then it dawned on me. Derbah was not asking me to report anything that was untrue. Wim was genuinely suspected of using other merchants' credit card services to receive holiday pack payments. I had no idea whether he was guilty of fraud, but he was undoubtedly *suspected* of it. And because of that, as a corporate services provider to Wim, it was likely that local police would want to speak to me during any investigation. I knew Goldcrest's paperwork was in order. But by going to the police with Mohamed at an early stage, I'd have the reassurance of knowing exactly what was being said about Wim, his company and alleged frauds. I had a solid local reputation to protect.

Mohamed knew the most senior officers at the police station, so I figured it would be easier to deal with them on his terms. A little reluctantly, I agreed to accompany Mohamed.

* * *

I expected a police-led discussion about Wim's business and questions designed to establish what I knew about alleged credit card fraud. What I experienced was extraordinary.

Mohamed dominated the meeting. He dictated the precise subjects under discussion, read through sensitive materials about Wim the police had obtained and, at one stage, even removed from the police's possession documents that specifically mentioned him. On occasion, the officer compiling my statement took instructions directly from Derbah. At one stage, Tenerife's chief of police even popped in to check that everything was to Mohamed's satisfaction.

One man appeared to be in control of the meeting. And he was not a policeman.

I provided a statement and stuck to the facts, despite pressure from Mohamed to include other gossip about Wim. The officer taking my statement spoke little English, while my Spanish lacked precise legal terminology. We had an interpreter present but, at times, multiple people would be speaking at the same time – some trying to make statements of fact, some trying to suggest alternative wordings and some trying to ask questions. In two languages. The whole situation was chaotic.

By the end of the process, a statement had been agreed and signed. I felt content that I had stuck to the facts as I understood them. But I had a sick feeling in the pit of my stomach as we left. Mohamed looked delighted.

Any police or state action against Wim meant that Mohamed would be free to target De Groote's sizable share of the holiday pack market. Derbah and his entourage could bag Wim's customer base and well-trained staff – and keep all proceeds from the Millennium Club Card sales associated with the business Wim had worked hard to build.

On the other hand, Wim faced a possible jail term if the police proved the suspected fraud. It did not seem right that we had played such an active part in discussing allegations against a man Mohamed and I had regularly socialised with.

As Mohamed and I made our way back to his office, I felt low. Derbah sensed it.

"Wim is not the man we thought he was, Paul," Mohamed said, breaking an uneasy silence between us. As he spoke, I could see Derbah eyeing me cautiously as though trying to assess what I was thinking.

"These frauds with the credit cards..."

"Alleged frauds, Mohamed," I interrupted. "We can't say for certain."

"Yes. These alleged frauds...these are very serious issues for police on Tenerife," Mohamed replied. "The authorities here remember John Palmer. Bad for business. Stigma. The police, the council, the government: they now watch us all closely. Wim was bad for business. That is why I acted. He cannot get in the way."

"Of who, Mohamed?" As I spoke, I realised my instinctive retort was louder and firmer than I had intended.

I glanced up, and Derbah had fixed a menacing stare on me. If looks could kill. Suddenly, I was getting a sense of who the real Mohamed Derbah was and how he treated people. I had to tread carefully.

"Why are you are angry with me, Paul?" Mohamed barked out his question, pointing his index finger towards me. Suddenly, Derbah looked a foot taller. And angry.

"You think the police did not already want to speak to you about Wim? About Goldguard? You also had questions to answer and you have done that with my help."

Mohamed walked towards me as he spoke? He drew close and said: "I take you...us...to the police station to clear this up quickly. Before it becomes *our* problem. Yes? Are you not grateful? Goldcrest will have less hassle now, Paul."

Now was not the time for confrontation. I reminded myself that Wim was genuinely under suspicion by the police, even if this was all rather convenient for Mohamed. Besides, if Derbah's associates on Tenerife could stitch up Wim, then they could do it to anybody. Suddenly, and for the first time since I'd arrived in the Canaries, I felt small and exposed so far from England.

"Look, Mohamed, I understand what you're saying. I'm just tired. Work has been hectic recently, and this...well...all this stuff with Wim came out of the blue. I am not ungrateful."

It was enough to placate Derbah. He thought for a moment, then nodded. The tension dissipated.

Mohamed looked to the floor, looked back at me, and suddenly burst into a deep, loud and guttural laugh. "Hahaha! Look at us, Paul. Two friends acting like we are enemies! Wim wants to divide us. We will not let that happen. Come, my friend, you have Goldcrest work to do..."

Mohamed Derbah gave me an almighty slap on the back. It hurt. But relief washed over me.

***

Back at my apartment that evening, I sat down on the bed and realised I'd had a lucky escape outside the police station. My instinct was to ask what the hell Mohamed was doing treating Wim so badly. But that would not have been wise. If the events of the past month had taught me anything, it was that Mohamed was indeed the influential figure on Tenerife that Carlos had described.

Mohamed had been present throughout my police statement – a situation that would have been unheard of in the UK. Not only that, but senior police officers had kowtowed to him, allowing Mohamed to review sensitive documentation relating to Wim and others. He even removed statements that did not present him, as the Millennium Club Card supplier, in a good light. All in full view of senior and friendly law enforcement officials.

Mohamed was certainly more than he'd let on when he first contacted Goldcrest. But how much more? I knew from that moment that I would need to tread carefully when it came to Derbah and his entourage. Suddenly, other local gossip about Mohamed and his brothers came to mind. I still couldn't see the full picture. But I was beginning to join some dots.

I'd witnessed potential corruption involving Mohamed. But did that make him the gangster others claimed he was? I'd glimpsed his vengeful nature. But all that bar gossip about how Mohamed and his brothers were John Palmer's henchmen? How they were responsible for countless violent attacks? How Mohamed ran Tenerife's underworld with an iron fist? I had not seen any of that first-hand.

I sat up in bed to try to stop my head from spinning. You can over-think these things.

"Be rational, Paul," I told myself. "What's the actual evidence in front of you? Mohamed has a close relationship with some policemen? OK. But he's helping the police, and Wim could be a fraudster. Right? Is that it?"

"The documents. He removed documents from the police station. That isn't a minor issue, but he was allowed to by the officers..."

My head was still spinning as I lay back down. I stared at the ceiling and considered how to handle the situation.

* * *

With my new travel agency offering holidays approved by official regulators, I was concerned about what would happen if Mohamed suddenly turned against me – as he had with Wim. As I lay on the bed, my recent history flashed by. Since the drugs conviction, I'd come too far, rebuilt too much of my life and business to allow others to take it away. But Tenerife was more dangerous than I'd allowed myself to believe. I'd been naïve.

I decided to surreptitiously record critical phone calls with Mohamed from this day on. I'd been stitched up by a "friend", Richard Henson, once before and was not going to risk it happening again. I had no intention of using the recordings to go after Mohamed. That would be business suicide on Tenerife. If the gossipmongers were right, it could also lead to a very different form of death.

No, I told myself the tapes would be an insurance policy if Mohamed repeated his betrayal of Wim. I also vowed not only to carry on doing everything by the book but also to ensure that there were recordings of Goldcrest conducting business by the book.

At some stage, I concluded, I'd also need to distance myself from Derbah. But if I backed away from him immediately after the Wim incident, Mohamed would know what I was thinking and would almost certainly see it as a betrayal.

I benefited from operating between the UK and Tenerife, so I could bide my time and use trips back to Yorkshire to create distance between myself and Mohamed.

Or so I thought.

In the end, Mohamed made a bigger decision for me.

* * *

Shortly after I made my police statement, I received a phone call from Wim's fiancée, Anne Ritserveldt, begging me not to make an official complaint because, she believed, Mohamed was framing Wim. She also had a message directly from Wim, warning me that Derbah would eventually stab me in the back, too.

I felt like shit explaining to Anne that I'd already made a police statement after being pressured by Mohamed. I explained what I'd told the police and that I was sorry events had turned out the way they had. But I stuck to the facts about the credit card fraud allegations and how Wim could disprove those if he had kept clean records.

But there was a lot more going on behind the scenes.

On 2 March 2000, days after the call from Ritserveldt, Wim was arrested on Tenerife, charged, flown to Madrid and detained at Alcala-Meco prison – a maximum security facility north-east of the capital in which many notorious criminals reside.

Not long after Wim's arrest, I learned that he had been found in possession of fake banknotes and counterfeit credit cards. Detaining Wim at Alcala-Meco seemed heavy-handed, but European states do not take kindly to the distribution of counterfeit currency. Many observers on Tenerife suspected that either Wim had been up to something none of us knew about, or timeshare rivals had intensified a campaign to see him off.

I was determined to find out more about Mohamed, his entourage and his businesses. Not the idle gossip, not the bar-room banter – the facts. Who was Mohamed Derbah? Exactly how much power did he exercise on Tenerife? And how? I wanted to be ready if Mohamed came after me next.

But I would do it all from a distance.

* * *

After he had been in Alcala-Meco for five months, Wim De Groote's lawyers managed to secure his release on bail. Wim had cut a deal with a hot-shot investigative magistrate in Madrid, Baltasar Garzon, under which De Groote gave Spain's prosecutors information on alleged criminal networks operating from Tenerife.

Wim told the judge he feared repercussions from criminals who effectively controlled the island. So, in return for his help, Wim was released from prison and placed under police protection. Despite a guarantee of personal security, Wim still felt unsafe in Spain. He quickly boarded a train to Belgium, breaching his bail conditions in the process.

It wasn't a smart move.

Spain's judicial authorities responded by demanding that Belgium extradite Wim to Madrid to face prosecution. Under the law at the time, European Union members states which were also part of the Schengen Area – in which mutual border controls had effectively been abolished – were expected to return fugitives to fellow EU member states from which they had fled.

Wim fought hard against extradition and used media interviews to make his case. It was around this time that I first saw the word "mafia" used to describe Mohamed Derbah and his associates.

From Belgium, Wim argued that he would be targeted by Tenerife's violent Lebanese-led "mafia" if he was returned to Spain. He publicly proclaimed that the mafia-controlled Tenerife's lucrative timeshare market, as well as prostitution and drug trafficking on the island. Wim argued that he would not be safe even in jail on the Spanish mainland because underworld figures could get to him via other prisoners.

"I am guaranteed to be killed out there," he told one Belgian newspaper.

De Groote had been more of a player on Tenerife than me. While I travelled back and forth to my family in England, the Belgian socialised hard – in the island's many pubs, bars and restaurants – and he knew the gossip about who ran Tenerife. What I could not figure out was whether his account of Derbah's "mafia" was based on genuine experience, or whether he was building a story based on legends.

Wim settled back into life in Belgium and, for more than a year, it seemed his mother country would not deport him to Spain. But in August 2002, as he prepared to board a plane to the Philippines from Brussels, Wim De Groote was detained by border police responding to an international arrest warrant.

Upon being returned to Madrid, De Groote was incarcerated while awaiting trial. He was later found guilty of fraud and sentenced to six years in prison, despite claiming that he remained under threat of death from Spain's underworld.

* * *

Judge Baltasar Garzon, with whom Wim De Groote had shared information on Tenerife's underworld, was a rising star within Spain's judicial ranks.

The charismatic lawyer was appointed to the Audiencia Nacional, Spain's central court, in 1988 and established a reputation as a fearless investigative magistrate by pursuing members of the Basque separatist terrorist group Euskadi Ta Askatasuna, or 'ETA'.

After a brief political career in the early 1990s, Garzon returned to the Audencia Nacional determined to ruffle more feathers.

In 1998, he made international headlines when he issued an international warrant for the arrest of former Chilean dictator Augusto Pinochet. Garzon exercised a legal nuclear option, known as universal jurisdiction, in an attempt to prosecute Pinochet for the torture and deaths of Spanish citizens in Chile. The world reacted with wide-eyed wonder at Garzon's chutzpah when he issued the arrest warrant – which forced British police to detain Pinochet in London in October 1998. The ex-dictator had travelled to the UK for medical treatment and was placed under house arrest.

But to Garzon's disappointment, the British government decided not to extradite Pinochet to Spain due to the former dictator's ill-health. Pinochet was instead allowed to return to Chile, where he died in 2006. He was never prosecuted.

Despite failing to nail Pinochet, Garzon became a household name in Spain. When Wim provided his information, Garzon was the examining magistrate at Madrid's high-profile Central Criminal Court Number 5, which deals with terrorism, organised crime and money laundering. And he was determined to continue to make a name for himself.

Little did I know that I would later get to know Spain's 'super-judge'.

* * *

Mohamed's treatment of Wim de Groote was the final straw for Carlos.

My great friend had repeatedly warned me about Derbah and I had not wanted to listen because I saw dollar signs. In my defence, nobody had produced firm evidence that Mohamed was a mobster or criminal. But I can't avoid the fact that I was warned about the risks. Carlos had made sure of that – and I had let him down by ignoring him.

Sure, I'd dressed up my dalliance with Mohamed by saying that Goldcrest Hispania was still a relatively new business that needed a steady flow of legitimate, wealthy clients – and pointing out that Derbah had passed all due diligence checks. But why had I not listened to the one experienced businessman I truly trusted on Tenerife?

Carlos quit Goldcrest following the Wim debacle. As he closed the door, my great friend repeated his warning that my venture could all end in tears.

We parted company on good terms, but I'd be a liar if I said that our friendship was unaffected. Carlos knew that I'd provided a statement about Wim to the local police, and at Derbah's request. He couldn't believe that I'd been so foolish to agree and, in the cold light of day, neither could I.

Carlos felt strongly that Derbah was dangerous to be around. Yet, Goldcrest was still providing services to Mohamed and other members of his entourage. I said it would take me a while to unpick the mess, but Carlos was not prepared to wait. I don't blame him: he had a wife, daughter and a permanent life on Tenerife to think about.

We said our goodbyes and went our separate ways.

I thought that we would still see each other socially, but I have not been in the same room as Carlos since that day. We've been in touch and we know where to find each other. One day, over a cold beer, I'll meet with my Argentinean pal once again and we will laugh about it all. But tainting our friendship remains one of the biggest mistakes I ever made.

***

Replacing Carlos and his encyclopaedic knowledge of Tenerife's laws, regulations, and business practices would not be easy. But I desperately needed somebody at Goldcrest Hispania who spoke fluent Spanish. By pure chance, I stumbled upon Sarah Hill.

Sarah was twenty-three, as sharp as a tack and sociable. She was highly organised, highly efficient and spoke fluent Spanish. She was also an extremely attractive blonde who could handle unwanted attention from Tenerife's many self-declared Casanovas. You'd be surprised what a useful skill that was in the Canaries.

Although Sarah was born in England, her parents – both teachers – moved to Tenerife when she was nine. Sarah had studied economics at university for two years before taking a break to work at a local travel agency.

I poached Sarah by offering her more money and responsibility before she signed up to complete her degree. She joined Goldcrest in April 2000. It was one of the best decisions I have ever made.

***

Having watched Wim de Groote's demise from the inside, so to speak, I planned to keep a watchful eye on Mohamed Derbah while gradually unpicking myself from him.

I'd lost Carlos, but I still wanted Goldcrest Hispania to thrive. Naively, I thought that I could simply start to have less contact with Mohamed and his associates, begin to pick up a portfolio of new and reliable clients elsewhere on the island and across Europe and take Goldcrest to a lucrative new level. That was certainly how we proceeded once Sarah Hill was on board.

In the meantime, I had unfinished business with Mohamed. Literally: Goldcrest was still completing work already commissioned by him. It was vital that I did not give my intentions away. Particularly as I was already trying to find out more about Derbah, his entourage and influential contacts on the island.

* * *

It did not take long before the phone rang and Mohamed's voice was on the other end of the line. He wanted to meet, informally, to discuss some minor administrative issues.

The phone call was pleasant enough, and Derbah was undoubtedly friendly with me. It was as though the walk back from the police station had never happened. But when I asked after Mohamed's general welfare – as I did every time we spoke – he said he was "unhappy with what is going on in the UK".

I knew exactly what he meant, so agreed to meet with Mohamed because I knew he'd want to let off steam about something unrelated to Wim.

* * *

"I can't fucking believe it! He has walked away from court, Paul. Not a single offence prosecuted yet! He's fucking...laughing at British justice. Everybody is laughing at British justice!"

Mohamed was sat opposite me at his favourite table in the corner of his restaurant. He wore an open-necked shirt and was slumped back in a comfortable chair. He looked disconsolate and his *misbaha* beads were getting a working-over.

On the table before us was a pot of fresh Lebanese tea, a selection of savoury dips and warm bread straight from the restaurant's ovens. I'd been offered wine, but politely declined. It was lunchtime, I had work to do later that afternoon – and I didn't want the social lubricant of alcohol to loosen my tongue during any discussion with Mohamed.

It was May 2000 and Mohamed was talking about a man he now hated, but whose day-to-day trials and tribulations had become another of his obsessions. His former friend and employer, now his greatest enemy.

John Palmer.

To the surprise of just about everybody on the planet, an eight-month Old Bailey fraud trial of 'Goldfinger' and his lover, Christina Ketley, had collapsed for legal reasons.

Palmer, Ketley and others had been arrested and charged over a £30m timeshare fraud on Tenerife – although island locals believed the total value of the fraud was significantly higher. The Old Bailey judge quickly ordered a retrial for Palmer and Ketley, but that meant it was unlikely either would be back in court for another year. In the meantime, British taxpayers had to swallow the multi-million cost of the failed prosecution.

It was the talk of Tenerife.

"That lucky fucking pig! He is the biggest criminal in Britain – Europe! – and he walks away every time. He was bad for business on Tenerife. No friend of this island. Can you believe it, Paul?"

Mohamed looked over at me and his face burst into what I can only describe as a reluctant smile. The sort you put on when you're not enjoying something you're supposed to enjoy. Like watching your kids plays at school. Mohamed wasn't angry, just utterly mystified.

"He's certainly one of the luckiest men I have ever read about. The judge hasn't even said why the case against him collapsed. It all sounds odd. But they are going to put him back on trial," I replied.

Unlike Derbah, I didn't know John Palmer. But like everybody on Tenerife, I knew the press reports and local gossip. I also knew many people who worked closely with Goldfinger. I'd been following the trial in Britain and the discussion seemed like a good way of falsely re-building bridges with Mohamed following the Wim incidents.

"Sheesh! He is one lucky son of a bitch! You know he is guilty, Paul, right? John Palmer is a criminal."

Mohamed started to gesticulate wildly, arms flailing. "Everybody here knows it: me, my brothers, my friends, the public, the police. Everybody! He is lucky."

"But he cannot come back to Tenerife because he might get killed. People here wish him harm," Mohamed said, nodding.

I wondered whether that meant *he* wished John Palmer harm? Mohamed's rant continued for some time. I sat, listened, nodded and placated. It was a useful meeting, because – to Derbah – I appeared to be firmly on his side.

* * *

After Wim De Groote's demise, I had made some significant but discreet inquiries about Mohamed – approaching only reliable contacts who were not prone to exaggeration or gossip.

To a man, they had confirmed Carlos's suspicions. Derbah was widely alleged to be a mafia boss – and a good and very wealthy one at that. I was warned to be careful because Derbah's gang were reportedly violent and vengeful. Allegations of beatings, assaults, threats and intimidation were commonplace.

As I made further inquiries, I learned more about allegations that Derbah's gang had engaged John Palmer's men in a bloody turf war on Tenerife after the two men fell out – with the lucrative timeshare market at stake. Mohamed's brothers, Sam and Hatem, were reportedly part of his muscle on the island and had a fearsome reputation.

Derbah's mafia was also allegedly involved in the island's lucrative prostitution, drugs and sex trafficking markets. Mohamed, it was claimed, had scrambled his way to the top of the Tenerife underworld.

He was, one source alleged, a dark force on Tenerife.

Guayota.

At the time, I still had no way of verifying these claims. But this was not the idle bar gossip I'd heard previously. These were the informed and sober views of sensible, senior and respected Tenerife residents who had no apparent reason to exaggerate. One also explained the background to the relationship between Derbah and John Palmer.

The two men reportedly met in Sierra Leone – although some people suggest it was Liberia – in West Africa. Palmer, then operating from Tenerife, had travelled to Africa to assess Sierra Leone's lucrative diamond mining industry. He happened upon Derbah, who was one of many Lebanese diasporas in the region. Palmer offered Derbah a job as his head of security on Tenerife. The two men forged what was, initially, a strong friendship.

It did not last. Derbah had always been an ambitious man and quickly tired of his mentor. He eventually considered Palmer and his British gangland cronies as weak and parochial businessmen.

Palmer was uneducated and, according to those who knew Goldfinger, conducted business like a boisterous market trader. By contrast, Derbah was intelligent, well-travelled, spoke fluent Spanish and adopted an international outlook. He was well-connected in Africa, the Middle East and the European mainland and saw the potential for greater cross-border business than Palmer.

Allegedly, challenging Palmer's status as the underworld kingpin on Tenerife wasn't as difficult for Derbah as other rival gangs found it. As Palmer's head of security, it was believed Mohamed controlled a fearsome and disciplined unit willing to confront Tenerife's less-disciplined British hoodlums. He had used his inside knowledge of Palmer's operations to undermine his former friend. Finally, unlike Palmer, he ingratiated himself with senior public officials on Tenerife and in Spain – the result of speaking the language fluently – and allegedly brought corrupt figures onto his payroll.

While Derbah's turf war with Palmer was allegedly violent, it did not take Mohamed long to displace his former boss. Of course, he was helped by the fact that Goldfinger had been arrested in England.

Mohamed's real power allegedly lay in his close relationship with members of the police department in Playa de Las Americas. An extremely well-placed source claimed that senior police officers took regular bribes from Derbah and, as a result, several official complaints about Mohamed were shredded by the time the complainants had left the police station.

These allegations were beginning to sound eerily familiar.

* * *

I was kicking myself. It was amazing how quickly I had learned all of this when I finally asked the right people the right questions. Carlos, it seemed, had been right to raise concerns.

Initially, I beat myself up about my naivety. But those close to me at the time were supportive and reminded me that I was not a detective: I was a corporate consultant from York trying to do legitimate business on Tenerife. Why should I have known all about the alleged dark arts of underworld figures?

The reality, I'm now quite sure, lay somewhere between naivety and blissful ignorance.

Regardless, the situation was now delicate. I had skin in the game. After the catastrophe of my drugs conviction, I was trying to build a new life and wealth. I'd come a long way since those long days cooped up in a cell in HMP Durham. Without Tenerife, I'd have nothing. So I was damned if I would be chased out of the Canaries like Wim de Groote and John Palmer.

I had not done anything illegal. And, superficially at least, I was still on reasonable terms with the man now allegedly in control of the island's underworld. I would bide my time, quietly distance Goldcrest from Derbah and go about my legitimate business.

At least, that was the plan.

* * *

It was a matter of weeks before Mohamed and Jeremy Sinclair were making a fortune out of Sovereign Gold Trust's 'cashback' venture.

Sovereign Gold Trust presented as a highly respectable corporation. Jeremy was a charismatic and friendly frontman, if a little quirky. Expensively produced and glossy brochures also helped. Mohamed paid a local firm £6,500 to print the literature and paid for it from a property company he owned, which banked at Jyske Bank in Gibraltar. I know, because I had created the company and saw the receipts.

But Sovereign's most significant asset was its well-drilled team of sales staff, who were adept at spotting signs of weakness in potential customers. If there was even the slightest possibility that a semi-retired and holidaying couple from Lincolnshire was considering an investment in Sovereign, then the sales team would leap on the opportunity and, verbally, batter the couple into submission before they could get back to the safety of Grantham or Skegness.

The cashback product promised customers a whopping three hundred per cent return, guaranteed, on any lump sum investment of three years or more. When customers inquired how that was possible, Sovereign's sales staff would hurl complicated financial jargon at them – before taking them to one side and, in the most patronising way possible, saying they would explain the whole thing in "lay man's terms".

The sales staff would then ask the holidaymakers whether they knew that there were two doors through which to enter a bank? Ordinary customers, silver-tongued staff said, use the front door. Then with a convincing smile on their face, they would claim: "The directors of Sovereign use the back door".

Customers were told that, by using Sovereign's close relationships with banks, funds deposited through Sovereign Gold Trust were used to finance bank credit cards – which paid an interest rate of 25% to 33%. In addition, Sovereign staff added, investments were managed by the Royal Bank of Scotland in Gibraltar – so returns were supposedly enhanced by professional investors.

Not only did these sales presentations convince many uninformed holidaymakers, but many professionals – including police officers, bank managers and accountants – were also won over and invested in Sovereign.

Such was the success of Sovereign that Wim De Groote's former associate, Thierry Boinnard, quickly asked me to incorporate an offshore company for him, through which he could also promote the cash-back scheme. The company involved became Hamilton Worldwide Limited. Another associate of Mohamed, Dennis New, also jumped on the bandwagon. I'd been told by some of my discreet sources on Tenerife to watch out for Dennis New, described by one local as a "two-bit gangster".

Everybody was rushing to help Sovereign reign supreme. Incredibly, while he was still on bail in the UK, John Palmer's Club Tenerife Sur Limited even began to sell the service without knowing that his arch-rival, Derbah, was behind it.

Deposits from customers ranged from £1,000 to £40,000. Mohamed was making so much money that he didn't know what to do with it. On one occasion, I had to visit Derbah's headquarters to discuss an unrelated company. As I entered Mohamed's personal office and greeted everybody inside, I glanced towards the corner of the room.

I couldn't believe what I saw.

Pile upon pile of high denomination banknotes were stacked on tables. There must have been several million pounds, just sitting there and waiting to be banked. As I turned around to make a disarming joke, I glanced at another corner of the room. Other towers of cash loomed large, this time stacked from the floor upwards. Multiple piles of elastic-bound cash, each about two feet high, were leaning against the wall.

I glanced back at Mohamed, who was stood next to his desk, watching some of his minions count cash.

Instinctively, I blurted: "What the hell?"

Mohamed wore the widest Cheshire Cat-style grin across his face. I'd never seen him look so happy. He shrugged his shoulders in mock modesty and laughed.

"Paul! My friend."

"Good to see you, Mohamed," I replied, still looking around the room. "Have you...broken into Fort Knox or something?"

Mohamed bellowed a huge laugh as he slapped me on the back.

"Hahaha! Paul, Sovereign is made of pure gold. Now I have the Midas touch! I want to thank you for introducing me to Jeremy. He is a fine salesman for me. You have missed out, my friend."

I couldn't help but glance back and forth between the piles of cash. I quickly surmised that the notes stacked in one corner of the room had already been counted, while everything in the opposite corner was still being counted.

"Jesus, Mohamed," I said, without even considering the irony of that line.

"Steady, my friend. We are Muslims, after all!" Mohamed jokingly waved his left hand towards his brothers and friends. His entourage joined the joke.

"Yes, quite...well...I don't know what to say," I replied. "Fucking hell, Mohamed! This is...incredible. Is this all Sovereign money? Collected recently?"

"Yes. I need to get this into a bank, Paul," Mohamed said excitedly. "Can you help?"

"Well...I can speak to some banks for you. But they'll need to see some paperwork," I replied, looking Mohamed directly in the eyes.

He nodded.

I continued: "You do know, don't you, that a million dollars made up of one hundred dollar bills weighs around ten kilos? A million dollars made up of twenties weighs around fifty kilos. You must have the equivalent of... heck...five or six million dollars here," I said, eyeing stacks of Euro notes.

"By my reckoning, that's between two hundred and three hundred kilograms of cash. Give or take. Roughly the same weight as two and a half heavyweight boxers."

Mohamed nodded in agreement. "So? What's your point, Paul?"

"My point is...I'm not fucking carrying it to the bank!"

Everybody in the room erupted with laughter. Derbah's Cheshire Cat grin returned and he laughed as loudly as Tenerife had heard in some time. Guayota inside the volcano had stirred.

* * *

As money poured into Sovereign, as well as Mohamed's other holiday-based products, his entourage consolidated their position as the timeshare and holiday-pack kings of Tenerife. Derbah moved his team to luxurious new offices in Los Cristianos, uncomfortably close to my headquarters.

At least I could observe them from up close.

Mohamed's alleged mafia was made up of a vast network of people, most of whom would pass through his offices at some point during the week. His closest confidants were his two younger brothers, Hatem and Sam. I'd met both men on early visits to see Mohamed and they had treated me with respect. Like Mohamed, they were polite in company, didn't drink alcohol and were hard working. They looked up to their older brother, Mohamed, and hung on his every word.

Sam, real name Hussein, was the older of the two brothers on Tenerife and was effectively Mohamed's second-in-command. More specifically, however, Sam was alleged by my more reliable sources to be head of Mohamed's "security" on the island – meaning he provided muscle for the organisation when required. Not alone, of course. Sam fronted several private firms which provided security at sites across the island, including holiday villages.

Sam's security businesses meant the brothers had a small army of heavily built, aggressive-looking pals at their disposal. I recognised some of the foot-soldiers from my visits to Mohamed's offices. In parts of Tenerife, Sam's security staff seemed to be on the streets more regularly than local police – particularly at night. They were certainly not averse to public shows of strength.

Hatem was the youngest of the three brothers. He was heavily built and looked the most intimidating of the Derbahs. He was a man of few words.

Dennis New operated on the fringes of the group. Alongside Mohamed, the former boxer from south London had been one of John Palmer's key enforcers. Since Palmer's split from Mohamed and arrest for fraud, however, New had been a regular visitor to Derbah's offices. But he did not appear to be working directly for Derbah.

I was aware that Dennis New, like Mohamed, did a lot of business on mainland Spain and had connections in France, Portugal and the Far East. To an offshore consultant like me, he should have been a potential client.

But New was a dislikeable man. He was a self-declared "gangster" and not a smart one: he openly used the term to describe himself. He was also unapologetically aggressive. Whenever I had the misfortune to be in the same room as New, I just ignored the loud and brag-heavy bullshit he would spew out.

Dennis New could start a fight with his own shadow in a dark room. He created enemies quickly. I remember thinking he wouldn't live to see his old age, and would be proved right.

Of course, alongside most alleged gangsters there is often a doting woman – and Mohamed Derbah was no different. Mohamed's partner was Djamila Berkaine, a French citizen. I can't say that I got to know Djamila, but she certainly doted on Mohamed. She seemed bright, was always impeccably attired and was extremely polite.

* * *

Shortly after the incident involving piles of cash in Derbah's office, I learned that Mohamed was also suspected of involvement in arms trading through his contacts in Africa. In normal circumstances, I would have laughed at the idea that one of my clients illegally traded weapons. But these were no longer normal circumstances.

I stayed sufficiently close to Mohamed to determine whether he planned to sacrifice me, as he had done with Wim. It was not paranoia. After all, I was a corporate consultant to Mohamed and Goldcrest had acted as a nominee director for some of his companies. In addition, I also ran a travel agency that had been approved by the industry's watchdogs.

It did not take long for Mohamed to identify his next rival. But it wasn't me.

Mohamed had cosied up to Thierry Boinnard after the latter decided he wanted a piece of Tenerife's timeshare market. I helped Thierry incorporate an offshore company for his timeshare business, and he quickly created two more. One firm was set up to offer cash-back services to timeshare owners wanting to sell their annual holiday entitlements to avoid paying the exorbitant maintenance fees mentioned only in the small print of contracts.

But just as I began to suspect that Mohamed planned to double-cross Boinnard, I also learned that the Belgian was an alleged conman. One of Thierry's new companies reportedly charged a fee for selling unwanted timeshares, banked the cash, then never contacting the owners again.

I couldn't believe the chaotic criminal allegations which now blighted Tenerife's timeshare, holiday pack and cash-back markets. Perhaps the scorching sun was frying everybody's brains?

The situation was getting out of hand. And that was before Mohamed pulled his next stunt.

* * *

In the first week of October 2000, Mohamed told me he would 'play a game with Boinnard' and sell Sovereign Gold Trust to him for a token payment of 10 million Pesetas, or £40,000. Under the plan, Boinnard agreed to assume day-to-day business management and Mohamed's firms continued to market their cash back and Millennium Club Card products to Boinnard's customers at the point of sale.

I didn't trust either man but, at this point, I was slightly confused as to who might be trying to screw who. I couldn't go to the authorities, because I couldn't prove that the whole arrangement involved at least one illegal scam.

Mohamed had effectively transferred liability for Sovereign's existing contracts to Boinnard. I wondered, therefore, whether Derbah was expecting trouble from disgruntled cashback customers? But if Derbah intended to ensure Thierry followed Wim as the next fall guy, Boinnard saw it coming.

Within weeks, Boinnard had diverted most of Sovereign's assets and income through a chain of offshore banks and into the United States: far out of reach of Mohamed and his customers. Mohamed was as furious as the distraught cashback customers who alleged they had been conned. Derbah had been played.

Based on feedback from his police connections, Mohamed advised that I block Boinnard's bank accounts at the Jyske Bank in Gibraltar. Backed into a corner by Mohamed, I put a temporary freeze on the accounts. But Boinnard's lawyers had them unblocked within hours. They had the legal power to do so, which just showed who the ultimate owner of the alleged scam company was at that point: Boinnard.

I now knew that I had to distance myself entirely from Derbah and similar businessmen. But I had one final piece of work to complete for him.

In early November 2000, I accompanied Mohamed to Beirut, Lebanon's war-scarred capital, to meet the country's energy minister. A firm run by the Derbah family had bid for a multi-million dollar government contract to put electricity meters into every home in Lebanon. Mohamed asked Goldcrest to act as corporate consultants on the deal and, with his entire family's reputation at stake, I had little intention of causing a fuss about the events of the past few months until the deal was completed.

At the meeting in Beirut, Mohamed jokingly introduced me as his "consigliere". For the uninitiated, a consigliere is an independent advisor to Italian mafia families, who is trusted to resolve family conflicts. It's a key position in major criminal networks, made famous by *The Godfather* film trilogy. Over time, its meaning in English has widened to become an informal reference to a no-nonsense close associate who operates in an advisory capacity. I didn't mind the reference: it was a bit of fun on

Mohamed's part and even the minister and his staff chuckled. But it was interesting that Derbah joked about the allegations that he led a "mafia" – even in the company of senior politicians.

After the meeting, we visited Mohamed's family in Tyre, south Lebanon. There, Mohamed introduced me to his mother and his Lebanon-based brothers, Mostapha and Ali. I was surprised to learn that the latter was a local politician.

The family home was surprisingly ramshackle. A crumbling façade protected spartan rooms painted brilliant white and kitted out with basic furnishings. At the back of the property, laundry was draped across a sagging clothesline. Nevertheless, the whole arrangement was cosy and Derbah's mother, who did not speak English, was demonstrably house-proud. While the house was spartan, it was also spotlessly clean.

Mohamed's family was a tight-knit group, but they received me warmly. The whole trip was disarming. There, in the peaceful and sun-scorched olive groves of south Lebanon, Derbah's life as the head of an alleged mafia on Tenerife seemed a million miles away. I've never seen Mohamed look as relaxed as when he sat softly chatting to his mother before gently grilling his politician brother about political matters. Gone was the steely authority and commanding machismo. Instead, I saw a man at ease with himself and his surroundings. Although he repeatedly told me that the local area had "little to offer" beyond his family, he loved his homeland.

One evening, after a luxurious home-cooked feast, Mohamed and I sat drinking tea on a white-washed terrace looking out across the gentle, rolling landscape and soaking up the sounds of nature. Bush crickets croaked and birds of prey shrieked overhead, scanning the landscape with forensic precision as they targeted their next meal.

Gently, almost softly, Mohamed broke the silence.

"You know...you meet my mother now, Paul,' he whispered. "So, I protect you forever."

I looked over at Derbah. He was sat, gently smiling, but somehow also looking serious. Reflective. Content.

"You are like family now, Paul. The people here in Lebanon – my family – they like you. They like what you have done for me, for my friends. For us."

I was thrown. Torn. I'd had the most extraordinarily positive experience in Beirut, Tyre and with Mohamed's family. The experience had been more in line with what I'd envisaged when I started Goldcrest. Yet sitting opposite me was a man suspected of running one of Europe's biggest, most violent and wealthiest criminal gangs. And he was as disarming as a family pet.

"Thank you, Mohamed. I...er...I don't know how to respond. Your family has made me feel so welcome in Lebanon. It has been my privilege," I said.

"You are a good friend to us, Paul."

Now seemed like as good a time as any to ask. "Do you...do you ever see yourself moving back here? You know, getting out of Tenerife? Out of Spain, and all that entails, and just putting your feet up?"

Mohamed looked at me like I was mad, then let out a characteristic belly laugh.

"Paul," he replied. "You are an amusing man! Tenerife is my business. My business is Tenerife. By the way, I want to introduce you to somebody in Spain..."

* * *

Once back in the Canaries, business threatened to return to normality.

Mohamed seemed content and less stressed about the Thierry Boinnard situation. I had to visit his offices regularly to sign various bits of paperwork and noticed that the number of coffee visits from local police had increased.

I had just one concern: Mohamed had begun to politely suggest that I sit at his main desk during meetings with potential new clients. I couldn't help but think of Wim. Was I paranoid? Mohamed had just described me as an extended family member. His *consiglieri*. On the flight back from Beirut, he'd talked about how much legitimate business was on offer in Tenerife and Spain.

Sat at Mohamed's desk during meetings, I began to notice paperwork and files relating to offshore banks and companies that I was unaware Mohamed used. Once outside his office, I wrote down as much of the information as I could recall.

It soon became apparent that I had been kept in the dark about Mohamed's wider financial affairs. The previously unseen paperwork indicated that Derbah was wealthy beyond even my imagination – and I think about money a lot!

Over time, I saw paperwork relating to a vast network of offshore banks, shell companies, trusts and other investments in jurisdictions such as Gibraltar, Russia and the British Virgin Islands. If these all belonged to Mohamed and his family, their wealth ran into tens of millions of dollars.

I couldn't help but question which activities lay behind these assets? I knew about Mohamed's timeshare firms, his holiday-pack and cashback businesses. I'd even seen up-to-date paperwork relating to properties scattered around the world. But these new documents pointed to other lucrative income streams.

* * *

The businessman who Mohamed wanted to introduce me to in Spain was 'Hugo' (a pseudonym), a European citizen with an estimated fortune of £750 million.

Hugo lived in a sprawling villa near Marbella that looked like something out of a Hollywood movie. Its outer perimeter was secured by a large wall. As we approached the site, armed security guards could be seen at the iron-gated entrance, which led up a driveway to a parking area for at least twenty cars. Hugo's vehicle collection consisted of a white Rolls Royce, a classic red Ferrari, three different Porsche models and several top-of-the-range BMWs. Each car shone so spotlessly clean in the scorching sunshine that I remember thinking you could fry an egg on them without getting a speck of dust on your meal.

Hugo's villa had indoor and outdoor swimming pools. There was also a private nightclub in a large basement on the complex. It was extraordinary.

I was, however, unprepared for what I saw once we passed through the grand entrance. The entire villa appeared to be staffed by a large group of stunning female secretaries and personal assistants – all from eastern Europe. Either the women were ripping off each other's style, or Hugo had a 'type'. It was like a scene out of MiLady's, only without the moody lighting and pack of drooling, drunken businessmen lusting over the women. Unless you counted me.

Derbah was not a close associate of Hugo but knew him well enough to recommend me when Hugo required advice on how to move assets between offshore jurisdictions. The Frenchman said he felt "over-taxed" under his current financial arrangements. One can only wonder what the size of his villa would have been like had he been able to 'splash out' following a tax rebate.

Hugo became my client and Elena Dontu, one of his assistants, was assigned to supervise any business I conducted on his behalf. To say that Elena was attractive would be an understatement of criminal proportions. She had long, flowing blonde hair, piercing blue eyes, high cheekbones and the figure and poise of a catwalk model. Indeed, the way she walked belied Elena's past: she had been an aspiring model in her native Moldova before travelling to southern Europe and joining Hugo's staff. I remember thinking that if she could not make it in the fickle, glamorous world of fashion, then ninety-nine per cent of people alive today should probably rule it out.

But Elena was not just eye-candy for Hugo. She was intelligent, organised and efficient. She spoke several languages – including fluent English and Spanish – and effortlessly switched between them during conversations. It was a pleasure to deal with her, and not just because she looked so elegant.

Hugo had little time to spare on most occasions when we met, yet, as a group, we always managed to cover all of the key issues I needed to clarify while working to secure and protect his vast fortune. Much of that was down to Elena's organisational skills. She worked hard and was ambitious. I could have done with appointing her to Goldcrest's staff, but I knew I wouldn't be able to compete with the wages Hugo paid. And I'm not sure Gill would have been too pleased if my firm had an ex-model wandering around the office!

* * *

Hugo was impressed with my work for him. In the absence of Carlos, I put in the hours and had the extraordinary Sarah Hill working overtime back on Tenerife. I found working for Hugo to be an enjoyable experience. Our relationship was purely professional: neither of us had time to socialise, yet we got on well.

Unlike many of my super-rich clients, Hugo was relaxed even when he was busy. He had a quiet authority about him, made firm decisions and stuck to them. Only on a few occasions did I witness the ruthless streak in Hugo that all top businesspeople possess. He chose his moments of authority carefully. That was one of the secrets of his success: his clients liked him and respected him. There was no posturing or bragging with Hugo, unlike Mohamed.

Goldcrest was moving up in the world.

One morning, Hugo contacted me and requested a discussion "in the strictest of confidence". He wanted to introduce me to a friend who also needed offshore services, but whose identity would need to be protected at all costs due to his seniority. Hugo stressed that his contact was extraordinarily reliable and somebody he admired greatly, but that the "highest level of discretion" would be required from me: I was not even allowed to tell Goldcrest staff about our potential new contact. I had no hesitation in agreeing, of course.

Edmond Hamid became my first billionaire client. But as I would later discover, he was no ordinary billionaire. His net worth was estimated at several billion dollars, and he was among the world's wealthiest people. Edmond was, by birth, from the Middle East. But he had strong connections among the powerful oligarchs and politicians inside Russia's rapidly re-emerging economy and state – including, it was said, the prime minister and soon-to-be president of Russia: Vladimir Putin.

He also had senior contacts inside the United States.

*　*　*

Edmond Hamid later proved to be a hard taskmaster. As well as complete privacy, he demanded excellence in everything Goldcrest did for him. He was extremely intelligent and fastidious, but somebody I could trust and do business with easily and honestly. He was a true gentleman – respectful, knowledgeable and humble despite his conspicuous wealth. He lacked the arrogance and ostentatiousness of Tenerife's *nouveau riche* gangsters.

I quickly developed a deep respect for Edmond because, in contrast to Mohamed, he never left me in the dark. Quite the opposite: I was expected to know everything about Hamid's firms swiftly and in great detail. Hamid treated me as a professional, and he expected extreme professionalism in return.

They say that 'money follows money' and, sure enough, no sooner had I met Edmond than he introduced me to one of his business associates from Russia.

Like Hamid, 'Viktor' (a pseudonym) was wealthy almost beyond description. He was also an influential figure in Russia, having made a fortune following the collapse of the Soviet Union and the switch to a controversial mode of capitalism dominated by a handful of oligarchs. When communism collapsed in Eastern Europe, Russia's economy initially withered to the size of the Netherlands'. Those who then thrived financially tended to be either powerful (often corrupt) politicians and their allies, ultra-violent mafias, or savvy individuals who had correctly interpreted Mikhail Gorbachev's *perestroika* movement as the chance to be in the vanguard of a new commercialism.

As Kremlinologists will tell you, many influential figures in Russia have a presence in all three of the groups described above. And a sub-group of that cabal often hijacked the legitimate offshore finance system to either launder their ill-gotten gains – or to flee Russia having upset those in power. For these reasons, I had always been wary of Russian clients bearing gifts.

It wasn't that I disliked Russians. But the economic chaos of post-Soviet privatization under Boris Yeltsin, and its replacement with Vladimir Putin's muscular and authoritarian capitalism, had the offshore finance world on alert. In the early 2000s, the quickest way to lose your reputation – or your head – as an international corporate consultant, was to get caught up in a murky deal involving the trillions of dollars of dirty Russian money flooding out of Moscow, St Petersburg, Novosibirsk and Chelyabinsk.

★ ★ ★

Thankfully, Viktor fell into the category of savvy businessmen who spotted significant commercial opportunities as Russia privatised. Like all successful Russians, he had ties with senior politicians in Moscow, which linked him tangentially to some underworld figures. But from what I could see, there was sufficient separation from criminality. My early due diligence suggested Viktor was a serious businessman who, as best you could in modern Russia, kept his hands clean.

I had been asked to create some shell companies for Viktor so that he could transfer a vast cash reserve, more than a billion dollars, to a bank in Monaco. I worked meticulously on the offshore arrangements, and the cash assets are now untraceable.

One evening over dinner, Viktor dropped a bombshell. He was aware, he said, that Mohamed Derbah had connections in Russia. In Moscow, it transpired, people had spoken of the alleged mafia active on Tenerife. John Palmer had travelled regularly to Moscow to do business – and, through Palmer, people became aware of Derbah.

Viktor went on to explain that he had some underworld contacts. He kept them well out of his business and his day-to-day personal life, he quickly pointed out.

"In Russia, everybody knows at least somebody who knows the mafias," he said. "And these people – they know your Mr Derbah and John Palmer."

According to Viktor, Mohamed was considered a relatively minor business figure by Muscovites – little more than a street-level security man and alleged minor arms dealer.

Wait...what?

"Arms dealer"?

This was the second time I'd heard such an allegation. According to Viktor's sources in Moscow, Derbah allegedly forged links with Russians seeking to sell Soviet-era weapons to West African states to support various governments and militias. Tenerife had become the stopping-off point for ships carrying illegal weapons smuggled out of eastern Europe. On the Canaries, the arms would be transferred to boats heading south past the Tropic of Cancer.

Mohamed, I knew, had strong connections among the Lebanese diaspora in western Africa – in particular, Sierra Leone. It is where he met John

Palmer. But until now, I had assumed that Goldfinger and Derbah's interest was Sierra Leone's valuable and controversial diamonds market.

I didn't quite know what to make of this new information. Was it true? Viktor hardly seemed the type to engage in idle gossip or speculation. He knew the risks involved in that.

CHAPTER NINE

Assets

Back on Tenerife, war had broken out.

On bail in England but unable to protect his illegal timeshare fortune from Tenerife, John Palmer had become a lame duck. Every gangster and wannabe mobster attempted to seize Palmer's share of the lucrative market while he was absent.

While I ploughed into Goldcrest's work for its ultra-wealthy new clients, Hugo and Hamid, Tenerife was awash with gossip about the gangland warfare, power grabs and vacuums that followed Palmer's demise. According to local gossip, Mohamed was at the head of the queue to replace his former boss. But even from a distance, Palmer had ordered his men not to give up his patch easily.

Late on Friday 10 November 2000, Sam Derbah was making his way back to his car when he noticed that the tyres had been slashed. As he bent down to inspect the vehicle, two men on a high-powered motorcycle bore down on him. The pillion rider pulled a handgun, fired off three shots at close quarters and yelled: "It's me!"

Acting on instinct, Sam threw himself to the ground. He crawled around to the blind side of the car, scrambled inside and took cover in the well of the passenger seat. By this time, the motorcycle had shot past Sam's Mercedes. Suddenly, it doubled back. Pointing the pistol into the car's interior, the man riding pillion fired two more shots, neither of which hit their target. As the bike pulled past, Sam recognised one of the attackers as a German associate of Palmer's gang.

Sam Derbah survived. Just.

Shortly after the incident, in the north of the island, a string of attacks on street-level criminals who ran prostitutes for the tourist trade was attributed to a powerful and ruthless Russian mafia that had seized control of key parts of the Canaries' underworld. Soon the Russians started to buy up development sites, too, and began to expand into the lucrative holiday and timeshare markets.

John Palmer and Mohamed Derbah had competition – and Tenerife was becoming a dangerous place to do business. The negative publicity surrounding gang violence quickly made its way back to Madrid, where Spain's politicians and police stirred into action to protect crucial tourism.

* * *

At Goldcrest Hispania, business was relentless. During the early months of 2001, Sarah Hill and I worked longer days just to complete paperwork so that I could return home to Gill and the kids regularly.

Sarah had already shown she could assume greater responsibility within the company. She was a huge asset and I would not have coped without her.

But Goldcrest was not yet free of Mohamed Derbah. We were still mid-contract on several of his important deals in Spain and Lebanon, and I was shortly due to travel to Beirut on his behalf to complete some work. I also had to field queries relating to Derbah's companies – sometimes from disgruntled customers who claimed they were not receiving the holiday pack or cashback services they were promised. There was only so much I could say: I had nothing to do with the day-to-day management of Mohamed's firms, so I instead referred complaints to Derbah's staff.

Unfortunately, I also had to spend time explaining what happened with Thierry Boinnard and the purchase of Sovereign.

Thierry had made an official complaint to Tenerife police after Mohamed directed me to freeze Belmar's bank accounts. I was potentially in the firing line even though I was acting under the orders of my client and the company's founder, Mohamed. But just as Derbah had used his influence on Tenerife to see off Wim De Groote via the police, so he used his contacts to address Boinnard's complaint.

Mohamed was sent a copy of Boinnard's police statement within minutes of the Belgian leaving the police station in Playa de las Americas. So, when I spoke to him about it the following day, Derbah had already made his own inquiries.

"The police will not do anything, Paul," he said. "But Boinnard's finished on Tenerife."

Three days before I was due to travel to Beirut, on 18 April 2000, I was summoned to the police station in Playa de las Americas to provide a statement on Boinnard's complaint.

The interview turned out to be a complete farce. The interviewing officers seemed unable to grasp that Mohamed had been the ultimate beneficial owner of Sovereign when it had been established. I was allowed to have a sworn translator, Alberto de la Maldonado, who also struggled to understand the offshore structures put in place to hide Mohamed as the ultimate owner of other companies. Nobody in the room seemed to comprehend the basic idea that the law allowed Mohamed to own a company that had been incorporated by somebody else. They just kept staring, confused by incorporation documents with my name on them.

After an hour or so, I was deeply frustrated. For a group of policemen who lived and worked on Tenerife – a low-tax zone designed to attract offshore business – they seemed blissfully ignorant. And they kept staring at a print-out that had my personal details on them.

Then I made *the* error.

I was asked, somewhat innocuously, by one of the officers whether I had any criminal convictions in the UK. I answered honestly. Better to be honest, right?

Little else was said but, bizarrely, after the interview, I was fingerprinted and photographed. This was more than a mere filing of my statement in response to Boinnard. Suddenly, my mind rushed back several weeks to Wim de Groote.

My mind began to whir. Was this the sort of stitch-up I had been half-expecting? Was Mohamed behind it? Surely not – I was still completing work for him in Beirut, Spain and elsewhere. I couldn't make sense of it. Yet as the police officers spoke amongst themselves, I heard the name "Mohamed" mentioned several times. Each time Derbah was mentioned, the officers glanced at me with awkward looks on their faces.

The officers thanked me and, through the interpreter, said that they would be in touch again soon. But that was it. I was free to go. As I wandered out to reception to re-join Sarah Hill, who had been waiting patiently, I saw the island's chief of police.

"Mister Blanchard," he said as I wandered towards him. "My advice is for you to leave Tenerife in the next 48 hours – or I'll arrest you and remand you in prison."

What the hell did he just say?

"I'm sorry", I replied. "I didn't catch that." I had, of course.

"You should leave Tenerife, Mr Blanchard. Or I will arrest you."

The look on Sarah's face said it all. She was horrified. Nobody had been expecting this, least of all me. I can only assume that I wore the same expression. A thousand possible responses to the police chief whizzed through my mind. But I bit my lip. Anything I said at this point would just have made matters worse. I simply nodded to the senior officer, took my briefcase from Sarah and left the building in silence.

* * *

Outside, Sarah spoke first.

"Paul, are you OK? What just happened in there? Who was that man?"

I was struggling to find the right words.

"I think Mohamed Derbah just happened, Sarah," I replied.

I continued: "I don't know if he's stitching me up. But somebody, maybe the police, have got me earmarked to take the rap for what happened with Sovereign. The man in reception? That was the chief of police. An acquaintance of Mohamed's. You heard what he said. He wants me off the island."

Sarah's face dropped. But she wasn't one to panic. "Oh my god, Paul. This is serious. What exactly did they ask you about?"

Before I could even answer, Sarah was already rummaging through her handbag, looking for her address book.

"You need a lawyer," Sarah said.

"No, Sarah. Not yet," I replied. "First, I need to find out what the hell is going on."

"What do you mean? Paul, you heard the policeman: you've been given 48 hours to leave Tenerife. Around here, that doesn't happen by accident. Something is very wrong."

"Yes, I know. And that's why I'm going to see one man who may know what it is: Mohamed."

***

On arrival at Derbah's headquarters, I was kept waiting in the main reception by Mohamed's secretary. Usually, I would have been shown straight through to his personal office. Finally, after forty-five minutes, I was ushered in.

Mohamed was full of polite apologies, explaining that several police contacts had just left by the rear door.

He sat back in his leather chair. "I have a copy of your police statement, Paul," Derbah revealed, waving the paper in his left hand. "You should not have said you have criminal convictions in England. This will damage you in Tenerife. After John Palmer, English criminals are not welcome here."

He couldn't have been any more blunt.

"What? I had no alternative," I said, taken aback at the lack of support from Mohamed. "I was asked a direct question by your friends at the police station, so I answered truthfully. Anyway, the police already knew because they had my details on their desk."

Silence. Mohamed ran his hands through his hair, sighed and looked down at the copy of my police statement. He studied the details intently.

After a minute or so, he raised his head.

"I will try to deal with this", he said. "Go to Lebanon tomorrow, as planned."

***

I told Sarah what happened at Mohamed's office. I had to tell somebody, and I couldn't exactly call Gill – she would have panicked and asked me to come straight back to England. But there was too much still to do on Tenerife, in Beirut and Spain. If I went home, my other clients, some of the world's wealthiest men, would cast doubt on my ability and commitment. I would not let them down.

Sarah was her usual logical self, only slightly more worried. She agreed to carry on working as usual, but insisted I call the office regularly from Beirut. She was concerned about my safety in Lebanon – something that had not occurred to me until that point. I agreed to stay in contact.

***

Over the next three days, I rushed around like a headless chicken. Off one plane, into a cab, onwards to a meeting, back to the airport, into another taxi, another meeting, and back for yet another flight. In between, I made work calls, poured over documents, signed contracts, chased up banks and offshore jurisdictions and had very little sleep. Throughout, at the back of my mind was what happened with the police – and whether Mohamed was behind it.

By the time I arrived in Beirut, I was fatigued. After finalising business for Mohamed in Lebanon's capital, I travelled south to meet his brother Ali in Tyre. The idea was to complete some contract work before heading home. But my physical condition had deteriorated. The combination of overwork, intense heat, dehydration, cramped flights, travel food, lack of sleep and stress did for me. I began to feel faint and suffer chest pains.

To his eternal credit, Ali was concerned. The following morning, he drove me to the Najem Hospital in Tyre, where a sullen-looking doctor advised that I should stay until my condition improved. There was just one problem: I was supposed to fly home to the UK for the start of my perjury trial on 24 April 2001.

The trial had already been postponed once, in July 2000, and I knew the UK judge would not take kindly to a further delay. But in Tyre, the doctors forcefully recommended that I did not travel and contacted my solicitor so he could tell the court.

* * *

I eventually flew back to the UK, expecting to face the judge's wrath after my non-appearance at court in Manchester. But to my surprise, the judge was extremely sympathetic. After seeing the documentation which proved that I had been ill, he even inquired after my health.

Back at home in England, I continued to make a full recovery and caught up on my work from a distance. I also set aside a couple of hours each day to work on a project of my own.

After events at the police station on Tenerife, I feared that I could become the next fall guy with links to Mohamed. So, I began to remove all documentation that Goldcrest held on Derbah from my office in Los Cristianos and sent it to England. I then prepared dossiers on Mohamed's firms, just in case they were ever investigated for criminality.

Once bitten, twice shy. I'd been turned over in the past for being too trusting of my business partners and associates.

After assessing all relevant paperwork on Mohamed, mapping income and asset flows in and out of his offshore entities, I realised that there was no sign of funds put aside to pay his customers when their Millennium Club Card benefits were due. Where were the crucial 'client accounts' that would cover such costs? I could see a lot of money entering Lebanon via Mohamed's offshore companies that I had helped to incorporate. But the accounts from which Mohamed would meet his legal cash liabilities were nowhere to be seen.

The significance of this did not pass me by. Without a client account from which to pay customers, Mohamed was potentially committing fraud – in the same way that John Palmer had. It was possible, of course, that he had accounts in Lebanon, or another offshore jurisdiction, which I was unaware of and from which Derbah could meet his liabilities. But I couldn't see one.

I wanted to be one hundred per cent sure about what had happened to Derbah's money and, of course, wanted to cover my own back. So, I decided to ask Mohamed about it once back on Tenerife. I was already in touch with some disgruntled Millennium Club Card customers, so I knew it was the right thing to do legally and morally.

However, I also knew that Mohamed would not take kindly to me asking sensitive questions.

* * *

After several weeks in England, I returned to Tenerife.

The chief of police had suggested that I leave the island and, while I had effectively complied by heading to Yorkshire after my trip to Lebanon, I knew that returning to the Canaries was fraught with danger. Mohamed had assured me that he would handle the problem with the police on Tenerife. But I'd heard nothing.

On the evening of Friday 18 May, I visited Derbah's office and was kept waiting again. Eventually, Mohamed emerged. But instead of being stand-offish, as I had expected, he greeted me in a state of jubilation.

"He's guilty! He's guilty!"

Mohamed's face was a picture of joy.

I asked: "Who?"

"John Palmer, Paul. He's guilty! In England. He gets sentenced on Monday!"

Derbah, a muscular man, floated around the room in delight at the news of his former boss's demise. With Palmer out of the way, Mohamed held a tighter-than-ever grip on Tenerife's timeshare market and, reportedly, the broader underworld.

Derbah delighted in telling everybody in his office about Palmer. It was as though he had taken an adrenaline shot – and was so distracted by the news from London, that when I plucked up the courage to politely ask him where the client account for Millennium Club Card disbursements was, he either didn't hear or pretended not to.

I got no answer and knew that trying to get one from Mohamed that day would be a fruitless task. With Derbah elated and distracted, I quietly left the building.

As I walked back towards my apartment in the late evening sun, I realised that was almost certainly the end of my relationship with Mohamed Jamil Derbah. I had completed most of Goldcrest's work for him and his associates. We hadn't even discussed whether Mohamed had spoken to the police about me, as he had promised. Derbah was too distracted by something which mattered more to him. All that talk in Lebanon about me being "like family", was just puff and bluster. Deep down, I'd known that anyway.

I didn't like the fact that the situation with the police remained unresolved but knew that I'd done little wrong in my dealings with Boinnard. I acted on Mohamed's orders when Thierry's bank account was frozen, and Boinnard's lawyers resolved the problem anyway. Ultimately, the row was between Mohamed and Thierry. I just hoped that, legally, I could continue to operate on Tenerife unaffected by police pressure. Despite the stresses of the past few months, I was in a decent position providing that the Boinnard situation was resolved. I had new, wealthy clients and was finally easing away from Mohamed Derbah.

But the cold, hard reality was about to hit me again.

Over the next few weeks, what had been a drip-drip of complaints to Goldcrest about Derbah's holiday pack and cashback schemes suddenly turned into a flood. Customers from across Europe were furious they were not receiving the reported benefits. I handled some calls directly and could sense the anger and frustration within Derbah's customer base. Many alleged they'd been ripped off.

The volume of complaints meant one thing: I now had a mandatory legal duty under European money laundering regulations to ask Derbah how he intended to pay his customers.

* * *

The crunch meeting came ten days later, on 28 May.

Mohamed knew I was coming because I'd had to make an appointment. But, this time, the reception was crammed full of his muscle-bound henchmen, a move designed to intimidate me. The friendly faces I knew, staff from Sam's security operations, looked a little awkward and conflicted as I took a seat. I could tell that some of them did not want to be there. I had always treated Sam's staff with respect and a friendly smile when I saw them patrolling around Tenerife or on the doors of bars and nightclubs. One or two of them shuffled awkwardly and glanced down rather than meet my eye.

But I'd be a liar if I said I was nerveless while sat in Derbah's offices clutching copies of dossiers on his companied that I had compiled.

I wasn't panicking – I'd reconciled myself with the thought that, legally, I had to ask the questions I was about to put to Derbah. But I wasn't exactly comfortable. Mohamed was, after all, now alleged to be the head of Tenerife's powerful underworld. So, I kept telling myself to stay calm and stick to simple questions. Then politely and quietly leave.

My heart rate increased.

* * *

"Paul. I am sorry for the delay. Please, take a seat," Mohamed said without a smile.

After an hour-long wait, I had finally been ushered into Derbah's main office, where several henchmen – including Sam – were also seated.

"Please, it is a very busy day today. I have many people to see, so we must stick to business. Goldcrest, Belmar and other things," Mohamed said, casting aside any idea of small talk.

"Sure," I said. "I don't know how long this will take, though."

To begin, I presented Mohamed with a letter from Goldcrest, which included an invoice for £200,000 in unpaid bills for offshore consultancy work my firm had completed for him. The letter also reminded Derbah of Goldcrest's legal duties under Europe's money laundering regulations.

Mohamed scanned the documents, snorted an ironic laugh and looked up.

He spoke firmly. "There is a problem, Paul?"

Hell, just cut to the chase.

"Well, Goldcrest has received many complaints from Millennium Club Card customers, who claim that they have not received their holidays and other benefits – even though they paid fees directly to your company," I started.

"As a corporate director, Goldcrest has a legal obligation to check these matters. But as the ultimate beneficial owner of the company, Mohamed, you and your management teams must set aside the cash to cover the services you have promised."

Mohamed stared at me with nothing but fury in his eyes. He nodded slowly.

After a short while, he broke an awkward silence.

"The money is in Lebanon, Paul. What is the problem?"

"The problem is that the complainants, your customers, say that they have not received the services or payments due to them. Some say that they've not heard from your company about how their holiday will be delivered. Some say they have not heard, at all, from your team since they made their payment – and that they cannot now get in touch with your firms. So, they have come to Goldcrest. We are receiving many calls from angry customers because Goldcrest Hispania is listed as corporate director at some of your other firms," I explained.

Mohamed snorted another reluctant, dismissive laugh.

"The money...it is all there. In Lebanon," he reiterated.

"Sure, but I can't see where that money is, Mohamed."

I slid the dossiers across Mohamed's desk towards him.

"From what I can see, there appears to be no disbursement account linked to any of these companies," I said, nodding towards the files. "Your companies have taken millions in payments. But I can't see a single payment or disbursement made in return."

Mohamed didn't even look at the files. He stared straight through me – as though trying to light a fire on the wall behind me with his eyes.

"What is *your* problem, Paul?"

His question said everything. Did he genuinely want me to turn a blind eye to the complaints?

"It is essentially this," I said, trying to keep the tone reasonable. "John Palmer was prosecuted for fraud because he took money from his time-share customers and provided little or nothing in return. Your companies are being accused of the same thing, Mohamed. When that happens, I have a duty, as an independent consultant, to review the situation and ensure that you have a client account from which you are making the promised disbursements. All I need, Mohamed, is to see evidence that such accounts exists."

Silence.

"It is in Lebanon."

"Sure," I replied. "But where are those accounts in this web of companies and accounts? There is no mention of it, no payments to customers made from it." I pointed at the dossiers.

Derbah was now visibly impatient. He tutted loudly, waved a hand dismissively and glanced around the room at his henchmen. Sam, leaning against an office wall, watched the entire exchange like a hawk.

For a brief moment, I wondered if I'd overstepped the mark.

"Mohamed...this is serious. You could encounter trouble from the authorities if this is not resolved," I explained. "This could be deemed illegal. That is what happened to John Palmer. You are my client. I incorporated some of your other companies. I have a legal duty to remind you...."

Suddenly, I was interrupted.

"Legal duty. Legal? Do you think this is illegal, Paul?"

His question threw me. I wasn't expecting to have to express an opinion. I sat silently for a few seconds, thinking. Trying to choose my words carefully.

"Without an obvious client account, from which you make payments due to your customers, it is potential fraud, Mohamed," I said without directly accusing the head of Tenerife's alleged mafia. "If I could see a client account, then I would know it is most likely legitimate. But I can't."

Mohamed leaned forward. He breathed deeply, exhaled loudly and the anger on his face became clear.

"So, you think it *is* fraud?"

I glanced around the room. Everybody was now staring at me.

It was time to be brave.

"I think it could be *perceived* as fraud. That is the difference. If it is, Mohamed, I have a duty under anti-money laundering laws to report this situation. In these matters, that would involve the authorities in Madrid and not Tenerife."

Mohamed did not like my answer. He pursed his lips and a look of disdain erupted across his face. I saw Sam lean towards me, and he made a point of catching my eye. I knew that Mohamed had some influential contacts in Madrid. Nonetheless, talk of going over his head to national bodies that were not based in Tenerife – where he was influential – clearly caused him discomfort.

I was trying to channel the brave Paul Blanchard Snr, the stone-faced Clint Eastwood type I'd presented at HMP Durham. I had no idea, though, whether I was simply coming across as a gibbering wreck and potential grass. It was hard to tell: beneath the thin veneer of confidence, my heart felt like it was about to explode.

I was in a stand-off with the alleged head of the Lebanese mafia, surrounded by his henchmen – including his brother, a renowned hardman. I'd just asked for £200,000 in unpaid bills and, in the politest way possible, threatened to report him for potential fraud. In that situation, I defy most men not to, figuratively, shit themselves.

Mohamed broke the silence.

"The authorities in Madrid?"

Derbah sneered as he spoke, picked up the dossiers in front of him and idly flicked through one of them before sliding the files back across the table towards me. Slowly, purposefully, he stared directly into my eyes.

"Paul...you haven't got the balls."

* * *

There's something about people from Yorkshire.

If you tell us we can't do something, you tend to find that we will go and do it. Sometimes, just for the hell of it – sometimes simply to show that we will not be ordered around! We are a stubborn, determined, contrarian and prickly breed. To a fault.

* * *

Derbah's bluff could not have been more misplaced.

But before I performed my legal duty to report the complaints against his companies, I needed to ensure that my other clients did not get caught up in any investigation into Mohamed. Foremost among these were Viktor and any clients with business links to Moscow. Contrary to popular belief, my Russian offshore clients were clean, reliable and loyal towards Goldcrest. I owed them a discreet heads-up about what was coming.

After making some checks, I was informed that Mohamed's traceable dealings with Russia were minimal and that any investigation into his finances would not turn up anything that would compromise people considered important in Moscow. That was good news, as I didn't fancy making enemies of Putin's allies or Moscow's bone-crushing mafias.

Better still, it appeared that none of Goldcrest's current clients would be directly affected by an investigation into Mohamed.

* * *

I needed to tread carefully during my approach to the Spanish authorities and figured the best place to start would be from the safety of the UK. Sarah Hill and I reasoned that it was unlikely Mohamed would cause her problems on Tenerife. Her family were well-regarded locally, she had avoided any personal involvement in my dispute with Derbah and he would not want to draw further attention. So, I knew that Sarah could safely run the Tenerife office until matters were resolved.

Through Tenerife's grapevine, I also discovered that Mohamed had quickly found a new corporate adviser. He was Jose Esteban Garcia Gonzalez, a director at the BSCH bank in Los Cristianos.

The events of the previous few months – Mohamed's increasingly stand-offish attitude towards me since the Wim de Groote incident – suddenly made more sense. Gonzalez also had a private consultancy business, Kara Consultores, trading as a corporate service provider. He could offer Mohamed the same services as Goldcrest and provide him with direct banking expertise. Canny move by Derbah, I'll give him that.

Thierry Boinnard also left Tenerife after his dispute with Mohamed, leaving thousands of angry Sovereign customers clutching worthless cash-back certificates. Derbah simply created a new firm called Royal Crown Investments, carried on using the same aggressive sales techniques and raked in further millions. I had no idea if he intended to make good the pledges made to his customers.

Despite being small fry to the mega-rich Russians, there was little doubt that Mohamed was becoming more powerful. Using a Lebanese company he co-owned with a Russian associate, he purchased a Boeing 757 parked at Madrid's Barajas Airport. It was an ostentatious show of wealth and power, right under the noses of Spain's law enforcement agencies.

But he hadn't reckoned with the most feared judge on the planet: the flamboyant Baltasar Garzon, the man who had pursued Chilean dictator General Pinochet.

* * *

I decided to contact the Spanish authorities via Scotland Yard and took the precaution of recording key telephone calls.

On 18 June 2001, I spoke with a Detective Constable Benson in London, who directed my enquiry to Detective Constable Fryer. A week later, DC Fryer asked if a "Mr Raul" from the Spanish intelligence service could contact me. I agreed and quickly arranged to meet the Spaniard on 4 July at 3pm inside the Hotel Novotel on the outskirts of Madrid.

After landing in Spain's capital, I checked into the Crown Plaza Hotel in the city centre and then took a taxi to the Novotel. I'd arrived early and, as I waited in the reception, scanned duplicate copies of the dossiers I'd shown Derbah. I wasn't expecting to feel a sense of unease, but I did. A small part of me worried that Spanish officers might arrest me for doing business with Derbah if they suspected he was a fraudster. After all, I'd worked closely with the alleged new head of Tenerife's underworld.

Minutes ticked by, and the agreed meeting time loomed. I glanced at the clock in the hotel reception, wondering whether I could still catch a return flight if I changed my mind and headed for an easy life back in the UK. But I was damned if I was going to let Derbah, or anybody, chase me from Tenerife just when my business had started to thrive.

Mr Raul arrived on time, introduced himself in a friendly manner and revealed that he spoke fluent English.

Over the next four and a half hours, I explained Goldcrest's activities and my role as a freelance corporate adviser to Mohamed Derbah. Gradually, I explained the complaints I had received, and broader allegations that at least one of his companies was engaged in fraud. Mr Raul nodded along, taking in everything. He browsed the dossiers I had brought with me, handed them back, and said he would contact me the following morning. He then arranged for two police officers to give me a lift back into town.

Later that evening, I phoned Gill to say the meeting went well. I didn't let on, but I really just wanted to hear her voice after a nerve-wracking day.

The next morning, Raul phoned around 8:30 am and asked if I would be willing to meet inspectors from the intelligence unit of the Spanish national police – known as the General Commissariat of Information (CGI) – which was "already investigating the affairs of Mohamed Derbah".

I had not been expecting that twist. Raul hadn't mentioned that Derbah was already a national police target. But the CGI is often referred to colloquially in Spain as the 'secret police'. The unit's budget and staffing levels are officially classified, and CGI employees specialise in undercover, information-gathering and counter-terror work. So, knowing what I now know, I should not have been surprised to hear that an alleged major criminal on Tenerife was already known to a professional police 'ghost' unit.

Raul asked again whether I would meet the two agents and, after stumbling over my answer, I replied: "Er, of course."

Within an hour, a team of Spanish CGI agents descended on my hotel. They had been briefed the previous evening and waited for me to agree to Raul's request. I was nervous, to say the least, when Raul arrived alongside eight plain-clothed officers. Well, I say plain-clothed: it wasn't difficult to guess what they did for a living. Some of them stood out like a sore thumb and were there as security, moving shoulder-to-shoulder with Mr Raul through the hotel lobby. I guessed that this was not the undercover surveillance unit. It was like a scene out of *Reservoir Dogs* – just without the smart suits. I'd never seen such an extensive collection of expensive sunglasses.

Raul smiled and quickly put me at ease.

"Good morning, Paul. And thank you for agreeing to see us," he said, giving my hand a firm and enthusiastic shake.

"This is Inspector Fernando Munoz," Raul said, indicating the man next to him. "He is leading the investigation into Mohamed Derbah and others in Tenerife."

Fernando Munoz leaned forward, arm outstretched, and shook my hand firmly while maintaining what I can only describe as intense eye contact. He wore a serious expression.

"I'm very pleased to meet you," Fernando said in slightly broken English, before asking whether I would be willing to accompany him to his office so that we could speak in private?

"Yes, of course," I replied. Almost immediately, the remaining agents turned on their heels, surrounded the three of us, and swept us at ultra-fast pace towards the hotel's main entrance. Once outside, the guards stood on either side of us, before bundling us into two cars parked immediately in front of the building. It all happened so quickly that I barely noticed the two vehicles were also surrounded by a small troop of uniformed and armed police.

Unlike in the UK, police officers carrying guns was not an unusual sight in Spain. What was odd, was that several of the uniformed officers were nervously looking around the street with one hand clasping their gun.

Whatever I had agreed to participate in, it was sensitive or dangerous.

* * *

With five men in each car, the two vehicles pulled smoothly away from the hotel before accelerating swiftly northwards through the Madrid traffic. There were no sirens, no fuss, yet both drivers weaved through tiny gaps in the traffic as we sped along busy roads. Initially, the car in which I was sat – flanked on either side of the back seat by Raul and Fernando – followed the second vehicle full only of agents. But as we stretched further north through the city, the agents' car settled ominously behind us, following our every move.

Few words were spoken, beyond an intermittent, reassuring "it's okay" sent my way by a smiling Raul. "This journey will not take long," he said. There was no small talk. No guide to the sights and sounds of Madrid's suburbs.

After less than half an hour, we arrived at the entrance to Spain's intelligence headquarters. Armed security staff operated the outer gates.

Once inside, we passed the barriers to the gatehouse building. There, I was checked in, had my passport swiped, was screened through a metal detector, and had my briefcase searched. The car then proceeded down into an underground car park below a separate building, and we accessed a lift to a second security point at ground floor level. At that point, Raul said he would leave me in the care of Fernando and his team. Within seconds, he was out of sight.

Fernando immediately introduced me to his deputy, Enrique Esteban, and a civilian English interpreter called Susana. The introductions were very formal and highly efficient. We made our way through several adjoining offices. As we passed through the area, I glanced at several filing cabinets pushed tight up against an internal wall. Row upon row of cabinets were marked 'John Palmer'. It was only then that it dawned on me: I was being walked through Spain's intelligence HQ – the nerve centre of its entire information-gathering, surveillance and spying operations.

This was crazy, like a scene out of a film.

To have accumulated that much information on John Palmer, there's no doubt that Spain's authorities would have had to have been investigating him for years. Spain and Britain had most likely shared information on Goldfinger as the net closed around him. And if they had that much information on Palmer, then they must already have at least some on Mohamed Derbah. For a brief moment, I felt small and insignificant. I wondered whether I was out of my depth approaching senior Spanish intelligence officials with just a few files of half-investigated information.

I was not a professional intelligence agent. The people around me were the big fish in this pond.

While I considered that fact, our group came to a sudden halt outside a meeting room. Fernando swung open the door and politely gestured to me to sit down at the table inside. Within seconds, a tray of coffee and water arrived and we were down to business. It all felt strangely unceremonial.

Fernando opened the meeting by saying that I was not viewed as a suspect or co-conspirator in Derbah's affairs – and that Spain needed me on its side as a potential prosecution witness. A wave of relief washed over me. When you know you're not guilty of something, you still worry when questioned by authority figures about the issue – and, given my history, I wasn't always confident that law enforcement agencies would make the correct judgement about me.

Interestingly, Fernando didn't explain exactly why his unit was already investigating Mohamed Derbah. It went unspoken. The officers just assumed that I knew. So I surmised that alleged fraud was part of it. I suspected that was only half the story, though.

After a short while, I was left in no doubt that the officers before me represented a unit which was, effectively, a combination of police and intelligence work – but which leant towards the secretive intelligence function. Each nation has a bespoke approach to policing and intelligence, of course, including bodies that represent the interaction between these two distinct functions. But from an early stage, I surmised that the CGI team was loosely comparable to the UK's Special Branch – units within the police force dealing with sensitive intelligence and security matters.

I could also tell that the CGI agents who were present had little detailed knowledge of the offshore world: incorporations, ultimate beneficial owners, company structures, trusts, transfer pricing, tax arrangements and so on.

During our initial discussions, I was asked repeatedly to explain basic concepts – and often smiled politely as blank faces stared back at me. No doubt, some of the agents' confusion was down to the fact that they were not always speaking in, or listening to, their mother tongue. But I also sensed that much of my information was new to them. I soon realised that the files on Mohamed's companies I had collated would be of significant interest to the CGI.

Maybe I wasn't quite the smallest fish in this pond.

I handed over the Derbah dossiers and told the agents that I had boxloads of other accounting ledgers, invoices, correspondence and even audio recordings of telephone conversations between myself, Mohamed and other members of his organisation.

The mention of further documentary evidence caused an excited stir. I'd overlooked the fact that intelligence officers value 'intelligence' and documentation above everything else. That may sound like an obvious point, but the discussion was a sharp reminder that while intelligence agencies may investigate criminal activity, they generally leave the prosecution of criminality and administration of justice to the police and courts. They trade in information – and I had it in abundance.

Suddenly, I didn't feel quite so insignificant. I agreed to disclose further materials and, provisionally, indicated that I would be prepared to give evidence against Mohamed Derbah if Spain ever charged him.

I had fulfilled my legal obligation to report alleged fraud to the relevant authority – but the discussion with agents reminded me that I also had a moral duty to those who may have been defrauded by Mohamed or his associates. Any successful prosecution against Derbah would mean his assets would be confiscated to compensate his victims and I knew he had millions invested in banks, land, and properties in Lebanon. The agents reminded me that Derbah was, of course, innocent until proven guilty and I agreed. I then told Fernando I would assist his department with anything they needed and he looked delighted.

From Spain's perspective, they suddenly had access to somebody who had been, until recently, a trusted confidant of Mohamed Derbah and who knew about his vast offshore money flows.

I was Spain's offshore 'asset'.

At the end of the meeting, Fernando excitedly shook my hand and beamed a huge smile. He also said that my security would be of the utmost importance to his team and that we would discuss suitable arrangements soon. In the meantime, he advised, I should not visit Tenerife until Derbah or his associates had been arrested, or the investigation was dropped. He did not indicate whether either outcome would take place soon.

We agreed, however, that I would return to mainland Spain on 15 July 2001 for three days to provide a detailed witness statement. Fernando then arranged for a police car and two officers to take me directly to the airport.

Despite assurances about my security, the significance of what I had just done hit me as we made our way to Barajas. I recalled the nervousness of the armed police officers outside the hotel that morning, and the fact that Raul and Fernando had turned up with a small army of security agents. I was already in this deep, and damned if I was going to hang around in Madrid!

* * *

Back home, Gill also became concerned about potential reprisals. She worried that I would be viewed as a "grass" and targeted.

I explained that I had a legal duty to report alleged fraud or money laundering – and that I would have got into trouble if I did not because I could be arrested and prevented from trading. Gill understood my dilemma. But like any loving wife, she was worried.

I didn't let on that I shared Gill's concerns. But I agreed to take additional precautions in Spain and Tenerife. I also needed to update Sarah Hill about what had happened in Madrid, so that she maintained a low profile on Tenerife.

After that, I collated reams of new information for Fernando.

* * *

Enrique: *OK – when you arrive here in Madrid, you stay while [sic] with another colleague to go with you.*
Blanchard: *OK.*
Enrique: *OK. And always, for your safety.*

The recorded call to Madrid was made to confirm my flight to the Spanish capital on July 15. I had initially spoken to Fernando to give him a DHL parcel number so that he could monitor the safe delivery of my documents – there had been too many to carry. Fernando had passed the phone to his colleague, Enrique, because he spoke better English.

Ahead of my arrival, the CGI agents had again become concerned about my safety. I knew then that the risk of reprisals from Derbah's alleged mafia was considered severe. CGI staff were worried about internal leaks: Derbah had senior contacts inside local and Spanish national police, and Fernando did not want to take risks with witnesses.

In Madrid, I spent three days furnishing Fernando and Enrique with the details of Mohamed's offshore activity. The agents were not experts in offshore finance – although they clearly understood some issues – so I tried to break down my evidence into easily understood chunks. I felt like a lecturer trying to relay complex theory to his students. To their credit, some of the investigative team grasped complex concepts quickly. I was, after all, briefing some of Spain's finest law enforcement minds.

It would have been easy to assume that personnel who had already investigated John Palmer would easily understand Mohamed's finances.

But that wasn't the case. I knew how Goldcrest operated as offshore corporate consultants and – without getting too egotistical about it – we were extremely good at 'hiding' money, businesses and ownerships legally. Probably better at it than Goldfinger.

Every offshore consultant uses subtly different methods of moving cash and, until now, Fernando's team was not familiar with my approach. Their eyes lit up with excitement when I showed them how to legally construct an almost impenetrable offshore trust which could not be traced to the ultimate beneficial owner.

Well, I say that the agents' eyes 'lit up'. That was until it dawned on them that it was indeed possible to construct such an impenetrable entity. At that point, they looked a little deflated!

"Don't worry," I told them. "I can get you as close to that trust's door as you can be. After that, you'll have to kick the door down!"

Even the high-minded agents raised a smile.

Thankfully for Fernando, Mohamed Derbah had paid for a network of offshore companies and bank accounts which I would describe as 'bronze' service, rather than 'gold'. The difference is all about accessibility and the cost customers are prepared to pay to hide their cash away safely. Mohamed was not a cheapskate, but he didn't pay top dollar like clients such as Viktor. In practical terms, this meant that with most of Derbah's companies and accounts, it was possible to track essential parts of his offshore network.

I handed to Fernando entire files displaying the day-to-day accounts for some of Mohamed's firms. Intelligence agents could begin tracing vast sums back to their sources – or as close as possible. As Mohamed's corporate service provider, I was only required to establish basic company and bank accounts for him, rather than create a complex web of legal transfer pricing arrangements or loan-back deals.

Of course, Mohamed Derbah was smart. As well as my services, it was likely he had used other corporate advisors who created parallel networks of companies and accounts. So, on occasions, my money trail ended abruptly once cash was transferred from the network I created to these alternatives. What we could often see from my documentation, however, were the names of corporate services providers, companies or banks which Mohamed may have used elsewhere – giving Fernando's team a handy starting point from which to continue their painstaking mapping exercise.

Soon, it became clear to the CGI team that there was a vast amount of cash entering Mohamed's financial network without sufficient evidence that payments to cover the services promised to his customers were going the other way. In short, we could find little evidence of the client accounts that Mohamed assured me were in Lebanon.

Sure, Mohamed had bank accounts in Lebanon. But we could see no evidence of the volume of disbursements required to satisfy his customers' contracts. Which meant Spain's authorities were staring at a potential fraud running into tens of millions of Euros.

After three days of viewing and discussing reams of material, we were exhausted.

At 10 pm on the third day, 18 July, Fernando drafted a detailed statement for me to sign. It was fifteen pages long. The Spaniards also arranged a Madrid-based lawyer, Vidal Velasco Merchan, to represent me and paid his expenses.

At the end of the evening, Fernando reaffirmed that I was not considered a suspect in any future case against Derbah and introduced me to the Director-General of Police, Juan Cotino. The director-general described me as a 'protected witness'– a statement that would come back to haunt Spain's CGI and prosecutors many years later.

* * *

The following morning, Fernando requested that I sign a separate document. He explained that I was undertaking to give evidence if any investigation into Mohamed ended in court. I agreed, on the assumption that I was a protected witness.

Fernando and Enrique then drove me to Court Number Five at the Central Courts in Madrid to formally present my documents and sign the declaration. Oddly, however, there was no sign of Vidal, my new lawyer, or my interpreter. Instead, Fernando said he would translate for me.

Before our arrival, I had not paid much attention to the name of the judge we were about to meet. As we arrived, I was hurried through to a plush and ornate looking private office within the main Central Courts.

Behind a large and luxurious desk, sat in a giant leather seat, was none other than Judge Baltasar Garzon: the same high-profile lawman who had pursued Chile's General Pinochet to Britain and heard Wim de Groote's case.

In the flesh, Garzon was a mesmerising figure. Handsome and sophisticated, he would not have looked out of place in a 1930s Hollywood film noir. On looks alone, however, he might be cast as the debonair villain. His once-dark hair was greying at the sides, and he confidently pulled off a near-white stripe set to one side of a broad fringe slicked back with oil. He looked like a wealthy badger.

Garzon stood to greet me, a pair of spectacles dangling from one hand. From his body language, I could tell that he knew Fernando and Enrique. The trio exchanged pleasantries in Spanish, uttered a few sentences to each other and, within seconds, a two-page document was handed around the group. Garzon maintained eye contact with me throughout, like he tried to see through my eyes and into my mind. I wondered when the stare would end, but it didn't really. After a while, it was a little un-nerving – what does an awkward Yorkshireman who speaks only broken Spanish do in response? I just nodded repeatedly and smiled back.

Garzon handed me the two-page document, which Fernando requested I sign. My intelligence agent-interpreter explained that the paper was an undertaking for me to attend court to give evidence as a potential prosecution witness against Mohamed Derbah.

I signed the document, as requested, but noticed that no other signatures appeared on it. Judge Garzon then shook my hand and, through Fernando, said he appreciated the assistance I had provided to Spain. I was then asked to wait outside the office while Fernando and Enrique held a brief, private conversation with the judge.

Once we were all back outside, Fernando thanked me again for helping his department. If I needed any help on any matter in Spain, I had only to ask, he said. The agents then handed me personal mobile phone numbers before driving me to the airport for my flight home.

On the way to Barajas Airport, Fernando was in high spirits. He explained that, once I had signed my statement, 'Operation Cedro' had been officially re-opened. The operation, he said, had been on hold for some considerable time because its remit overlapped with John Palmer's court cases.

I didn't know it at the time, but the statement I had just signed – and the entire meeting we had just held in Judge Garzon's office – would turn out to be potentially illegal.

* * *

I sent Fernando's team copies of telephone conversations I had with Mohamed and his entourage during the early days of the Spanish investigation. In early September 2001, I telephoned Fernando to let him know that I was going on holiday to St Lucia, in the Caribbean, in November. At that point, he said he needed to see me before I left the UK. He wanted any intelligence I had on a Russian associate of Derbah. The discussion would later be heard in a UK court.

Fernando: This man Boris...
Paul: The Russian?
Fernando: Yes, who is he?
Paul: He is the Russian associate of Derbah.
Fernando: Oh – he has properties on Tenerife?
Paul: He has business interests in Tenerife.
Fernando: Uh – 'business interests' in Tenerife?
Paul: Correct!

The 'Boris' in question was linked to a namesake and one of Russia's most influential men – Boris Berezovsky: the billionaire media mogul who later had a spectacular fall-out with Vladimir Putin. Fernando's team had discovered links between Derbah and his Russian associate but had drawn a blank when trying to connect their finances.

I figured that, during my visit to Madrid to discuss the Russian, I might pick up intel on Mohamed's associates that I could pass on to my Russian business contacts.

When I arrived, Fernando and Enrique explained that their case was progressing smoothly. But they asked for details of other offshore accounts or companies controlled by Derbah – and any disgruntled customers of Mohamed who would be willing to provide witness statements. I said I could provide both.

"Great. Any information on Mohamed and the Russians will also help considerably," Fernando added.

The investigation might well have been going smoothly, but it was also expanding.

* * *

I had lost Mohamed Derbah as a client, to say the very least, and needed to replace him. So with some reservations, in October 2001, I agreed to do some basic offshore work for Eric Reiner.

The brash American was still interested in securing investment for several major schemes, including a mining project in the Nevada desert which promised significant returns. But Reiner was struggling to identify potential investors and kept asking me to approach people I knew. More pressingly, however, the American wanted an offshore company to act as the primary vehicle for a film and entertainment business he fronted.

I agreed to create a Belize-based firm, Stargate Ventures Ltd, to fulfil the role. But soon I was concerned that the specific film industry projects Reiner had in mind would, in part, be paid for by cash he wanted to raise through methods finance professionals might describe as "credit enhancement".

To explain, credit enhancement is a method of raising cash commonly used by fraudsters – as well as legitimate businesses. The basic model involves paying hefty sums into a new bank account for a brief period, so that the same bank provides a generous credit facility based on the value of what is deposited. The cash on deposit can then quickly be moved back to its original accounts, but the borrowing or overdraft facility on the new account remains in place.

As you can imagine, fraudsters are then in a position to withdraw or transfer the value of the new borrowing limit and, hey presto, they can make off with it. In the offshore consultancy world, we were always looking for suspicious-looking 'credit enhancement' proposals – as were banks and law firms. But, despite some careful due diligence rules, such as minimum time limits for some bank deposits, it was not always possible to separate dodgy deals from legitimate use of credit enhancement.

Reiner appeared to have all relevant paperwork, and assets, to justify his plan. So I informed Hugo about the potential investment project, but reiterated that we would need to monitor it carefully before he committed. Hugo was interested in the proposal, which promised lucrative returns, and asked Elena Dontu to liaise with Eric Reiner and me on his behalf.

* * *

Gill and I enjoyed an incredible trip to St Lucia.

The lush, forested Caribbean island is stunning in every sense of the word. Gill and I stayed at what was then the Hilton hotel, overlooked by the island's iconic mountainous plugs: volcanic spires known as The Pitons. We travelled in style across the Atlantic and planned a thrilling arrival at the hotel. We chartered a helicopter, the pilot flew in low and we enjoyed a bird's-eye view of spectacular rainforests before landing nearby.

Lord Glenconner, the man who bought the island of Mustique for £45,000, ran a boutique restaurant adjacent to our resort and he made Gill and I welcome guests. In 2000, St Lucia was a fully-fledged offshore jurisdiction, so I used the opportunity to research local rules and regulations. Lord Glenconner gave me some pointers on the bespoke offshore services offered across the island and referred me to his local accountant and lawyers.

Later during the holiday, Glenconner also sought my advice on restructuring his property holdings to avoid inheritance taxes. At one stage, I even considered relocating Goldcrest to St Lucia because local laws provided strict confidentiality towards owners and directors of companies. Luxury yacht owners can also register their boats through a St Lucia-based company to mask the ultimate beneficial owners.

Alas, two weeks in the Caribbean passed quickly. On our return to the UK, on 22 November, I phoned Fernando for an update. In his broken English, the CGI agent dropped a bombshell.

Mohamed Derbah had been arrested and was languishing inside a Madrid prison.

CHAPTER TEN
Isabella

On 20 November 2001, while Gill and I were relaxing in the warm waters of the Caribbean, Judge Baltasar Garzon and a small army of Spanish police and intelligence agents landed planes in north Tenerife. They carried out a series of raids, the like of which the island had never seen.

At 9am that day, scores of armed National Police officers operating under the judge's direction simultaneously stormed Mohamed Derbah's offices, his home, other properties connected to the Lebanese businessman and those of his brothers. The raids were carried out with militaristic precision. Police and intelligence officers wore ski masks to hide their identities, scaring the living daylights out of passers-by. The 'search and seize' operation went until late in the evening.

By the day's end, sixteen people had been arrested – all on suspicion of links to an organised criminal group or mafia.

The arrested men included Mohamed and his Tenerife-based brothers, Hussein (Sam) and Hatem. Jose Fernandez, the senior officer of the Guardia Civil who had endorsed Mohamed's passport, was also arrested – along with Derbah's new corporate adviser, Jose Gonzalez.

Fernando informed me that several arrests had also taken place in Madrid. But two persons of interest to Garzon's team – Omar 'Tano' Francionis and London-based gangster Dennis New – could not be found. International warrants were issued for their arrest.

Officers seized a lorry load of documentation, as well as crucial assets linked to the Tenerife mafia. Envelopes stuffed full of cash, which officers suspected may have been used to bribe local officials, were also discovered. Investigators also found a cache of weapons, including shotguns, stun guns, pistols and revolvers. They even impounded two planes at Madrid's Barajas Airport, owned by a company belonging to Mohamed Derbah and a Russian associate.

Press reports said politicians on Tenerife viewed the police operation positively. Local leaders also praised the fact that Judge Garzon, who enjoyed pop star status, led the operation. Many saw it as a sign that Madrid wanted to rid the Canary Islands of alleged criminals.

Fernando told me as much as CGI bosses and lawyers allowed. Before he put the phone down, the agent also urged me to take extra security measures and to avoid Tenerife for the foreseeable future. I could hear the buzz of activity in Fernando's office during our discussion.

***

Despite my chat with Fernando, key questions remained unanswered.

Had I unleashed this? If so, what exactly had I unleashed?

Dialling furiously, I called everybody I knew on Tenerife and urged them to send me as much information about the raids as they could. In the meantime, I sat at my computer and read the Internet-based news coverage. I wanted to know everything. The CGI had known much more about Derbah before I met them. The filing cabinets full of information on John Palmer indicated that. But how much more?

***

International press coverage described Mohamed Derbah as the alleged head of the Lebanese Mafia and claimed he had laundered £500m for gangs from Britain, Russia and South America.

But there was a problem with the media coverage. An article in the Spanish newspaper *La Opinion*, published on 21 November, named me as a witness who had provided law enforcement agencies with information on the reported crime syndicate.

Had I been foolish to initiate all of this? I suddenly felt vulnerable and worried that my family could be targeted by Derbah's organisation. Now I knew what Fernando was referring to at the end of our phone call.

I poured over newspapers and websites, and what emerged was a string of sensational allegations about Mohamed Derbah that few people outside his close circle of family and friends would have known.

Firstly, he was accused of supplying weapons and money to the Amal and Hezbollah militias in Lebanon. Amal (meaning 'hope') is a Lebanese political movement associated with the country's Shia Muslim community. It was co-founded by the charismatic Iranian cleric Musa al-Sadr, who went missing after visiting Libya's ex-dictator Muammar Gaddafi in 1978. Perhaps significantly, al-Sadr's base in Lebanon was in Tyre – Mohamed Derbah's hometown, where I had been entertained by his family and treated in hospital.

According to press reports, the intelligence and police operation against Derbah included phone taps. Agents are even alleged to have listened to a discussion between Derbah and Nabih Berri – who was elected leader of Amal in 1980 following al-Sadr's disappearance and the resignation of the party's other co-founder, Hussein el-Husseini.

Berri led Amal during the violent Lebanese civil war. On the covertly recorded tapes, Mohamed and the Amal leader are alleged to have discussed the delivery of "chairs" – believed to be a code word for weapons.

Separately, the press coverage also alleged that Derbah was linked to Hezbollah – the Shia Islamist movement defined as a terrorist organisation by many western governments, including the USA and UK.

Hezbollah acts as a proxy for Iran in the long-running Iran-Israel dispute and has a paramilitary wing called the Jihad ('holy war') Council. It waged a long-running and bloody guerrilla war against an Israeli-backed group in south Lebanon between 1985 and 2000.

Even though both groups represent Shia Muslims, Amal and Hezbollah share a love-hate relationship and history. Hezbollah was initially formed as an Amal spin-off in the 1980s and the two militias fought on separate sides of Lebanon's civil war until 1990. Since then, however, the two groups have at times reconciled and been part of a broader alliance. So, while the two organisations are different – Hezbollah is now arguably the most powerful force in Lebanon – Mohamed Derbah might have been linked to both.

Allegations that Mohamed may have been an arms trader and supplied major terrorist organisations was startling.

I had been aware of unproven local claims that Mohamed held small caches of arms on Tenerife – and the odd unsubstantiated boast that Mohamed himself had made during discussions. But the new press reports took these matters to a new level. What's more, it was now apparent that despite the intelligence services' reticence to tell me more, *somebody* was supplying the Spanish newspapers with detailed information on the Derbah case,

In the weeks after the raids, more press coverage emerged linking Mohamed and his associates with serious alleged criminality.

The revelations reached a peak when Derbah was allegedly linked to Al-Qaeda (meaning 'The Base'): the Sunni jihadist extremist network led by Osama Bin Laden and the most feared terror group on the planet.

Among the reported links to Al-Qaeda was Derbah's alleged role in the theft of 1,300 French passports on behalf of the terror group.

Just two months before the raids on Tenerife, Al-Qaeda launched the most devastating terror attack in history when eleven men hijacked four passenger airliners and flew three of them into iconic buildings on the east coast of the United States. The fourth plane crashed in a field in Pennsylvania.

The attacks on 11 September 2001 came to be known as '9/11' and saw almost 3,000 innocent people killed, a further 6,000 injured and around $10bn worth of damage to the United States' infrastructure.

The most dreadful, but unfortunately iconic, images of the attacks were those of two planes crashing into the Twin Towers of the World Trade Centre in south Manhattan, New York, within seventeen minutes of each other. One and a half hours later, both towers had collapsed. Within days of the attacks, the USA and its allies began preparations for controversial wars in Afghanistan and Iraq, citing the 'war on terror' as their justification.

* * *

Mohamed Derbah was allegedly linked to the terrorist group which had attacked the United States and played a part in kick-starting wars?

Mohamed? Whose mother I'd met? Whose brothers I knew? Who declared that I was "almost family"?

I genuinely struggled with the magnitude of those allegations.

But this was also the same Mohamed Derbah who betrayed close associates such as John Palmer and Wim de Groote. The Mohamed whose business empire was supposedly linked with timeshare scams, arms trades and other criminal activity worth up to $10m annually.

My head was spinning. Being English, of course, I went downstairs and made a cup of tea. In the kitchen, I leaned on the sideboard, head in hands, and tried to process what I had just read.

British and Russian gangsters. Lebanese mafia. Amal. Hezbollah. Al-Qaeda. Just who had I been involved with? These groups were not natural bedfellows, to say the least. So if the allegations and reports were true, what was Mohamed exactly? A mafia boss? A London-style gangland geezer? A terrorist mastermind? A money-oriented opportunist? Intelligence? An *agent provocateur*?

All of the above? None of them?

Mohamed Jamil Derbah has always categorically denied involvement in any criminal activity on Tenerife or elsewhere. While he has been named as an alleged criminal on Spanish indictments and European Arrest Warrants, he has not been convicted of any crime mentioned above or elsewhere in this book.

* * *

In early 2002, I accepted Fernando and Enrique's offer of assistance in obtaining an NIE certificate. In the aftermath of 9/11 and, more locally, the John Palmer scandal on Tenerife, governments had clamped down on businesses that operated secretively, including offshore firms. The NIE system in Spain wasn't solely aimed at offshore operators, but it required anybody opening a bank account or creating a Spanish company to be registered with the police – and the NIE certificate would be attached to bank account applications and company documents for official identity purposes.

I had delayed obtaining a certificate during the application period because any checks with the UK police would have revealed my criminal convictions. I wasn't avoiding the new requirements – I couldn't – but I was waiting for the right time to lodge an application that would not be automatically rejected. Despite the heat which followed the Derbah raids, I was enjoying working in both Spain and the UK. Hugo, Viktor and Edmond were great clients and others were coming on board. But I needed to remain legal. To my surprise, when I mentioned my imminent NIE application to the intelligence officers, they offered to help. At the time, I thought it was merely a favour in return for my help – the endorsement of Spain's CGI guaranteed that I would receive the certificate, despite my past offences. But I now realise their rush to help was probably a well-calculated and canny move.

On 20 January, I travelled to Madrid and stayed at the Crown Plaza hotel. The next morning, I was picked up by a youthful-looking officer called Danny and taken to the CGI's HQ. There, Fernando and Enrique greeted me like brothers and said my NIE application was already being processed.

Since our last meeting, I had gathered material that potentially implicated Thierry Boinnard in fraudulent deals with Derbah. After providing a general update, the two agents drove me to another police department in central Madrid, where a long queue had formed outside. It was the queue for NIE-related interviews.

We pulled up and parked directly on the road outside the main entrance. There, we were immediately approached by a uniformed police officer who intended to move us on. Fernando waved his police badge and said we would be a matter of minutes, so the officer ended up guarding the car until we returned. We then bypassed the queue, found the issuing office, and collected my certificate. It was that simple.

Suddenly, and thanks to Spanish intelligence officers, I was a fully endorsed businessman in Spain. The two agents then took me to the airport departure point for my flight back to Liverpool.

* * *

By this time, I had a reputation within the offshore industry as somebody who could be trusted with his clients' most sensitive financial secrets and who could ensure that my clients stayed on the right side of the thin line between tax evasion and tax avoidance. Thanks to people like Hugo, word of my skills had spread.

I took pride in my reputation, but it is a hard 'rep' to maintain – so I worked diligently to ensure that I stayed up to speed with all key legal requirements that would allow my clients to minimise their tax requirements despite the post-9/11 clampdown on offshore services. When I wasn't dealing directly with clients, or spending time with Gill and my children, I could be found with my head in a book about offshore laws, or on the phone to regulatory contacts and banks around the world. It wasn't glamorous, but I put the hours in. You don't succeed in life unless you are prepared to work like a sleigh dog.

* * *

Working hard kept me focused on making money and putting my family back in a solid financial position after losing my original fortune. Gill and I were enjoying married life, despite my long hours. But there was one thorny issue that I could not, initially, discuss with my wife.

Throughout 2002, Elena Dontu – Hugo's beautiful assistant – became increasingly flirtatious. I met with Elena occasionally to brief her on Eric Reiner's mining investment proposal. Super-sharp Elena quickly familiarised herself with the plan. One evening, over coffee, we arranged to discuss how Hugo could help fund the project. We met at Ristorante Los Bandidos, an upmarket restaurant in Puerto Banus. As I entered the joint, my jaw almost dropped.

Elena wore a full face of subtle make-up, sported pouting lips softened with lipstick and hair draped over her shoulders. She wore an elegant, figure-hugging dress with thin shoulder straps. The flowing lower part of the dress stopped above her knees and revealed long, tanned legs. It was a very different outfit from what I had seen her in since we began working together.

A NETWORK OF TERROR

Osama Bin Laden

LINKS TO SPAIN

  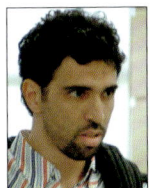

Mohamed Atta   Mohammed Khan   Jamal Zougam

THE 7/7 LONDON BOMBERS

  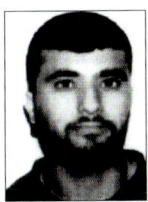 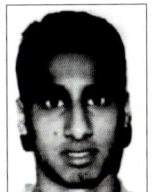

Hasib Hussain   Germaine Lindsay   Mohammad Sidique Khan   Shehzad Tanweer

THE CREVICE GANG

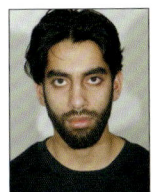    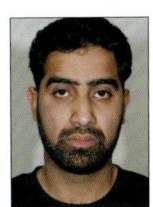

Jawad Akbar   Omar Khyam   Salahuddin Amin   Anthony Garcia   Waheed Mahood

Mostapha Jamil Derbah
Lebanese Businessman

Mohamed Jamil Derbah
Alleged Mafia Don

Ali Jamil Derbah
Lebanese Politician

Chamel Fabel Chamseddine
Trusted nominee

Jeremy Sinclair
'Sovereign Gold Trust' nominee

John Palmer

Veronique Daures
Derbah's trusted PA

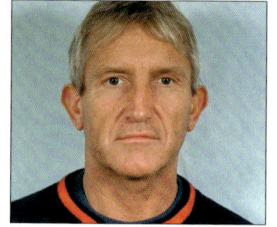
Kenneth Noye
Derbah said Noye 'was just a man for business'

Mohamed Derbah
in fake Masonic regalia

Jeremy Sinclair
Taught Derbah secret Masonic signs

Derbah's
Lebanese Associates

With Mohamed
and Wim De Groote

With Mohamed
and his Mother

With
Mohamed's Mother

With Mohamed
and Family friend

With Mohamed
in the Lebanon

With Carlos

Wedding day with
Tommy Hindmarch,
Jeremy Sinclair and Carlos

Scot Young
Trumped-up dealmaker

Boris Berezovsky
The Oligarch

Baltasar Garzon
Disgraced Spanish Judge

Vladimir Putin
The Godfather

John Palmer
Assassinated

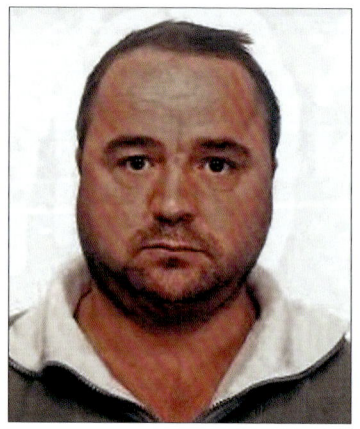
Sonny Fletcher
Convicted Drug Dealer

'Grass 1' Richard Henson

'Grass 2' Darren Steadman

London
7/7 Atrocities

London
7/7 Atrocities

With Sarah Hill

In St Lucia with my multi-millionaire client Lord Glenconner

With world champion Alex 'Hurricane' Higgins

With Carlos getting 'rat-arsed'

The Cheavours

Elena Dontu

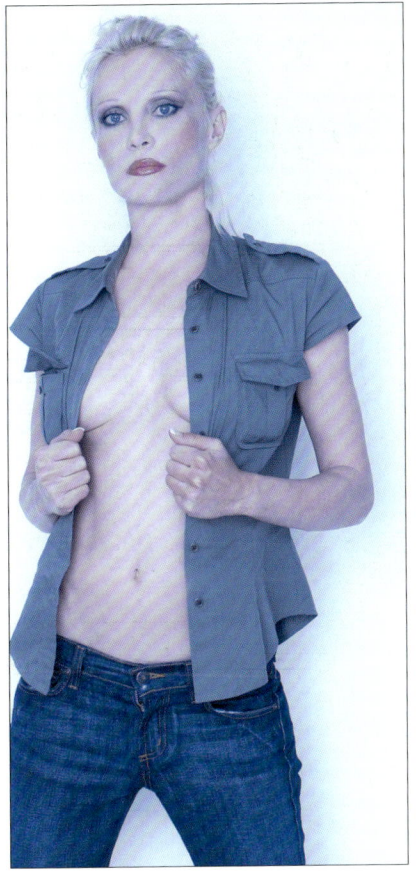

Elena returning to her
modelling career in Los Angeles

Vidal, my Spanish Lawyer,
testifying for the defence

Spain never challenged Paul's
'Offshore asset' claims

PAUL BLANCHARD SNR
THROUGH THE YEARS

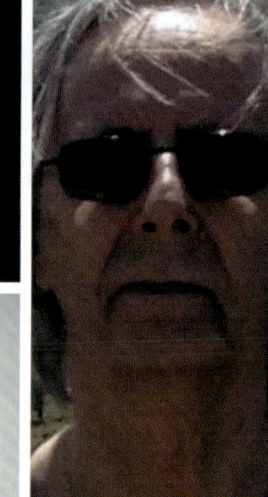

I was a happily married man, without temptation, but would freely admit that Elena looked stunning. Almost every red-blooded male in the restaurant turned his head when she stood to greet me.

"Paul, so lovely to see you again," she said, kissing me softly on both cheeks. Her deep blue eyes caught mine as we embraced.

This was a little different from Elena's usually cool, professional demeanour.

"I thought we might have wine. Do you think?"

"Oh, well...er...I might just stick to coffee tonight, Elena. I'm trying not to drink too much these days," I replied, caught a little off guard. "But by all means, please, you order wine. Are we celebrating something special?"

"Just another day at work completed," Elena said, smiling broadly. She leaned forward slightly across the table. "Everybody else seems to be having fun in Marbella, so I think I will also have fun tonight." As she finished speaking, Elena raised her carefully plucked eyebrows and scanned the drinks menu in an exaggerated manner.

It was a comical moment and we both chuckled.

Elena asked again, head tilted and one eyebrow raised: "I cannot interest you in a small drink, Paul?"

"Haha! You are very insistent, Elena. But I am going to politely decline. I've got a mountain of work to do tomorrow morning and need a clear head. Your boss will not thank me otherwise."

"Oh, such a shame! What do they say in England? All work and no play!" As she teased me, Elena leaned forward, flicked a lock of her loose hair back behind her ear and, again, our eyes met.

She was flirting. I had to pause, mentally, to make sure that I hadn't misread the signs. But I hadn't.

In other circumstances, and as a single man, I'd have been overjoyed at the attention from such a woman. But I was married and dedicated to my beautiful wife, Gill. Elena was drop-dead gorgeous and I was significantly older than her.

This was all a little surreal, but not entirely unexpected. I had heard from other contacts who did business with Hugo and his associates that you had to keep your wits about you around some of his glamorous assistants. It was not clear whether Hugo encouraged his staff to flirt with male clients, but it was well known that it happened.

Still, I didn't want to spoil Elena's upbeat mood, so I played along. We had an enjoyable chat about non-work-related matters over drinks: Elena's family, Moldova, the UK, countries we'd like to visit and a few we agreed neither of us would set foot in. I'd never seen Elena look so relaxed.

The mood became a little more professional when we turned to Hugo's finances but, once in a while, Elena would lighten the technical talk with a quip or flirtatious smile. She was enjoying the attention, that was for sure. As I leaned over to politely pour some more wine into her glass, Elena gently touched my hand to indicate that she had enough – her fingers lingering on mine just longer than would be reasonable. As she did, our eyes met again.

I reminded myself to be on my best behaviour. But what the hell was going on?

***

Whenever Elena and I met during 2002, things would blow hot and cold: she would look and act hot, and I would invariably have to go cold on her. It was beginning to get a little awkward because I valued Hugo as a client and liked Elena – but I was not interested in having an affair with her. I knew the trouble that would cause and, after the incredible loyalty Gill had shown during my imprisonment, there was simply no way I would betray my wife.

Not that Elena seemed to get the message. Her flirting was sometimes subtle, sometimes not, but she knew never to take it too far. What I wondered, however, was whether it was genuine? Had she been asked to butter me up? Perhaps by her boss?

I had read tales of how some businessmen in Spain had been victims of 'honey traps' by glamourous women, or men, working for wealthy investors. There were cases reported in local media, in which businessmen had been set up so that rivals gained leverage over them during negotiations or property deals. But those cases involved women working for underworld figures. The criminal gangs would pay the women to seduce and sleep with targets and then use photos or videos of the affairs to blackmail their 'mark' by threatening to release the images to wives and girlfriends.

Hugo, however, did not strike me as a criminal. I'd always assumed he surrounded himself with beautiful women for his enjoyment – and to encourage more innocent compliance amongst his clients.

***

Late on the morning of 22 July 2002, I received a call from Aunt Lilly. She sounded distressed.

"Come as quickly as you can. Uncle Paul's collapsed and is in a lot of pain. I'm on my own."

"I'm on my way," I replied.

From his home, Uncle Paul was rushed to the hospital. He was taken to an emergency operating theatre while myself, Lilly and Paul Jnr were ushered into an adjoining waiting room. Uncle Paul had only recently been diagnosed with stomach cancer, but we lost him that day.

Shortly before he passed, a nurse entered the waiting room and asked if we wanted to be with him in his final moments. Lilly and I were shown into the operating theatre and sat at the bedside holding Uncle Paul's hands. We whispered words of comfort for several minutes and in a soft, permanent blink of an eye, he was at rest.

The family was devastated. The gentlest, kindest soul amongst us – a man who had seen and survived the atrocities of war – had gone. While I was growing up, Uncle Paul had always said it was essential to enjoy life. "You never know which day will be your last," he would say with a smile.

His death was a sharp reminder that life is fragile. I had lost the man who had been my father figure.

***

Weeks before Uncle Paul's death, in June 2002, Tenerife experienced the might of Judge Garzon for a second time, when he led further raids on the island and neighbouring Gran Canaria. Among the 35 people arrested was Richard Cashman, a close associate of John Palmer.

Garzon, already a popular figure on mainland Spain, was fast becoming a legend on Tenerife: the man sent by the motherland to clean up the Canaries. Never one to miss an opportunity to enhance his reputation as a crime-fighting crusader, Garzon played to the crowd through his statements to the media.

Battle lines were being drawn across Tenerife: those supporting law and order on one side of the divide and those trying to undermine it on the other. Opportunistic criminal gangs new to Tenerife, including Russian and Italian mafias, filled the void created by a fresh wave of gangland arrests. What had been a simmering war between gangs, including Mohamed's alleged Lebanese mafia, threatened to boil over into something much more significant as the net closed around the island's dons, hoodlums and wise-guys. A string of attacks committed by foot-soldiers for each of the gangs, acts of gangland retribution, were reported.

Thankfully, I was advised to stay well away. York seemed like a safe haven. That is until I took a trip to the city centre one afternoon in August.

As I wandered among the summer crowd, doing some afternoon shopping, I caught a fleeting glimpse of a loping giant on the busy street ahead of me. I recognised him immediately.

'Tano' stood at least six foot six inches tall, and the Argentinean was built like the proverbial out-house. He had the height, reach and ability to crush bones of a heavyweight boxer. And he was Mohamed Derbah's personal bodyguard.

Thankfully, while I had spotted him, Tano had not seen me. I slid into a nearby shop doorway, keeping one eye on the street ahead of me. Tano strode purposefully through the crowd but seemed to be looking around, his eyes not fixed on any person or building. As he neared, I slipped inside the shop.

What the hell was Mohamed's most trusted bodyguard doing in York? This was not a coincidence! If he was on holiday in Britain, he'd have been in London or Edinburgh: not York, beautiful city though it is. I felt my heartbeat increase and my breathing grew louder.

Within seconds, Tano wandered into view. He turned his head to peer inside only as he sped by the end of the store's front window – but his view of me was blocked by advertising pasted onto the display. I could see his giant frame, but Tano could not see me. Almost as quickly as I'd seen the Argentinean, he was out of view. We'd missed each other by mere seconds.

After a few minutes of loitering, I left the store and made my way back to my car, checking over my shoulder and taking only side roads as I walked. I turned on the engine, hit the accelerator and sped straight to my office in Heslington. As I weaved through the back streets, I tried to rationalise what had just happened. There seemed little doubt that Mohamed had sent Tano to find me. But why exactly was he here – and was he alone?

When I got back to Heslington, I parked up a little further from my office than usual and scanned the area to ensure that nobody was lurking. When I could see that the coast was clear, I dashed up the stairs, into the maisonette and locked the door tight behind me.

The first thing I did was dial the office in Tenerife.

* * *

"What? You're serious? When did that happen?"

"Yesterday," Sarah Hill replied calmly. "I've just found out myself, Paul."

"Christ! And the police didn't think to tell me? Okay...okay. It's happened. Not much we can do now. Any other news?"

"No, things at the office are fine. Paul..."

"Yes?"

"Stay safe. People here say that things are heating up," Sarah warned.

"Sure. You too, Sarah. They'll leave you alone but, still, keep your wits about you."

"Of course. I haven't lost them just yet, boss."

I put the phone down and exhaled.

Mohamed Derbah was out of prison. He'd been bailed and had returned to Tenerife. Sarah had picked up the news around the same time I saw Tano in York.

Surely Mohamed would not try to target me so obviously after being released? No. I figured that Tano's visit was more likely to be a show of strength. A message, rather than an action. I figured? And hoped.

I called those who needed to be warned. Then I phoned Fernando in Madrid, but the call went straight through to an answering machine. Where the hell was he? And why had nobody warned me that Mohamed Derbah was out?

I jumped into the car and sped home. When I got there, I warned Gill not to open the door to any giant Argentinean salesmen carrying violin cases. She got the message.

* * *

I was calmer than I expected over the following few days. There had been no further sightings of Tano, and I began to wonder whether he had tried to visit my office or home in the days preceding our near-encounter in town – perhaps when Gill and I had been out.

Even more promisingly, a Tano-sized figure had been spotted back on Tenerife. Perhaps his visit to the UK had been a fact-finding mission? Or maybe Tano was smarter than I had given him credit for – and had seen me that afternoon at the shops. Perhaps he had achieved what he came for: to put the wind up me?

Fernando and I finally spoke on 22 August. He apologized for the delay in returning my call, explaining that most government departments effectively closed during the August holiday period. After I described the near-miss with Tano, Fernando advised me to contact the police in York if I had any concerns.

I didn't want to tell Fernando but, given my history, there was little chance of that. I asked why the Spanish authorities had not contacted me to tell me that Mohamed had been released. Fernando said his unit believed there was little risk to me in the UK, despite Tano's recent guest appearance.

The CGI officer added that he was going on holiday but would like to see me when he returned in October. He had new information about Mohamed.

"I want to speak with you about this, all in secret. Your safety is very important for us," he reiterated.

I guess being a "protected witness" only applied to Spain.

★ ★ ★

When Sonny Fletcher was released from prison, he vowed to go straight. On my advice, he created a used-car company: Fletcher (Car Sales) Limited. Sonny worked hard and the business quickly made a profit, which he sought to invest in lucrative development deals – including a harbour renewal programme in Cornwall. He had also persuaded many of his associates to place their cash in the same development. Sonny couldn't read or write, but he was canny – and acutely aware of the opportunities the UK's property market offered.

In business, one introduction leads to another and my work on Sonny's development portfolio led the reformed ex-con to introduce me to three gentlemen: John Allin, Darren Steadman and Mohammed Khan.

I agreed to meet the three new faces on 18 September 2002 at Warrington Lymm Services – an unglamorous motorway service station on the M6 near Manchester.

Over a lukewarm service station coffee, I did my usual presentation: explaining the services I could provide to clients. Mohammed Khan, or "Mo", as he liked to be called, listened intently. He lived in the heart of Birmingham's Asian community and boasted that he was well-connected among business groups in the West Midlands. At the end of the meeting, Mo said some of his other friends might also want to use my offshore services and asked whether he could contact me later. I nodded.

At the time, the meeting on the motorway seemed innocuous, even if the venue was a little weird. Just like scores of pitches I had made to potential new clients. But driving back over the South Pennines into Yorkshire, Sonny piped up.

"Them lads could bring us a lot of business, Paul. Mo knows everybody."

I smiled. I'd heard similar claims from my prison friends before. Some turned out to be accurate. Others turned out to be baseless-but-harmless chatter.

"Good, let's hope so," I said as we turned off the M62 and headed towards Sonny's home city of Bradford. We quickly turned the discussion back to our prison days, swapping inflated tales in the way old inmates do. While my past behind bars seemed like a lifetime ago, catching up with Sonny was always fun. He was now a legitimate businessman, but his background also meant he always had a hair-raising tale or two to tell.

***

On my next visit to Madrid, 17 October 2002, I learned from Fernando and Enrique that one of Derbah's bodyguards had boasted locally that he would kill me for speaking to the authorities. It was not Tano.

None of us knew how seriously to take the threat. It could have been just another bit of braggadocio by bored bodyguards who had little to do with Derbah. But it was not a nice message to receive.

After further discussion about my safety, the agents and I talked more generally about our work. I casually mentioned my encounter with Allin, Steadman and Mo Khan – and their connections with allegedly wealthy Asians from Birmingham, Luton and Yorkshire. The two agents' ears pricked up. They glanced awkwardly at each other before turning to me.

Spain's intelligence service, they said, would be interested in any Asian businessmen moving money through mainland Europe and into offshore jurisdictions.

This was the aftermath of 9/11. Osama Bin Laden, Al-Qaeda's figurehead and the mastermind behind the attacks, was still a fugitive. The use of offshore banks, companies and trusts to move terror funding had soared to the top of the political agenda. The whole world was on alert while Al-Qaeda and its affiliates remained an active terror threat – and senior politicians from the USA, UK, Spain and their allies appeared to be heading inexorably towards war in Iraq. I assumed the intelligence agents were, like many law enforcement bodies during that period, a little jumpy about Asian businessmen moving cash. So, I forgave the slight xenophobia.

"Paul, any information, no matter how insignificant it may seem, we would like to know," Enrique said.

***

After lunch that day, I gave a long-planned presentation on offshore finance to a select group of attentive CGI officers.

Fernando had asked me to brief his team on the latest financial and regulatory developments. "Just in case there are any gaps in our knowledge," he said. There were gaps, of course. To be frank, there were some gaping holes!

Several officers looked gobsmacked when, through my interpreter, a stern-looking Spanish woman named Mar, I explained the latest legal loopholes which allowed offshore businessmen to stay one step ahead of global tax authorities – such as complex lease-back arrangements or the transfer of assets to an offshore foundation and the recruitment of its creator as a well-paid consultant. All legal at the time. All common occurrences among wealthy elites.

The legitimate offshore sector is almost always ahead of regulators or law enforcement agencies when it comes to tax minimisation. But I figured that Fernando's team might get close to some more genuine criminals with my help – and saw the briefing as me returning the favour over his help with the NIE certificate.

After the presentation, the spooks gave me a generous round of applause and told me that the briefing had opened their eyes to some offshore methods. I was, well and truly, Spain's offshore asset.

* * *

Once back in the UK, I got my head down and prepared for my trial on two perjury charges, which was due to begin at Manchester Crown Court on 19 November 2002.

The judge overseeing the case was Mr Justice Douglas Brown. But three more prestigious judges were due to appear in court as witnesses for the Crown and against me: Sir John Christopher Blofeld QC; John Barry Mortimer QC, and His Honour Judge Angus MacDonald QC.

Prosecution lawyers had also lined up a stellar support cast of witnesses, including His Honour Judge John Blackburn Gittings QC, the registrar of criminal appeals for England and Wales, Michael McKenzie QC; Patrick Cosgrove QC; Hong Kong magistrate Robert Bruce McNair; and DI Trevor Wells from the Special Intelligence Section of Scotland Yard. An expert from British Telecom had also been asked to give evidence on the authenticity of telephone records which *The Observer* newspaper and I had obtained.

The Crown was certainly throwing its weight behind saving the reputation of the three judges – an attempt to discredit the telephone records was planned. The prosecution argued that I had only produced the phone records four years after my arrest – the implication being that I had forged them. Never mind that *The Observer* had separately obtained the very same records!

But the prosecution's case fell apart once the expert from BT, Stephen Wren, was called. Historical files of the phone records, which indicated potential collusion by the three judges, had been deleted by BT by the time of the trial. Nonetheless, on seeing my defence team's copies, Wren admitted to the court: "The information appears in a format standard at the time of its alleged production."

In layman's terms, the BT expert believed that my defence documents looked real.

John Mortimer QC was questioned and asked whether he had informed me that he was a relative of Wilson Pullyne when he represented me back in 1978. Under oath, the judge acknowledged: "I certainly didn't tell him anything about the relationship."

Regarding my companies being insolvent when I was arrested in the 1970s, Mortimer added: "It seems to me that if he [Blanchard] was owed money, he certainly would not be insolvent."

When Blofeld was cross-examined about a meeting he had with Peter Taylor, the then Lord Chief Justice (who legally had no interest in my case), he reluctantly admitted: "There, I have said it: I spoke to the Lord Chief Justice."

The implication was clear: judges had been discussing my case with other senior members of the legal profession – despite claiming they had not.

After the prosecution had presented its case, I was able to give my defence from the dock. It was the moment I had been waiting for. I reminded the court that I could not have faked the documents because *The Observer* had paid an agent £5,000 to obtain the records in 1994. It therefore followed, I argued, that the phone records showed contact between the three judges.

David Rose, home affairs correspondent at *The Observer*, confirmed he had obtained the telephone records in 1994: six years before I had allegedly forged the documents. Rose said he had also acquired an identical second set of records in July 1995, from a separate agent.

In summing up, Mr Justice Douglas Brown revisited the prosecution's claim that the phone records were forgeries. "That is, at the end of the day, an issue for the jury to decide."

It was indeed.

The jury took less than forty-five minutes to acquit me. It was a unanimous verdict.

I had stood in court, accused of perjury, and accused three senior judges of lying – and won.

* * *

After the perjury trial my solicitor, Mark Foley, said the legal establishment and UK police would never forgive me for my victory in Manchester. "You've made them all look like a bunch of idiots, Paul," he warned. "If ever the police have grounds to come through your door again, they will nail you to the wall."

He would be proved right.

* * *

In early 2003, I discovered why the Spanish police and intelligence service had been so determined to help me secure an NIE certificate. Fernando called and offered support for my plan to open an office in Marbella on the southern Spanish coast.

I'd been thinking about Marbella for a while and had mentioned it to the intelligence officers. I was *persona non grata* on Tenerife. But opening an office elsewhere in Spain meant that I could maintain a presence in a country I was growing very fond of.

I quickly clocked why Fernando was so supportive.

Of course the CGI approved of a British businessman, with expertise in tax avoidance and identifying money laundering, establishing an office on the 'Costa del Crime'. I had already briefed Madrid about alleged criminals – if I set up in Marbella, home of some of the world's wealthiest underworld figures as well as legitimate billionaires, I would be a gold-plated asset.

Fernando was after his pound of flesh. Nonetheless, Marbella was an appealing prospect. Provided I stayed on the straight and narrow, which I had since leaving prison, then the spooks would support me – and I'd be able to live and work among some of Europe's wealthiest people. In exchange, I'm quite sure Madrid would expect regular updates on any illegal activity I spotted.

You scratch our back, Paul, and we'll scratch yours.

But could I tolerate my business being a front for multiple Spanish police and intelligence operations?

It wouldn't put my wealthiest clients at risk, because their documentation was not stored at my offices. But exactly how much would Madrid want from me? A few informal briefings here and there would be tolerable. But would it stop there? The intensity, regularity and detail of my disclosures about Mohamed and his associates indicated that the authorities demand a lot more than informal chats. I could end up spending large chunks of time effectively working a second job. In those circumstances, the risk of being targeted by criminal gangs was higher.

And what if Spain already had one eye on my clients? I was confident about Hugo and my higher fee-paying clients. But how well did I know some of the others? I thought I knew Mohamed.

Yes? No?

Thankfully, I hadn't yet committed to anything.

* * *

In early February 2003, Eric Reiner confirmed he would meet me in Los Angeles to assess several potential investment projects. I was still wary of Reiner and told him that, given the investment he wanted from my clients, and the amount of work involved in preparing documents, he should put up a "good faith" deposit worth $225,000. To me, a deposit of that kind would signal whether Reiner was serious about his proposals because it would force him to invest his own cash.

I travelled to Los Angeles in April. There, I met Reiner and several other contacts – including a wealthy businessman named Larry Osaki. Between them, Reiner and his friends had proposed four projects worth a total of $450m – including Eric's plan to raise $44m to finance a sodium bentonite mine in Nevada. Sodium bentonite is the absorbent clay-like substance used in cat litter production – a surprisingly lucrative global market. The more I learned about the potential mining project, the more interested I became.

Later in 2003, Reiner introduced me to the two American businessmen behind the Nevada mine – Tom Copeland and Larry Creek. He also arranged the $225,000 "good faith" deposit I had suggested, to be paid into Goldcrest's Isle of Man account.

* * *

Throughout early 2003, I helped Fernando and Enrique unpick more of Mohamed Derbah's complex web of offshore companies – including his decision to move bank accounts from the Isle of Man to Gibraltar.

Despite my briefings, some CGI officers were still struggling with aspects of offshore finance – often complicated by regulatory issues. That's where people like me add value to our clients and make our money, so there was no shame in crime-fighters not understanding it.

On 12 February 2003, the extent to which Spain was keeping one eye on me, as an asset, became apparent. Shortly before that date, I had won my perjury trial in Manchester. As I entered a meeting room in Madrid,

Fernando and Enrique stood and greeted me a little more enthusiastically than usual.

"Congratulations, Paul," Fernando said, shaking my hand vigorously. He seemed genuinely pleased to see me, rather than just pleased out of politeness.

Enrique also reached for my hand and, smiling, gave me a hearty slap on the back.

I must have worn a puzzled expression. Fernando explained: "You not guilty in Manchester – you win [sic] three judges! We heard the day after you were acquitted."

They knew about the perjury case. Yet, I hadn't told them.

I explained the background to the court case and shared a laugh at the folly of the prosecution's case. When I'd finished, Fernando said he had a more detailed proposition for me to consider.

"We would like you to work for our intelligence services, Paul. We have much confidence in you as a businessman and you have shown your loyalty to Spain.

"You care in a good way. We view you as a credible witness, someone who we can work with. In return, we will assist you in any way we can."

I knew this was coming, of course. This was about Marbella, but I didn't kid myself that I would be a fully-fledged "agent". I guess my perjury case, which boiled down to whether I was telling the truth, had shown the agents I could be trusted.

"Okay, I accept," I said. No sooner had I finished the sentence than I wondered whether I would live to regret it.

"There is also something you could help me with, Fernando," I added. "I want to apply to trade and deal in currencies."

Enrique looked a little puzzled. "Sure, for your clients. But why in Spain and not the UK?"

"A UK application would be rejected because I have criminal convictions," I explained.

"That won't be a problem here," said Fernando. "We can help. I also want to share some information we have on your client Sonny Fletcher and others."

Now it was my turn to look puzzled. They already knew that I helped Sonny?

We began to walk as Fernando spoke.

"They are known to law enforcement agencies throughout Europe as being part of a drugs cartel. You must be very careful not to be implicated in any of their actions. It will have serious consequences," the agent explained.

Now that was a shock.

Sonny and drugs? I'd recently spent the afternoon with Sonny, jokingly discussing our time in prison, and he looked and sounded like he was going straight. Things were taking bizarre turns – and quickly.

"Oh...er, of course," I said, still processing the disorienting information. "How do you know this?"

"Haha! Paul, you are clever man. But you have much to learn, my friend. Much to learn," Fernando chuckled as he smiled, turned on his heels, put an arm over my shoulder and guided me towards the door.

* * *

On the flight back to Liverpool, I kept looking out of the window and shaking my head. What a crazy world. Me of all people? Effectively running a front company for Spanish intelligence? I was, in turn, elated and terrified.

And Sonny? Fernando revealed little of what Spain, Interpol and the UK authorities knew. But it sounded serious. Sonny had been good to me inside prison, so I was not going to grass on him. But I made a mental note to double-check all documents relating to his car firm.

* * *

Fernando's assurance that my safety was important to him would soon be tested.

I needed to visit Tenerife to complete the annual accounts for my Spanish companies. On the morning of 28 February 2003 – and with my recording device switched on – I phoned Fernando to tell him. He said the new chief of police on Tenerife would organise protection for the duration of my stay.

"I will get Sarah Hill to telephone you because she speaks fluent Spanish and can arrange everything," I told the agent.

The day before my arrival on 4 March, Sarah Hill made arrangements for the visit. When I arrived on Tenerife, I would be in the hands of Inspector Trinitario. He had replaced the chief of police who had warned me to leave the island.

My daughter Sarah accompanied me on the trip. The moment we landed, we were given armed protection by plain-clothed police officers. Fernando had been true to his word so, on my return home, I telephoned Inspector Trinitario and Munoz to thank them.

I recorded the call to the CGI agent.

"If you go back [to Tenerife], call me. Call me before. Because we have other information about Mohamed and I want to be sure about your safety," Fernando warned.

I was careful to heed the warning about not travelling to the Canaries regularly. But in the meantime, I wanted to develop my portfolio of clients in the UK and on mainland Spain.

* * *

When Chris Eyre was sober, he was an excellent solicitor. The problem was keeping Chris's hands off the bottle. He had a severe drink problem and, when drunk, could become irrational, illogical and unreliable.

Before I met him, Eyre had been jailed for his part in a minor scam and was almost forced to close his practice in Selby, Yorkshire, where he lived. He was later cleared on appeal, which allowed him to continue to practice.

Through me, Eyre met Simon Eldritch: a long-term school friend of Paul Jnr. Simon won't mind me describing him as a likeable wheeler-dealer. He worked several jobs and boosted his income through casual roles –

including courier and delivery services used by my British-based firm, Chris Eyre's practice and others.

In 2003, I introduced Simon to John Allin and Darren Steadman – two men I had been introduced to at the motorway service station. At the time, I wasn't sure what, if any, business Allin and Steadman would do with my UK or international companies: the introduction to Simon was merely a networking opportunity.

I regret the introduction to this day because the two men from the Midlands immediately seized the opportunity to use my son's school friend as a "patsy" in a fraud which would have a significant impact on Simon, my life and health – and that of my family.

Allin and Steadman introduced Simon to their associate, Paco Lizarran, in Marbella. Paco told Simon he had previously worked for a yacht broker but wasn't allowed to undertake any deals for eighteen months due to a Europe-wide exclusion clause in his contract. Simon agreed to a deal under which he would effectively act as a nominee to conduct Paco's business until his exclusion clause lapsed. Lizarran told Simon that his previous clients wanted to do business with his new firm, but knew they could not deal with Paco directly.

The deal also involved Simon setting up a company, Colesport Limited, which Lizarran agreed to purchase at a later date. To convince Simon that the project was legitimate, Paco arranged to produce a high-quality promotional video featuring a yacht supposedly intended for an American firm based in Dublin called Lucent Technologies. The story sold to Simon was that Lucent wanted the boat to entertain prospective corporate clients in London.

Secretly, however, Allin and Steadman were behind the whole project and it was a scam. Allin, Steadman and their partners planned to rip off Lucent Technologies to the tune of £4.3m. The plan was to steal the cash from the firm's funds, using an insider, and transfer the money to Simon's Spanish bank account before anybody noticed. The idea was to lead Simon to believe the money was for the yacht. In return for handling the cash, the scammers had promised Simon £50,000. Naturally, Simon and I discovered this much later.

At the time, when Simon explained Paco's version of events, I was pleased for him. After all, £50,000 was a lot of money. The deal sounded needlessly complex but, at the time, I was familiar with more complex legitimate operations.

* * *

On 24 March 2003, I caught an early morning train from York to London for a meeting at the Meridian Hotel in Piccadilly. I planned to stay overnight, so I also booked a room at the hotel.

Mo Khan, the man I had met over lukewarm coffee at Warrington Lymm motorway services, had organised the meeting to include Allin, Steadman and a group of seven other Asian businessmen I'd never met. I was there to explain the benefits of legitimate offshore structures to the group. Mo Khan already had some knowledge of the offshore world. I was there to convince his friends.

It was an odd meeting. At times, the Asian men looked confused and struggled to understand even basic financial concepts – so I slowed things down. Meanwhile, Mo Khan was preoccupied – often standing away from the main group to make and receive calls on his mobile phone.

I could hear that he was relaying information to a contact known as "Aminie". After one of Mo's calls, another member of the group asked after "Salahuddin".

Despite the confusion and distractions, the meeting proved fruitful. As it came to a close, Mo said his friends wanted to use my services. By late afternoon, it became apparent that I did not need to stay overnight in London. So I told the group that one of them was welcome to use my hotel room that night.

* * *

When my daughter Sarah checked my American Express account two days later, she discovered several unauthorised transactions charged by the Meridian Hotel.

I made enquiries with Bob Stanbridge, head of security at the hotel, and he traced the charges to my room. I eventually discovered that one of the group had stayed in the room and, from there, booked other rooms for his associates – and charged them to my account. I was fuming. Stanbridge said the entire group was visible on the hotel's CCTV system and offered to contact the police if I wanted to make a complaint.

Ordinarily, I would have severed all contact with Mo and his associates there and then. But I didn't know what Fernando's stance would be – he had asked me to monitor British-Asian businessmen running large sums of cash through Spain. So, I decided to wait until my next meeting with CGI agents before making a decision. In the meantime, I would try to discover who was responsible for my credit card charges.

Mo Khan was full of apologies when I called him. He defused the situation by undertaking to repay the money into my account. But I wanted to know more. After all, whoever was responsible had used my credit card details.

I explained to Mo that I had made a formal complaint to the hotel and that the Meridian staff had checked the CCTV footage. He immediately became nervous and angry.

"To be honest with you, I'm going to get to the bottom of it anyway," Mo said. "But obviously I mean, with all the fucking guys...and myself. I mean, I am in there...the lads that were with me in there and I don't want...and the last thing I want is a fucking picture. Myself showing up on a fucking camera with these people," he blurted nervously. I recorded the discussion.

He seemed more worried about his associates being caught on CCTV than the fact that somebody had misused my credit card. Three days later, somebody paid £919 into my account from a branch of HSBC bank in Halesowen, just outside Birmingham.

During the following week, 14 April 2003, I met Fernando and Enrique in a cafe at Madrid Barajas. I was on my way to Marbella to find a new office. I explained the events at the Meridian Hotel and Mo Khan's concern that his group was caught on camera. Fernando urged me to maintain contact with the group, despite their disrespect towards me.

"Any information on Asians from the Birmingham area will assist our intelligence gathering," Fernando said. "When you open your office in Marbella, I will introduce you to the local chief of police. I must be satisfied about your safety."

* * *

When I next saw John Allin, he was pleased with the introduction to Simon. It was, he said, a bonus that Eyre was also Simon's solicitor. At this point, he also divulged his Irish background, foolishly revealing that he had a second passport in the name of John Donnelly.

Allin also hinted at connections with the Irish Republican Army (IRA) but, initially, I thought little of it. If I had a pound for every Irishman or wannabe Irishman in England who boasted of paramilitary links, well, I wouldn't be in England: I'd be living it up on a Caribbean island. I also learned that the Lucent 'loan' contract was being arranged by Thomas Canning, another Irishman, who had connections at the firm. I later learned that Thomas Canning also used the aliases John Canning and Thomas Cannon.

Clearly, something was not right.

Under the informal terms of my deal with the CGI, I was compelled to tell Fernando about the plan to move Lucent's money through Simon's bank account in Spain. But I was worried for Simon that he was being used.

At a meeting in Madrid, Fernando produced a flow chart showing the money route from the source to its intended destination in Simon's account at the Banco Atlantico at Benalmadena, close to Torremolinos. While Fernando meticulously linked the personalities involved, Enrique left to check for any intel on Thomas Canning. The younger agent later reappeared with a smile on his face: "The name Thomas Canning is known both to MI6 and MI5 and has connections to the IRA," he calmly announced.

The agents recognised the potential significance immediately and warned me not to over-interfere in events – or ask too many questions about the Lucent plan – for fear of being exposed. Simon, they inferred, would be OK. I nodded in agreement.

Spain would be watching events unfold. But nobody had figured on Sonny Fletcher.

* * *

Sonny was initially ecstatic at the prospect of a hefty fee for introducing the men involved in the Lucent deal. But during his talks with Allin and Steadman, they'd let slip that Simon was to withdraw the entire 'yacht' payment in cash over three days.

Sonny planned to take it all and use his underworld connections to scare the living daylights out of Allin and Steadman. What he didn't know was that behind Allin and Steadman stood a more fearsome group who would threaten gruesome revenge unless Sonny repaid the cash.

Sonny arranged for his private bankers from Israel to meet him in Marbella once the money landed at Simon's bank – and asked me to accompany him to that meeting because he couldn't read or write. In normal circumstances, knowing what I knew, I'd have found a reason not to attend. But the request suited my agenda because I could monitor events for Fernando.

The planned date for the transfer from Lucent was 11 June. That day, three people attended Simon's office in York to sign the non-existent loan agreement between the two parties. They included a lady introduced to Simon as Anne Fox. A woman by that name had been employed by Lucent, but the woman standing in the office was not the real Anne Fox.

The two other figures were male. One had an Irish accent, the other was English.

On the evening of 11 June, Simon telephoned me to let me know the money had landed at his bank in Spain and that he would travel to Malaga the following day.

★ ★ ★

The following day, I travelled to southern Spain and checked into a hotel. Sonny Fletcher owned an apartment in Puerto Banus and made separate arrangements to arrive early.

Simon planned to withdraw the money from his account on 16 June, which was the following Monday. But with too much time on his hands, Sonny spent the evening before the withdrawal at Milady's getting drunk and snorting cocaine. He was a useless, uncoordinated bundle of bones by the early hours of the morning. So I took the keys to his Bentley and drove him back to his apartment, leaving him slumped on his bed.

As the day of the withdrawal neared, I had a bad feeling about what would unfold. My main concern was Simon. But, having told Fernando I would monitor the situation, I felt trapped by events.

Unbeknown to Sonny, Steadman was on his way to Marbella – and under threat from more powerful Irish underworld figures to seize the cash.

On the morning of 16 June, I drove Simon to Benalmadena. He wandered off to the bank, and I holed myself up inside a coffee shop. I couldn't tell Simon what I was really doing, and exactly what I knew, but on the drive down we discussed how he should stay away from the likes of Sonny and Allin after the deal.

★ ★ ★

I spotted Simon from a distance. He was walking with purpose along the sunny side of the street, unconcerned about seeking shade on a scorching day, heading towards me. As he crossed the road to enter the café, he looked happy. He would soon get his £50k fee.

When Simon entered the café, I didn't even get time to ask how he was.

We were immediately surrounded by plain-clothed police officers. Simon was handcuffed and led towards a car parked outside. When two officers approached me, I explained my relationship with the CGI. The officers nodded to indicate they understood but said they would need to confirm my story at the local police station. The officers beckoned me to follow them but did not cuff me.

* * *

"Okay, what is the name of your contact at our security services," the police officer asked.

"Fernando Munoz. *Inspector* Fernando Munoz. I have his number on my mobile," I replied, handing the officer my phone.

"No need. I have my own contact numbers, thank you," came the stern reply.

When the officer was put through to Enrique, he had a smirk etched on his face. It quickly disappeared. I watched him listen as the unlikely reality of the situation dawned on him.

"Okay," he said at the end of a brief conversation. "Yes, sir."

Minutes later, I walked out of the police station.

* * *

By the time we met in Madrid the following week, Enrique already had full details of the cash Sonny had paid to get Simon released. During a matter-of-fact meeting, he then debriefed me on the Lucent scam.

When the accounts department at Lucent discovered the fraudulent transfer, one of their European directors had flown to Spain and made a *denuncia* – an official complaint – to the police resulting in Simon's account being frozen. Enrique also knew that Lucent's head of security, Barry Heath, was conducting an internal investigation. I knew that Heath was due to meet Chris Eyre, the drunken solicitor, the following day.

Enrique suggested I meet with Heath at Eyre's office to glean further intelligence on the criminals who were really behind the scam.

"Phone Eyre now and try and make the meeting," Enrique said.

I remember sitting in the boardroom, thinking that my role as the unit's asset had moved to a different level. This was far more than just giving information – this was actively going undercover. But what the hell? If it meant the agents would look after my business on the Costas then all the better – and I needed to ensure Simon would be OK.

"I think with all this, we need to up your level as an agent," Enrique mused.

I looked puzzled. "What does that entail?"

"It means MI5 knowing of your status, and you will have a code name for emergencies should you need to contact us. We cannot risk your security been compromised," he explained.

"Of course."

"You will have a codename. Can you think of one now?"

"Let me think about it," I said.

At a later meeting, I chose the codename 'Isabella'. The intelligence agents looked amused when I told them, but using a woman's name seemed like a smart move. For the record, it is also my granddaughter's name.

***

I contacted Chris Eyre to talk my way into attending his meeting with Heath. Eyre told me that there would be a second attempt to transfer the Lucent cash to Spain. The plan made no sense whatsoever, given that we all knew the police in Spain had been monitoring everything. Had I not been monitoring the attempted scam for the Spanish authorities, I'd have cut loose the losers behind their crazy plot.

Nonetheless, I called Enrique and told him what I knew. At the end of the call, in his typically broken English, Enrique suggested that we find a 'more safety way of communicating'.

"We will do it. We must be very cautious now," he added. The inference was obvious: 'Isabella' should continue to feed information to Spanish agents.

CHAPTER ELEVEN
Terror

After gate-crashing the meeting with Heath, it did not take me long to work out that he was poised to finger me, Eyre and Simon for the £4.3m attempted Lucent Technologies fraud.

We were the 'low hanging fruit' – easy pickings to a corporate investigator. In a later statement on the case, Heath acknowledged that while he believed the three of us were the perpetrators, it was strange that we were so open about our identities.

I would not have expected Heath to guess that I was monitoring the scam for Spain's CGI. But it worried me that he failed to see that Simon had been identified as a patsy by far more organised and dangerous criminals.

Elsewhere in his statement, Heath added that, following the attempted scam, he was contacted by a mysterious Irishman using the name 'John Rodgers'. The mystery man called from a withheld number and allegedly tipped off Heath with crucial details. Heath's statement also revealed he passed the information to the UK police at an early stage, meaning there would most likely be a full-blown criminal investigation.

The case ended up with North Yorkshire Police because Simon, Chris Eyre and I all lived locally.

* * *

Shortly after the meeting with Heath, John Allin arranged to visit me in York.

I didn't want to see Allin – things were spiralling out of control because of the Lucent scam, and he was trouble – but had promised Enrique that I would monitor the men connected to Mo Khan.

When asked what he knew about the Lucent fraud, Allin was elusive but eventually revealed that Thomas Canning and a "Glasgow gang" were behind it. I logged the reference for Fernando and Enrique. Slowly, Allin divulged the alleged details of a classic double-cross.

Once the Lucent cash had hit Simon's bank account, Canning's henchmen allegedly held Allin captive at gunpoint until the deal was finalised and the money transferred to a separate account. While extraordinary, Allin's tale seemed just about plausible – not least because nobody trusted Allin or Steadman. I'm not a violent man, yet I could understand why somebody would threaten the noxious and slippery pair!

Allin continued. Once the deal had gone wrong, and it became clear to Canning's gang that they could not obtain the money, he was released.

I had no idea whether Allin was telling the truth. All I knew was that somebody had set out to stitch up Simon and should be held to account for it.

I didn't want to spend too long asking about the failed fraud in case Allin became suspicious. He could see that I was unimpressed with what had taken place in southern Spain and insisted that any future deals he brought to Goldcrest would be "one hundred per cent" legitimate. I doubted that but was committed to monitoring him and his associates.

* * *

Following the Lucent debacle, I remember being inundated with requests from Asian businessmen operating what looked suspiciously like 'carousel frauds'.

Such frauds had been prevalent across the European Union since the establishment of a standardised Value Added Tax (VAT) system in 1993. In short, if a company in one EU member state (XCo) buys goods from a second firm within a separate member state (YCo), the purchasing company does not need to pay VAT. But if XCo then wants to sell its goods to a third company operating from the same country (ZCo), then XCo must add VAT on the transaction price and later pay that VAT to the tax authority in its own country.

Carousel frauds occur when firms that should make the VAT payment do not, and are then quickly dissolved or closed down: so-called 'missing traders'.

Fraudsters often establish chains of companies through which the goods are passed on by firms that do not declare VAT. This acts as a buffer against scrutiny by tax authorities by complicating the supply chain and increasing transaction prices. To complete the circle – or carousel – the final firm in the chain would sell the goods back to a company in another EU state. Under EU rules, the last firm in the chain could then ask its domestic tax authority to reimburse the value of VAT on the final deal.

The losers in carousel frauds were domestic tax authorities. At its height, the value of EU-based frauds was $50 billion annually. For years, tax consultants had been warned to look out for carousel frauds.

In the case of Mo Khan's associates, many of their transactions looked suspiciously like carousel arrangements. But I had been asked to monitor the gang by Fernando, so I couldn't exactly challenge every deal.

Mo Khan's associates needed offshore companies and bank accounts, but they seemed to lack credibility. Right down to their names at meetings: 'KJ', 'G', 'Jugga' and other non-titles. By setting up the companies and viewing the paperwork for some trades, I learnt that the group had links with a mega-rich Yemeni national and a well-known family from the north of England who appeared on the Sunday Times' annual Rich List.

But what Fernando and Enrique wanted from me was any indication that the group was group moving dirty cash through Spain.

* * *

Eric Reiner was so sure that he had my complete confidence that he visited my York office on 19 and 20 August 2003 and effectively declared that he was involved in a scam using my clients' money. The brash American suggested that once Hugo's $100 million was deposited and blocked in an account for his film company, Seventh Generation, for credit enhancement purposes, then those funds could be unblocked for a short period. That would enable Eric to claim that the funds represented equity in his company. In other words, Reiner could gain unrestricted access to the cash without Hugo's knowledge.

He must have thought I was a complete fool! But that's what these two-a-penny scammers are like: they delude themselves into thinking that professionals like me will play along with their games providing we get paid. What Eric Reiner didn't know during our meetings was that his every word was being recorded. The valuable tape now sits in the vaults of the FBI's offices in Los Angeles.

* * *

On 21 August, I received a phone call from one of Mo Khan's associates using the name 'Mike Singh', a likely pseudonym. Singh asked whether I had checked my client account at HSBC bank on the Isle of Man. I hadn't.

Two days earlier, £192,000 had been credited to my client account from a Glasgow-based company called Starmack. Singh said he was on the way to York with Sonny Fletcher and Mo Khan – and that I shouldn't part with the money because it belonged to them.

As soon as I put the phone down, I received a call from John Allin. He claimed the £192,000 belonged to people he knew in Glasgow. Allin added that he would attend my office the following day to explain everything. He wanted to introduce me to somebody called Brendan Keeley, who represented the Glaswegians.

When Sonny, Mo and Singh arrived at my office that afternoon, Fletcher appeared anxious and insisted I divert the money to an account under his control. I refused and said the money was going nowhere until I'd met Allin and Keeley the following morning.

Frankly, I had no idea what was going on. But somebody was up to no good.

At 9am the following day, Sonny was back at my office – with Mike Singh and Mo Khan in tow. The three men promised to reimburse me for any losses to my account and claimed the £192,000 should be returned to a different Glasgow-based firm. I'd never seen Sonny so agitated and fearful.

I insisted the money was going nowhere until I'd had a chance to work out what was going on.

John Allin, Darren Steadman and Brendan Keeley arrived at my office around 2 pm. Keeley explained that he represented Thomas Canning, a name he knew would be familiar to me.

Suddenly, I sensed exactly what was going on. And I did not like it.

Keely explained that Thomas Canning was involved with a Glasgow-based company and claimed the money in my account should be sent to the firm immediately.

"I can't do that," I explained. "I've already sent the money back to its source – so that there are no misunderstandings. I'm not getting involved, Mr Keeley. Whatever this is about, it has nothing to do with me."

A cacophony of noise erupted, voices talking over voices. When things calmed down, Keeley explained that Mr Canning would be "most displeased" because the cash was his.

"Well, I've already returned the money to Starmack. So that's the end of the matter, as far as I'm concerned," I said.

"No, that's not the end of it. You can phone your bank and recall the wire transfer," Keeley claimed.

Knowing that the bank could not recall the transfer, I decided to play along to make it look like I assisted the Keeley-Canning cause. The three men listened to my telephone conversation with bank officials, and Keeley's jaw dropped when the bank confirmed that the transfer could not be returned.

While Keeley was put out, he believed that I had tried to help. So as he left, Keeley said he could use my services in the future and would be in touch. Even after the three men left, I could not work out the links between Keeley, Canning, Allin and Mo Khan – and whoever the Glaswegians were. It would be many months before all would be revealed.

* * *

In early October 2003, I flew to Los Angeles to meet up with Elena Dontu and Eric Reiner and discuss Hugo's possible investment in the mining project. We caught up on the proposal over dinner at the Beverly Hills Hilton and, the following morning, Eric and I flew to Nevada to visit the mine. A week later, Tom Copeland and Larry Creek sent Goldcrest U$300,000 as a security bond to cover any fees my firm incurred during this project phase.

Elena looked as stunning as ever in Los Angeles. After dinner, she revealed how she wanted to move to the United States or Britain – and how she had begun to tire of her life in Spain. She seemed desperate to do something else. Elena was generally professional, but something about her on that trip made me wary of her. She repeatedly expressed her frustrations that she could not settle in the countries she wanted to be in, her non-existent love life and getting away from Marbella. It wasn't subtle – she was telling anybody who would listen that she was available to start a new life. Eric Reiner piped up when he realised that!

Who were we kidding, though? If this wasn't a 'honey trap' on behalf of somebody, Elena's unsubtle messages indicated that she might just be a gold-digger.

* * *

After the Lucent Technologies debacle, Allin and Steadman felt they owed Simon Eldritch for carrying the can for the attempted fraud. The irony, of course, is that they had identified Simon as the patsy. But I guess that they wanted to keep him sweet – and silent.

Simon should not have gone anywhere near the duo again, but he needed money. In October 2003, he agreed with Allin, Steadman and Mo Khan to transfer a £375,000 payment through his bank account and onto a Spanish account run by Steadman – having received assurances that it was a legitimate tax minimisation move. Simon's commission was £7,000, and Steadman would receive £368,000.

On 23 October, Steadman and Allin arrived in Spain to withdraw their share of the cash. I was already in Marbella to meet Eric Reiner. Later that evening, I introduced Reiner to Allin and Steadman in a hotel bar, and the group of us chatted about everything and nothing. Secretly, I wanted to update Fernando on what the British duo's associate, Mo Khan, was up to: Spanish police and intelligence were beginning to take more of an interest in British-Pakistanis operating in southern Europe.

I flew home to the UK the following day.

Mo Khan arrived in Spain and checked into the Andalucía Plaza hotel in Puerto Banas. On 28 October, he was joined by John Allin, who handed Mo £368,000 in crisp new Euro notes. It was not the only money Khan had diverted through Spain in October 2003. A total of €10 million had been cashed by Mo's associates, often using bureau de change outlets on the Costa del Sol.

Wherever the cash had come from, any electronic money trail had now been broken. These looked like classic laundering and smurfing tactics.

* * *

Back in York, I received a desperate phone call from Mo Khan. It was the same day, 28 October.

"I've been let down, big style, by a lawyer in Marbella", Khan said.

Mo claimed that a lawyer he had been using had refused to move some money for him and that he was now "stuck" with €10m in cash.

I could think of worse situations.

"Paul, I need your help," Mo said. "Have you got a contact here in Marbella who can bank cash and then wire nine million euros to Dubai for me?"

"Possibly", I said.

In his usual laid-back manner, Mo then dropped a bombshell. "Paul, I'll give you one million euros in cash if you can help me. If the police catch me with this lot, they'll link me to Al-Qaeda."

What. The. Fuck?

Al-Qaeda? I had no intention of going anywhere near that money. It was toxic and almost certainly illegal.

Suddenly, I understood why Fernando, Enrique and the wider CGI were so keen to receive information about Mo Khan and his associates.

But did Mo honestly think that I would rush to help a man who, by his own admission, could be linked to the world's most feared terror network? I decided to play it cool, so let the Al-Qaeda reference slide without comment.

"Phone me back in one hour," I said.

I put the phone down and considered how to handle the situation. Spain's agents needed to know the information – and soon. But there was no way that I could handle Al-Qaeda's cash, even as part of a surveillance operation for Spain.

Since 9/11, the Americans and their close allies had been engaged in a worldwide search for Al-Qaeda's leadership, fund-raisers and supporters. They were leaving no stone unturned. If I left a fingerprint on Mo Khan's cash, however tangentially it linked him to Bin Laden's men, then the CIA would be crawling all over me within weeks. And the Pentagon does not give a shit about other intelligence services – if the US wanted to arrest me for knowingly moving terror finance, they would just do it. And I wouldn't blame them.

No. I wouldn't touch the money, despite the attractive reward offered by Mo Khan.

As it transpired, the decision was made for me anyway. Less than an hour later, Mo phoned back. He no longer needed my help – he'd sorted the problem. But in his earlier panic, Mo had let the cat out of the bag.

* * *

In early November, shortly after two meetings with Eric Reiner in Marbella, I received a phone call from him at my office in York. The discussion was un-noteworthy, except for one revelation: Reiner casually revealed that his contact Larry Osaki had been charged with running a $250m 'Ponzi' scheme by the US Attorney's Office for the District of California.

I wasn't surprised to hear the news. I'd long been wary of some of Reiner's contacts. But I had been named in court papers covering the case against Osaki.

Neither Reiner nor I were accused of wrongdoing, but the discussion with Eric left me feeling uncomfortable. I wanted to find out more about what was going on across the Atlantic. I had clients who conducted a lot of business with the US and the last thing I, or they, needed was to become embroiled in any scandals inside the world's biggest market.

Unbeknownst to Reiner, I contacted the District Attorney's office in California and spoke to Assistant District Attorney David Willingham. That discussion involved more significant revelations than my earlier chat with Reiner – and gave me cause for concern about Osaki and Eric.

The DA's primary interest was Osaki and any financial interests he had in the Cook Islands. Law enforcement agencies suspected that Osaki's fortune was hidden in the South Pacific. Once they realised what I did for a living, the DA's office asked for my advice on penetrating the Cook Islands' secrecy. My response was not encouraging, but I bonded with Willingham – who I found to be an impressive, inquisitive and intelligent man. When asked about Reiner, I explained my long-held suspicions.

By the end of the call to Los Angeles, I had agreed to send a file on Reiner to the US. I had instinctively defaulted to 'Isabella' mode, despite not dealing with the Spanish.

* * *

I sent the Reiner file to Willingham's office and, within a few days, the DA's office had arranged a conference call with me.

On 10 November 2003, I dialled into a discussion between Willingham, Stephanie Miller from the Internal Revenue Service (IRS) and Audrey Berry, an FBI agent who specialised in finance. The subjects under review were Osaki and Reiner.

Willingham began by explaining that the group had seen my files and found the contents "illuminating". At that point, I heard everybody chuckle. It was evident that the group was interested in what I had sent through.

After I outlined Reiner's suspicious investment proposals, I agreed to meet Reiner in Los Angeles and covertly record the discussion to see whether he would admit that Osaki was a conman.

Unlike most of Europe's law enforcement agencies, those in the United States tend to move quickly. On 18 November, having arranged to meet Eric Reiner and Elena Dontu two days later, I found myself on a flight to Los Angeles.

I checked into the Beverly Hills Hilton hotel in the upmarket district west of the city centre ahead of a meeting the following day, at which Willingham and a federal agent were due to talk me through how they wanted to secretly record Reiner – and what information to extract from him.

Dontu contacted me several times that day while she worked on Hugo's part of the potential Reiner deal. I had not been able to tip-off Elena that the authorities in L.A. were investigating Reiner – let alone tell her that, for my part, the trip was an attempt to 'out' a potential fraudster.

The bigger problem I faced with Elena, however, was that she was still flirting wildly with me. She had inquired whether I had some spare time to "chaperone" her around Los Angeles for some sightseeing. I'm not sure precisely what Elena had planned, but cocktails at one of Hollywood's trendy bars was mentioned. So was dinner for two at what sounded remarkably like a romantic getaway close to my hotel.

Beautiful though Elena was, and quite aside from the flirting, she was generally good company. But random visits to trendy bars were the last thing I needed while the FBI and district attorney prepared to pounce on Hugo's potential client. To the best of my knowledge, the FBI did not know about Elena's involvement with the Reiner talks – and I wanted to keep it that way. A succession of late-night calls from Elena followed that evening, during which she openly suggested spending the following evening 'together'. It could have meant anything. It sounded like an offer of sex.

To say this trip was getting complicated would be an understatement.

* * *

On the morning of 19 November, I was picked up by two FBI officers and taken to the eleventh floor of the District Attorney's Office where I met David Willingham, Stephanie Miller and Special Agent Clint Wilmsem representing the FBI. I disclosed details of my association with Reiner and explained my previous history – including my dealings with Mohamed Derbah, his links to terrorists and my battles with the British legal system. I played the tape of Reiner implicating himself at our earlier meeting in York and, upon request, agreed that the FBI could keep it.

Willingham, Miller and Wilmsem were courteous, professional, efficient and determined. I could sense that these were not people to cross. They were also well-informed and told me what they could about the information they held on Reiner. They pointed out that on every faxed letter Reiner had sent to me, the name 'Michael' appeared at the top of the page. Another name used by Reiner, and known to the US authorities, was 'Michael Heartsong'.

It seemed that the US authorities had been on to Reiner for a long time – but had always been one step behind his money trail, which often led offshore. That is where I came in. Using me as bait, they hoped to catch Reiner discussing his dealings with Osaki and where he'd hidden millions of dollars. I was to record the whole meeting.

After the initial discussion, Clint took me to the FBI's main office in Los Angeles to advise me on how to handle the meeting with Reiner the following day.

My security, Clint said, was of the utmost importance – so the hotel room would contain several listening devices so that agents holed up in a nearby room would be able to burst into the meeting if things took a turn for the worse. As far as I could tell, Reiner was not a violent individual. Quite the opposite – he was something of a coward. But the Feds were taking no chances.

The officers told me what to wear to cover the wire they would attach to my body under my clothes. They told me where to sit during the meeting, what to drink, not to eat because it creates additional noise on recordings, what to say, what to avoid saying, which posture to use and how to control the natural human instinct to feel and look nervous about what was taking place.

I hadn't given any of it much thought until Clint reminded me what was at stake. Suddenly, I felt a little nervous. But I knew that having previously covertly recorded meetings with CGI agents, Derbah and other suspected criminals, I would be able to handle the situation.

There was just one problem nagging away at the back of my mind – Elena. I had to keep her at arms-length of the sting operation. So I requested a private meeting with Eric and explained to Elena that I needed to speak candidly with Eric about issues that did not relate to Hugo's potential investment. Of course, I secretly hoped that it was Reiner who would speak candidly.

***

By mid-afternoon on 19 November, I'd rehearsed what I thought was a foolproof plan for the sting – including dealing with Elena. But plans are just that: they exist in your head, or on paper, and not in the real world.

When I returned to the Hilton hotel that evening, FBI agents were busy bugging my room. They were taking no chances, either. Every sound would be heard from across the corridor the next day. Every word spoken, every footstep taken: so that agents could 'map' who moved around the room and when – in case they had to burst in. The FBI's equipment was so advanced they would even know who was breaking wind or peeing too loudly during toilet breaks!

Elena had been pushing for another face-to-face to discuss Hugo's potential investments. So, despite my plan for the next day, I met her for coffee in a café near my hotel that evening. When I arrived, Elena was slightly drunk, and the flirting started. I couldn't believe her timing! She lamented her lack of 'opportunities' and love life in Spain. It was very self-indulgent. In Spain, I knew, Elena was lauded as the sort of woman you would burn your own house down for. Other married men had openly told me that.

As she gazed into my eyes, I noticed that Elena's were a little glazed. The alcohol had kicked in. I stirred my coffee.

"Walk with me up to Hollywood, Paul," Elena said. It's a lovely night. You have nothing planned, surely?"

"Well...actually...I do have a lot on, Elena"'

"Okay. If you must go back to the hotel, I will wait for you in the hotel bar," Elena suggested. "For a nightcap."

No chance. The hotel was crawling with FBI agents. The bar would probably be full of them. But I didn't have the opportunity to explain before she spoke again.

"Come on, Paul. Back to your hotel. I will stay at the Hilton tonight. It's too far back to my place."

"Well...you...you can't stay at the Hilton tonight, Elena," I said, a little panicked. "You don't have a room."

Elena was having none of it. She grabbed me by the arm and began to walk us towards the lifts. Suddenly, she stopped and turned on her heels, looking directly at me, smiling and gently moving her head towards me. The beautiful blonde Moldovan, buoyed by Dutch courage, was making her move.

"I could stay with you tonight, Paul," she said. Her head stopping just centimetres from mine, lips pouting, head tilted slightly to the side.

She giggled at the thought of what had been suggested and casually raised an eyebrow, inviting a response.

Jesus. How to test a man.

"Please don't take this the wrong way, Elena. But the answer is 'no'. That would be inappropriate – on so many more levels than I could even begin to explain right now."

"We could always take another room. You know, for discretion?"

"I don't think that would avoid all of the problems I'm talking about, Elena," I said.

Silence. Elena looked at me, puzzled. One of the most beautiful young women I'd ever set eyes on, somebody who I liked despite her desperation, wanted to go to bed with me. That much was now clear. But for what reason? She could have her pick of almost any man in the world. I was a 58-year-old offshore finance consultant from York. Call me a cynic, but the whole thing left me asking about her real aim.

Elena was miles from her hotel and in no fit state to go back alone, so I booked another room for her at the Hilton. Her expression gradually eased into a passive smile. I have no idea whether, at that moment, a carefully planned honeytrap had been rumbled, or whether a naïve and lonely young woman simply felt rejected.

"Maybe another night, then, Paul?"

I let that one hang. There was no response that wouldn't insult somebody.

It worked. The slightly tense atmosphere lightened. A few minutes later, Elena kissed me on the cheek, turned on her heels and headed towards the lift. I needed to prepare mentally for the following day. So, I waited until Elena was out of sight, then wandered slowly towards my room.

* * *

When I met Reiner the following morning, 20 November 2003, we walked past two FBI agents positioned in the Hilton hotel's lobby. To unsuspecting guests, the two men were merely deep in conversation and minding their own business. Instead, they watched our every move.

Eric and I proceeded through the reception area and took the lift to an upper floor, exchanging small talk as we walked. Eric looked a little pale but was otherwise his usual brash self.

The sting didn't work.

Utterly oblivious to my suspicions of him and his contacts, Reiner nonetheless never once implicated himself in Osaki's frauds. Quite the opposite. Throughout our long conversation, he maintained it was the US authorities' fault that Osaki had fallen from grace. Without sounding desperate, I repeatedly tried to get Reiner to admit prior knowledge of Osaki's activities and to discuss other potential crimes. But Eric would not bite. I don't think he had rumbled me – Eric seemed blissfully unaware that the discussion was being recorded by a group of agents huddled in a bedroom along the corridor.

After Reiner had left, a group of disappointed FBI agents emerged from their hiding place. They were polite and appreciative of my efforts, but I felt like I had let them down. "Welcome to our world, Paul. Don't beat yourself up – happens all of the time," one agent said, trying to force a smile.

After the failed sting, I gradually severed contact with Eric Reiner. At some point later, he wrote to me and attempted to re-pitch his investment proposals. The letter, which I still have, was full of his usual bluster and hot air. But by that point, Eric Reiner was a lame duck, so I ignored him.

It took many months before Reiner gave up chasing the return of his deposit bond and, in May 2004, he contacted North Yorkshire Police to lodge a formal complaint about it. Of course, his complaint did not mention his plan to scam my clients or the six-figure costs I had incurred travelling around the world assessing his proposals. He was not going to get his money back.

However, I did want to stay in contact with Tom Copeland and Larry Creek. They struck me as genuine businessmen in need of investment in their mine. So, I arranged to meet both men in York in January 2004.

Larry and Tom signed a brokerage deal with Goldcrest, under which I sought to raise $44m through investors. If I achieved the target, I would receive a whopping $4m fee. I knew that was unlikely, but I stood to gain significantly if I helped raise anywhere near that amount.

I still had Hugo in mind as a potential investor. However, disaster struck weeks later when Hugo discovered through his US-based lawyers that Reiner was a suspected fraudster. Even though Reiner had been ditched from the mining proposal, Hugo associated the project with him and wanted nothing to do with the deal.

Hugo was also unhappy that I had not told him about Reiner's suspected frauds. It was the beginning of the end of our professional relationship. Within weeks, Elena had left Hugo's employment and re-started her modelling career. Despite the awkwardness of the evening we shared in Los Angeles, I stayed in touch with Elena and wished her well.

* * *

I wasn't able to meet with Fernando and Enrique in Madrid until mid-November. The agents wanted any information which linked Mohamed Derbah and Thierry Boinnard. I agreed to undertake a global search for offshore firms that connected the two men. It was clear from the discussion that the Spanish were making significant progress with the Derbah investigation, often based on information I'd provided.

After the Derbah discussion was exhausted, I raised the issue of Mo Khan and his associates. In particular, the telephone call I had taken from Mo when he sought to transfer millions of Euros to Dubai.

Al-Qaeda.

Jaws dropped and the room fell silent. The mention of Bin Laden's terror group focused the agents' minds like nothing I had seen before.

Fernando said the authorities in Madrid knew that Al-Qaeda and other Islamist extremist groups moved money through Europe before the 9/11 attacks. They also knew that Al-Qaeda cells were active in Spain because of intelligence gleaned by Germany's BND federal intelligence service.

Key members of the terrorist cell that planned and carried out 9/11 had been based in Europe before the attacks – including in Hamburg, northern Germany. These included Mohamed Atta, the Egyptian-born 9/11 ringleader who crashed United Airlines Flight 93 into a field in Pennsylvania. It was believed that the plane hijacked by Atta was heading for a critical target in Washington, possibly the Capitol Building or White House, before brave passengers – aware that two airliners had been flown into the World Trade Centre – fought to regain control.

Atta had left Hamburg in 1999 and 2000. The CIA now believes he travelled to Afghanistan, where he met Osama bin Laden and other Al-Qaeda leaders. Upon returning to Germany in early 2000, Atta made inquiries about flight training.

In May 2001, Atta visited Spain. There, he met up with his close friend from Hamburg, Ramzi bin al-Shibh, who was among Osama bin Laden's closest advisors. In the city of Tarragona, south of Barcelona on Spain's east coast, it is believed the pair retreated to an Al-Qaeda safe house and planned 9/11.

Spain was a known Al-Qaeda hang-out. It was linked to 9/11, it was linked to the hunt for Osama bin Laden and it was linked to the global search for Al-Qaeda's money designed to cripple the organisation's capacity to carry out further terrorist attacks.

Fernando and Enrique told me what they could about Spain's role in the hunt for terror finance. They were disciplined and did not disclose sensitive information. But they wanted what I knew.

At the end of the discussion, Enrique said it was important my information was assessed in detail so that Spain could build a profile of Mo Khan and his associates. They would examine his emails, phone records, text messages, travel history, bank accounts, credit card use, contacts, and social media activity. I knew they'd examine more than that, too. Let's not kid ourselves: even in 2003, major intelligence services had a surveillance and information-gathering capacity that ordinary folk would find frightening. Phone taps, physical surveillance, mobile intercepts, computer trojans, undercover work – the list was long.

The most notable name in my initial intelligence report on Mo Khan's associates turned out to be Salahuddin Amin. However, his identity did not stand out at the time: it was just one name among many. Mo Khan's power base in the UK was the city of Birmingham, but he also had contacts in Yorkshire – including Leeds, Bradford and Dewsbury.

Khan had made no secret of his fear of being caught on camera at the Meridian Hotel in London. But it was Mo's desperate attempt to transfer €9m to Dubai, which he declared would help him to avoid being linked with Al-Qaeda, which became the focus of our discussion.

Where had Khan's money gone, we wondered? Could I help trace it? How? I quickly learned that, when it comes to terrorism, the intelligence services consider dirty money the most dangerous weapon of all.

Enrique complimented me on my report and said he would pass it to his director of intelligence. I assured the agents I would continue to monitor events.

* * *

I had a mountain of work to get through in late 2003 and early 2004. I remained keen to open an office in Marbella and was confident that Sarah Hill could continue to manage my affairs on Tenerife. That arrangement would keep me out of Mohamed Derbah's way while building a more extensive client base.

In early March 2004, I travelled to Marbella to speak to a local law firm about the office contract I wanted.

On the morning of 11 March 2004, I boarded an early flight from southern Spain to Liverpool. As I flew over Spain's beautiful patchwork of chocolate earth countryside, interspersed with lush green vineyards and busy cities, I was oblivious to the horror unfolding 30,000 feet below.

* * *

When the plane touched down on Merseyside, passengers discovered the horror of what had unfolded in Madrid. Travellers gathered around a TV screen at one of the tiny airport's counters, dumb with shock. One Spanish woman was in tears, comforted by her young son and airport staff.

The first bomb had exploded on a train inside Madrid's Atocha Station at 07.37. Three minutes of carnage followed across the capital. Nine further explosions ripped through a total of four trains on the same railway line running east out of the city.

As I stood at passport control in Liverpool, I could hear my fellow passengers receiving updates from Spain. At least twenty people were dead, one said. No, it was forty, another interjected solemnly. The number of casualties reported by local hospitals and police was increasing. Hundreds of people were injured and Madrid's emergency services were overwhelmed.

Once outside, I made straight for my car and flicked on the radio. It was one of the most awful days in living memory – a crushing blow, coming so soon after 9/11. The drive back to Yorkshire passed quickly as the world's media reported the uncomfortable details.

A total of 193 people lost their lives in Madrid that day. A further two thousand were injured.

I thought about Spain and realised I had developed a strong sense of loyalty to the country. It felt like somebody had attacked my friends. I thought about calling Fernando and Enrique, to make sure they were safe, but knew that police and intelligence units would be working flat-out after the attacks.

But who was behind the atrocities?

Within hours of the bombings, Spanish Prime Minister Jose Maria Aznar began his infamous political sleight of hand – he suggested that the feared Basque terrorist group Euskadi Ta Askatasuna (ETA) was responsible. Spain was poised for a general election on 14 March, just three days after the bombings, and Aznar's nationalist People's Party government did not want his unpopular support for the Iraq war to swing votes towards the opposition socialists.

The day after the attacks, ETA's political wing, Batasuna, denied any involvement in the bombings. Terrorism experts quickly pointed out that ETA usually provided advanced warning of its attacks and tended to target specific state agencies or personnel – not the general public. Experts instead warned the *modus operandi* and evidence suggested radical Islamists had struck at the heart of Europe. And the name on many people's lips was Al-Qaeda.

My thoughts turned to *that* phone call from Mo Khan.

* * *

I later learned that, in the immediate aftermath of the Madrid bombings, intelligence personnel had told Aznar's government the attacks were most likely the work of an Al-Qaeda-inspired terrorist cell.

However, Aznar's government continued to insist that ETA was most likely responsible. Amid public outcry over Aznar's handling of the situation, the government's vote collapsed. The opposition socialist party, which had pledged to withdraw Spain's troops from the unpopular Iraq war, won the general election and Spain entered a new political era.

But the political fall-out from the bombings continued long after Aznar departed. In December 2004, an official Spanish inquiry revealed that Aznar's office had destroyed all of the computer records covering the period from the day of the bombings through to the general election. Indeed,

Spanish government officials loyal to Aznar's party destroyed many years' worth of documents relating to the PP's period in office.

To this day, despite all of the evidence, some PP members and supporters still insist that Al-Qaeda did not act alone over 11-M.

* * *

Four months before the Madrid attacks, I had told Spanish agents that a British-Asian businessman told me that he was running cash, potentially linked to Al-Qaeda, through Spain and onto Dubai. I'd handed over information on the network of people involved. Not only that, but I was aware through discussions with Spanish agents that the authorities were monitoring other potential Al-Qaeda-inspired terror cells on the mainland.

Six weeks after 11-M, I travelled to Madrid on the way to Marbella. It was the first opportunity I'd had to see Fernando and Enrique since the bombings. The agents had been working flat out since the attacks.

While Spain's politicians had argued over the likely organisation responsible for the bombings, the country's police and intelligence services had leapt into action. On 13 March, two days after the bombs exploded, fresh intelligence led officers to the door of Jamal Zougam, a Moroccan from Tangiers who owned a mobile phone shop in Madrid.

Zougam was suspected of supplying the mobile phones which detonated the train bombs. Three bombs placed on trains during the 11-M attacks failed to explode, and a fingerprint found on a SIM card in one of the unexploded devices later linked Zougam to the attacks. When law enforcement agencies delved into his background, they discovered links with a terrorist group from Morocco – a Salafi jihadist outfit called the Moroccan Islamic Combatant Group (known by the French acronym GICM). The group was responsible for a deadly bomb blast in Casablanca in 2003 and raised its terror finance through drug dealing, arms trafficking throughout North Africa and Europe, robbery, fraud and extortion. It was also a known affiliate of Al-Qaeda.

Zougam was linked to the GICM through trips he had made to the UK, where he received logistical support and forged documents ahead of the 11-M attacks. The GICM had supporters in London, including visitors to the controversial Finsbury Park Mosque where the radical preacher Abu Qatadah, described by critics as the spiritual leader of Al-Qaeda in Europe, was based. Spanish and British intelligence agents also linked money flows from the UK to the Moroccan group.

Zougam was also linked directly to another man, Imadeddin Barakat Yarkas, who used the alias Abu Dahdah and was believed to have led Al-Qaeda's Madrid cell. Yarkas was arrested by authorities in Spain in 2001 and later prosecuted for helping to fundraise for Al-Qaeda ahead of the 9/11 attacks. But it is alleged that he maintained contact with the Madrid bombers and helped to co-ordinate 11-M from inside prison. One Spanish intelligence officer, Rafael Gomes Menor, would later tell the country's parliament that the Madrid bombings were the work of "Abu Dahdah, without any doubt".

In early April, members of the suspected GICM-led terror cell behind 11-M were tracked to an apartment in Leganes, a suburb south of Madrid. Armed police surrounded the property on 3 April. As they prepared to storm the building, the seven people inside exploded another bomb – killing themselves and a member of Spain's elite police assault unit. Four of those inside were officially identified as terrorists.

Among the rubble in Leganes lay the remains of Sarhane ben Abdelmajid Fakhet, known as 'The Tunisian' after his country of origin. He was understood to be the ringleader of the Madrid plot.

Also discovered in the apartment was the body of Jamal Ahmidan, a convicted murderer, drug dealer and cleric who bought the volatile Goma-2 explosives used in the bombs. Police later discovered that Ahmidan, a Moroccan known as 'El Chino' ('The Chinese'), had procured the explosives from a retired miner in northern Spain.

Goma-2 had previously been used by ETA in high-profile attacks dating back to the 1973 assassination of Spanish prime minister Luis Carrero Blanco – a close ally of General Franco. So, to be fair to Aznar and the PP, in the immediate aftermath of the Madrid bombings, there was at least one reason to believe that Basque separatists may have been involved. The majority of evidence, however, pointed away from ETA's involvement.

* * *

Unbeknown to Spain's intelligence service at the time, in 2002 a collection of north African terrorist leaders met in Turkey and discussed their determination to bring holy war, or jihad, to Europe following Al-Qaeda's 9/11 attacks. The groups present hailed from Morocco, Tunisia and Algeria, but were guided by Abu Musab al Zarqawi – the Jordanian radical who led Al-Qaeda in Iraq.

According to a report published years later by the Institute for Security Studies, an African security think-tank, the meeting in Turkey "spelt serious consequences for European security forces".

Among the many repercussions was an intensification of efforts by Al-Qaeda affiliates to raise funds for a campaign of terror inside European Union states. That led to a spike in illegal activities designed to fund terror networks – fraud, extortion, drug dealing, arms trading, sex trafficking and bootlegging – and the associated laundering of these funds.

All intelligence agencies were on the lookout for groups plotting attacks – as well as fund-raisers and money launderers hidden in plain sight. In particular, British and Spanish intelligence were in regular contact over suspected links between Al-Qaeda sympathisers sheltering in Britain and some of the North African men behind the Madrid bombings.

I learned all of this in the aftermath of 11-M. Considering what Mo Khan had told me over the phone when he wanted to move €9m to Dubai, it now seemed obvious why Fernando and Enrique were so keen for me to monitor Mo and his associates.

* * *

On 29 April 2004, I was inadvertently handed an opportunity to obtain more information on Mo Khan and his group.

Incredibly, John Allin appeared to have successfully arranged a loan for Tom Copeland and Larry Creek's mining project through Nicholas Leach, a financier acting on behalf of his wealthy parents. Leach had stipulated that his parents wanted an upfront fee of €100,000 for expenses involved in arranging the loan facility, so Larry Creek wired the money to my Goldcrest account in Marbella. I withdrew the money in cash and gave it to Creek.

Allin, Tom, Larry and Leach agreed to exchange contracts for the deal at the office of Mr Romero, a lawyer in Marbella. I didn't need to attend the meeting, but Goldcrest had helped with the deal and, like everybody, I wanted to celebrate its completion. I didn't suspect underhand activity because the paperwork went through a professional lawyer.

I couldn't have been more wrong.

At 2pm, I set off from my hotel towards the meeting venue and saw Allin and Nicholas Leach heading towards me – travelling in the wrong direction. As soon as Leach spotted me, he sprinted down a side street. Allin, however, continued walking.

As John neared, I asked: "What's the matter with Leach?"

"Don't know, Paul. He...er...he just set off without saying a word," came Allin's reply. As he spoke, Allin looked back towards the street onto which Leach had turned. He looked alarmed. Like he'd been caught off guard.

Something was amiss and, given Allin's background, I suspected foul play. Allin denied any wrongdoing but gave the game away when he said he would get Leach to return the money.

"Oh, here we go," I said in response, rolling my eyes. "John, what the hell is going on here?"

Allin rushed past me – not aggressively, but certainly panicked. I called after him, but he kept walking.

As soon as Allin was out of sight, I rushed off to contact Tom Copeland and Larry Creek. They were good men and I wanted to warn them that they had been conned. Unbeknownst to Tom and Larry, I then phoned Fernando. He advised me to go to Malaga police and arranged for us to meet senior officer Juan Fernandez to file complaints against Leach and Allin.

* * *

When we arrived in Malaga, Juan Fernandez was puzzled about my relationship with Fernando. Nonetheless, he allowed me to sit in the room while Tom and Larry made their complaints.

Allin, meanwhile, had travelled to Malaga to try to prevent complaints being made against him – but he was not under arrest. Initially, Allin waited in the police station's reception area. Brazenly, under the noses of the police, he began to send information to Darren Steadman via the fax machine on the station's reception desk.

It was only when Juan Fernandez believed he had enough evidence from Tom and Larry that he sent his officers out to arrest Allin, confiscate paperwork and seize mobile phones. I'm no expert in policing, but I couldn't help but feel that Malaga police's efforts were a little amateurish.

With Juan Fernandez's permission, I was then allowed to go through Allin's papers and mobile phones, make notes and photocopy documents linked to the suspected fraud.

Ploughing through Allin's materials, I quickly came across contact details for Mo Khan and his associates. The men named could have been entirely innocent for all I knew. But lists of British-Asian businessmen linked to Mo Khan was what the CGI agents had asked for – so that was what they were going to get.

From Allin's documents, I also learned that the £375,000 deal that had been processed via the bank account of Simon Eldritch looked like another scam. Simon had been used for a second time by a group of accomplished and meticulous fraudsters.

The documents and money trail led from Simon's corporate bank account in the UK to Darren Steadman's account in Spain, where he withdrew part of the cash before transferring the balance to Allin's account at La Caixa bank in Marbella. I also learned that Allin withdrew the money and paid the full amount to Mo Khan.

Mo's telephone number was in Allin's mobile phone memory, and there was also a text message discussing the transfer of cash to Dubai. Allin had been foolish in bringing the information into a police station.

The names I copied from Allin's documents included Salahuddin Amin, which I recognised as the likely identity of "Aminie" – the man on the other end of the line when Mo Khan made several mobile phone calls during our meeting at the Meridien Hotel in London.

Other names I took down included a Birmingham-based businessman called 'Suleman' and two men named Mohammad Sidique Khan and Shehzad Tanweer.

*　*　*

After finishing Allin's documents, I told Juan Fernandez that he should retain the paperwork. He started to get annoyed that this mysterious Englishman was wandering around his police station, giving him instructions.

That's when I made the mistake that changed my entire relationship with Fernandez, Spain's intelligence services and judiciary, and Europe's law enforcement agencies.

When Fernandez pressed me over the potential importance of Allin's papers, I inadvertently breached my remit of confidentiality with Spain's intelligence agents – and told the officer that Allin's documents contained information on suspected terrorist activity.

The use of the word "terrorist" caused a stir at the police station and resulted in the chief of police contacting Fernando. I also reported back to Fernando that evening. He sounded angry, but we were both busy and our discussion was brief.

A quick word here about John Allin. While I removed the names of people like Mo Khan, suspected of links to Al-Qaeda, from Allin's phone and documents, I doubt that Allin knew much about the men involved. Allin's due diligence was poor and, to him, these men were just potential business contacts. It is extremely unlikely he knew about suspected links to the world's most feared terror group.

* * *

After returning to the UK, I discovered that Darren Steadman was on bail for allegedly attempting to steal money from Terence Conran, the founder of furnishing company Habitat, He was also suspected of other offences using tactics similar to those involved in the £375,000 deal linked to Simon's bank account.

I immediately phoned Simon to alert him that there could soon be a knock at his door – and advised him to tell the police everything about his dealings with Allin and Steadman. Simon had been used as a patsy again, and his best chance of avoiding trouble would be to come clean about who was behind the scam.

* * *

On 6 May 2004, I faxed Fernando a memo in English advising him to keep Allin's paperwork and mobile phones. Sarah Hill also translated the memo into Spanish and faxed the second version to Fernando's office.

The following day, I called Fernando to arrange a visit to Madrid. I sensed a degree of reticence in Fernando's voice when I also told him that I had other information I intended to provide to Malaga police.

"I only ask you something?"

"Yes," I replied.

"Don't...er...don't speak...with other people about...er...about...about our issues."

"Yes, of course. Of course."

"Er, about...er...about, er..."

"Just the fraud," I said, trying to reassure the agent.

"Er, about Mohammed or Terrorism."

Thankfully, I recorded the discussion. Many years later, the significance of that phone call would be recognised in a British court.

CHAPTER TWELVE

Heat

Shortly after my discussion with Simon Eldritch, he was contacted by the police over the £375,000 NatWest scam. Simon gave them chapter and verse.

Around this time, I learned through private intelligence sources that York Police, working with colleagues in Derbyshire, had been investigating my financial affairs for two years. I also discovered that detectives from York fraud squad had approached Silvia Harvey, a neighbour at Peel Close, and asked if they could set up an observation post in her back bedroom that overlooked my office entrance.

My name had been mentioned to detectives concerning the Lucent Technology fraud and the crazy-sounding £375,000 deal that Allin, Steadman, Mo Khan and Simon were involved in. I couldn't blame UK police forces for being unaware that I'd monitored both scams for Spanish intelligence.

It was time for me to cement my defence against any accusations that could emerge from the UK-based police investigations, and to help out Simon by paying a visit to contacts in Madrid.

* * *

As I booked the travel arrangements, instinct told me this Madrid trip could turn out to be my last meeting with Fernando and Enrique. They had started to go cold on me after the incident at Malaga police station when I'd mentioned my relationship with the CGI.

Gone were the offers to collect me from Madrid airport. There was just one cursory and business-like phone call from the agents, letting me know we should meet at the Novotel Hotel at 1 pm on 17 May 2004.

I reflected on Fernando's response to the Malaga incident. It seemed evident that his unit wanted to distance themselves from me, so I travelled to Madrid equipped with a recording device. It felt strange covertly recording a face-to-face discussion with Fernando and Enrique. Still, I needed more references to my relationship with the CGI on tape. I believed that the agents dared not deny all contact with me, because I had already recorded vital phone calls. But I wanted more.

* * *

After a cursory exchange of pleasantries, the three of us took seats around a small coffee table in the hotel lobby. The officers wasted no time explaining their frustration with me. Fernando, agitated, was annoyed that I had mentioned 'terror' or 'terrorism' when I spoke to police in Malaga. I told the agents I understood their frustration – but reminded them that I was not a professional intelligence officer and promised not to mention the subject to anybody again.

After a barrage of criticism, I warned the intelligence officers that there was now an English police force investigation into Allin, Steadman and Eldritch – and asked that they speak to the UK authorities to confirm my role in advising their unit, so that I would not get caught up in any prosecutions.

I could tell by Munoz's body language that he no longer cared about my welfare. He point-blank refused to speak to anyone from the UK:

"Nah...nah...impossible. The relationship...it's not...not working," he said dismissively.

"At the end, we will. But not in the immediate future. We are working with you, but they [the UK authorities] know nothing. They can know that you are a witness in Mohamed [Derbah]. But if the [English] police suspect our relationship...we'll take a break then."

I was furious and felt betrayed. As I sat there, it dawned on me that I was being completely hung out to dry by the very agents I had worked so hard to assist over four years. Finally, I'd seen the real Munoz. He stared at me intensely, revealing himself as the hard-assed senior intelligence figure – and no longer the friendly finance geek he'd played since I met him.

Munoz then warned Spain was in a position to deny any knowledge or involvement with me – other than to confirm that I was a witness in the case against Mohamed Derbah. The agents were clear: they would not allow me to use the CGI as cover for anything.

There was just one major problem. It had been my legitimate cover for many months, upon the agents' request.

Blood rushed to my head. After everything I had done for Fernando, Enrique, the intelligence services and Spain, this felt treacherous. I was sat in the same spot where my relationship with CGI officers had begun, yet agents were openly stating they would pretend none of this had ever happened.

I had to be careful not to sound like I was intentionally leading a recorded conversation. But I wanted further confirmation that my relationship with intelligence officials was not merely about Derbah. We talked about me providing information generally and I casually said I'd provided valuable intelligence to them before the Madrid bombings. Years later, the tape remains in my possession and I can be heard reminding the agents how I tipped them off about Mo Khan and his associates.

Blanchard. "Two or three months before the Madrid bombings, I tell you about the [CCTV] video. I tell you about other things, I...we discussed this."
Enrique: "I know."
Fernando: "Your actions, they [Malaga police] have not heard who you are, for example. I have papers that say you are a very good friend of the police department."
Blanchard: "I've always given you everything. I put myself at risk over what has happened with John Allin and all these people. That's the bottom

line – I put myself at risk! Now, all these people who are linked with Allin, Derbah: they're the worst kind of people. They're all criminals!"

I was worried about the repercussions in the UK if Spain's agents ditched or denied our arrangement. But Fernando's body language became more confrontational. He could sense that I was not going to be silenced easily. He puffed out his chest.

I continued. "I sent you a fax. Outlined it. I put it down on the paper. The bigger problem is that, in England, I can be approached by someone, whoever, and I can be asked all these questions about what I'm doing with all these people. So, what I feel, and why I'm here asking you…this either comes from you or I can telephone them [MI5] myself. Whatever you wish – but the time has come."

Fernando: "Are you worried?"
Blanchard: "What I'm worried about is that the police come and raid my offices. Take my computers and everything. I've got my business to run and I [will then] have no computers. I already can't go to Tenerife. I've got…"

Fernando had lost interest at this point and looked away. Seconds later, he stressed it was essential to stay in touch only because of the Derbah case. They needed me if they were going to prosecute Derbah because nobody else understood his financial affairs, and they wanted me to give court evidence.

With every fibre of my being, I wanted to shout "fuck you". But the agents knew that I needed to keep them onside. I wanted to continue trading in Spain, and contacts within the intelligence and police services would help. Besides, there was always a chance that if I continued to prove useful to him, Fernando would eventually put in a good word for me if the Lucent and NatWest issues became more problematic. Maybe this was a bluff by them. Leverage.

I swallowed my pride. "I am still here to be a witness against Mohamed Derbah," I said, handing my updated reports on the Malaga incident to Fernando. The report contained several names of Asian businessmen linked to Mo Khan.

The meeting ended cordially enough but, beneath the surface, I was raging. This was no longer a two-way relationship. I'd been a fool to trust the intelligence officers.

Thankfully, I'd caught the exchange on tape.

* * *

On my journey home, I considered the potential consequences of failing to get Spain to officially recognise my role. I planned a second attempt, this time in writing.

The following morning, I asked Sarah Hill to translate a memo.

* * *

"Dear Fernando,

I wish to respond formally to the issues raised yesterday at our meeting at the Novotel Hotel, Parque Ferial, Juan Carlos I, Madrid.
I would be pleased if you would confirm Enrique's full name and police number, and also your full name and police number. My lawyer, Mr Vidal Velasco Merchan, is to request a meeting at the earliest opportunity with the director-general of the police and the director of the Spanish security services.

You are aware that you have breached the terms of my engagement as an agent for the Spanish Security Services and placed me at risk as a result of your actions. Both you and Enrique at all times stressed and assured me that my personal safety would be of the utmost importance to the Spanish authorities in the work I undertook on your behalf.

Please reply by return to fax number: +44 1904 [number withheld]."

* * *

In the meantime, I asked Vidal and Sarah to request a meeting with the director-general of police.

Vidal, Sarah and I met with Jesus Nieto Rodenas, a senior police official representing the director-general of police and the security services, on 1 July 2004.

The meeting took place at Rodenas' office in central Madrid. He greeted us with a translator in tow. Speaking in Spanish, Vidal outlined my relationship with Munoz and Esteban and Rodenas confirmed he was aware of it because of the Derbah case. He acknowledged that I had provided information and documents on Derbah and expressed concern for my situation. At an early stage, he also asked what my feelings were towards both officers. Speaking through Vidal, I explained that I felt betrayed.

Initially, I thought Rodenas asked after my welfare out of genuine concern. But I quickly realised that he was gauging my hostility towards Spain's police and intelligence services.

The meeting lasted two hours. I presented copies of the reports I had supplied to Fernando and Enrique, as well as recorded discussions and my faxed memo from 3 May. Rodenas could tell that I was worried about being implicated in the Lucent and NatWest scams and asked me to explain them in detail. In doing so, I mentioned that Mo Khan had linked himself to terrorism and a money trail that led from the UK through Spain and onwards to Dubai.

To my surprise, Rodenas agreed that my role had been to gather information on individuals who could be linked to terrorism. As he confirmed it, I glanced first at Vidal, then Sarah, smiled and clenched my fist in celebration.

At the end of the meeting, Rodenas requested that we did not discuss our meeting with anybody else until he had completed his enquiries. He promised to contact Vidal.

I left the meeting feeling upbeat. Eight days later, any confidence that I had left was shattered.

* * *

On 9 July 2004, I was having breakfast at my home in York. It was Friday and I had a lighter workload than usual that day, so I was looking forward to enjoying some summer sun and a restful weekend.

Suddenly, several police cars screeched to a halt directly outside my house. Officers jumped from the vehicles and stormed up the garden path.

My mind flashed back to the drugs case in 1992.

When I opened the door, I was greeted by Detective Sergeant Adam Harland. Like DC Kenneth Wilkes many years before, DS Harland looked like a dog that had just discovered it could lick its testicles. He smiled while telling me that I was being arrested on suspicion of fraud, waved a search warrant in my face and gestured to his officers to enter my home. Within hours, the police had stripped my office of computers, files and other records – including copies of my Derbah dossiers.

Although I didn't know it at the time, simultaneous raids were underway at the offices and homes of Chris Eyre and Simon Eldritch. Later that morning, I was shoved into the back of a police car and taken to York police station.

I had prepared for this development. So, while I waited to be interviewed, I requested a meeting with an MI5 officer. At 8:43 am, I was introduced to Andrew Blain from Special Branch – the intelligence arm of British police. I informed Blain of my association with Derbah, revealed that I was a witness in the case against him in Spain – and that I had also been working for Spanish intelligence officers monitoring possible terror finance.

To his credit, Blain did not look at me like I was insane. Instead, he said he would check my information with officials in Madrid. The interview concluded at 8:58 am.

Later that day, Blain interviewed me for a second time. He said Spanish police had confirmed that I was a witness in the Derbah case – but nothing else.

I was not surprised. Fernando had told me as much.

Blain added, however, that after speaking with his colleagues at MI5, they'd asked him to talk to me again because the names of some individuals I had provided – notably Thomas Canning – were of interest to the British.

I explained the *modus operandi* behind the Lucent fraud and how my CGI brief was to gather information on potential terror finance – in particular, a group of British-Asian businessmen of interest to Spain. Blain took extensive notes. When the discussion finished, he suggested it would be better if somebody from MI5 contacted me directly, so that I could make a full disclosure. The second interview lasted thirty-four minutes and concluded at 17.58.

Three hours later, I was interviewed by York police. My usual solicitor, Mark Foley, was not available to attend. Sat alongside Foley's replacement, I read a pre-prepared statement outlining my role with Spanish intelligence and added that I was not prepared to answer questions relating to the Lucent or NatWest incidents until my relationship with Spanish police and intelligence had been confirmed. I also offered an interview with MI5.

Late that night, I was bailed. Upon returning home, I sat down at the kitchen table and reflected over a steaming hot cup of tea. I wasn't one to turn to the bottle when clear-thinking was required. Gill was extremely upset about what had unfolded. I tried to reassure her.

* * *

On 13 July, I received a phone call from a gentleman at MI5 who used the name 'Chas'. I assumed it was not his real name.

I met 'Chas' and a gentleman known as 'Stewart' on 16 July at the Hilton Hotel in York, but decided against recording the meeting in case they searched me before the meeting. I showed Chas copies of the dossiers I had given to Rodenas in Madrid, including the information on the Lucent and NatWest incidents. I then briefed him on Mohamed Derbah.

To highlight my willingness to co-operate with British intelligence, I later contacted Blain directly. Over two days in July 2004, I faxed him details of what I knew about Thomas Canning and Mo Khan's associates – including the names I had copied from John Allin's phone at the police station in Malaga.

That list of names included Mohammad Sidique Khan and Shehzad Tanweer.

* * *

Earlier in 2004, British police and intelligence services had launched a major counter-terrorism operation codenamed Operation Crevice. The case, led by the Metropolitan Police Service in London, centred on extensive surveillance of an Al-Qaeda-inspired terrorist cell that planned to explode homemade bombs at busy venues in England. Potential targets included the Bluewater shopping centre in Kent, one of Europe's largest retail sites, and the Ministry of Sound nightclub in south London.

Unbeknown to the terrorists, MI5 surveillance teams watched as they planned the attacks. British and American intelligence agents had obtained crucial information from jihadists arrested in Pakistan and the United States. These later included the Al-Qaeda 'supergrass' Mohammed Junaid Babar, who explained how the most senior jihadists in Asia trained and communicated with their foot soldiers across Europe. Similar information led British intelligence officers to the door of a well-organised terror cell operating from Bedfordshire and Sussex.

While they had kept a low profile, the Crevice cell was planning high-profile attacks. Its leaders had stockpiled half a tonne of ammonium nitrate fertiliser, which could be used to make bombs. But they had been followed, filmed and recorded throughout their plot. Over months, intelligence agents collected 24,000 hours of surveillance video, CCTV and audios. They even replaced the fertiliser chemicals, hidden by the terrorists in a commercial storage unit, with an identical but harmless substance.

Members of the Crevice cell were linked with Al-Muhajiroun, an Al-Qaeda affiliated extremist group headquartered co-founded by the Syrian-born radical Omar Bakri Muhammed and British-born activist Anjem Choudhary. Omar Bakri Muhammed was widely known in Britain for his sickening praise of the 9/11 attackers, whom he described as "magnificent". In the late 1990s, he had sent envoys from Al-Muhajiroun to Pakistan and New York to foment support for his organisation's radical causes.

British intelligence agents believe the networks which emerged from Al-Muhajiroun's international visits were used to support scores of British jihadists who travelled abroad for terrorist training. They also established links with Al-Qaeda's leadership. Al-Muhajiroun would later be banned in the UK.

In 2003, members of the Operation Crevice terror gang travelled to an extremist training camp in Pakistan. There, they met a young British-Asian man called Mohammad Sidique Khan and learned how to make explosives.

During the Crevice surveillance period in the UK, intelligence officers also witnessed the plot leader, Omar Khyam, meet with Mohammad Sidique Khan and another British-Asian, Shehzad Tanweer in February 2004. Intelligence officials assessed that Khan and Tanweer were not part of the Crevice plot – and did not have the resources or manpower to keep the two men under surveillance. A year later, that would prove to be a fatal judgement call.

Operation Crevice came to a dramatic conclusion on 30 March 2004 – just three weeks after the Madrid bombings. Fearing that the terror cell intended to carry out an attack of similar proportions, intelligence and police officials swooped. Almost 700 officers from five forces were involved in simultaneous raids.

Those arrested and prosecuted as part of the Crevice plot included Khyam, Anthony Garcia, Jawad Akhbar and a man in Canada whose role was to build bomb detonators. Another member of the terror cell, Salahuddin Amin, was not in the UK at the time of the raids. Amin was viewed as the link between the UK-based terrorists and Al-Qaeda operatives in Pakistan. He was later picked up by police in Pakistan and arrested upon returning to the UK in February 2005.

It was long after Amin's low-key arrest in the UK, and the gang's subsequent prosecution in 2007, that I made the connection. Salahuddin Amin was, in all likelihood, 'Aminie': the man Mo Khan had telephoned from the Meridian Hotel in London when his associates used my credit card details.

The picture was becoming clearer: Mo Khan was moving money around the world on behalf of groups linked to Al-Qaeda – he had more or less admitted as much when he made his panicked phone call, asking me to help him move €9m to Dubai.

During the Operation Crevice trials in 2007, it emerged that Omar Khyam had discussed with Mohammad Sidique Khan how the "brothers" (fellow jihadists) raised cash for terror causes through frauds and "scams".

"All the brothers are running scams and I advise you to do the same," Khyam told Khan during one phone call.

In phone calls recorded by British intelligence agents, Khyam explains how jihadist fundraisers set up accounts with banks and loan companies using false names, before running off with borrowed cash. Another scam involved using credit accounts from builders merchants to buy thousands of pounds worth of materials such as kitchens and boilers, with no intention of settling the debts. Terror sympathisers would then sell the goods on the black market for half the price – and send a sizable chunk of the cash to their jihadist "emir" or leader.

Interestingly, when considering whether to intensify their surveillance of Muhammad Sidique Khan and Shehzad Tanweer after the pair met with Khyam in February 2004, MI5 concluded that they were most likely not a direct threat and were instead "petty fraudsters in loose contact with members of the [Crevice] plot".

"Petty fraudsters". The kind who might be linked to suspected terror fund-raisers such as Mo Khan?

Salahuddin Amin was clearly in Mo Khan's orbit. Mo Khan had linked himself to Al-Qaeda, the group which inspired the Madrid bombings, and was moving dirty money through Spain in the months before 11-M. Through John Allin's phones and documents in Malaga police station, I had linked Mo Khan to Mohammad Sidique Khan and Shehzad Tanweer. I handed their names to Spain's intelligence agents long before 11-M and the Operation Crevice arrests.

To this day, I have no idea whether Mo Khan or his associates were linked with the Moroccan jihadists behind the 11-M plot. But it seems increasingly certain that at least two Al-Qaeda-inspired terror gangs shifted money through Spain under the noses of the country's intelligence services before the horror which unfolded in the capital.

*   *   *

There is an important clarification I should make concerning Operation Crevice.

During the police and intelligence investigation, surveillance teams tracked Omar Khyam to Luton, Bedfordshire. There, Khyam met with a man named Mohammed Quayyam Khan – referred to by the group and police as 'Q'.

I had heard the code-name 'Q' on occasions but did not know his name until later. The mysterious figure had been mentioned by several people I had monitored, and I passed the details to the CGI. Judge Lawler later requested those same notes.

Mohammed Quayyam Khan was suspected of having links to Al-Qaeda and is an associate of the radical preacher Abu Hamza. Some reports have even suggested 'Q' was Al-Qaeda's chief recruiter in the UK. He was never arrested as part of Operation Crevice, and he remains a free man. British journalists have long suspected that 'Q' was a police or intelligence informant – something Peter Clarke, former head of counter-terrorism at Scotland Yard, refused to clarify when asked by the BBC. If 'Q' had been an informant, it might explain why he was not arrested along with the rest of the Crevice gang.

One thing is clear, though: Mohammed Quayyam Khan, or 'Q', is not the same man as the Mohammed Khan, or 'Mo', who I first met at a service station close to the M6 and, later, at the Meridian Hotel in London.

* * *

Goldcrest's Marbella office opened in January 2005 and looked every inch the headquarters of an upwardly mobile financial institution. Sarah Hill managed what remained of my office on Tenerife and I recruited an assistant PA in Marbella.

Initially, we were inundated with clients on the Spanish mainland who needed to ring-fence their financial affairs to avoid paying unnecessary tax.

However, we soon discovered that there was also an appetite for my services from local customers seeking to illegally hide their wealth from their wives, business partners and the taxman. Many of the Costas' con artists, fraudsters, petty criminals, unfaithful husbands, scammers and gangsters discovered that a new corporate services provider was in town.

A friendly local banker in Marbella warned Goldcrest to look out for criminals seeking "fresh meat" through which they would attempt to wash their dirty money. It wasn't long before a few tried their luck. However, due to my many discussions with CGI agents and other security experts, I knew many of the tricks used.

In 2005, one common ruse used by criminals was to attempt to open bank accounts and establish offshore companies, using high-quality false passports. In particular, I'd been warned that Belgium had become the global centre of counterfeit identity documents.

There were two reasons for this.

Firstly, Belgium acted as an accessible gateway to the European Union's three largest economies – Germany, France and the UK (via ports) – since the EU had dispensed with most border checks.

But secondly, and more interestingly, Belgium used a less formal way of distributing passports than its European neighbours. In the UK for example, the Home Office – a centralised government department – monitors passport applications and dispersals through arm's-length agencies such as the Passport Office. The process is generally considered secure.

But in Belgium in the early 2000s, local councils were often responsible for producing and distributing passports. Which meant thousands of blank passports were locked away in insecure town hall cupboards – making them easy targets for well-organised criminal gangs.

Passports could be stolen to order in Belgium. How good they were depended on how much criminals were prepared to pay. Somebody else's stolen passport, with amended details, cost around $1,500 in 2001. In contrast, a high-quality document produced from a blank official Belgian passport would cost closer to $10,000: peanuts to cash-rich criminal gangs.

Goldcrest stopped several attempts to establish offshore bank accounts and companies using stolen Belgian passports. There were often giveaway signs – such as re-sealed photographs on older documents, or faked and unusual immigration stamps inside pristine passports.

Despite what some authorities will now claim, I didn't accept any old client. I did, however, take on some clients who made clever use of my offshore services.

* * *

In July 2005, I received a call from Kateryna, a young PA to Edmond Hamid. Mr Hamid wanted to speak to me in private, so I made arrangements to see him at his home in Greece as a matter of urgency. Few details were discussed – I was told only that I could expect to stay for several days.

Such was the secrecy surrounding my meeting with Mr Hamid that I travelled to France and flew to Greece from Charles de Gaulle Airport, Paris, so that there would be no record of my travel arrangements in the UK.

* * *

Paris, July 2005.
I had never travelled in such luxury. To this day, I still pinch myself to remind me that the journey was not some sort of dream.

As I approached Hamid's private jet, I was greeted by his cabin crew – a tall, elegant twenty-something woman with long dark hair tied up under her hat, and a willowy, impeccably mannered forty-something man.

As I entered the plane, I glanced inside the open cockpit door to see the pilot addressing more flight staff.

"Welcome on board, Mr Blanchard," a smiling man said, introducing himself and reaching to shake my hand. "Please, take a seat. We hope to be in the air shortly."

I entered the main body of the jet. I'd never seen so much space on an aircraft. Beyond the entrance, the fuselage opened out to reveal a seating area based around tables or workspaces. The seats were luxurious soft leather and the entire cabin was kitted out with thick, lush carpet. Along one side, under several windows, ran a small, comfortable sofa that looked like it doubled as a bed.

Speakers had been built into the 'wall' panels to boost an in-flight entertainment system that included a sizable TV screen, controlled remotely from the seating area. Next to some of the seats was a small cupboard for hanging business jackets and coats, as well as a magazine rack full of recently published newspapers and magazines.

Beyond the main cabin was a galley area. At the back of the galley, behind a partial partition, was the entrance to a discreet toilet. Ahead of that, along a small corridor, stood two refrigerators full of expensive drinks and food, as well as a small ice freezer. Neat, stable cupboards full of glasses, plates and cutlery were attached to the panels above the fridges and a small basin was next door.

It was a luxurious apartment in the sky. This is how Edmond Hamid travelled the globe – in style.

A smiling female crew member broke the silence, quite possibly to lift my jaw from the floor! "Please, Mr Blanchard, make yourself comfortable. Would you like anything to eat or drink while we await take-off clearance? Some coffee or freshly-squeezed orange juice, perhaps? Some wine?"

"Coffee would be lovely, thank you. This…well, this is quite something," I said, nodding back along the cabin. "I've never seen anything like it. Would it be OK for me to use the table once we are in the air? I have some work to do?"

"Of course, Mr Blanchard. Make yourself comfortable anywhere. No doubt it will be a smooth flight," came the reply.

And so it proved. I placed my files on the table, sipped a cup of fresh coffee, ate some surprisingly good food and worked as we drifted above white clouds towards Athens.

* * *

I've never had a guard of honour, but the closest I came was when I left Edmond Hamid's private jet and descended the stairs to the limousine which had been sent to pick me up. The faultlessly polite flight crew lined the entrance to the plane and thanked me for being their passenger. It was all quite surreal.

Formal security in Athens consisted of a uniformed officer examining my passport through a rear window of the limousine, followed by a nod to the driver. Once cleared to leave, the car accelerated past the airport gates, through the suburbs of Athens and into the countryside's warm evening air.

* * *

On arrival at Hamid's magnificent home, two enormous security guards escorted the car through a huge iron-gated entrance. Once we eased up the driveway, another well-built assistant opened the limousine door just outside the luxurious-looking villa and greeted me. After changing into my summer clothes, I joined Mr Hamid in glorious sunshine at the side of a south-facing swimming pool with breath-taking views out towards the sea.

"Paul, my friend," Edmond said as he shook my hand. "I trust you had a pleasant journey?"

"It was the most comfortable journey I've ever made, Mr Hamid. Your staff were extremely helpful – thank you for everything."

"You are welcome, Paul. And you are most welcome to my humble home," Hamid smiled. We all knew that the villa was far from humble. Spectacular. Beautiful. But hardly humble.

Edmond Hamid put an arm around my shoulder and discreetly walked me away from his staff, alongside one edge of the pool.

"I was delighted that you could come to Greece so quickly, Paul. It is a matter of some urgency and requires an informed, meticulous mind. Your knowledge of the law, as well as financial instruments, has always impressed me," Hamid explained.

"Please, follow me."

We walked away from Hamid's staff towards a private garden within his grounds.

* * *

Mr Hamid wanted somebody he trusted to make his wealth 'disappear'. All of it – including his cash assets and investments, which ran into billions of dollars. Not only that, Mr Hamid wanted his liquid wealth moved to offshore jurisdictions and made accessible to him under a completely new identity. He wasn't just making his wealth disappear – he was going to disappear with it.

With teams of lawyers and accountants scattered around the globe, in both onshore and offshore jurisdictions, what Edmond needed was somebody who was detached from his inner circle to restructure his entire empire without giving away what was happening.

The fees involved were incredibly generous. I had no hesitation in accepting his offer.

* * *

I knew it was not my place to ask, but I couldn't help but wonder why Edmond Hamid wanted to change his identity and move his wealth so suddenly. I could think of some former clients who, had they made the same request, would most likely be doing it for illegal reasons.

But Edmond Hamid was unlike any other client I had represented. He had never struck me as corrupt or "dodgy", as us Brits like to say. I had grown to admire the man. Sure, he was well-connected in Lebanon and Russia: two states with chequered business reputations in the offshore world.

With Edmond, I always sensed that he was at the legitimate end of the business spectrum. Extremely intelligent and quick to spot commercial potential? Yes. A ruthless operator? Certainly. But, unlike with Mohamed Derbah, I'd seen nothing in Hamid's business dealings which caused alarm.

Had Edmond, like many wealthy oligarchs before him, fallen out with the wrong people in Moscow? That summer, the world's media was full of stories about feuds between Russia's all-powerful president, Vladimir Putin, and wealthy businessmen – many with political ambitions. And while he was the most influential figure in Russia, Putin was not the only extremely powerful individual.

I had contacts in Russia but had not picked up any gossip involving Hamid. In Moscow and St Petersburg, the boundaries between the legitimate business world, politics and the country's powerful gangsters and mafias are often blurred – so Edmond might have stepped on the wrong toes. But that explanation seemed out of character for a man who was so clearly adept at negotiating Russia's complex power relationships.

Perhaps Edmond just wanted out of the rat race? Being adept at balancing potentially internecine relationships does not mean it is an enjoyable or sustainable situation. Even the smartest of men must tire of it. Maybe the client I admired so much was getting out while the going was good?

No – I told myself to stop thinking about it. Some level of intrigue was natural but, unless it was obviously illegal, then it wasn't my place to ask.

* * *

"I'm not a lawyer, of course. But offshore incorporations, banking, trusts? That is what I do for a living and your requirements will have my full attention," I assured Edmond.

"You are a kind man, Paul. You will also understand that this matter requires a great deal of discretion – for which you will be rewarded?"

"Absolutely, Mr Hamid. The only people who will know about this are standing here now," I said. We both looked around and, thankfully, nobody else was in sight.

"Naturally, I will ensure that only you have access to all passwords and documentation that will protect your assets under your new identity. You have my word on that. Once established, even I will not be able to access information on your assets, because only you will sign-off the required passwords and codes."

"Thank you, Paul. You are a gentleman. I knew that I could trust you. We have much to discuss." Hamid smiled. "But where are my manners? You have travelled very far on my request. So, first, some refreshment..."

With that, Hamid guided me back towards a shaded, secluded dining area on a terrace overlooking the vast expanse of warm sea below. With the merest of nods from Hamid, nearby staff busied themselves as we discussed his plan to make himself disappear.

That conversation will forever remain private. When it ended, I understood a little more about why Edmond Hamid wanted to become a ghost.

∗ ∗ ∗

I set to work the following morning.

The Greek summer was scorching hot, but the villa was perfectly constructed to throw convenient shade on Edmond's guests.

Over a week, I studied a mountain of documentation relating to Edmond Hamid's financial affairs. Initially, I worked out his existing company structures – including who appeared to own which company, who controlled which trust, which accountants and lawyers had fronted companies and who controlled scores of bank accounts scattered around the world.

Edmond's plan to restructure his finances had primarily arisen out of the need to keep pace with changes in legislation surrounding so-called tax havens. In the aftermath of 9/11 and an escalation of terror attacks, the likes of the United States and OECD had put the squeeze on countries or jurisdictions with secretive financial rules. In particular, so-called "tax havens" were under pressure to be more transparent about the ultimate beneficial owners (UBOs) of offshore companies and accounts – usually through demands for a transparent registry of owners.

Transfer pricing agreements, which I had used regularly on behalf of my clients, were also coming under heavy scrutiny. Influential revenue authorities were keen to ensure that charges for goods or services provided between companies under the same ownership were realistically priced. Several standard arrangements were recently ruled illegal because they were deemed financially incestuous and considered excessive tax avoidance.

In practice, this meant I had to dismantle some of Edmond's firms, trusts and foundations – and then reorganise them to keep them in line with new legal requirements. I devised a system that would not only satisfy accountants and lawyers, but also the world's most influential tax authorities. In layman's terms, I made it look like Mr Hamid was selling up and retiring, then restructured his affairs with the firms involved under 'new' ownership. Of course, Mr Hamid ultimately retained a rather considerable interest in the firms.

It was essential to get the new structures right from the outset, so I began by creating a Cook Islands trust that acted as the founder of a Panama Private Interest Foundation – an asset protection tool favoured by the super-rich.

With the attacks on offshore structures globally, the new reality is that there are fewer jurisdictions today which guarantee complete secrecy, or bullet-proof asset protection. Lawyers and offshore consultants are often not forthcoming about the potential risks involved if a major government or law enforcement agency makes a formal request to a jurisdiction for information on a company or client. A handful of jurisdictions do, however, remain steadfast in their determination to protect their clients – and it is to those centres that I turned when I restructured Hamid's finances.

Of course, even if you are up to speed with the new arrangements, as I was, there is always a risk that information on a client's offshore dealings will be leaked – as happened at Mossack Fonseca with the 'Panama Papers'.

In my early years as a consultant, I had been taught to utilise small and family-based law firms to minimise the risk of a Mossack Fonseca-style leak. So that's precisely what I did for Edmond Hamid.

During that week in Greece, I felt like Hamid's consigliere: the independent, trusted family friend who offered a dispassionate view of why a course of action should be followed. I connected with Edmond more than any of my other clients. We respected each other, so I felt compelled to do the best job possible despite the challenging circumstances. I wanted to show Edmond how good I was at my job.

Hamid knew that, too. He gave me the time and space to get on with the task. That week felt like a month – they were long, hard days on the telephone to jurisdictions across Europe, the Caribbean and the South Pacific.

Moving Edmond's billions was like completing a giant jigsaw. I had to find the right combination of trusts, foundations, holding companies and trading organisations to dovetail with his vast assets already placed around the world. At each stage, there were various legal, financial, contractual and jurisdictional requirements to consider. And, throughout, I had to keep in mind that the whole purpose was to help a man 'disappear'.

The 'warm up' for this began before I arrived in Greece, and involved Hamid changing his name in his country of residence. Using the new name, he then obtained a passport from Cyprus: one of many tax havens which issued official documents to people who invest heavily in their jurisdiction.

Mr Hamid then changed his name in both jurisdictions. Using a second Cypriot passport, he then obtained a further passport in a Caribbean offshore jurisdiction. Key to this process was ensuring that any files identifying Hamid in Cyprus were destroyed – so that nobody could trace his 'starter' identity. Incredibly, after strenuous checks, I determined that all of this was done without breaking a single law. And then attention turned to the 'money magic'.

Stage One
The process began with the establishment of an offshore trust in the Cook Islands. For the uninitiated, the Cook Islands, a tiny archipelago 3,200 kilometres north-east of New Zealand, is among the world's most secretive offshore centres. If you have substantial assets or serious potential financial enemies, then it is arguably the safest jurisdiction in which to place your assets.

The Cook Islands' ability to withstand foreign judgments, or foreign government agencies seeking to claim assets held in trust locally, is well-documented. Any claims against a Cook Island trust can only proceed if the claimant files their lawsuit locally. Even then, the law tends to favour established trusts and trustees.

Also, there is a one-year statute of limitations on claims against a Cook Islands trust, as well as a total two-year time limit on legal action. In practice, these rules have severely hampered attempts by powerful states to access information on Cook Islands-registered trusts. In every major case in which the jurisdiction's rules have been challenged – usually an attempt to discover the ultimate beneficial owner (UBO) of a trust – the legal ruling has favoured the trust. Even when the application was made by powerful authorities in the United States.

Stage Two
However impenetrable, I knew that a Cook Islands trust would provide just a single firewall against potential intrusion into Mr Hamid's financial affairs. So, the second stage of my plan was to use the Cook Islands trust to establish a separate offshore entity registered 9,200 kilometres away in Panama and known as a 'Foundation'.

A Panama-based foundation is an extraordinary offshore creation. They are similar to offshore trusts but, unlike trusts, foundations are separate legal entities that own – legally and beneficially – any assets they hold. In practice, this means the foundation owns the assets held within it and not any individuals. In a trust arrangement, of course, a trustee holds the property or assets for a third party – usually the UBO.

Some foundations also allow for investment income created within its structure to be reinvested before any tax is due, meaning those making decisions about the foundation's assets can quickly grow the organisation's wealth.

Panama-based foundations can also have a stock-brokerage account, deposit account and own real estate. You can donate or transfer assets to the Foundation for an annuity – and any individual can be employed by the organisation as an asset manager, for example, allowing them to draw a generous income, as well as expenses and other benefits. These employment contracts can be held in secret, so they do not appear in any public registry or database. This means that the person behind the foundation could transfer legal ownership to the foundation itself, but still access its assets.

A further reason for using a Panama-based foundation was that they were exempt from other states' attempts to freeze an individual's assets while that person was under investigation for suspected tax evasion or money laundering.

In many countries, people charged with money laundering or tax-related offences are often subject to an asset freeze imposed by a court while an investigation into their finances is undertaken – and they would be in contempt of court if they remove cash or assets without court approval. They must also declare whether they have other hidden assets.

Naturally, I hoped that none of my clients would find themselves in the unenviable position of having their assets frozen pending the outcome of an official investigation. But by using a Panama-based foundation, I could ensure that any client managing the assets of a foundation would avoid such problems. This meant that, even if the taxman was not aware of the Panama-based foundation, my client could accurately declare that they had no hidden assets.

So now I had created a Cook Islands trust which had established a Panama-based foundation.

Stage Three
The next step was to use the Panama-based foundation to establish multiple trusts in different offshore jurisdictions around the world. Let's say that (theoretically) there were four: one each in the Isle of Man, British Virgin Islands, Jersey and Cayman Islands.

Stage Four
Each of these new layers of trusts, established by the foundation, would then hold a 25 per cent share of further holding companies registered in other jurisdictions around the world. Let's say that the jurisdictions in which the holding companies were registered were Gibraltar, Monaco, Belize and Malta. Each holding company would have multiple nominee trustees and directors (lawyers etc.), giving the appearance of them 'running' the companies. But separately from these trustees and directors, an unrelated individual, or set of individuals, would hold a private legal contract stating that they were the UBO of the company – and guaranteeing their access to the company's assets.

Stage Five
Finally, the holding companies would each be linked to a separate trading entity, a company, based in yet another layer of offshore jurisdictions. Let's say there were four new trading entities: in Mauritius, the Seychelles, Anguilla and Cyprus. Again, these trading entities would have several nominee trustees or directors and, privately, a legally recognised UBO.

At the end of this fifth stage, I had created a complex web of trusts, foundations, holding companies and trading entities across (in this example) no fewer than fourteen different offshore jurisdictions spanning the globe. I've kept this example simple. But I could create layer upon layer of trusts, foundations, holding companies and trading entities. The potential combinations are almost endless.

Then add further complexities created by transfer pricing arrangements between many trading organisations in this giant loop. At this point, the flow of trade, monies, assets, benefits, contracts and salaries circulating the world would become mind-boggling.

Yet, ultimately, there may be just one individual, company or group controlling most of the assets of these organisations.

In the example I have provided, that person was Edmond Hamid.

Stage Six.
Now recall that Edmond changed his name: something hundreds of thousands of people annually do through organisations such as the UK's Deed Poll service. Most of the assets previously registered under his former name are now flowing around the globe, having passed through foundations that now technically own them. At each stage of this money flow, there is a new offshore jurisdiction with its own rules and laws over transparency and disclosure, and its own taxation system.

Nobody will ever find 'Edmond' and his assets unless he wants to be found. To even begin to do it, any authority would need to drag multiple offshore jurisdictions – as well as entire networks of law firms, trusts, foundations, trustees, directors and companies – into a giant disclosure lawsuit. The cost of such a lawsuit would be astronomical, and the logistics of it impossible to deliver.

* * *

After five days of the most meticulous offshore incorporation exercise I had ever undertaken, my temporary office at Edmond's villa looked like Winston Churchill's Cabinet War Room before D-Day. Maps, paperwork and numbers were strewn all over the desk and floor.

Hamid left the villa on several occasions to attend to more immediate business. When he did, he made sure that his staff were briefed to provide me with everything I needed.

On the sixth evening, I heard a gentle knock on the office door. It was Edmond and, unusually, he was carrying a large tray of drinks and snacks. I had not even realised that he was back from Athens.

"Paul, I have brought you some fresh coffee and orange juice. It is late, but I figured you would like some refreshment." As he spoke, Edmond looked around his feet at the office floor. What had been messy stacks of documents were now organised in more orderly piles that would soon be moved to individual cabinets, lawyers' offices and personal safes.

"I can see that you have been busy," Edmond said. "How far away are you now?"

"I've broken the back of it now, Mr Hamid," I replied. "It has been hard work. Lots of paperwork, as I'm sure you can understand. But I've restructured your assets in line with all new rules and requirements. You can rest easy that you are tax-efficient, as well as legally compliant. It will not be long now before most processes are completed, save for those procedures which are time-limited. I have drawn up a list of those for you."

I grabbed the relevant file from a nearby desk and handed it to Edmond as I finished speaking. He flicked through it.

"Paul, I cannot thank you enough. You have done the work of five men – and I'm sure it is of your usual impeccable standard. I wanted to thank you personally," Hamid said, patting me firmly on the shoulder.

He turned and looked me directly in the eyes. "If you ever need anything to help your business, you just have to ask," he added.

That was quite an offer, coming from somebody as influential and respected as Edmond Hamid.

"It has been my pleasure, Mr Hamid," I replied. "This is what you pay me for. Besides, you and your staff have been incredibly hospitable since I arrived. There is more to complete, but I see no reason why I can't deliver exactly what you requested by the end of this week," I explained.

And that is how one of the world's wealthiest men outsmarted his business rivals, as well as tax authorities across the globe, and legally 'disappeared'.

On parting, Mr Hamid asked me to memorise a secret mobile phone number. If it ever changed, he said, I would be notified. The number, he added, was provided to me in case I ever needed his protection of his powerful associates in Russia and elsewhere.

In the global war on tax avoidance, nation-states and regulators often have misplaced beliefs. They assemble armies of tax inspectors and investigators and run around like headless chickens obtaining search warrants and restraint orders to catch low-level criminals. But the smartest and wealthiest businessmen avoid any scrutiny because they become ghosts.

And ghosts don't exist, even offshore.

★ ★ ★

Around the time I opened an office in Spain, I was approached by an intelligent and sharp-witted man, Mr Thornton, who had an ulterior motive for using Goldcrest.

Thornton was a successful medical professional who had also inherited a tidy fortune from his wealthy family. He was married, had two children and an idyllic life.

Or so he thought.

Around the turn of the Millennium, Thornton discovered that his wife of many years was having an affair. Worse, she was serious about her lover and planned to divorce Thornton once the kids became adults. After that, she could claim up to half of his wealth.

On my advice, instead of confronting his wife over her affair and diving headfirst into a protracted and bitter divorce, Thornton stayed calm and planned the sort of financial revenge only a calculated soul would undertake.

We designed a legitimate method of moving his money, including his inherited wealth, offshore on the pretence of minimising Thornton's tax liabilities. I established a primary offshore investment firm for Thornton, complete with nominee directors and shareholders. That business then invested Thornton's money in other offshore investment companies with separate nominee directors and shareholders.

On paper, Thornton's offshore primary investment firm started to make bad investment decisions and it soon looked like he encountered financial difficulties. Thornton's wife was kept up to date on the whole situation, of course. To an outsider, it looked like poor Mr Thornton was on his knees. Letters started to arrive from his offshore company, revealing that most of his £5m wealth had been lost and that he was effectively penniless. His wife even began to feel sympathetic about his plight – while she continued her affair.

Soon enough, the couple filed for divorce. His soon-to-be-ex-wife believed her husband to be skint: a view verified by all paperwork for Mr Thornton' Belize-based offshore investment business and accepted by Mrs Thornton's lawyers.

Once separated, Mr Thornton then rebuilt his life. After a little while, he started to make much better investment decisions and rebuilt his fortune. Taking stock of his finances sometime later, he estimated his net worth at £5m.

The whole arrangement had been a ruse designed to prevent Thornton's unfaithful wife from running off with half of his fortune. In reality, Thornton had continued to pass his wealth through his primary offshore investment company and into other offshore vehicles with unrelated nominee directors and shareholders – but him acting as the UBO.

This financial foxtrot is unfortunately common among savvy offshore investors. It is also legally watertight if executed correctly. Readers may well be familiar with a high-profile case believed to involve this same ruse.

* * *

In 2014, a 54-year-old property developer named Scot Young fell to his death from the fourth-floor window of his girlfriend's luxury apartment in Marylebone, north London. Young's body was found impaled on railings at the front of the property.

At the time of his death, Young – who counted billionaires such as Sir Philip Green among his associates – was involved in a bitter divorce case brought by his wife of eleven years, Michelle. Young had been diagnosed with bipolar disorder after a stint in prison and battled drug and alcohol problems. He reportedly telephoned his girlfriend, the American model Noelle Reno, shortly before he fell from the window of her flat – allegedly telling her that he was going to jump.

But suspicion still surrounds his death.

Young had close ties to wealthy Russian businessmen, including several oligarchs who fell out of favour with Russian president Vladimir Putin.

These included the now-deceased billionaire media mogul Boris Berezovsky. Young had also been involved in a controversial collapsed property scheme in Russia, known as 'Project Moscow', which turned out to be a scam.

In 2006, Michelle and Scot Young separated and their divorce proceedings turned into a bitter, long-running legal battle. Michelle believed Scot was worth between £400m and £2bn – and she demanded a considerable settlement as part of the divorce. In 2013, Michelle was awarded £20m by a UK court, although she had requested significantly more. Young insisted he had lost most of his fortune due to his failed Project Moscow investment – and Michelle never received a penny from him.

Sound familiar?

During the couple's legal battle, Michelle persuaded the court that Young had failed to reveal full details of his financial affairs. Young was promptly sentenced to six months in prison for contempt of court.

Through my consultancy, I met several men familiar with Scot Young and his controversial dealings in Moscow. These included Edmond Hamid, a business partner of Berezovsky until the latter fell out with Putin and came to the UK in 2001. Hamid saw no reason to sever ties with Russia and stayed loyal to Putin's allies in Moscow – choosing instead to ditch Berezovsky.

Berezovsky settled in England and, through Scot Young, purchased a £19m property on the leafy Wentworth Park Estate in Surrey.

Young and Berezovsky were involved in numerous deals together, including the ill-fated Project Moscow. Initially, Hamid had also invested in the doomed project – but he withdrew following advice from contacts within Russia's security services. Powerful Russians feared that Project Moscow was a scam and that Young and others were skimming profits from investors and hiding the money in offshore accounts. Which proved to be the case.

Documents later leaked during the 'Panama Papers' scandal revealed Young used lawyers Mossack Fonseca to place cash in Russia, Monaco and the British Virgin Islands – suggesting that Russia, and Michelle, had correctly concluded he was playing loose with money. Other people's money.

Several of my intelligence contacts have suggested that Young was, by this time, way out of his depth. He also knew that Berezovsky's involvement in Project Moscow would anger Putin and his powerful allies in Russia. My intelligence sources confirmed that Young was defenestrated by Bulgarian hitmen on the order of senior figures within Moscow's brutal underworld.

These Bulgarian assassins, three brothers known in Moscow as 'Nia Sofiya Tri' (The Sofia Three) carry out assassinations on orders from high-level Russian Mafia groups. They have specialist skills in administering deadly and untraceable poisons, and never leave any trace or evidence. They live in Moscow, travel the world on assignments, and have Moldovan passports. When instructed to shoot a target – as in the case of John Palmer, they execute military style planning that leaves police forces across the globe baffled by the wall of secrecy surrounding their identity. I can say with absolute certainty that my intelligence contacts have never once provided me with duff information.

The Metropolitan Police Service in London is now investigating that possibility, alongside suggestions that other businessmen involved in Project Moscow – including Berezovsky and several of Young's close friends – were murdered on the order of Moscow-based gangsters.

Four of Young's closest friends died in unusual circumstances between 2010 and 2014 – one fell from the upper floor of a shopping centre, and two were hit by tube trains in London. The deaths of Johnny Elichaoff, Robert Curtis and Paul Castle were all reported as likely suicides. But another close associate of Young told *The Daily Telegraph* that he feared the men were murdered because 'they all owed money to the wrong people'.

Berezovsky was found dead in the bathroom of his ex-wife's Berkshire home in 2013, with a ligature around his neck. A post-mortem examination found that his death was consistent with hanging and no apparent signs of a struggle. Nonetheless, the coroner recorded an 'open verdict' – and my own Moscow sources have suggested that he, too, was the victim of the same Bulgarian assassin who dispensed with Scot Young.

Scot Young's life was a complicated mess, and the circumstances surrounding his death are fast becoming another of the underworld's myth-laden tales. On Hamid's behalf, I scrutinised the accounts for Project Moscow and its filter company, Parasol Participations Limited. In doing so, I re-wrote Hamid's capital account ledgers for monies initially routed by him via a Latvian and Cypriot bank – then diverted his investment to a trust in Gibraltar.

I can categorically state that having analysed those finance flows, Vladimir Putin had no financial involvement or connections to Scot Young and his cohort.

Young lost his fortune after he diverted money from the British Virgin Islands to a Cypriot bank. The cash was then confiscated by influential figures in Moscow.

* * *

A final word on the fall-out from Project Moscow and the deaths of Scot Young and Boris Berezovsky.

John Palmer, Mohamed Derbah's former gangland boss on Tenerife, was among the many business associates of both men. 'Goldfinger' is believed to have met Young when the property developer sought protection from UK-based gangsters with their links to Russia.

Palmer had used his knowledge of the timeshare industry to help his Russian connections set up timeshare resorts on the Black Sea. The Essex-based gangster borrowed heavily from Russian associates, hoping to make a new fortune, but his plans perished when he was imprisoned in the UK for timeshare fraud on Tenerife. The problem was, while in prison, he remained heavily in debt to his Russian contacts, who are more ruthless and cold-blooded villains than those Palmer had previously experienced.

John Palmer was found dead in the garden of his Essex home on 24 June 2015, shot in the chest six times by a gunman who had watched him through a spyhole drilled through Goldfinger's perimeter fence. To date, nobody has been prosecuted for Palmer's murder – but Essex Police said they believe it was "a professional hit". Detectives are looking into Palmer's business associates and "his links to organised crime". That could take them a while, but I know where I would start. The City is situated on the Moskva River in the Central Federal District of European Russia.

CHAPTER THIRTEEN

Cleanskins

Luton, 7 July 2005.

Four casually attired backpackers made their way slowly through Luton railway station's busy walkways, barely exchanging a word. It was 7.22 am. The rush of commuters from Bedfordshire into London was underway and, as the four men approached the ticket gates, they were quickly separated by the crowd.

Three of the group had set off by hire car from Leeds, Yorkshire, at four o'clock that morning. In Luton, they met the fourth member of their group, loaded tightly packed rucksacks onto their backs and left two vehicles in the station car park. Two of the young men wore baseball caps which obscured many of their features.

At 7.24 am, a south-bound Thameslink train arrived at Luton. The four figures squeezed themselves on board, ready for the forty-minute journey into central London. The train would be delayed in reaching the capital.

At 8.23 am, the group disembarked at London King's Cross and weaved their way through the concourse down into the capital's iconic and hectic underground railway network. Backpackers passing through London on public transport is a regular occurrence – so the crowds around the four men paid little attention to their hefty luggage. It was just another frantic summer rush-hour morning in a capital city still celebrating the previous day's announcement that London would host the 2012 Olympic Games.

As the group entered Kings Cross tube station, one man headed for the westbound Circle Line platform. A second figure headed east on the same line. A third man approached the westbound Piccadilly Line platform. The fourth and youngest member, an eighteen-year-old, lingered inside Kings Cross.

* * *

Shortly after 9 am, the UK's media reported explosions caused by a possible power surge on the London Underground network. But details from one hundred feet below ground were sketchy.

Within minutes, as injured, shocked and terrified crowds of commuters began to spill onto the streets around six of the capital's tube stations, reports of far darker events began to surface.

At 8.49 am, three men had detonated suicide bombs inside tube trains at Edgware Road, Aldgate and Russell Square stations. Each train had left Kings Cross minutes before the explosion. As London's train networks were placed on lockdown amid news of a significant terrorist attack, commuters made their way through the capital's streets to escape potential target areas. Many boarded buses.

At 9.47 am, a fourth suicide bomber – the eighteen-year-old who had lingered at Kings Cross – exploded a device on one of London's iconic red double-decker buses in Tavistock Square, south of the station. The blast was so powerful that the roof of the bus was blown off. Doctors gathering for a conference at the nearby British Medical Association headquarters ran towards the explosion to treat the injured. Once there, they discovered a large body count.

* * *

When the smoke had cleared on that fateful morning, London's emergency services announced that 52 innocent people were dead and almost eight hundred more were injured. The *triacetone triperoxide* bombs were packed with shrapnel – coins, nails and screws – ensuring that maximum damage was inflicted after each device exploded. Many survivors had to piece their lives back together with 20 pence coins stuck inside their bodies, too dangerous or difficult for doctors to remove.

With the events of Madrid's 11-M attacks still fresh in people's minds, attention immediately turned to an Al-Qaeda-inspired group as the likely perpetrators.

At 11.40 pm on the day of the London attacks, amid the blood, bags and twisted metal inside the stricken tube carriages at Edgware Road and Aldgate stations, police forensic teams discovered the remnants of bank cards and personal items bearing two names:

Sidique Khan and Mr S Tanweer.

Within hours, detectives had established that "Sidique" Khan was most likely Mohammad Sidique Khan. Tanweer's full first name, they discovered, was Shehzad.

When the names of the two 7/7 ringleaders were later made public alongside those of the other bombers, teenagers Germaine Lindsey and Hasib Hussain, I should have clocked them. But it would be several years before my lawyers re-examined copies of the documents I handed to Spanish and British intelligence agents in 2004, containing the identities of two 7/7 bombers: Khan and Tanweer. Their details had been among many names I had copied from mobile phones and documents at Malaga Police Station after John Allin's arrest.

Khan and Tanweer were undoubtedly the 7/7 ringleaders. They were older than the two other bombers, Germaine Lindsey and Hasib Hussain, and had attended several terror training camps. While both men were home-grown radicals, they were inspired by Al-Qaeda's fundamentalist ideology. Before the bombings, both men recorded video messages describing themselves as jihadist "soldiers" and outlining their intention to kill civilians. Months after 7/7, the recordings were broadcast by Qatar-based TV station Al-Jazeera.

Charles Clarke, UK Home Secretary at the time of the London attacks, initially described the four bombers as 'cleanskins' – a term used by intelligence services to indicate that the perpetrators were previously unknown to the authorities.

Bullshit.

Twelve months before 7/7, I had linked the two ringleaders to 'Mo' Khan – who was suspected of moving terror finance for members of the Al-Qaeda inspired Operation Crevice gang including Salahuddin Amin. Moreover, while MI5 had the Operation Crevice bomb plotters under surveillance, intelligence officers had observed Mohammad Sidique Khan and Shehzad Tanweer meeting with the group.

And there was more.

In January and February 2005, British police twice made inquiries relating to Mohammad Sidique Khan. On one occasion, officers took a statement from a garage owner who had loaned the terrorist a courtesy vehicle. These inquiries most likely resulted from Operation Crevice surveillance.

The grim and uncomfortable truth is that two of the 7/7 bombers had been under the noses of Europe's intelligence and police services for at least a year. I know this, because on two occasions, I provided their names. I handed the names Mohammad Sidique Khan and Shehzad Tanweer to Spanish agents on 17 May 2004; and on 22 July 2004, sent the same list to Special Branch officer Andrew Blain who provided a witness statement on 10 May 2007, confirming he passed on those names to MI5.

CHAPTER FOURTEEN

Betrayal

After I was arrested and bailed over my alleged roles in the £4.3m Lucent Technology and £375,000 yacht-based scams, I found myself up against some old foes inside the local police.

Much water had passed under York's bridges since I was jailed for trading while insolvent in 1978 and following Henson's drugs claim in 1992. I'd taken both convictions on the chin – the drugs charge in particular because I was not, and have never been, a drug dealer. Nonetheless, I'd bounced back from the financial, emotional and family turmoil that conviction had created.

Through a combination of my convictions and intermittent financial success, which had allowed me to enjoy a luxurious lifestyle, I had long been on the radar of local police and media.

And I knew that I divided opinion in York. The fact that I'd enjoyed the high life led one newspaper to dub me a fast-living "playboy": a description which, to those who knew me, never fairly reflected my character – but which has never gone away.

Local media were not interested in the fact that I was a committed father who loved his family, or a hard-working entrepreneur who, at times, employed many people and contributed significantly to the local economy. They cared about my offences, how much money I had made then lost, business failures and even my love life. Those issues sold newspapers.

My run-ins with judges and regional police meant I also had a prickly relationship with the boys in blue. I have nothing against the police – most officers do a brave and challenging frontline job. But my offences meant some officers perceived me as an arrogant, wealthy lawbreaker – and were champing at the bit for another chance to go after me.

So, it was no surprise when, shortly after my arrest in July 2004, I discovered that local detectives had been calling my Goldcrest-related contacts and encouraging them to report any concerns about me.

I also discovered that the police investigation was codenamed Operation Penthouse – a reference to the fact that I'd once bought the most expensive penthouse in York. The codename smacked of the petty jealousy and 'bring him down a notch' mindset of officers who begrudged the fact that an ex-con had become successful.

There is a fine line between a legitimate police investigation in which detectives actively seek evidence to determine the truth of allegations – and, however inadvertently, distorting evidence by encouraging the reporting of false claims.

***

Through some private intelligence sources, I learned in mid-2005 that the police investigation into me involved four strands:

- The alleged Lucent Technology and yachting scams.
- Allegations that I'd helped Elena Dontu secure a false passport.
- Claims that I'd planned an "upfront fees" scam with Goldcrest client Nicholas Peckham and Tom Copeland.
- And claims that I'd defrauded three separate businessmen through Goldcrest.

I had been aware of the first two strands. My role in assisting the CGI was my primary defence against the alleged frauds. The passport problem seemed minor – I'd helped Elena, but only to fund her expenses and the due diligence that Hugo requested before he would consider investing in any project.

The alleged 'upfront fees' scam emerged because the police had misunderstood how my fees and payments worked. So, while I was uncomfortable with the claim that I was planning to make off with clients' fees, I felt sure that a more detailed explanation to detectives would get the claim dropped.

The strand which worried me most was the allegation that I'd undertaken a series of small-scale frauds against former clients or potential clients. I knew the names of the parties involved. To my mind, the complainants were simply trying it on to make a compensation claim later. Two complainants, Alan and Carol Cooper, who I'd never met, claimed I'd made off with just £12,500 of their cash. Another, Nigel Cox, said the sum involved was a more meaningful £73,950.

Without trying to sound arrogant, such sums were small change to me after years of dealing with the likes of Edmond Hamid, Viktor and Hugo. In the case involving £73,950, the complainant was an ex-client who had asked me to create a company for him into which that sum was deposited – only to change his mind and instruct me to accept most of the cash (£62,950) as fees for creating a further four offshore vehicles for him. Cox had even visited my office in York in 2005 to sign the relevant paperwork – requesting an £11,000 cheque for the balance.

There is simply no way I would risk prosecution for fraud, and the end of my lucrative offshore career, by stealing relatively paltry sums. I could make even the £73,950 figure from one wealthy client in a matter of weeks. It just wasn't logical.

I knew from people who had been interviewed by the police that detectives were effectively briefing the broader allegations against me. Was it any surprise, therefore, that some interviewees subsequently signed statements which alleged I'd committed crimes similar to those the police had described? The witnesses were simply telling detectives what they wanted to hear. In my opinion, it was a blatant case of 'confirmation bias' with potentially far-reaching consequences.

Detectives had inquired whether Tom Copeland would provide information relating to the incident involving Allin, Leach and Steadman in Malaga – even though Tom had already provided a statement to police in Spain which did not implicate me.

One British detective even sent Tom an error-strewn email to use as the basis for a new statement. Tom took offence to the detective's approach.

In a curt response to the detective, Tom states: "In reference to this email and our conversations on the phone [it] makes me feel you are trying to get me to represent events in a fashion that fits an agenda that is not correct."

Tom's response: questions why the UK police did not simply use his Spanish police statement; criticises detectives for attempting to draft a statement (for Tom) based on discussions with a third party, Larry Creek; and points out basic factual errors.

The entire Operation Penthouse investigation had a whiff of desperation about it. But that was of no comfort to me.

* * *

In September 2006, I was re-arrested.

In simultaneous raids, detectives also arrested Simon Eldritch and Chris Eyre.

That evening, I was interviewed at York police station about the alleged passport offence and, later, the alleged series of small-scale fees thefts. It was an exhausting process that ended long after 9 pm. In between formal interviews, my solicitor Mark Foley and I were shown questions or themes which would be raised during the following discussion – so that I could take legal advice over what information, if any, to disclose.

During interviews and breaks, I could see some of the other arrested men, including Simon Eldritch and Chris Eyre, coming in and out of police interview rooms. We exchanged nods and the odd smile whenever we caught each other's eye. Foley joked that there must have been a "revolving door" in the interview room!

When confronted with the claim that I'd conspired to procure a false passport for Elena Dontu, I denied the accusation through a pre-prepared statement. On Foley's advice, I answered "no comment" to all other questions.

In response to the alleged fees theft, I denied the offences but provided detectives with some much-needed background. I could have given a "no comment" interview. But, in this instance, it was more helpful for me to explain why client monies sometimes remained in my accounts. One example I gave was that clients sometimes re-categorised previous payments so that I could establish further offshore companies on their behalf. In those circumstances, the money in my account was simply my fees.

Unfortunately, the interviewing officers seemed more concerned that I told them they had not collected all relevant documentation about the alleged fees thefts when they raided my home and office at Peel Close. I told detectives that some of the documentation that would show what happened was held abroad and elsewhere in the UK. Initially, one of the detectives,

DI Harland, accused me of "concealing" the paperwork – implying that I was being deceptive. The detective soon received a polite ear-bashing from Foley, who reminded the police that I could disclose the documents later.

It seemed to come as a surprise to detectives that a man who ran companies in the UK and Spain and dealt with offshore jurisdictions all over the world legitimately held paperwork in multiple countries. These men didn't strike me as the most sophisticated detectives, but I knew that could become more of a problem for me than for the boys in blue. I needed the police to understand some complex financial issues and had little confidence that they did.

It was 9.21 pm when the detectives concluded their interviews on the alleged passport and fees offences. I was tired due to the lack of natural light and fresh air and was looking forward to being bailed and going home. But instead, one of the detectives took great pleasure in telling me that I would be held in police custody overnight. I was to be interviewed about the Lucent and NatWest allegations, as well as the alleged upfront fees scam, the following day.

Mark Foley was furious, but the police were allowed to detain me. So, I spent an uncomfortable and sleepless night in a cold, dark cell in the bowels of York Police Station. The stale air, the stench of cigarettes and constantly slamming doors reminded me of my days inside HMP Durham. At least I didn't have to shit in a bucket.

* * *

The detectives knew that I would be cold, tired and hungry the following morning.

After a toilet break, the station sergeant provided a simple breakfast of lukewarm tea which, on an empty stomach, made me feel quite sick. There was nothing that passed as food. I knew it was all part of the police's plan to create discomfort – they hope it will wear you down before you are questioned.

Mark Foley arrived early in the morning and detectives immediately began to interview me about an alleged plan to steal $225,000 from Eric Reiner.

Once again, Mark had prepared a statement on my behalf, which he read aloud. After that, I answered "no comment" to all questions. My statement outlined past dealings with Reiner and made it clear to detectives that I held a significant amount of paperwork abroad that could be provided later.

* * *

During a break for lunch, I asked one of the friendlier female detectives, Melanie Spanton, whether she could locate some fruit. Melanie promptly returned with two large bananas, a fresh cup of coffee and some water. As she handed over the items, she wore a knowing look on her face which said: "I don't blame you for asking!" I felt a hundred times better after getting some food into my stomach.

In the afternoon, I was challenged over my alleged roles in the £4.3m Lucent Technology fraud and the £375,000 NatWest scam.

Through a third pre-prepared statement, I denied any involvement in both incidents.

Later in the same interview, a detective constable called Winnard revealed that he was aware I'd acted as an "adviser to the Spanish government" on money laundering. While I replied with my pre-determined "no comment" response, as agreed with Foley, it dawned on me that North Yorkshire Police must have been in touch with the CGI. Mind you, the detective had still got the information wrong – I had not advised Spain's "government" at all. Perhaps the mistake was a ruse by the detective designed to get me to correct him and break my silence?

But if UK police knew about my involvement with Spain, why was I being questioned about the Lucent and NatWest scams? Surely British detectives, upon discovering that I was monitoring the scams on behalf of their Spanish counterparts, would drop that line of questioning? It concerned me that they did not. What, if anything, had the authorities in Spain told the British?

I felt a sense of unease.

★ ★ ★

After a second full day of interviews, denials, "no comments" and the odd bit of information divulged to the police, I was tired but still determined to see off the allegations. As questions from the officers flew thick and fast, hour after relentless hour, it certainly began to feel like a frenzied attempt by the police to nail me for something. Anything.

After the final interview, DC Winnard and DI Harland briefly left the room. As the door closed behind them, Foley looked at me and warned: "Prepare yourself, Paul. Their evidence is thin. But I've never seen a group of detectives so determined to make something stick. If they charge you, stay calm. We have plenty of time to fight this."

His words were suitably reassuring yet slightly burst my bubble. I'd been feeling a sense of satisfaction at having got through so many interviews. At that moment, I felt like the police had no firm evidence of any wrongdoing on my part. They would, I assumed, have to release me.

Mark, however, was to be proved right. When the door to the interview room re-opened, Winnard and Harland entered the room looking determined.

"Mr Paul William Donald Blanchard," Harland began. "You are hereby charged with the following offences..."

★ ★ ★

After rattling off the list of alleged crimes I'd committed, Harland's face burst into a broad smile. He also seemed to take pleasure in telling me that I would be remanded in custody because the police considered me a flight risk.

I glanced at Mark. He had not been expecting me to be remanded, and contested the decision on the grounds that my business and family were in York. In reality, Mark argued, there was no risk of me running off. Foley warned the detectives that he would contest the decision and apply for bail at the first opportunity – and then asked the officers to leave the room so that he could brief me in private.

"This is not a good sign, Paul, as you know," he said. "I was not expecting this, and I am sorry that you will be remanded in custody locally. You do understand what this means?"

"I do – and you do not need to apologise, Mark. You've done everything you could today," I replied. "But these guys...Jesus!

"I'm hardly a fucking flight risk, am I? Gill is here in York, Sarah and Paul are here. My main business is here. What is wrong with these officers? Have the Spanish even told the British that I was advising them about the Lucent and Malaga frauds? Something is not right. I need you to find out what."

Mark let me finish my rant. He replied: "Sure. In the meantime, if Gill, your family or friends need anything, then just let me know. You going to be OK until we can get you out?"

"It's not ideal, but I'll be fine. There's not a lot to do inside those cells. Might need a good book or two," I joked. "Preferably something about prison breaks."

Foley momentarily dropped his professional manner and laughed. Despite the gallows humour, we both knew we now had an epic fight on our hands.

* * *

Chris Eyre and Simon Eldritch were also charged for the passport offence and the Lucent Technology fraud. Simon was also jointly charged over the alleged £375,000 scam, along with John and Jeanne Allin and Darren Steadman.

Chris, Simon and I appeared at York Magistrates Court on 18 September 2006 and were remanded in custody at HMP Hull. Harland told the magistrate that there was a risk I'd dispose of assets and accused me of having already sold one property owned by my stepson, Chris. Harland also claimed I had the means to abscond if I was bailed. Many alleged criminals have the means to flee, and I knew the police had provided no evidence that I either needed to, or intended to, dispose of assets to tackle the allegations.

A week later, Mark Foley exposed and then dismantled the police's flawed logic at a bail hearing inside a judge's chambers at York Crown Court. Hours later, I walked out of HMP Hull, having been bailed. Paul Jnr was waiting for me, sat on the bonnet of his new sports car. Paul Jnr's business was doing well and I couldn't help but feel proud of him, despite my problems.

Eyre and Eldritch also made successful bail applications. So began the task of preparing my trial defence – and I knew that hinged on my relationship with the CGI.

* * *

The authorities acted quickly to freeze my assets. A court order was issued following a police application to Leeds Crown Court in late September 2006. I'd been expecting it – Mark Foley had warned it would come.

What I did not know at the time, however, is that the asset freeze would effectively be in place for a further thirteen years and would include the longest running Proceeds of Crime Act (POCA) claim in British legal history. All of my wealth, everything I'd worked for and which I knew had been legitimately earned, was now effectively under the control of a court and judge. I hated the idea.

The police also convinced the court to issue production orders, which meant I was compelled to hand over reams of documents that officers had not discovered or removed when they searched my properties.

Production orders are strange beasts. For an order to be issued, the court must have reasonable grounds to suspect that an indictable offence has taken place – and, whether I liked it or not, they had that in my case.

The production order materials – which did not include information on my most sensitive clients – would significantly influence my life for the next fifteen years. At the time, however, I treated the orders as a basic legal request for the disclosure of information, which would help clear my name. Thankfully, I took photocopies of every page I handed over.

* * *

After a series of directions hearings at York, all future hearings and trials relating to Operation Penthouse were transferred to Sheffield Crown Court, to be overseen by His Honour Judge Simon Lawler QC.

Judge Lawler was a stickler for detail and a fastidious manager of court proceedings. But he was also a fair, if at times blunt, judge. He treated the Crown prosecutors and my defence team with perfectly equal disdain whenever they misinterpreted law or facts! The judge did not suffer fools gladly, yet I think all parties involved in my proceedings appreciated his authoritative legal mind, as well as his clear and concise directions.

Aged fifty-seven when he took on the cases, Lawler seemed dogged by a bad back throughout court proceedings. It was possibly the result of years of sitting in an uncomfortable-looking chair for hours each day without moving freely around the room. His physical discomfort was, at times, an obvious distraction, and his impaired vision was also an issue inside the courthouse. Judge Lawler would squint through his glasses when addressing the jury during trials, but often struggled to find the appropriate range of vision for any of the accused who stood in the dock. That would lead him to tilt his head forward, look down his nose and peer over his glasses when addressing me or others. It made for moments of comedic confusion in court – mainly when it was unclear who the judge was addressing – even though the issues under discussion were extremely serious.

During a private discussion with a mutual contact, the judge once described me as 'dangerous' because of my tenacious approach to contesting charges against me. All things considered, though, I respected Judge Lawler. Having been imprisoned as an innocent man once before, I was instinctively sceptical of, and cynical about, the judiciary. But I could have had many worse judges overseeing my cases.

Besides, my future was in the judge's hands, so I took a conscious decision to be extra friendly and polite in court despite my instincts.

* * *

The first Barristers Mark Foley instructed on my behalf were Robin Frieze (my senior barrister) and Gill Batts (as junior counsel). Robin immediately drafted advice, imploring our team to transcribe all of my covertly recorded audio material because, as he put it in typically understated fashion, it "went to the heart" of my defence.

Frieze also suggested we obtain a response from the Spanish authorities – the CGI or a court in Madrid – confirming my role advising agents, a move that could negate the key charges against me. In reality, there was little prospect of the CGI confirming my role: Fernando had said as much during our tetchy final meeting in May 2004. Instead, I wrote to Judge Garzon setting out the issues. I included copies of my discussions with CGI agents, recordings, faxes, documents and the intelligence reports I'd provided.

My letter and attachments were dated 12 October 2006 and hand-delivered by Vidal Merchan, my lawyer in Spain, to Garzon's court in Madrid. Foolishly, I believed the flamboyant Spanish judge would investigate matters, intervene, and confirm that I'd acted at the behest of Spain's intelligence agents. I couldn't have been more wrong: Garzon was about to face his own professional crisis.

In the meantime, Mark Foley and I were gobsmacked when Robin Frieze quickly returned his barrister's brief and said he could not represent me. Frieze had taken on too much work and, after seeing the reams of documents involved in my case, said he could not commit sufficient time to my case. I appreciated his honesty but was disappointed. Time was of the essence, and I could have done without the false start.

Mark then approached a second barrister, Paul Brooks, on the basis that he would "think outside the box". Paul had an impressive CV and could certainly talk the talk. After much discussion, he set to work – drafting an application for assistance from the Spanish authorities to disclose all the documents, memos, reports and tape recordings I'd provided to the CGI and judicial bodies since 2001.

Brooks believed his request laid the groundwork for an 'abuse of process' argument if the material wasn't disclosed ahead of trial. He felt we may even get cases thrown out on that basis. That was music to my ears. I knew that, if disclosed, Spain's materials would lead to my acquittal over the key charges – and now my barrister was telling me there was a chance that cases against me could get thrown out even if the materials were not disclosed. For a brief moment, it seemed like a win-win situation. Too good to be true.

Which is what it turned out to be.

* * *

In 2006, Tom Copeland received a substantial offer to sell his interest in the Nevada mining venture – so he no longer needed investment. Tom was looking around for his next business opportunity, and we decided to get together with Nick Peckham, another Goldcrest client, and offer loan facilities backed by a group of American lawyers.

When PC Melanie Spanton searched my office back in September 2006, she found a Goldcrest business card with Tom Copeland's name on it. Previously, DC Harland had inquired whether Tom and Larry Creek could become prosecution witnesses. But North Yorkshire Police later performed a *volte-face* and decided to re-arrest me, along with Tom and Nick. We were charged with obtaining up-front fees for non-existent loan facilities.

The allegations were ludicrous. How could I not conclude that Mark Foley had been proved right when he warned me, after the perjury trial, that the police would try to "nail me to the wall"?

* * *

In April 2007, I turned up at Sheffield Crown Court for what I believed would be a simple directions hearing at which an application would be made to combine my legal cases. But on arrival, I received a phone call from Mark Foley during which he revealed the passport trial would commence on 16 May 2007 – which was just three weeks away – and could not be postponed.

I warned we could not be "trial ready" in time because the application for materials from Spain was still outstanding. Without that material, I couldn't corroborate the claim that I'd been assisting the CGI. And in the absence of firm evidence, I would be laughed out of court and be found guilty.

Suddenly, my situation was a lot more complicated than any of us had envisaged. Up until this point, I'd been naively labouring under the view that the authorities in Spain would eventually do the right thing and confirm my assistance. As I put the phone down after speaking to Mark, I felt alone and insignificant. Sick to my stomach. This was not what Paul Brooks had anticipated. Why couldn't the passport trial be delayed? And why were the officials in Spain who knew the truth still playing God when my liberty was at stake?

Brooks had warned that the prosecution would argue, ahead of my trials, that the alleged passport offence was unrelated to my work for Spanish intelligence. But while there was some logic to that argument, I believed *all* allegations against me could be disproved once Spain acknowledged the extent of my involvement with intelligence agents. Even Elena's passport application was linked to people and activities I'd been monitoring for the CGI – such as John Allin, Darren Steadman and Chris Eyre. That context was crucial, in my view.

A directions hearing followed, during which Paul Brooks did not attempt to delay the passport-related trial. I sat seething in the dock, caught between acting politely towards the judge and outright anger over recent developments.

You rarely think straight in such circumstances.

The following day, 25 April 2007, I sent an email to Mark Foley outlining my concerns. I questioned the direction in which the legal cases were heading, how the evidence-gathering processes had appeared to slow down and the omission of crucial statements made by Vidal Merchan that supported my claims. I also asked why my legal team's application for documents from Spain had still not been sent to Judge Lawler.

Foley and I were friends, so I was careful to keep my language as constructive as possible. But the email contained the line: "The important representations to make to the judge, which we have spoken about over the last weeks and months, were not even touched upon by Paul Brooks in court."

The decision of the court to refuse to delay the passport trial was, in my opinion, down to Brooks' reluctance to highlight the significance of the material we had requested. After all, the application referred expressly to its relevance to the passport charges. The UK courts, and Spain in particular, were playing a rough game and had pushed me to the brink of imprisonment. But I felt that I did not have a 'streetfighter' barrister in my corner – and needed one.

My message to Foley continued: "I hate to be critical, Mark, as I regard you as a friend and will continue to do so. But I am feeling really down about the whole situation at the moment."

Inevitably, the email led to a breakdown in my relationship with Mark. Shortly after sending it, I decided to switch solicitors after the imminent passport-related trial. It was too late to do anything about the passport-related evidence with a new solicitor, and Judge Lawler would not have taken kindly to last-minute changes of representation. But, rightly or wrongly, I was now worried that Foley and Brooks, while no doubt fine lawyers, were not quite the legal team I needed for trials involving the alleged Lucent and NatWest frauds.

* * *

In May 2007, just days before the passport trial, I met with Jude Lanchin – a solicitor at the prestigious London-based law firm Bindmans. Jude informed me that she could accept my later cases. But she also advised that I should retain Foley and Brooks for the passport-related trial.

* * *

On the day of my passport-related trial, Brooks notified me he had still not finalised the application to Spain for all relevant materials relating to my cases. Brooks said his request was not ready, but he'd been working on it for some time. Life has taught me that there are many different tactical approaches to legal proceedings. So I don't doubt that Paul Brooks had a solid, professional strategy in mind. But I would have preferred my barrister to have submitted the application before the 'minor' trial – or to have tried to negotiate a delay to court proceedings.

I also decided not to give evidence at the passport trial because, without any response from Spain, I would be a lame-duck defendant. Under questioning, and without the relevant evidence in court, any decent prosecutor would rip holes in my claim that I was assisting Spain. I would look like a fantasist.

* * *

The passport trial took place on 16 May 2007.

Judge Lawler ran a tight ship during the trial – allowing time only for the essential details. The prosecution's case was simple: Elena Dontu and I had been lovers, and I'd used Chris Eyre and Simon Eldritch to obtain a false passport for her.

It was complete nonsense: I'd never sought a fake passport for Elena, let alone slept with her. Truth be told, Elena was a troubled soul – something which would become evident over time. So while she was good at her job, and looked like she'd walked straight off the catwalk, I had never given in to temptation.

But while there was no direct evidence of my alleged role in the offence, there was circumstantial evidence linking me to key players – including Elena. I'd paid cash into Elena's bank accounts, usually to cover flight costs when Elena and I were scoping potential investments for Hugo. The prosecution claimed that those payments to Elena, and other evidence, indicated that I supported her financially and that we had a relationship.

* * *

But all of this begs the question – what was the real crime? How had Elena ended up with a British passport? The answer was straightforward.

At Chris Eyre's request, Simon had introduced him to Jane Lancaster. Eyre had wanted a woman to act as secretary for a company owned by Darren Liversage – a client of the solicitor. But unbeknown to Simon, the real reason was to use Lancaster as a means of obtaining a false passport in Elena's name. The Passport Office issued the document before the identity scam was uncovered.

The biggest problem that Simon and I faced throughout the trial, however, was that Chris Eyre pleaded guilty on the opening day. There's little doubt that, in the jury's mind, that cast doubt over our separate pleas of not guilty.

The trial was further complicated because neither the prosecution nor the defence could call Elena to give evidence. She'd suffered a breakdown and was being treated in a recovery centre in Moldova. She was, by all accounts, in no fit state to attend a UK court.

Unsurprisingly following Chris Eyre's plea, the rest of the trial did not go well. After Judge Lawler's summing up, the Jury retired for only a short while before returning to reveal their verdict. Simon and I were found guilty. We were not immediately sentenced because both of us faced further trials – meaning we were remanded in custody with no prospect of bail.

At the time, the UK's prison service was experiencing an overcrowding crisis – we joked that it was because the courts were sentencing too many innocent people. So Simon and I were moved around various police station cells before ending up at Strangeways in Manchester, one of Britain's most notorious and harsh prisons.

Thankfully, our time in Manchester was short. I won't linger on Strangeways or claim to be an expert on the place – but the conditions there were shocking. They bordered on Third World. TV depictions of south American jails often look similar!

Simon and I were soon transferred to HMP Leeds across the Pennines in Yorkshire. It was still a prison, and porridge should never be easy for those who are genuinely guilty. But HMP Leeds, known locally as Armley Gaol, after the western suburb of Leeds in which it stands, was a better environment. Unlike Strangeways, it was not as close to breaching prisoners' basic human rights.

* * *

Mark Foley had inadvertently informed Judge Lawler that I was sharing a cell with Simon when we entered Armley. Shortly after this revelation, prison guards moved me from the cell. You can get paranoid about these things, but I suspected that the court was unhappy that Simon and I would have months to discuss and co-ordinate our defence.

After Simon and I were split up, I was moved around single-bed cells on E Wing. The frequent moves to tiny cells meant there was nowhere to store my case notes, which became a further hindrance.

Armley's E-Wing suffered from a distinct lack of fresh air – the place had its very own *parfum* far worse than HMP Durham – the food was awful, and it was ridiculously noisy. I began to suffer from migraines. Ordinarily, I would tackle migraines by exercising. But there were few opportunities to take a regular, uninterrupted walk in the exercise yard. Unusually, I began to feel claustrophobic and stressed out – partly because Gill and the family were also struggling with me being inside again. With each visit from family members, I could sense a loss of confidence in me and the legal system, as well as uncertainty about our futures.

Gill became ill with stress. My bank accounts had been frozen, so money was getting tight and my mortgage was in arrears. The bank was threatening to repossess our home. Gill deserved more than this in life. Thankfully, Paul Jnr again stepped in with the mortgage payments.

It was time for a fresh approach to my legal cases.

* * *

It's a small world, prison.

You never know who you're going to bump into. But it's rare to meet and befriend somebody who was recruited to smash in your kneecaps.

On E Wing at HMP Leeds, I shared a cell with a notorious convicted drug dealer from Bradford called Fariman Khan. He was doing twelve years and passed his days inside as a cleaner. I'd landed the same role, so the two of us shared a cell.

Fariman already knew who I was. I'd barely had time to sit down inside our cell on my first evening when he struck up a firm-but-friendly conversation.

"Paul, I need you to help me move some money when I get out," he said, looking me directly in the eyes. "People say you know about these things?"

I was taken aback: "How do you know that?"

"I know everything that goes on in Yorkshire," Fariman smiled. "You used to travel to Malaga, didn't you?"

This was freaky. I didn't know what to make of it.

"How the hell would you know that?"

"Sonny Fletcher had us lying in wait for you, a few times, at Leeds-Bradford Airport," Fariman said.

"Lying in wait? What for?"

"To put you in hospital," Fariman smiled. "Or worse. He thought you would grass on him for them frauds in Spain."

A shiver ran down my spine, but I was in no mood to show any weakness. I was inside a prison cell with a man who had been recruited to attack me – or 'worse'. Slowly, I clenched the fist of my right hand behind my back. If this kicks off, at least I'd go down swinging.

As it happened, there was no need to prepare for a scrap.

"Haha! Don't worry, Paul! We were his paid protection," Fariman said. 'It was nothing personal. If you're in my camp, there'll be no problems for you or your colleagues here. Besides, you didn't grass, did you?"

Little did he know!

"According to Sonny, you kept schtum and that's why I wanted to see you. I'm told you're a man I can trust. I need your help. In return, you'll get mine. In here." Fariman looked at me expectantly.

"It seemed like a fair offer, but I was damned if I was going to help move dirty drug cash while telling the prison authorities that I was an innocent offshore consultant. I was caught between a rock and a hard place.

After a few seconds of silence, I spoke up. "When you get out, right?"

"Yep – can't do fuck all while I'm in here. Too much heat, innit? I'm told you're a loyal, discreet sort?"

I laughed ironically.

"Ha! Perhaps a little too discreet, mate. Might have done me some good to have spoken publicly about some of my 'work'."

Fariman looked confused.

"Never mind," I said. "It's a long story, and most of it doesn't relate to Sonny Fletcher. Yes – I know how to move money offshore, legitimately. I'm happy to talk to you about how it is done."

"Brilliant. That's all I ask," Fariman said, raising a large hand and slapping me hard on the shoulder. It was a friendly gesture, although I'm not sure it felt like one. He was a beast of a man, Fariman Khan, and could have crushed me with his bare hands. So it was probably helpful that he hadn't realised I'd made no promises to touch his cash.

That night, as we chatted about prison life and our backgrounds, Fariman explained more about Sonny Fletcher's concern. Sonny had indeed asked Fariman and his brother, known locally as 'Meggy', to keep an eye on me just in case I implicated Fletcher in anything. The brothers had been recruited to give me a good pasting and warn me off – if it came to that.

Thankfully, it had never come to that. My knees and I remain grateful to this day.

* * *

In August 2007, 'Meggy' Khan was shot in the stomach at his home in Bradford. He spent two weeks in hospital. The bullet perforated his colon and liver, but Meggy survived. Police believed the shooting was a drug-related hit organised by rival gangsters. Sonny Fletcher and his nephew, James, were later arrested and put on trial for the attack – but the case against them collapsed.

Sometime later, the Serious and Organised Crime Agency (SOCA), an offshoot of the Home Office, approached me asking for information on Sonny and his associates. I was even offered an incentive to co-operate with investigators.

I rejected SOCA's offer. As a former adviser to Sonny, I had a duty of confidentiality towards him. Besides, I had no desire to insert myself into an alleged row between rival Yorkshire-based gangsters who were closely monitored by the state. I felt I'd be viewed by all parties as a "grass" if I co-operated with SOCA – and, after everything that had happened in Spain, I had no desire to go back down that route.

* * *

Resigned to custody in HMP Leeds, I set about trying to find a way through the crazy web of legal issues facing me. Rightly or wrongly, I'd already decided that I did not want to use Mark Foley and Paul Brooks as my team for the remaining legal cases.

But you could argue that I jumped out of the frying pan and into the fire.

Bindmans LLP and Jude Lanchin seemed to be a natural fit. The influential London-based firm of solicitors was established by human rights expert Sir Geoffrey Bindman in 1974, and quickly developed a reputation as a fierce defender of 'ordinary' people in the face of legal authority or power.

Lawyers at Bindmans specialised in complex criminal cases, including alleged financial crime and money laundering, yet still had an excellent record defending the accused. Their solicitors, I was told, were extremely intelligent and less 'snobbish' than those found at some other London firms. The firm came highly recommended.

Jude Lanchin appeared to be Bindmans' archetypal street-fighting solicitor. She was bright, of course, but had a pre-law background in local community work. As a result, she focused as much on a visceral, practical approach to cases as she did the academic side of the law when dealing with clients. She had for many years worked with youngsters on the Broadwater Farm estate in Tottenham charged with offences after the infamous riot in 1985, during which PC Keith Blakelock was killed with a machete. Through that, Jude had earned a fearless reputation – and her record indicated that she got results. I thought she was just what I needed.

Jude advised, however, that if I was going to engage Bindmans, the case's complexity necessitated regular face-to-face meetings. So she recommended that I should be moved to a prison in London: HMP Belmarsh. I agreed.

In my opinion, and in retrospect, it was an appalling decision.

* * *

I hadn't done my homework.

HMP Belmarsh was built in 1991 on the site of the old Royal Arsenal in Woolwich: the former munitions factory and research centre for the British armed forces. The modern prison is a maximum-security facility and, in the aftermath of 9/11, it had become known as Britain's Guantanamo Bay because it was used to detain suspected terrorists indefinitely without charge or trial. The controversial practice was later banned by British judges. But the prison continues to be used to incarcerate high-profile terror suspects on trial at the adjoining Woolwich Crown Court.

Almost immediately after I arrived, I discovered that Belmarsh had a reputation as Britain's most brutal jail – and conditions were as harsh as I'd ever encountered.

Belmarsh felt wild, unsafe. The guards were barely in control of the facility, and violence was common. I'm not talking about standard prison punch-ups, either. This was regular serious, targeted and bone-crushing violence between the most hardened men I'd had the misfortune to meet.

If you wanted to survive unscathed in Belmarsh, you kept your head down and offended nobody. I thought I'd been in harsh prisons before now, but none of them compared to the 1,000-man facility perched close to the muddy southern banks of the River Thames.

The move was a huge mistake, a decision made in haste while my head was filled with optimism about the future. And, to cap it all, I was now two hundred miles away from Gill, Sarah and Paul Jnr.

My health began to deteriorate shortly after I arrived at Belmarsh. I lost weight, my asthma returned and I began to suffer regular heart palpitations.

On Jude Lanchin's recommendation, I also appointed Selva Ramasamy of Hollis Whiteman chambers as my senior barrister and Huzla Rawat of Carmelite Chambers as my new junior. But with new legal representation, there was little time to lose. The trial for the alleged £4.3m Lucent Technology fraud and separate £375,000 NatWest scam was set for 26 November 2007. When the prosecution served their papers, the bundle contained thousands of pages – including witness statements. These included statements from Spanish police officers detailing Simon's arrest in Torremolinos and one each from the officers who interviewed and then released me – on the instruction of Enrique.

Among the prosecution papers were statements from Andrew Blain, the Special Branch officer I had spoken to, and an MI5 employee referred to in the documents only as 'Officer 9040'. These statements confirmed my contact with both intelligence bodies and would, I thought, prove extremely useful.

However, the principal evidence against Simon and I were police interviews and statements from Darren Steadman – who had also implicated his friend John Allin. The early signs for Simon and I were good: the evidence was certainly contestable.

Steadman had provided five interviews to investigating officers, as well as three statements, during which he laid the blame for the Lucent scam directly at the feet of the IRA. Brave move, and partially correct. There was a snag, however. Critical aspects of Steadman's story changed with each telling of the tale, and he had opted to implicate me at every opportunity.

★ ★ ★

Judge Lawler was forced to delay the Lucent and NatWest-related trial date when it became evident that Madrid was dragging its feet over my legal team's request for files. Initially, we believed it was just a matter of time before the documents would be released.

In the meantime, the judge re-arranged the sequence of trials – bringing forward the final hearings relating to the Cox, Cooper and Starling allegations to February 2008. This was a significant blow because part of my defence to those allegations also relied on undisclosed files we had requested from Spain.

We would just have to fight the other allegations with the evidence I already held. I remained confident and was more concerned about obtaining the Spanish materials to see off the Lucent and NatWest allegations. But something was about to happen in Madrid which would shatter that confidence.

★ ★ ★

We're all brought up to trust in authority, particularly the state institutions – and certainly the courts. After my conviction in 1992, I knew that such trust was misplaced. But because democratic cultures require us to believe in the public-spirited nature of politicians, the police and the courts – and condition us to think that way – it is all too easy to default to a trusting mindset. After all, liberal democratic societies have checks and balances in place to keep those in power on the straight and narrow. Right?

We normalise such trust because we do not want to think that the powerful institutions of the state are, or can be, corrupt. Of course, that isn't the version of liberal democracy we are sold as children!

So despite everything that had already happened to me before 2007, it came as a shock when Judge Baltasar Garzon – regarded as a pioneering and fearless pursuer of criminals globally – acted less-than-admirably when faced with a dilemma over how to deal with my role as a Spanish intelligence asset.

★ ★ ★

On 27 December 2007, several months after Judge Lawler had finally sent my legal application for documents to the courts in Madrid, Judge Baltazar Garzon added my name to the Spanish indictment against Mohamed Derbah and his associates.

According to Garzon's revised indictment documents, I was suddenly and criminally responsible for laundering the ill-gotten gains of the Lebanese-led "mafia" running Tenerife – and he was seeking a fifteen-year sentence for my conviction.

There was no mention in the indictment of the enormous help I'd provided to Garzon, intelligence officers and Spanish police – all at massive risk to my safety. There was no mention of the fact that I'd taken seriously my duty as an offshore consultant and referred concerns about Mohamed Derbah's alleged frauds to Spain's authorities. There was no mention of how I'd helped Spain's CGI unpick the labyrinthine network of offshore companies, trusts and bank accounts Derbah used to stay one step ahead of

Spain's authorities. And there was no mention of how I'd assisted Spanish investigators by exposing other criminal activities taking place under their noses – including the likely movement of terror finance through Spain.

No. According to Judge Baltazar Garzon's hastily revised indictment, compiled almost six years after his initial warrants against Mohamed Derbah, I'd been the financial architect of a vast criminal empire involved in fraud, money laundering, coercion, extortion, prostitution and other activities. The indictment linked individuals across Europe from Russia, Lebanon, Spain and France. In a thinly-veiled attempt to get the UK criminal justice authorities interested in the case, Garzon had even shamelessly included members of the notorious 'Adams Family', or Clerkenwell Syndicate, on the indictment. I'd never met a member of the Adams Family or Syndicate.

The document issued by Judge Garzon was ludicrous. It could not have been more ludicrous if it had also named Jack the Ripper or Michael Corleone as part of the same mafia! I'd gone from being Spain's 'offshore asset' and a protected witness, to one of Europe's most wanted men. Why?

The answer was simple. My lawyers were demanding from Madrid's criminal court, information that would confirm my role as a CGI asset to defend me from false allegations in the UK. It is common knowledge that the world's powerful intelligence services – from the CIA and MI6 through to Mossad – do not reveal information about their assets, let alone their paid officers, as a matter of policy.

Faced with such a legal application, Garzon and Spain responded by going on the attack. Adding me to a revised indictment, some six years after the original warrants were served on Tenerife, immediately created distance between me and the Spanish authorities. Legally, it placed me at loggerheads with the very organisations I'd actively sought to assist. It gave Spain, Garzon, Fernando, Enrique and the secretive CGI 'plausible deniability'.

To me, however, it was a betrayal of the highest order. One of the world's most senior judges was prepared to throw me under a bus to protect himself, Spain and its intelligence services.

I was furious. I have never been a member of a "mafia". I'd certainly advised Mohamed Derbah on offshore finance and helped create business and banking structures. But all such activity was legal, and I could prove that I was unaware that Derbah's money may have been illegally earned.

Hell, I'd documented every transaction, kept every account and invoice for scores of clients. And as soon as I became suspicious of Derbah's business activities, I'd reported him to the relevant authorities.

I'd even invoiced Derbah for my consultancy services and retained documents to prove it. Derbah paid me just £60,000 to establish companies and accounts for his businesses. The tightwad still owed me a further £200,000.

Does that sound like the behaviour of, and reward for, the financial mastermind of an international "mafia"? Quite the opposite: it was what I did for a living! People may disagree with offshore business and consultancy, but it is not illegal. I wasn't even hiding my activity, like some criminals: I handed out business cards telling the world what I did for a living!

Spain was trying to fuck me over. Garzon was fucking me over. All to protect Spain's institutions and keep me from revealing my role inside a British courtroom. It was no coincidence that the revised indictment arrived during a period when Spain's intelligence agents and courts were scrambling around trying to avoid my requests for their sensitive files, the disclosure of which could have undermined their case against Derbah.

Paul Brooks, my barrister, had eventually finalised and sent requests to Spain – but the authorities in Madrid appeared to ignore him.

Years later, I discovered that Garzon's decision to include me on the indictment may also have been because, on the day he recruited me in his fight against Tenerife's alleged 'mafia', he had potentially broken Spanish law.

* * *

I suspect Garzon's decision to include me on the Tenerife 'mafia' indictment triggered something in Jude Lanchin at Bindmans because, in early 2008, our client-solicitor relationship soured. While most discussions focused on the upcoming Cox, Cooper and Starling cases, the tone of our chats often became prickly, awkward. Only Jude would know precisely what she was thinking, but I sometimes got the impression that my solicitor figured I might be guilty.

Garzon was, after all, a famous figure within the legal industry – even in England. His reputation had sky-rocketed after his attempt to prosecute General Pinochet, and lawyers spoke about him in revered tones. Now Garzon was after me, and perhaps that changed people's perception of my cases.

In response, I claimed to be a Spanish intelligence asset recruited by Garzon to help nail the very mafia boss I stood accused of assisting. I must have come across as half-crazed. On one occasion, in response to observations made about my successful perjury trial, Jude even compiled a file note, stating: "All this sounds as if it is out of a film."

At one meeting with Jude, I referenced the many files I'd provided to North Yorkshire Police following the force's production order demands.

I'd taken copies of the files, while the originals went to the police, and I knew that Mark Foley, my previous solicitor, had forwarded them to my new legal team. So I assumed that Bindmans and the Crown Prosecution Service were working from identical sets of documents. Yet Jude often seemed to become confrontational when I referred to specific evidence contained in those files, which I knew could be exhibited as part of my defence. Initially, I thought little of it – thinking merely that Jude had yet to familiarise herself with the information. Closer to trial, I surmised, she would know it all.

In retrospect, Jude's lack of knowledge about the files should have been more of a red flag. One reason it was not, was that I was distracted by my deteriorating health inside HMP Belmarsh. I'd lost weight and the heart palpitations I'd experienced had become more frequent. At night inside my cell, I often found it hard to breathe or regulate my breathing. Initially, the guards thought I was making it up. But my body was failing just when I needed to be physically strong.

The stress of being inside Belmarsh made matters worse. The unbearable noise, under-staffing and constant violence left many inmates on edge – not that you could show any weakness. I'd not had a solid night of sleep for many months, a grim reality that played havoc with my immune system. Sleep is crucial to effective recuperation – if you don't get enough of it, your recovery from illness and injury takes a lot longer. It is also vital for concentration and, in my zombie-like state, I was finding it hard to focus on my defence cases. Distracted by poor health and unable to break the cycle, I reacted too slowly to threats posed by my upcoming trial.

* * *

Seven days before my second trial, 29 January 2008, my legal team gathered at Belmarsh for a pre-trial conference. The group comprised solicitors Jude Lanchin and Laura Higgs, senior counsel Selva Ramasamy, Sean Larkin, and Huzla Rawat.

Ramasamy began by explaining that my legal team had not been provided with a copy of police production orders dated 13 September 2006, and neither had they been disclosed in unused material. He was concerned because it appeared we now held more documents than we'd given to the police – making it look like I'd not handed over everything required under the law.

I explained that I'd provided all the information requested in the production orders and, on the advice of Mark Foley, had voluntarily provided additional records for Goldcrest Hispania's client account from August 2003 onwards. Naturally, I added, there were other defence materials I'd not provided to the police because they hadn't requested the documents in the production orders. The whole situation seemed straightforward to me, but then I understood my documents better than anybody.

But Ramasamy was explicitly concerned that I'd produced in defence material a letter dated 9 December 2005 and signed by Nigel Cox, one of my accusers. The letter confirmed that £62,950 could be deducted from Cox's monies held by Goldcrest.

Selva said this document concerned him because it was not clear whether it had been provided to the police despite the production order. Ramasamy warned a jury would find it odd that Nigel Cox had not mentioned this document in all of his statements. He said this appeared to support the suggestion that the police were unaware of it.

These were all fair points: I had no idea whether the police had discussed the document with Cox – but I knew that I'd disclosed it. But Ramasamy was worried that I would be accused of falsifying the Cox documents. He needed a rock-solid explanation, yet all I could offer, repeatedly, was that I'd disclosed the papers to the police and therefore, it should have formed part of the prosecution's evidence.

I began to get upset and a little angry.

I'd entered the conference with a severe headache and, by this time, had a full-blown migraine. I was getting annoyed that my legal team appeared to not believe me. Of all things, Ramasamy then warned me that I ran the risk of additional charges – such as perverting the course of justice – if it was believed that I'd forged the Cox documentation or failed to disclose key material following a production order. Such sentences, he observed, could also run consecutively: meaning more prison time.

None of this made any sense. I knew the document existed and had been handed over – and even began to wonder whether the police had destroyed it or conveniently 'lost' it. But the reality was that, without the Cox receipt and documents being accepted as court evidence, we had little with which to win a case. After a lengthy stand-off, we moved on to discussing the Starling and Cooper charges – and Ramasamy expressed similar concerns.

Next on our list of themes to discuss were the developments in Spain now that Garzon had added me to the indictment against Derbah. I explained that I believed Garzon had done it to silence me because I'd provided information to the CGI about potential terrorist activity.

During the discussion, it dawned on me that none of my lawyers had read all my documents. Lanchin and Ramasamy thought the two intelligence officers, Munoz and Esteban, had been indicted as rogue officers during the Spanish proceedings. I had to explain the whole situation again. At one point, Lanchin said: "You will be accusing Garzon and Spanish intelligence of corruption next."

If I had, of course, I would have been proved right.

The discussion went round in circles: me explaining my innocence, my legal team concerned they could not evidence key claims.

"I feel I'm pleading guilty to things I'm not guilty of. Lucent, I was monitoring on behalf of Spanish Intelligence," I protested. But it was to no avail.

At the end of the conference, I was in a heightened state of confusion and my protestations that I'd provided the police with all relevant material seemed to fall on deaf ears. My legal team advised that I should plead guilty and cut a deal with the prosecution. They did not want to fight key issues in court without documented evidence.

In those circumstances, none of us could see a way out. I was ill, suffering from the most severe migraines and chest pains, and at one of the lowest points in my life. Against every instinct I had, I caved in and accepted my lawyers' advice and agreed to plead guilty.

When I got back to my cell, my chest pains worsened and I felt sharp pains down my left arm. That evening, I later discovered, I'd suffered a heart attack that permanently damaged one of my heart muscles. I was in a mess – physically and mentally. Broken.

***

The following week passed by in a heavily medicated haze. I told my family to prepare for the worst in court. Up until that point, all they had seen was my usual optimistic self – telling them that I'd beat the rap because I had the evidence to prove the prosecution wrong. They couldn't understand why my lawyers now advised me to plead guilty.

When I look back at this period of my life, it feels like an out of body experience. I was ill and extraordinarily stressed. Not my usual, decisive self. An emotional and physical numbness had enveloped me.

Close friends have since said that they could never imagine me admitting to something I did not do. In those circumstances, the normal me would have fought, hustled and engaged with my adversaries until the uncomfortable truth emerged. It pains me to write the words even now, but for the first time in my life…I quit.

* * *

One week later, on 5 February, I was taken to Sheffield Crown Court to meet my legal team and finalise my plea. On arrival, I had a further conference with Lanchin, Ramasamy and Huzla Rawat, during which Selva said he'd re-read the case papers and that his advice was to "do the deal" with the Crown.

On 6 February 2008 at Sheffield Crown Court, I pleaded guilty to all charges in the scheduled case, including the Cooper and Starling offences. The Cox charge was dropped.

Ramasamy struck a deal with the Crown, effectively packaging all alleged offences into one case – including the Lucent and NatWest-related allegations. The US-style plea bargain erased any possibility of my sentences running consecutively, meaning I would spend less time in jail.

I can't say I was pleased or proud of the outcome. My lawyers were delighted to have pulled off what, in circumstances where their client had admitted guilt, would be viewed as a legal coup. But I knew I was innocent. So I was devastated.

Judge Lawler sentenced me to six and a half years in jail, meaning I would serve just over three. I'd already spent some time in prison, so I was eligible for parole in two and a half years.

When my prison cell door slammed shut that night, I stood alone in silence. Head bowed, defeated.

CHAPTER FIFTEEN
Fightback

The metallic clang of a nearby cell door shook me awake. I shot bolt upright and looked across the bed, expecting to meet Gill's eyes. Nothing.

Déjà vu.

I was feeling better after getting moved to HMP Doncaster in Yorkshire after sentencing. Having effectively abandoned my legal battle, there was no need for proximity to my solicitor or barrister. In fact, I wanted to be as far away from them as possible. Rightly or wrongly, I couldn't shake the feeling that they had let me down.

"Fuck you all," I thought, the fire inside my stomach beginning to reignite. "I'm not spending another day behind bars without fighting this betrayal with every fibre of my being."

The old Paul Blanchard had returned.

I'd been put on new medications following my heart problem and, steadily, made a physical recovery. I still suffered migraines, but they were more manageable now that I could take fresh air without being attacked by psychopaths inside Belmarsh. The general mental haze which often smothered my rational thoughts during the intense, stressful build-up to my fraud trial had lifted.

At Doncaster, I was given a single-occupancy cell with the luxury of floor space. It meant I could store my legal files in my cell and scour them during the day. I'd been spurred into action by the realisation that I faced hefty confiscation proceedings. The British state was using the Proceeds of Crime Act (POCA) to attempt to seize my assets, cash and properties: everything I had worked for.

What the hell was I thinking when I agreed to plead guilty? I couldn't immediately free myself, but I was damned if I was going to sit idly by and allow an injustice to take Gill's lifestyle and my children's inheritance from them.

With all defence material and prosecution exhibits to hand, I combed every document for peace of mind. Now reinvigorated, I figured that, regardless of what was in my files at this point, I'd achieve some sort of closure. The documents might even indicate whether the police had ignored evidence that could have cleared me.

I carefully unpacked forty-five boxes of paperwork before identifying the Cox prosecution exhibits. It took days. Eventually, my documents confirmed that each numbered prosecution exhibit matched precisely the materials I'd given to the police. That ruled out any lingering suspicion that the police had tampered with evidence. Something else was most likely amiss – but what?

I spent weeks reading and re-reading the legal material. Long days alone in my cell stretched into nights and, without even thinking about it, I blocked out the entire background noise of prison life. Food breaks at the servery were an annoying inconvenience rather than a social escape. I even took paperwork with me while I exercised in the yard. Nothing else mattered. A bomb could have exploded inside HMP Doncaster, and I wouldn't have noticed – I was so utterly focused on finding the anomalies I knew must have existed inside those evidence boxes.

And then...bingo! After a relentless and forensic search, I found it.

Tucked away within reams of invoices and accounts was a receipt from Cox. It had been assigned the exhibit number 3489 – and proved that, contrary to the prosecution's claim, Cox had OK'd Goldcrest's use of his funds.

I had a good reason to be angry, but forced myself to stay calm. I was thinking rationally again, albeit from behind bars. After assessing the situation, I concluded there was only one likely reason for the reported (by my legal team) inconsistencies in the court documents: my lawyers hadn't read all the paperwork. But they were experienced professionals, so how could that have happened?

I contacted Jude Lanchin to let her know what I had found. In her reply, sent to me on 21 February 2008, Jude confirmed that she had spoken to Selva, and that they accepted the Cox receipt had been missed. But Jude added that Ramasamy would still have advised me to plead guilty and cut a deal with the CPS.

Lanchin's letter stated: "[Selva] accepts that he missed this within the Crown's exhibits.

"He did so, however, as you had not provided any comments on it in that schedule, only in relation to it as a defence document – hence his focus on the document as a defence material only.

"Having said that, he understands your concerns and says you are right to have raised this matter. You made it clear to us that the document had been handed to the police and we did accept that, and Selva was pleased that his concern in that respect was misplaced.

"However...this was only one of very many factors in your cases and that we were considering at the start of that week. It does not in any way affect the advice that Selva gave as to the problems which were affecting the cases globally. The issue as to whether the police had the Cox letter was a secondary concern. The main focus was whether the Crown would claim the document was a forgery and use it against the defence."

Jude's letter also made it clear that she "fully endorsed" Selva's view. I was not happy with my legal team's response.

Five days after Jude's letter, she and Ramasamy visited me in Doncaster. Ramasamy belatedly acknowledged that the Cox receipt was part of the prosecution exhibits. But to my anger, he confirmed that his advice would not have changed.

During my prosecution, I'd reassured everybody that Cox had agreed to a settlement for an invoice raised by Goldcrest. I'd even provided the police with the receipt, signed by Cox, and would have been content for the signature to be analysed to verify its authenticity. So I couldn't understand why Ramasamy claimed his advice would have been the same if he had known about the receipt.

In my view, it disproved a key claim against me: that I walked off with Cox's money. It was an example of how I had been telling the truth about the criminal allegations against me, despite fears that I had not, and was something my lawyers could perhaps have seized upon in their broader legal arguments.

The discussion with Jude and Selva at HMP Doncaster seemed, to me at least, like an arse-covering exercise. But I was still wedded to both lawyers for a while longer. The confiscation proceedings were about to begin, and we knew that Judge Lawler would not take kindly to another change of legal representation. I was lumped with Jude and Selva, at least for the time being.

* * *

Simon Eldritch pleaded guilty for his part in the Lucent Technology and NatWest scams and was sentenced to four years in prison. His lawyers felt Simon had little choice.

Chris Eyre also pleaded guilty and received a two-year sentence. Darren Steadman was halfway through a four-year sentence for trying to steal almost £1m from Sir Terence Conran, and had his role in the NatWest scam taken into account by the Crown Court. John Allin was given a twelve-month sentence in addition to the five-year stretch he was already serving.

As each case concluded, I felt increasingly angry that official records would show Simon and I were convicted alongside the likes of Steadman and Allin. Media coverage of the convictions gave the impression we were all close allies, which was far from the reality. I despised the likes of Allin. But once I had pleaded guilty, I knew I would forever be associated with those I blew the whistle on. To this day, that fact hangs over me like a dark cloud.

* * *

My 'package deal' guilty plea also meant that Nick Peckham and Tom Copeland were forced to prepare without me for their trial in June 2008. Both men were subject to strict bail conditions. But Copeland, a US citizen, had no intention of sticking around.

One evening in late May 2008, a small Cessna 170 plane landed on a tiny grass runway at East Winch Airfield in Norfolk. It took off again minutes later. The private airfield is so remote that most planes that land there are simple crop-sprayers. But onboard the departing flight which headed out across the North Sea that night was a tall, 54-year-old American.

After landing in the Netherlands, Copeland travelled by train to the US Embassy in Paris. He obtained a new passport in France, claiming he'd lost the original, then boarded a flight for Mexico before crossing the US border into Texas. It was an elaborate escape from justice, particularly since Tom had a good chance of being cleared of all charges. Some might say that Tom was a fool to flee but, like me, he had lost all confidence in the UK's courts.

When the trial began the following month, Nick Peckham stood alone in the dock. One of his co-accused had pleaded guilty as part of a package deal, and the other had fled. Once that was disclosed to the jury, the odds were stacked against Peckham.

Incredibly, though, Nick Peckham walked out of the courtroom a free man. Perhaps more astonishingly, Tom Copeland was cleared in his absence. I'm sure Tom raised a glass to UK justice at that point! Technically speaking, Tom is still wanted in the UK for having skipped bail. But given that he was back home, with his feet up, it seemed clear that nobody was chasing him hard.

While I was pleased that Nick and Tom had rightly been cleared, it made me even angrier that I had been advised to plead guilty. Deep down, I knew that Nick, Tom and I would have disproved the charges if we had just stood our ground.

I was beginning to regret ever having met Jude and Selva.

* * *

On 24 June 2008, I was called to HMP Doncaster's reception and handed a large box of files containing thousands more documents. The Crown's case against me under the Proceeds of Crime Act (POCA) had arrived. Included in the case papers was what is known as a 'Section 16' statement prepared by the police's Regional Asset Recovery Team (RART). The statement allows the state to value a criminal's assets and assess how much of that wealth can be attributed to criminal activity. The state can then attempt to recover that 'criminal' sum.

Astonishingly, the RART calculated that I'd benefited from my "criminal" career to the tune of £11.2m. At this point, I couldn't deny the RART's use of the term "criminal" because I had pleaded guilty.

More than eleven million pounds! I was also informed that any failure to pay the sum requested meant I faced a further ten years in jail.

There are three parts to a 'Section 16' statement. The first covers 'particular criminal conduct' – in my case, the guilty pleas – which the state somehow estimated at £4.8m. The prosecution claims that the 'particular criminal conduct' figure is non-negotiable, although I would later disprove that.

The second section covers the rather vague area of 'general criminal conduct'. This is the amount a person is alleged to have benefited from through other illegal activities conducted over six years before being charged. At best, it is guesswork by the state. At its worst, this section could be viewed as attempted theft by the state because the POCA calculation often falsely assumes that other income results from crime. Interestingly, the traditional burden of proof within UK law – that the state must prove criminality – is reversed for this second section. Under the POCA, the defence must prove that the figures quoted are not the proceeds of crime.

The third section deals with a defendant's realisable assets: houses, cash, cars. That sort of thing.

Of course, the RART calculation was utter nonsense. It was an inflated figure designed to make me and my lawyers panic into handing over millions of pounds to a desperate and under-funded public sector. I had never earned £11.2m from criminal activity. My businesses turned over more than that figure and made substantial profits. But from that turnover, I had to pay staff, taxes, operating costs, rent, travel and many other costs long before any profit was earned.

I knew then that my POCA proceedings would be a long and drawn-out affair. I did not realise in 2008 that it would go on to be the longest-running POCA case in British legal history and would not be settled until 2019.

* * *

Six days after receiving my POCA papers, I received a visit from Vicky Brown at Bindmans – a young paralegal assisting Jude Lanchin. I liked Vicky. She had a calm demeanour and took the time to listen to clients. I told her that I was upset that I'd agreed to plead guilty and explained the background to the Cox documents and how I felt it undermined the evidence used to prosecute me.

During several visits, Vicky admirably fielded my complaints about Jude, Selva and what I considered their poor preparation for my court hearings. I explained that I was furious with them for missing the crucial Cox receipt and wondered what else they had overlooked. Poor Vicky had to sit there, taking notes, listening to me bad-mouthing her senior colleagues. I put her in an unenviable position, but she dealt with it all with good grace.

Vicky's notes from the visits, which I have retained, state. "*PB was still very upset about the Cox exhibit and the fact that Bindmans and barristers had not picked it up in the prosecution exhibits.*"

Another note adds: "*PB confessed that he was sorry he had entered the guilty plea especially in the light of the fact that in the £375,000 case the only evidence against him was Steadman, who was unreliable.*"

"PB said his solicitors and barristers did not know his case... that he had been given negligent advice in respect of the guilty plea."

A third note reveals the tensions between the legal team and me at the time. "*PB was incredibly upset about the fact that he was accused of forging defence documents by JL [Jude Lanchin] and barristers in conference – he said that if his team had known his case, they would have known that he had disclosed these same documents to the prosecution at the beginning of the case in 2006 and therefore had not made them up,*" Vicky writes.

* * *

In September 2008, I was downgraded from a Category B prisoner to Category D. It meant I was assessed as less of a risk and was eligible to attend an open prison. Consequently, I was transferred to HMP Moorland Open Prison (now Hatfield Prison). There, I was allowed town visits and the odd home visit – all on the proviso that I returned to the prison at a stipulated time. I delighted in seeing my family regularly and continued to use my cell time to work on clearing my name.

The food at Moorland Open Prison was far better than any jail I had been in. It contained many more fresh ingredients, and the cooks did not boil the nutrients and vitamins out of meals before serving them. That made the grub bearable, rather than inedible: a noteworthy upgrade on the congealed sludge I'd been served everywhere else. Consequently, I felt fitter and stronger.

During one family visit, Paul Jnr remarked that I "had some colour" back in my face for the first time since my heart problem. I couldn't tell whether he was taking the piss, but we rolled about laughing at the thought that a prisoner could be complimented on his tan! Dark humour continued to get us through tough times.

From early 2009, I was granted home visits, including one which lasted five days. It was such a joy to see Gill and to sleep in our marital bed again. We spent the time visiting Filey, strolling along the coast and planning what we would do once I was released. On other occasions, Gill hosted small dinner parties for our friends. The evenings spent sipping wine and eating rich food undid some of my physical improvement at the prison, achieved through regular exercise. But it was worth every mouthful.

It began to feel like old times again. I didn't even mind returning to the open prison. Life at HMP Moorland was manageable: I got on with my fellow inmates, and even some of the officers were friendly types with whom you could share the odd joke. They were a refreshing break from the stern-faced authoritarianism of Category B facilities.

In February 2009, however, my freedoms came to a sudden end.

At Moorland, inmates returning from home leave were ordered to attend the prison reception area to join the queue of people waiting to be re-admitted. The procedure mainly consisted of being searched – personal property was examined for any illegal items such as drugs, mobile phones or dangerous weapons. As I joined the queue one grey February morning, a senior prison officer spotted me and bellowed: "Blanchard! Come to the desk."

At the reception desk, I was surrounded by five officers and led to a nearby cell. I wondered what the hell I'd done to be banged up again after returning on time and sticking rigidly to the strict rules governing periods of leave.

I glanced at one of the junior officers, a puzzled look on my face, and asked: "What's going on?"

"You're being returned to closed conditions on the Governor's orders," the senior officer interrupted.

"Me? What did I do?"

"The police have concerns that you'll abscond," he said, handing me an official document spelling out the prison governor's reasons.

I browsed through it: *"Yadda, yadda, yadda...the police have received concerns that Mr Blanchard's risk of absconding is high due to outstanding confiscation order issues. He would therefore be located in closed conditions until the issues are resolved."*

Glancing back up at the senior officer, I spoke calmly, but firmly. "You're kidding me? I've just returned from home leave. If I was going to abscond, I wouldn't be here now – would I? I've never run away from anything in my life. This is bullshit!"

I tossed the letter back towards the guard, a little petulantly.

In fairness to the officer, he looked at me sympathetically. But it was no use. The decision had been made by the boss of bosses: the governor himself.

I was locked up for two hours, after which the heavy cell door swung open. In the doorway stood a small group of officers assembled to take me to HMP Moorland Closed Prison (now HMP Moorland) a couple of miles away. The officers made it clear they disagreed with the decision and said I'd been one of the easiest prisoners to manage, but none of us had a choice. I was handcuffed and shoved on a prison bus with several large bags crammed with personal possessions and legal papers. At the new site, I was allocated a single cell and was forced to settle back into the mind-numbing and disheartening routine of closed conditions.

In 2005, three years previously, inmates at Moorland Closed Prison had rioted. A report into the incident, published in 2006, warned that the prison's culture was "over-punitive" and "under-motivating". Yeah – and the cells needed a fucking good clean, too. It was the filthiest facility I had seen.

I appealed the governor's decision to relocate me and, in the absence of a justifiable reason for it, I won.

Bindmans' civil claims department oversaw my appeal against the prison move, and I received first-class advice and support. The prison was even forced to pay my £42,000 legal bill: the cost of keeping a violent criminal in a high-security prison for a year. It was a complete waste of taxpayers' money, but I'm glad the liability was not mine.

* * *

The prosecution in my POCA case had alleged that more than 100 companies I'd created, including 72 offshore entities, were my "alter ego" and used for money laundering or to hide assets overseas. Despite the thousands of pages of documents, accounts and transactions, the Crown's case couldn't have been summarised any more simply than that.

There was just one problem: the Crown's case was complete tripe and failed to understand how offshore finance works. Quite the opposite, the Crown's prosecutors appeared to make the schoolboy error of assuming that all offshore activity is illegal. A small part of me was reassured by how badly wrong the prosecution had got it. As an offshore consultant, I knew the relevant laws – and knew that I had abided by those laws. But a bigger part of me knew at this point that, given the prosecution's apparent lack of knowledge about the offshore world, the POCA case would take far longer to settle than anybody had previously anticipated.

One complicating factor was that the Crown had also asserted that I had "hidden assets". Again, by placing that unsubstantiated claim in the POCA document, the Crown knew the onus was on me, and my defence team, to disprove it. In some circumstances, particularly involving non-existent "hidden assets", this equated to us trying to prove a negative: an impossible task. But I was damned if I was going to just hand over my legally-earned assets. So I threw myself into challenging the prosecution's claims – and my first act was to ditch Jude Lanchin.

The split from Jude had been a long time coming. Our relationship had become increasingly fractious. Jude knew that I resented the advice – formally provided by Selva, as my barrister – to plead guilty and that I insisted I was innocent. She also knew that I felt she did not know my case papers well enough to defend my innocence.

To be fair, for my part I knew that, so far as she and my legal team were concerned, they wouldn't have advised me any differently. In fact, they were sure they'd served me well in ensuring, ultimately, a lower sentence.

It left us in a stand-off over the POCA case. Each time I protested my innocence and wanted to frame a response to the POCA documents to reflect that, Jude would point out that I had pleaded guilty on legal advice.

One example was my alleged role in the £375,000 NatWest scam. That sum formed part of the Crown's POCA claim – yet I knew for sure that my paperwork showed that I had not received a penny of the money. So how could it be included in the POCA claim?

Jude, however, repeatedly reminded me that the NatWest case formed part of my guilty plea. She wanted me to negotiate a deal over the POCA case, and I had no intention of doing that if the prosecution insisted my 'criminal' acts could be valued at £11.2m.

Jude and I would go round and round in circles. Our discussions became characterised by unyielding views. I urged Jude to review my criminal cases, this time taking into account all of my paperwork. But Jude insisted it would have no bearing on my POCA case.

It couldn't last.

* * *

My confiscation trial was listed for 16 August 2010. So in the first week of January 2010, I contacted Aziz Rahman, a solicitor from the firm Rahman Ravelli based in Halifax, West Yorkshire.

Rahman visited me in prison and agreed to take on my case subject to Judge Lawler's agreement. I then informed Bindmans that I would drop Jude, a move that triggered a meeting of my entire legal team in London. Attempts were made to get me to stick with Bindmans, Selva Ramasamy and Huzla Rawat. But my mind was made up. "Solicitors should read their client's entire case and then take instructions," I told a puzzled-looking group of lawyers. And with that, I was gone.

* * *

By the time Bindmans sent my case papers to Rahman Ravelli and my new legal team had familiarised themselves with the POCA proceedings, I was approaching my prison release date of 13 August 2010. The initial POCA trial date had been delayed to give my new lawyers some extra time to master their brief. And so it was that, in late July, I was visited by a senior paralegal from Rahman Ravelli, named Helen Lynch.

Helen was a game-changer.

From that very first meeting, my whole history took on a different legal perspective. Helen was a breath of fresh air. She left no stone unturned and meticulously mastered every detail of my case. Helen wanted to see every document, statement, account, email and judgment. She went through it all, line by line, and when things did not make sense to her, she asked detailed and probing questions. It often felt like I was being grilled by the police all over again, but I was reassured because I could sense that Helen 'got' it.

Helen would later reveal that she thought I was "off my rocker" when I first revealed my relationship with Spanish intelligence. But over time, the reality of my situation became clear. Through our chats, I realised that most people – even intelligent lawyers – could never conceive of meeting an intelligence asset. Instead, Helen politely reminded me, most people would find the idea far-fetched and unbelievable. But, as I would always point out, every major country globally has an active intelligence service. So, where do they get their information from?

People like me.

The day-to-day reality of intelligence work, particularly at policing level in states such as Spain, looks and feels nothing like a James Bond film. It is not fast cars, bikini-clad Halle Berry-types and midnight raids. Most of it is dull, grassroots information-gathering from people 'in the know' about a vital issue – including serious criminals and, in my case, those who encounter serious criminals. Helen grasped this reality quicker than almost any lawyer I have met.

There were, however, some concerns that arose from my long chats with Helen. In particular, she often looked confused when I referred to certain documents that I believed Bindmans held during my early legal cases. On occasions, Helen would respond by saying: "I don't know which file you're talking about, Paul."

My case involved thousands of documents, files, emails and ledgers. So I was not alarmed or suspicious when Helen initially responded with confusion: I just assumed the matter under discussion would be something she would grasp once she'd read the relevant paperwork.

Thankfully, these little inconsistencies nagged away. At Helen.

* * *

I walked out of HMP Moorland on 13 August 2010 and hoped it would be the last day I ever spent in prison.

It's funny: I never envisaged that I would be forced to go through the same period of re-adjustment into civil society that I had lived through in 1995. But here I was, following precisely the same path. Re-adjusting to civvy street was easier the second time around, though. I knew to be patient and not to get worked up when things at home became difficult. Not that being back home with Gill, and seeing my kids, was difficult – they were a joy to be around. Once again, they'd shown immense strength and support while I was behind bars.

No, the problems were in my head. I don't mean depression, mania or any other mental health condition. I mean the all-consuming feeling that

I had been betrayed by Spain's CGI and Judge Garzon. It was on my mind constantly and, naturally, that meant it impacted my home life.

Close friends would sometimes advise me to "let sleeping dogs lie". But the injustice of it all consumed me. I wasn't the same man. Spain had taken a piece of me – and, frankly, I wanted it back.

Before I ended my relationship with Bindmans, the Crown conceded that I hadn't benefited from the £4.3m Lucent scam because the cash had been frozen when it landed in Simon's Spanish bank account.

The figure for my recognised 'criminal conduct' in the POCA case was therefore reduced from £4.8m to just £543,500 – the bulk of which was reported to be the £375,000 NatWest scam cash, which I also intended to challenge. In total, the Crown now suggested that I had benefited more broadly from crime to the tune of £6.85m. It was still utter nonsense, but it was a lot less nonsense than before.

The balance of power in the POCA case had begun to shift towards me due to some sterling legal work. Helen Lynch, a humble and industrious paralegal from Halifax, Yorkshire, was proving to be a very effective brief. I just wish that I had discovered her, and Rahman Ravelli, sooner.

In terms of my realisable assets, the Crown also alleged that I held a beneficial interest in a property in Chelmsford, Essex, valued around £1.25 million, which they'd frozen alongside other assets.

* * *

My belief that Helen could get the allegation that I'd benefited from the £375,000 NatWest scam kicked out of the POCA case intensified when I transcribed a covert tape recording between Darren Steadman and Simon Eldritch.

Steadman had initially told the police that he withdrew the yacht scam cash from his Spanish bank account in Alicante on 23 October 2003. According to his original story, Steadman transferred £200,000 of the money to John Allin while in Marbella the following day: 24 October. Steadman also told the police that I had been in Marbella with my alleged co-conspirators when that money was withdrawn from Allin's account – and that I had been handed the cash.

But the police had since learned that the cash was withdrawn from Allin's bank on 28 October 2003. That was four days after Steadman claimed the cash had been handed to me. More importantly, the police confirmed that I flew back to the UK from Spain on the evening of 24 October. So I wasn't even in Spain when Steadman said I'd obtained the cash.

The police had relied on Steadman's initial statement during the early stages of my prosecution. Yet Steadman had misled the police, and detectives had belatedly caught him out.

In reality, Mo Khan had been the primary beneficiary of the £375,000 scam. The cash had eventually made its way to Khan, most likely as part of a 'smurfing' operation to launder a more significant sum. It was on 28 October, the day that John Allin made the £200,000 cash withdrawal from his account, that Mo Khan called me to ask for help in moving €9m to Dubai.

I could see the bigger picture, and the forensic Helen Lynch was beginning to piece it together. But it was a constant source of frustration that the UK authorities didn't give a hoot. To officials, the fact that I'd pleaded guilty to these alleged crimes when I was at the lowest point in my life meant that I was a perpetrator.

In my opinion, that was the cost of errors made by my legal team when key evidence went unread.

★ ★ ★

I needed more evidence that I had monitored the NatWest scam for Spain.

The team at Rahman Ravelli set about compiling transcripts for the recordings I had made of discussions with Fernando and Enrique. In addition, they transcribed audios of conversations I'd had with Steadman, Allin, Mo Khan and Simon. The point was to show that Steadman, Allin and Mo Khan had benefited from the plot.

Also included in the defence bundle was my version of events following the fraud perpetrated by Allin and Leach against mine owners Tom and Larry in Marbella on 30 April 2004.

I described how, initially, Allin was not arrested at the police station in Marbella and waited in the reception area – leaving him free to fax messages to Steadman. When Inspector Fernandez felt he had enough evidence, he sent his officers across the building to arrest Allin. That allowed me to go through Allin's paperwork and examine his mobile phone contacts – which confirmed links to Mo Khan and other British-Asian businessmen moving money through Spain.

In stressing to Inspector Fernandez the importance of retaining Allin's belongings, I had foolishly revealed my role as a CGI source. It was the beginning of the end of my relationship with Spanish agents. After my recent jail term, that was a painful memory and a sharp reminder that, while I was innocent, I was still in some way the architect of my downfall.

But Helen Lynch's superb work also highlighted how I had telephoned my intelligence handlers after the Malaga incident and that they were angry I'd revealed my role to police in southern Spain.

In 2019, that telephone discussion would be presented to a British court as evidence of my involvement with the CGI. But even in 2010, the importance of Munoz's words was unmistakable. He talked of my discussions, with his team, about 'Mohammed or terrorism'.

The 'Mohammed' to which Munoz refers is not, as has sometimes been claimed, Mohamed Derbah. It is Mo Khan.

By 7 May 2004, I had long disclosed what I knew about Mohamed Derbah and Tenerife. Instead, in the aftermath of 11-M in Spain, my handlers were far more interested in the terror threat facing Madrid and wider Europe.

Besides, I had never directly connected Derbah to terrorism. I had no information of use to Spain on that issue. Allegations about Derbah's links with terrorist groups were not made by me – and I was unaware of many of them until years later. What I had done, was disclose to CGI officers Mo Khan's reference to Al-Qaeda when he sought help to move money to Dubai.

I reiterate that point to avoid any confusion about which 'Mohammed' Fernando Munoz referred to on the audio recording.

The indefatigable Helen Lynch also oversaw the transcription of the covert recording of my final meeting with Fernando and Enrique in Madrid on 17 May 2004: the agents' ultimate betrayal, following which Spain cut me loose and warned Madrid would deny all knowledge of me.

During that meeting, Fernando revealed that police in Malaga had put some tough questions to the CGI because I'd mentioned Allin's tangential links to potential "terrorism".

A twenty-two-page witness statement from Sarah Hill – detailing how, as my personal assistant, she dealt with Fernando's unit in Madrid – further supported my evidence. Sarah's statement included her recollection of my relationship with Derbah and his associates. It also referenced my meeting in Madrid with the sub-director of the national police, Don Jesus Nieto Rodenas, on 1 July 2004 – at which I handed over dossiers on Mo Khan, Salahuddin Amin and other British men with suspected terror links. It was all witnessed by Sarah as a third party.

Sarah Hill still lived on Tenerife, where Derbah and his entourage operated. So, there was a significant risk attached to the assistance she bravely provided to my legal team. Yet Sarah firmly believed that assisting me was the right thing to do. I will be grateful to her until my dying day – a true friend and colleague.

Vidal, my lawyer in Spain, also provided a statement which included details of the meeting he attended, with Sarah, at the office of Don Jesus Nieto Rodenas.

My defence against the POCA claim grew stronger by the day. Helen Lynch coordinated a superb legal campaign, drawing on hard-hitting and corroborative evidence that proved beyond doubt that I had been a CGI asset. But the fact is, most of Helen's evidence had been available to my previous legal team before I was advised to plead guilty and spent a further two years in prison.

* * *

In idle moments after my release, as I sat reflecting on the maelstrom of events before my guilty plea, my mind would wander back to pre-trial briefings I'd had with Jude and Selva. Regularly, I was struck by how none of my legal team appeared to have complete knowledge of my files. Don't get me wrong: I appreciated the fact that my case was complicated – and that I probably sounded like a fantasist to those unfamiliar with all of the evidence. But my pre-trial legal team had seen and heard all the evidence. Right?

* * *

When my legal files arrived at Rahman Ravelli from Bindmans following my change of solicitor in April 2010, Helen Lynch compiled a detailed inventory of every document. But there was no sight of my original audio recordings.

For weeks, I told Helen that Mark Foley sent Bindmans more material. Helen checked with the Bindmans team, who were adamant that they'd sent everything they had.

Initially, Helen was busy familiarising herself with what had been delivered. So, I think she just assumed that I was wrong and was too polite to say. But after several months, I was still adamant: key material was missing from my files. Gradually, Helen sensed that I was not bullshitting or inventing convenient excuses for my conviction that would assist the POCA case.

Then she had a hunch.

During a hastily-arranged visit to the London chambers of Huzla Rawat, Helen discovered most of the missing material – including crucial audio recordings and a file marked 'Spanish Intelligence'.

Not everything that was missing was recovered on Helen's trip. But it finally seemed clear what had happened, and I had been right all along: Jude and Selva had not read all of the material related to my case before advising me to plead guilty. They couldn't have read all of the files because at least some of them had been gathering dust elsewhere.

You couldn't make it up. Crucial evidence which would have proved my relationship with the CGI – and disproved allegations that I helped to co-ordinate the Lucent and NatWest-related scams – had been stuck inside the office of Huzla Rawat the whole time.

In an email to Jude Lanchin on 14 March 2012, Helen summed up our thoughts in beautiful, understated fashion. She wrote: "I have to say that I found Huzla's efforts in this matter a little remiss...given the importance of the material to Mr Blanchard's case."

To my mind, Huzla Rawat should have told Jude Lanchin when the material had arrived from my previous junior counsel, Gillian Batts. Perhaps that's what happened – I simply don't know to this day. But in my opinion, this extraordinary oversight, however accidental, had the effect of sending me to jail. And for that reason, there is no forgiving what happened.

I remain angry almost beyond words at what happened. At the time, I fumed for months without really knowing who, if anyone, was to blame. There were days when I'd be all-consumed by the injustice, ill-health and stress which followed such an oversight by professional lawyers. But after a year or so, I realised that the issue was eating away at me from the inside and that, rightly or wrongly, I was the only person who felt so angry about it. That's the problem with injustice. It's always the victim who has to deal with the horrific fall-out. I'd already had one heart attack because of the stress – so I resolved to let my anger dissipate just enough to get on with my life.

* * *

Incredibly, I learned of a second positive legal development shortly after my missing files were re-discovered.

Vidal came to York for three days in February 2011 to compile and sign his witness statement for use in my POCA case. My Spanish lawyer was already viewed with cult-like status at my home, due to his generosity in coming to England to support me. His reputation in Yorkshire was about to soar further.

Vidal spoke little English, so Sarah Hill also travelled to Yorkshire to act as our translator. Within minutes of beginning our first meeting, we learned that, while I languished in prison in December 2009, Vidal had appealed Garzon's decision to add me to the Derbah indictment. Vidal had gone straight to the High Court in Madrid – and won!

His grounds for appeal were mind-blowing. It transpired that the undertaking I'd provided to Judge Garzon on 18 July 2001 was void. Judge Garzon, Fernando and Esteban were supposed to counter-sign the document in my presence and with an official translator and other judicial representatives present. But none of those critical requirements were in place back in 2001. According to Vidal, there were further breaches of Spanish law, too, which invalidated the entire document.

But more than that, the court in Madrid was presented with firm evidence that I had assisted Garzon and the Spanish authorities with information on Mohamed Derbah – and that I had been considered a protected witness. One court paper states: "[Blanchard] himself made photocopies of some of the documents to give to the police".

It may not have seemed like a key development to the untrained eye. But that was a direct reference to the very documents, and proof of me assisting Spanish intelligence, which Judge Lawler in Sheffield had requested from Madrid before my conviction in 2007. Remember, I had been told by Fernando that Spain would not publicly acknowledge my role. Yet there, in black and white, was an official reference to my relationship with the agents staring at us from a court document.

The translated court document states: "*This person in synthesis, and this is how it appears in his personal testimony, carried out various appearances in the police department, informing civil servants of a series of facts and at the same time contributing relative documentation of which he decided to relate in the courts summons (chambers), statements which he made under the position as a witness, with the pretence that he would be granted the status of a* **protected witness**.*"*

Spain's conniving judicial authorities had been hoist by their own petard!

The tide was turning.

* * *

In January 2011, a month before he flew to the UK, Vidal also discovered that the Spanish authorities had issued a summons for me to attend court in Madrid on 15 February 2011, to provide a witness statement in the case against Mohamed Derbah.

The summons was processed by the UK's Home Office, which refused permission for me to fly to Spain because I was still subject to tight licence conditions following my release from prison. Instead, Vidal appeared in court in Madrid on my behalf. There, he was informed that, due to my absence, the proceedings had been suspended. Inside the packed courtroom sat Mohamed Derbah and seventeen of his alleged accomplices. Mohamed greeted Vidal and told my lawyer he was pleased that I hadn't attended.

Through Vidal, Derbah said he bore me no malice and wished me well. I had no idea whether what Mohamed said was true, or whether he was simply posturing from inside the courtroom.

Over the next few months, Vidal persisted with enquiries to the Spanish authorities.

On 9 May 2011, he visited the court in Madrid and spoke with a friendly official. To everybody's surprise, Vidal's source informed him that Madrid had responded to Judge Lawler's application for assistance on 11 September 2008 – after I had pleaded guilty to multiple charges. The official broke with protocol and let Vidal see the response, which was approximately ten pages long and marked 'Confidential'. However, as Vidal began to read the document, a second officer within the courthouse intervened and took it away.

So had Britain's Home Office or Crown Prosecution Service suppressed Spain's response to Judge Lawler? And what exactly did the 'Confidential' Spanish report say? More importantly, though, why were my lawyers unable to see it after I had been jailed? As was often the case, I had more questions than answers.

* * *

The next twelve months were swallowed up by directions hearings and legal processes while I settled back into family life in England. But my license conditions and the legal freeze on my assets were beginning to bite.

I couldn't travel for work or trade using my old companies and assets. Once again, my incredible family supported me financially and emotionally. My children had long become adults and led busy professional and family lives of their own. But the sacrifices they made to help me out were testimony to their undying love. And then there was Gill – my quiet, softly-spoken but extraordinarily determined wife – without whom I would not have made it through those years.

* * *

Don't say I hadn't warned you!

In February 2012, the rest of the world discovered what I had known for some time: Judge Baltasar Garzon, the Spanish 'super judge' who attempted to prosecute General Pinochet of Chile and led the investigation into the alleged Tenerife mafia, was corrupt.

Spain's supreme court ruled that Garzon was guilty of illegally ordering jailhouse wiretaps so that the authorities could eavesdrop on conversations between prisoners and their lawyers during a major investigation into alleged political corruption. Spanish law only allows such actions in cases involving terrorism. Garzon had acted beyond his remit and was barred from the bench for eleven years, effectively ending his career as a judge.

While unsurprised by the news, I was nonetheless delighted. My protestations of innocence were built upon the idea that Garzon and CGI officers had betrayed me when they engaged me as an informer, or asset, only to later add me to the Tenerife-related indictments once their betrayal was complete. Now there was a definitive legal ruling in Spain that showed that Garzon had acted in an *ultra vires* manner in a separate case. Garzon denied that he acted beyond his legal remit in the wire-tap case, but he was never cleared.

* * *

With my defence against confiscation proceedings progressing, the Crown requested that the confiscation figure should be determined before any assessment of my realisable assets. It was an odd request and one that Judge Lawler rejected. Instead, the judge demanded an early evaluation of my assets. My business affairs, he knew, were so complex and unwieldy that trying to determine the benefit figure first would be meaningless and would cost taxpayers a fortune.

The prosecution team claimed that I was the ultimate beneficial owner (UBO) of all offshore companies that I'd incorporated – a nonsensical assertion, which suggested the state's lawyers knew little about the offshore finance sector Britain had unleashed on the world. The judge was instinctively doubtful about the Crown's claim, but set a 'properties trial' for 14 August 2012. To the consternation of the prosecution, he also directed that a test trial take place, focused on just one company I had incorporated for a client named Andrew Moulden. The purpose was to determine whether I was the ultimate owner.

I knew the answer was no, of course. The UBO had always been Moulden, a traveller-turned-businessman from Bradford. I created Andrew's company in Belize for inheritance tax purposes and he used it to purchase a property for £250,000. At the test trial in July 2012, the Regional Asset Recovery Team (RART) leading the POCA investigation produced a graph showing money flowing via several of my bank accounts to the client account of the lawyers used for the property purchase. On that basis alone, the RART had concluded I owned the property and that it was a realisable asset towards my POCA settlement. That's how simplistic their thinking was. But life, and especially finance, is always more complicated.

Thankfully, I had kept a detailed record of all Goldcrest clients and a declaration of trust, revealing the UBO of every company I had created. Moulden was from a traditional traveller family and, when he wanted my services, had turned up at my office with £250,000 in cash in a plastic bag!

After performing tougher-than-normal due diligence checks because of cash involved, I was satisfied that the £250,000 had come from a property sold by Moulden's father – so the legitimate origin of his money was not in doubt. So I logged Moulden's deposit in my client account at HSBC on the Isle of Man, along with all subsequent transactions relating to the same client.

Paper trails I kept revealed to the court the movement of cash from Moulden's father, through to the plastic bag and the purchase of Andrew's property via his Belize-based firm, Inglenook. My defence team was able to show that Inglenook legally owned the property, a fact also borne out by Moulden's court evidence.

The prosecution had picked the wrong battle with the wrong man! I was, and always have been, meticulous in keeping financial records. That's my job, and I like the order and certainty that it brings to my life.

Judge Behrens, who oversaw the test case, found in my favour when it concluded – a decision which blew a giant hole in the prosecution's claim that I owned all offshore companies created for my clients as part of a money-laundering exercise.

In summing up, the judge concluded: "Andrew Moulden is to be treated as a man of good character. He was not known to Paul Blanchard before this transaction; there is no evidence of any subsequent transaction between them. If this was a money-laundering exercise by Paul Blanchard, Andrew Moulden is not the most likely partner for such an exercise."

Bring on the main trial.

* * *

Following my test case victory, Judge Lawler was of the view that prosecutors should consider a compromise settlement ahead of a lengthy and costly (for taxpayers) full trial at which a large volume of documentation, relating to hundreds of offshore companies, would need to be reviewed. To the apparent frustration of the judge, however, the prosecution demanded a full trial.

Judge Lawler, remember, had overseen several of my cases over many years. More than anybody in the legal world, he was familiar with the background to my argument – namely my allegation (as he saw it) that I had been a CGI asset who had also supplied a small, but potentially significant, amount of information to British intelligence. He was aware that my defence team made several attempts to get Madrid to confirm my role. Judge Lawler himself had made one of those requests before my guilty plea.

Those issues seemed to be on the judge's mind as my full POCA-related trial neared.

On the eve of court proceedings, 13 August 2012, Judge Lawler convened a hearing at which he made one final attempt to see whether a compromise settlement could be reached.

Significantly, the judge said he was "dismayed" to learn that prosecutors had received instructions to proceed to a full trial.

"It will be recalled, I am sure, that I have had conduct of this case now for several years and have presided at every trial and every hearing," the judge said.

"I make it clear that I have come to no definitive conclusion in this matter and if forced to a hearing will conduct it and will determine it on the evidence – and I pause there to say that, although I may be wrong, a good deal more may come out. However, I am bound to say, upon my reading, that the Crown would be well-advised to re-think their position.

"I merely express the Court's concern. And it is my view that this matter, as I have had it outlined to me on previous occasions, can reasonably and sensibly be settled with substantial benefit to the public purse, even taking into account the tax situation the State will still win, if I may put it that way, by a substantial amount."

"A good deal more may come out." The strong warning to the Crown could not have been more explicit. And it was not said by my defence team or me. It was uttered by the man in charge of proceedings. Judge Lawler

had been careful with his words to remain independent. But my defence team and I knew exactly what he meant.

* * *

The Judge's pre-trial warning shook the prosecution into action. Over the next few days, Crown barristers and members of the RART met with my legal team, led by Helen Lynch, and hammered out a deal that suited all parties. Once the Crown's lawyers drafted the agreement, I signed on the dotted line with a massive smile on my face.

At that point, I believed my POCA settlement was finalised and that, with my assets unfrozen, I would soon be able to trade freely again. Goldcrest would be up and running again within weeks, and I could get on with rebuilding my business and career.

However, a few months later, the proposed deal fell apart amid incessant squabbling between both legal teams – each convinced that their interpretation of the complex financial requirements which underpinned the agreement was correct.

Two years after the deal hit the rocks, in August 2014, I was dealt an enormous blow when the exceptional Helen Lynch left Rahman Ravelli for unrelated reasons. Within weeks of Helen's departure, the proposed POCA deal was in such a mess that it had to be scrapped. After years of hard work, everybody was back where we had started.

Judge Lawler was furious. He gave both parties until February 2015 to resolve matters. But attempts to reach a revised agreement quickly collapsed. To the judge's annoyance, the case was heading back to a full trial – which Judge Lawler then revealed he felt unequipped to oversee because it would be too complicated. To everybody's amazement, Judge Lawler circulated a memo explaining that he believed a full trial would be "outwith my area of competence". He transferred the trial to Judge Gargan, who had more experience overseeing complex financial cases.

With the POCA deal scuppered and a full trial beckoning, my application for information from Spain took on renewed importance because my time in Spain was relevant to the complicated court proceedings.

Time was dragging on due to both sides' legal wrangles. My files passed through two solicitors after Helen Lynch left Rahman Ravelli. The complexity of the case was unfair on both newcomers – but I had to find somebody who could master the brief as well as Helen.

* * *

Helen Lynch was an exceptional young lawyer. She was meticulous and took the time to understand my entire legal history. She was a diligent investigator and knew the law inside out. Helen was also humane, humorous and exceptionally bright – the sort of woman who intimidates some men. Not me. I cannot thank Helen enough for her hard work, compassion and her dry, northern wit. She cared about her clients and, because of her 'hunch' regarding the whereabouts of my missing files, she will always be held in the highest regard within my family.

CHAPTER SIXTEEN
'Fugitive'

In January 2016, shortly after his surprise decision to withdraw from my case, Judge Simon Lawler received Spain's abhorrently late response to his 2007 request for information from Madrid.

Proving my role as a Spanish asset was central to my cases, including the proposed POCA deal. So, in an ideal world, I would have wanted Judge Lawler to share copies of Spain's reply with my lawyers immediately. Instead, he sent it first to the Crown Prosecution Service (CPS).

That meant my lawyers were forced into a legal battle even to see the documents. In July 2016, the CPS wrote to my solicitor saying Spain's reply contained nothing significant.

That was an extraordinary claim, given what emerged later.

* * *

Neither my defence team nor the police's regional asset recovery team (RART) wanted the POCA case to end in a full-blown trial, so a compromise deal remained a possibility.

With that in mind, in 2016, I initiated the next stage of my attempt at exoneration and sought a solicitor to work on appealing my 2008 convictions. After careful research, I approached Keith Wood at Lewis Nedas Law in Camden, London.

Recruiting Keith was a masterstroke. Yorkshire born and bred, he is a thoughtful and friendly, yet pugnacious and hard-working, solicitor who doesn't pull his punches. Keith had significant experience handling complex fraud, organised crime and asset confiscation cases – and a reputation as a lawyer who never gave up.

Keith quickly mastered the complexities of my case and spoke with impressive clarity about case law. He doesn't butter-up clients, either: Keith was straight-talking but always offered solutions to problems. My kind of lawyer.

Working with Rahman Ravelli before I met Keith, I'd concocted a plan to use the POCA case to subpoena agents Munoz and Esteban: forcing them to give evidence under oath in the UK. Keith liked the idea and said he could base my appeal against convictions on any confirmation of my intelligence-related role that emerged from POCA proceedings.

At this point, the Crown still wanted £6.4m to settle the POCA case. I was innocent of the crimes I'd been jailed for in 2008. But I was also savvy enough to know that, having reluctantly pleaded guilty, I'd have to offer something.

My POCA trial was set for December 2016. But in November, and through the dogged determination of my legal team, the Crown finally handed over Spain's 'confidential' reply to Judge Lawler: ten months after it arrived. That and a mix-up over timetables delayed court proceedings further.

Madrid's files were revelatory. But they made for bitter-sweet reading.

***

Spain's response to Judge Lawler was dated 20 June 2008: eight years and five months before my legal team obtained it. Nobody outside Spain could tell when the letter was actually drafted. Irrespective, I'd been left with no alternative but to plead guilty to serious offences and was even in prison when Madrid claimed it replied to a senior British judge.

The covering letter accompanying Spain's documents was a confusing mess of contradictory and illogical claims, poorly explained references and carefully worded misdirections: the sort of correspondence you'd expect from a police-intelligence service that did not want to provide information on a former asset.

Spain's authorities denied, for example, that I was an intelligence 'agent' and claimed that I was seeking to mitigate criminal acts by *alleging* I'd collaborated with the CGI.

Although I have always used the generic term 'agent' to describe my role, more accurately it took the form of that of an 'asset': commonly defined as 'any resource utilised by an intelligence organisation for an operational support role'. There's little doubt that's what my expertise was used for.

So Spain's belated response craftily denied something I'd never claimed. The subtle misdirections were designed to make the British judges believe Madrid had never heard of me or was a liar. But there was a problem for the Spanish. The larger cache of documents included reports I'd handed to Fernando and Enrique, making a mockery of Madrid's stance.

Spain's evasiveness was made all the more ludicrous by a section that confirmed I'd provided intelligence on John Allin, including his connection to individuals allegedly involved in Northern Ireland and Islamist terrorism. The reply to Judge Lawler even mentions the British-Asian men I monitored for the CGI, referring to them as the "Grupo de Birmingham".

And Spain's reply contained an even more important reference. "He [Blanchard] was trying to use the possible protection offered by our relationship," it stated.

'Relationship'?

Gotcha!

That one word confirmed the reality of a situation Madrid had previously denied for years. I did have a 'relationship' with the CGI, and Spain had finally acknowledged it.

I should have been furious about the general evasiveness of Spain's reply. There was no acknowledgement of Judge Garzon's assurance that I was a protected witness, or that I had monitored suspected crimes for the CGI. In my view, Spain was trying to make the UK courts believe I was a criminal and fantasist. Denying things I had never claimed, implying I was the manipulator while simultaneously acknowledging our 'relationship': these misdirections are the tradecraft of experienced intelligence professionals who hide realities and create plausible deniability.

Spain's response also claimed its intelligence services had "no record" of phone calls between CGI officials and me. But that played straight into my hands.

It is possible Spain's evidence was misplaced or destroyed. But I had recorded more than forty of the seventy-two telephone discussions I had with Munoz and Esteban. Having retrieved my audio material, I could prove extensive contact with both agents. Spain may not have held the evidence, but my lawyers certainly had it.

I had to move fast, though, because my future finances depended on proving everything before any POCA settlement.

* * *

Through Spain's documents, I learned that in April 2013 a new Madrid-based prosecutor named Pedro Martinez Torrijos asked to interview me as a suspect in his continued case against Mohamed Derbah.

Torrijos's request came twelve years after I'd approached the CGI and been offered protected witness status, and six years after Judge Garzon's unforgivable betrayal.

My first thought was to dismiss Torrijos as naïve. Did he honestly believe I would now assist a trumped-up case against myself? I'd gone to jail because of Spain's betrayal, suffered a heart attack in prison and had my assets frozen for ten years. I'd lost millions of pounds, my livelihood, friendships and businesses – when all it would have taken to keep me on friendly terms was one letter from the court in Madrid acknowledging I'd been Spain's protected asset.

I considered Torrijos' motivations. It seemed evident Spain was still struggling to prosecute Derbah without my evidence. And if prosecutors in Madrid now correctly surmised that I was not prepared to assist them, they would have an obvious motivation for trying to prosecute me. That way, their lawyers could drag me into a Spanish court.

In April 2017, I received a visit from two North Yorkshire Police constables asking whether I'd answer a long list of questions attached to Torrijos' 2013 interview request. The tone of Torrijos' queries left little doubt that he was hostile.

Politely, I told the police officers that I had no intention of assisting. I wanted to say: "Tell the Spanish to go fuck themselves," but held my tongue. The officers were just messengers.

I predicted what would happen next.

* * *

The knock at the door arrived on 2 May 2018.

"Mr Paul William Donald Blanchard?"

I nodded slowly.

Police officers standing outside my apartment in York had become an all-too-common occurrence. But this time, there was a twist. Two officers, one in uniform, were accompanied by a television crew.

"You are the subject of a European Arrest Warrant issued by Spain on 13 April and received by North Yorkshire Police via the National Crime Agency. You are hereby under arrest and must come with us to York Police Station, where you will be held overnight. You are legally required to attend Westminster Magistrates Court in London tomorrow," the first officer explained.

While I had guessed that Spain might pull this trick, I was caught off-guard by the timing. And I was a little confused by the arrangement.

"I have no quarrel with local police, officer. But, just to be clear, am I under arrest? You didn't appear to read my rights. And what are those people doing here?"

I pointed over the policeman's shoulder towards the TV crew.

The officer's response was polite, but firm. "It is not a standard UK arrest, Mr Blanchard. But you are under arrest and legally required to come with us. The relevant authorities in Spain have issued a Europe-wide warrant and we are obliged to take you in to custody,"

"To answer your final question, these people are from the BBC. They're filming a documentary. Will you allow them to film inside your home?"

I looked back at the camera crew and asked: "They need my permission to film?"

"Yes, sir," one of the officers confirmed.

"OK. In that case, they most certainly cannot film," I replied. "They can switch that bloody camera off, thank you."

As I spoke, I leaned forward and pushed my hand over the camera lens. The cameraman let out a disappointed groan and stopped filming.

Senior managers at the National Crime Agency, which receives all extradition requests in the UK, and North Yorkshire police had invited the BBC to film a daytime documentary series called *Fugitives*. When I discovered the series title, I couldn't help but raise a smile. A 'fugitive' is somebody who flees from justice. Yet, I wasn't exactly on the run. I was at home and easily located at the property Gill and I had lived at for years. Until that moment, I'd not even been made aware that I was a wanted man. How could I possibly be a 'fugitive'?

Still, it was nice to discover that the police informed daytime TV journalists at the BBC that Spain had issued an arrest warrant before me, or my lawyers, knew about it. To make a serious point, I'm not sure that's appropriate. Reality TV is now awash with cheap programmes about the daily struggles of policing. Consequently, the police sometimes seem more concerned with their public profile – how they appear on the telly – than the natural course of justice. As somebody who has been on the receiving end of a miscarriage of justice, I find that concerning.

With the film crew waiting outside, the two policemen explained more about why they'd been sent to arrest me. One of the officers showed me a copy of Spain's EAW, while the other explained that he had "no choice" but to follow up on the request.

Calmly, I tried explaining to the officers that Spain's request was malicious and that I had "kept my head down" since leaving prison in 2010. But I knew the police were compelled to ignore any protest – even one as civil as mine. Thankfully, Gill was at lunch with a friend, so she missed the entire incident. I told the police I'd need to call her, as well as my lawyer, at the first opportunity – or she would worry when she returned to an empty apartment.

The lead officer nodded in agreement and explained a little more about what would follow. Once at Westminster Magistrates Court, he said, an extradition request would be formally lodged by the Crown Prosecution Service on behalf of Spain, and I'd be given the opportunity to appeal against it.

I asked: "What does Spain want to extradite me for, exactly?"

"Their argument is that you were the financial architect of a Tenerife-based organised crime group, Mr Blanchard," an officer volunteered. "It's all in the warrant."

I glanced at the EAW document and saw only Spanish before looking back at the officer.

"Is it? It's hard to tell," I replied. The officer shrugged.

After collecting medications for my heart condition, I was led downstairs and into the back of a police van. The officers declined to handcuff me, something I appreciated and thanked them for because, by this point, my neighbours were watching events unfold from behind twitching curtains. I was driven to York Police Station, where I was held overnight in a cramped, cold and damp-smelling cell. The pesky TV crew made another attempt to film me at the station, but I refused permission once again.

The police station staff were surprisingly polite. They made sure I had a supply of hot drinks and, later that evening, brought through some food. Some of the older officers were even sympathetic, especially when they saw my heart medication.

I'd not been inside York Police Station for several years. It would be fair to say that the aggressive, *Sweeney*-style attitude of past officers had changed. The new generation was more thoughtful and less jack-the-lad.

In the UK, I was first arrested in connection with my Spanish activities in 2004: fourteen years before Madrid issued an EAW naming me as a suspect. It had been eight years since I was released from a UK prison sentence I shouldn't have served. But after I was released in 2010, I simply got on with my life. Yet the Spanish remained determined to pursue Mohamed Derbah – who they had first arrested in 2001 but never prosecuted.

Derbah remained Spain's 'Public Enemy Number One', and a new Madrid-based judge had now made it obvious he would sacrifice me to get to Mohamed. Clearly, I still considered collateral damage by my former allies. This was a fresh betrayal.

I couldn't sleep at the police station. The cell was too uncomfortable and my mind raced. So I reflected on how to tackle Spain's latest betrayal from the UK.

* * *

The eerily familiar clang of a cell door jolted me awake. It was 5am. I'd been warned to prepare for an early journey south.

When the cell door swung open, a police officer strolled in, whistling while carrying a mug of tea and a snack. I gulped down the refreshments and soon climbed into a waiting custody van.

We hit traffic just outside London, delaying our arrival at Westminster Magistrates Court. The modern courthouse sits on the busy, polluted Marylebone Road and deals with all extradition cases in England.

Once inside, I was taken to detention cells beneath the courtrooms. Despite the early hour, the cells were crammed with prisoners or accused awaiting their appearance before a judge. I'd contacted my solicitor, Keith, the previous evening and he arranged for Ben Cooper, a barrister at Doughty Street Chambers, to attend court.

My relationship with Cooper got off to an inauspicious start. I struggled to hear a word the softly spoken barrister said in the court's noisy detention area and didn't really understand what my barrister's tactics would be.

Overnight, my family arranged to attend court. Paul Jnr was on a business trip to America, but he asked a London-based friend and journalist, Connor, to observe proceedings. Gill and Sarah travelled to Marylebone as early as they could.

My wife and daughter were angry that I had been arrested at Spain's behest. They had long known that Garzon was corrupt. And they still fumed over Madrid's refusal to acknowledge that I'd assisted Spanish agents before my 2008 convictions.

To most people, Spain is rightly considered an advanced western democracy and, diplomatic rows over Gibraltar aside, a solid pre-Brexit ally of Britain inside the EU. So many Brits instinctively trust Spanish politics and law, including its judicial process.

But my family knew the darker side of Spain. They knew that the Spanish judiciary could be as corrupt as any dictator or gangster. Garzon, a world-famous judge, was found guilty of approving illegal wiretaps to record prisoners' conversations. So my family knew about the questionable methods employed by the judge who initially oversaw the Derbah investigation.

Flustered but determined to hear the 'evidence' against me, Gill and Sarah arrived in London ahead of my court appearance and waited upstairs. And they waited.

Other hearings stretched long into the afternoon before a clerk finally called my case.

The courthouse itself was chaotic. Since my release from prison, Britain's criminal justice system had suffered from public sector austerity imposed following the 2008 financial crisis. Service cuts meant that courts operated on tight budgets and low staffing levels just as 'demand', in the form of alleged crimes, soared.

Moreover, Legal Aid cuts meant fewer prisoners or suspects received state help with legal costs. The knock-on effect was that many law firms laid-off staff or did not fill vacant positions, meaning heavier caseloads for the lawyers who remained and less time spent on each case.

Penny-pinching meant that, at times, the 2018 criminal justice system was a clusterfuck.

Prison transport arrived late arriving for hearings. Solicitors and barristers failed to show up on time amid scheduling mix-ups, and flustered lawyers would scurry around the courthouse frantically trying to find a quiet corner in which to brief clients during the seconds they could spare before hearings.

Inside courtrooms, paperwork was often misplaced and judges sometimes started proceedings only to find that they'd not received vital information. Satellite links to prisons, which allow the accused to 'appear' before judges remotely, often failed due to inadequate technology or a lack of trained court staff.

The system tottered on the brink of meltdown. And Westminster Magistrates Court, one of the UK's flagship courthouses, was not spared its problems.

On the morning of my appearance, Paul Jnr's friend witnessed a hearing in which the extradition judge had no way of communicating with a Hungarian defendant giving evidence by satellite link from prison, because the court-appointed interpreter had been double-booked. As farcical scenes played out inside the courtroom, one paralegal scoured the reception area outside, asking random members of the public whether they spoke Hungarian. To no avail.

So those in court watched helplessly as the confused-looking defendant on the screen laughed at a frustrated prison screw trying to mime the words 'postponed' and 'delayed'. Eventually, a second guard appeared on screen and unceremoniously shoved the prisoner through a door and out of sight.

"Well," the unimpressed judge sighed. "I think we'll just move on."

***

The wait for my court appearance stretched deep into the afternoon. But Ben Cooper was confident that I was not considered a flight risk and would make bail.

When my case was finally heard, it was explained to the judge that I had been detained under the EAW, which is valid across all EU member states.

Even though my arrest came after Britain's 2016 vote to leave the EU, the British government had agreed to process existing EAW requests during the 'Brexit' transition period – meaning I could not simply ignore the warrant.

There are, however, legal clauses that allow a suspect to contest an EAW. So unless an individual gives permission to be extradited, EAW applications can become a long and drawn-out process. After my arrest, I told Keith Wood that I would fight Spain's request and Cooper was briefed accordingly.

Initial extradition court hearings are designed to ensure the arrested person is the individual named on the warrant, and to inform the arrested person and their lawyers about the alleged crimes. The judge then sets a date for more detailed court proceedings and decides whether to grant bail or remand the suspect in custody.

Having been brought up from the detention cells, I was ushered into the courtroom and asked to sit in the 'dock' to the right of the judge's bench.

Respectfully, those inside the courtroom stood as the judge entered and took his seat. When everybody else sat down once the judge had his feet under his desk, I was asked to remain standing. I confirmed my name and date of birth, and only then was I allowed to sit.

CPS lawyers then attempted to guide the judge on my alleged crimes. But there were so few details on Spain's EAW that it was not immediately clear why I'd been arrested. Spain had not sent a fully translated copy of the warrant – an oversight seized upon by the unimpressed judge, who ordered that one should be sent to him within seven days.

Attention then turned to whether I would be bailed.

Initially, the CPS argued that – given my past convictions and the nature of the allegations against me – I represented a flight risk and should be remanded in custody. But the judge baulked at the idea of further overcrowding Britain's prisons and instead entertained the idea that I should be bailed, wear an electronic tag on my leg and report to police in York three times a week.

Buoyed by the judge's harsh instincts, the CPS lawyer suggested I should also be placed under strict curfew: between 7.30am and 9.30am each day.

The judge warned that any breach of such bail conditions could result in me being taken into custody. He concluded proceedings by setting bail at £50,000.

But I had another problem.

As I was led back to the holding cells, Sarah realised that she had just minutes to get to the bank and make the bail payment before returning to lodge my paperwork. Incredibly, the bail office at Westminster Magistrates closes shortly after the final court hearing.

Sarah sprinted along Marylebone Road towards Baker Street, where she completed the transfer of funds that she and Paul Jnr had put together. When Sarah returned to the courthouse, she was out of breath but delighted. But it was all in vain. In Sarah's absence, the bail office had closed, and 'jobsworth' staff refused to process the paperwork that would have allowed my release that evening.

Sarah and Gill were furious, but there was nothing that could be done. My wife and daughter travelled home alone. I was transported from Westminster Magistrates to HMP Wandsworth across the River Thames in south London, where I spent a cold and uncomfortable night back in prison.

HMP Wandsworth is a large Category B facility. Former inmates include Oscar Wilde, Ronnie Biggs and Ronnie Kray. But the prison's high walls hide an unusually macabre past. It is famous for being an execution site and was one of the last UK prisons to maintain a gallows – long after England's final hanging in 1964. The Prison Service maintained Wandsworth's gallows until 1993, just in case bloodthirsty British MPs voted to restore capital punishment.

My bail forms were finally processed the following day. It was a lonely journey home.

At a directions hearing the following month, July 2018, my continuing bail arrangements were re-discussed with the judge.

I fully expected Ben Cooper to fight hard for the withdrawal of onerous and regular arrangements under which I had to wear a tag and report to the police.

But in my view, Cooper's approach was too deferential. In the absence of stiff opposition, the judge simply dismissed the idea of fundamental changes to bail. Instead, my 'curfew' hours were amended to between 1am and 3am each night.

Superficially, it looked like the change would save me from having to stay at home until 9.30am every day. But immediately, I knew it would create a bigger problem: police officers would sometimes be forced to attend my home in the middle of the night to check I'd complied with bail conditions.

But Cooper said little in response. As the hearing progressed, I waved my hand to try to catch the judge's attention and speak for myself. But you can't 'hail' judges like taxis in UK courtrooms.

Before Cooper even sat down at the end of the hearing, I knew that I needed a different barrister. I'm not saying Ben isn't good at his job, just that his style did not match my needs.

The journey home that day also gave me some time to reflect on my arrest. After years of silence, police and judges in Spain were suddenly gunning for me again. Why?

* * *

"It's probably Mohamed Derbah's book, Paul."

Paul Jnr's journalist friend, Connor, was on the other end of the phone. "I asked around. Derbah's autobiography has seemingly spurred Spain's authorities back into action. They're incensed. Derbah denied everything, including allegations that he's a mafia boss, and presented himself as a legitimate businessman and adviser to West African states. All-round Mr Nice Guy. Spanish officials are incandescent with rage and are gunning for him. To get to Derbah, though, they must go through you: because you are still the key witness to his alleged frauds. Maybe they want you to turn QE. Maybe they will just sacrifice you. I doubt they care which it is – no offence meant."

"None taken," I replied. "But you know they are alleging I was part of Derbah's so-called mafia?"

"Sure they are. And everybody else, too," Connor said. "Several people on that indictment probably shouldn't be on it. But you created companies for Derbah. You also gave key financial information to authorities in Madrid but later said you wouldn't give court evidence. So they are going to trample over you to get to Derbah. You are collateral damage. It's Spain, Paul: you know what it's like."

I sighed. "Exactly! But the reason I won't give court evidence against Derbah is that officials in Madrid did nothing to stop me from going to jail when I needed their help – after everything I'd done for the CGI."

"Sure," Connor replied. "But do you think Spain gives the slightest shit about that? Rightly or wrongly, they want Derbah. They've wanted Derbah since before you went to them in 2001. And if you're not with them, then they think you're against them. If they betrayed you in 2007, do you think they are going to play nicely now?"

"No. I wouldn't expect that," I replied. "But they could have let sleeping dogs lie. I've had to since I left prison," I replied.

"I hear that. That's why Derbah's book probably has something to do with it," Connor suggested. "The authorities in Madrid think Mohamed is rubbing their faces in it. He's presenting himself as an innocent 'man of the people. He was arrested seventeen years ago, and they haven't been able to prosecute him. But with his book, he appears to have awoken the Siesta State!"

Despite the grave situation, I chuckled. "Droll. That one of your best?"

"Yup! Listen, let me do some gumshoe work. I'll see what we can find out about developments in Spain and Tenerife. I've got a contact at *El Pais,* the Spanish newspaper. In the meantime, are you holding up OK? Gill, Sarah and Paul Jnr?"

"Me and the kids will be OK. I'm used to being dragged through legal mud, and the kids are mentally tough. But it hurts Gill. She doesn't need this again. What did you think of Ben Cooper, my barrister?"

Connor paused. "Ben...doesn't seem to be the right fit for you. He seemed too 'nice' for a case involving a corrupt Spanish judge. You probably need a street-fighting lawyer. Ben is very bright. But his style might not be the best fit for your case."

"Thanks. I've been thinking the same thing," I replied. "I'm going to look elsewhere. I'll spend some time putting together a list."

"OK," Connor concluded. "But the way Spain is coming after you? You might need an army of lawyers."

I didn't know it then, but the hack's gallows humour would prove to be prophetic.

* * *

George Hepburn Scott was the street-fighting barrister I needed. Cerebral and impressively straight-talking, George was described on Church Court Chambers' website as a 'tour de force'.

Hepburn Scott was called to The Bar in 1999. By 2017, he'd developed a reputation as a fearless, unflappable and approachable barrister who specialised in extradition cases and complex criminal law.

He was also a winner. George once won back-to-back victories in separate Court of Appeal cases in London before heading to Sussex to continue a complex rape trial. He worked tirelessly, and I knew that my case required such commitment.

On paper, George seemed like the perfect fit. But what would he be like in person?

After calling Hepburn Scott's office, I arranged to meet him in London and offered to pay for the consultation. "No need, Paul," George said. "Let's meet to discuss your case and requirements, I'll give you my legal view and we can take it from there. If after that you feel I'm the right barrister, then we'll proceed."

He'd already adopted my favoured no-nonsense approach.

During that initial meeting at George's chambers, he listened intently while I talked him through my history. Every now and then, the lawyer nodded. When he interjected with a question, it was always forensic and showed he'd taken everything in. George didn't miss a trick.

Over the years, I've got used to being stared at by wide-eyed lawyers as though I'm crazy. I guess my unconventional history – ex-millionaire, three-time prisoner, Spanish intelligence asset who blew the whistle on organised crime – invites that response. But George was different.

"Wow, Paul! You certainly have cheesed off an impressive list of powerful people," he joked, leaning back in his chair. "But that doesn't worry me. My question for you is simple: what evidence, beyond your own words, do you have to support what you are saying?"

It was *the* killer question, and I was not surprised to hear it. Thankfully, this time, I was prepared. Ten years after I was convicted for fraud because I could not show that I was a CGI asset, I was back in possession of audio recordings and paperwork that proved it.

Hard, documented evidence. Not hearsay. George's eyes lit up and a smile broke across his face. We were in business.

* * *

I contacted Keith and told him about George. My solicitor contacted Church Court Chambers and the two men hit it off. I finally felt confident I had a legal team who could clear my name.

But things got even better.

After an early review of my material, Keith and George agreed: the fact that the intelligence services were involved in my case meant I also needed a Queen's Counsel (QC) on board. The title 'QC' indicates that a senior barrister is experienced and has dealt with challenging cases, including those at the Court of Appeal. George was an experienced and talented advocate, but not yet a QC.

In normal circumstances, I'd have had reservations about the cost of a three-man legal team for what promised to be a long battle. But because my assets were still frozen during POCA proceedings, I stood a good chance of receiving Legal Aid. Besides, Keith and George already suspected that my case could end at the Court of Appeal: making a QC essential. My lawyers made the Legal Aid application and the appointment of a QC, or silk, was approved.

Enter 'Mr Extradition'.

* * *

Mark Summers QC is a barrister who instils fear in opponents and judges alike. Fiercely intelligent, forensic, silver-tongued, and occasionally cutting: Mark knows extradition law inside out.

Summers' track record was unparalleled, earning him the nickname 'Mr Extradition'. He has been involved in some of the highest-profile cases in modern years, including extradition requests linked to the Enron scandal and the financial crash of 2008. Summers also defended in the case of

Shrien Dewani, a newlywed UK citizen cleared of arranging the murder of his wife.

Mark has defended hackers accused of breaching the computer networks of NASA and the Pentagon, as well as men on the FBI's 'Most Wanted' list. But I was won over by his significant experience in dealing with cases involving intelligence services and terrorism. Incredibly, these included three cases tangentially linked to mine: the 'Operation Crevice' fertiliser bomb plot, 9/11 and the Madrid bombings.

Summers' CV was gold standard. So when George recommended Mark, I did not hesitate to bring him on board.

'Mr Extradition's' status was cemented months later, when he represented the controversial Australian journalist and Wikileaks founder, Julian Assange, during the United States' attempt to extradite the alleged hacker from the UK.

In 2010, Sweden had issued an international arrest warrant for Assange following allegations of sexual assault. After a UK court agreed to Assange's extradition in 2012, he skipped bail and holed up at the Ecuadorian embassy in London, where he was granted asylum. Sweden dropped its case against Assange, but he stayed inside the embassy for seven years. He had by that time breached British law when he skipped bail and faced a local charge when he emerged.

Over time, in cramped embassy conditions, Assange's mental health and relationship with his hosts deteriorated.

In April 2019, Ecuador withdrew Assange's asylum status. UK police then entered the embassy and arrested him. The following month, he was sentenced to fifty weeks in prison for breaching the UK's Bail Act. He was incarcerated at HMP Belmarsh, where I'd suffered my heart attack.

Belmarsh is tough bird. Putting Assange inside one of Britain's most notorious prisons sent a clear message about not disobeying a court order.

On the day that Assange was sentenced for his bail breach, the United States unsealed an indictment against him for allegedly helping former soldier Chelsea Manning illegally access a US military computer system. The US requested that Assange be extradited after his UK prison sentence – and he was later charged in the US under the Espionage Act.

Assange claimed that attempts to extradite him were politically motivated. As the world prepared for the highest-profile extradition case in decades, the WikiLeaks founder turned to Mark Summers.

* * *

I now had a legal 'dream team'. But I would need all their expertise to convince a British judge to reject a request made under the powerful EAW. In many cases, an EAW issued by one EU member state simply leads the recipient state to rubber-stamp the warrant and extradite. In effect, there is a working assumption that most defendants would receive a fair trial anywhere in the EU, and that any wrongful arrest or prosecution would be dealt with in the prosecuting state.

It was the job of Keith, George and Mark to prove that my case should be an exception.

* * *

The remainder of 2018 and early 2019 flew by in a whir of legal activity. My team busied themselves with a detailed analysis of Spain's case and demanded fresh disclosures from Madrid through the Request for Further Information (RFFI) process.

Mark, George and Keith painstakingly worked through entire filing cabinets' worth of material. Gradually, they mastered my complicated brief.

I met with Keith at Lewis Nedas' office throughout the year, often taking time afterwards to catch up with Paul Jnr before heading back on the late train so that I didn't breach my bail curfew. After several months, my legal team successfully negotiated a relaxation of bail. The hours were amended so that police did not perform 'random' checks on me at 2am.

While bail is preferable to custodial remand, it is no cakewalk. Ben Cooper's failure to successfully challenge the original conditions hit hard when local police officers visited un-announced in the middle of the night several times, just to check that I was not breaking my curfew.

Once awoken by the police, I was always unable to get back to sleep. This may not sound like a major imposition, but I lost weeks of sleep during my bail period. Not a healthy situation for a man in his seventies with a heart condition. Gill's life and sleep were also severely disrupted. I'm forever thankful that I have such a tolerant and loving wife.

Curfew checks were not the only bail-related inconvenience, either. Wearing an electronic tag was also challenging.

As Britain's prisons have become overcrowded, the use of tags to support bail has become widespread. Some twenty-five per cent of people in the UK who wear tags are now on bail. Many are probably innocent.

I was fitted with an electronic tag within seventy-two hours of my curfew being imposed. The tagging process is straightforward, if somewhat bizarre. Officials arrive at your house and strap an unremovable plastic tag, with a microchip in it, to the top of your ankle. The bail officers then set up an electronic monitoring box inside your home, which looks a bit like a telephone answering machine from the 1980s. Finally, they ask the person on bail to walk around the perimeter of each room within the house in which you must be present during curfew hours – so that the tag and the electronic box in tandem 'map' and the area in which you must remain.

Once the monitoring box is operational, any perimeter breach during curfew hours means local police receive an alert. Likewise, any attempt to remove the tag also alerts the police.

Contrary to popular opinion, bail tags are not GPS devices and do not provide the police or courts with a real-time record of where you are. They simply send a signal to the monitoring box while you're inside your home. If you're outside your property when you shouldn't be, then you're in trouble.

For more than a year after my bail conditions were imposed, I was forced to wear a tag above my left ankle. Not only is it uncomfortable – the plastic rubs against your leg, making the whole experience sweaty and itchy – but the social stigma attached to wearing one invariably means you cover it up when you leave the house. Thankfully, now that I'm in my seventies, I hardly ever wear shorts!

Tags are worse at night. I rarely managed to sleep without rolling over onto the damn thing. On occasions, I'd be jolted awake by the pain. Worse, my entire lower leg would sometimes go numb if the tag pressed against flesh for too long. It is infuriating, uncomfortable and sleep-depriving.

So I'm sure you can imagine how relieved I was when my lawyers convinced the court to remove my tag and curfew after a year?

* * *

Keith Wood was determined to settle my POCA proceedings before any extradition trial. My solicitor wanted to show UK judges and Spain that I'd been a law-abiding member of society since leaving prison in 2010.

The problem was the state still wanted too much money to settle the dispute. As late as 2019, the RART was demanding £6.8m. So the ever-impressive Keith Wood set to work.

Meticulously, Keith unpicked the RART's demands. He successfully showed that none of my major assets had come from illegal activity. So we could have argued that I would pay nothing. But having pleaded guilty to fraud in 2008, Keith and I knew we'd have to offer something.

Keith's determination paid off. Eventually, both sides agreed I would pay just over £1m in final settlement of all POCA proceedings. In doing so, the state also accepted that I had no other assets hidden around the world that officials could later attempt to claw back.

It pained me even to offer a deal worth £1m. But the standoff had become the longest-running POCA case in British history. My assets had been frozen throughout the period, meaning I could not own or manage registered companies and, in the meantime, Gill and I lived on a significantly reduced income. As time dragged on, the financial challenges intensified. So I agreed to hand over a million pounds.

Keith and I insisted on a further clause in the POCA settlement, though: any deal would be agreed "without prejudice to my arguments in relation to any appeal against relevant convictions". In other words, I could reclaim the value of the POCA settlement if I overturned my 2008 fraud convictions.

I'd gone from wanting to let sleeping dogs lie after leaving prison in 2010 to wanting to clear my name entirely. Why? I'd learned to live with Spain's betrayal in 2007. But Madrid's more recent attempt to prosecute me had reignited a smouldering sense of injustice.

The POCA court accepted my appeal clause and, on 17 September 2019, I received a letter confirming the £1m settlement. Eleven years of financial hell was over! Within months, I'd be able to own a business again.

Having been surprisingly accommodating during legal negotiations, the RART and North Yorkshire Police PR machine swung into action. The police released a statement trumpeting the fact they had secured £1m from a convicted fraudster. Keith and I were furious: the reality was that the court accepted significantly less than the RART initially demanded.

But local media were not interested in the truth. Within days, reports appeared naming me as a fraudster and my family were forced to endure further slurs. It was a sharp reminder that some media struggle with nuance, and the police PR had not helped. I guess the RART needed to trumpet a 'success' after spending vast sums pursuing an eleven-year case and seeing its demand for £11m reduced to just £1m.

* * *

There was now just one, albeit massive, legal hurdle left in my life: proving I had been an intelligence asset and mafia whistle-blower to avoid extradition and a Spanish jail cell.

No distractions and hindrances. I was now armed with reams of evidence I'd collected over two decades.

* * *

"I want every key witness in that courtroom. Your former staff, your former lawyer in Spain – possibly even the CGI agents. I'm still considering that. We could yet request that they give evidence under oath. We may also want to play the recordings of your discussions with them. The court should hear first-hand evidence that you assisted with information on Mohamed Derbah's alleged crimes..."

Mark Summers QC was doing what he does best: directing affairs, spurred into action by injustice, but with his usual commitment to forensic-level evidence.

It was mid-2019, and I was sat inside Mark's office at Matrix Chambers with George and Keith. Through the Request for Further Information (RFFI) process, my legal team had discovered new information on my dealings with Spain's CGI. Reassuringly, Spain's reluctant disclosures confirmed what I had claimed for years: that I had approached Spanish police regarding Derbah in 2001, six years before Judge Garzon placed me on a revised indictment.

I had no reason to think my lawyers had not believed me. But it is always reassuring when lawyers receive independent confirmation, or a strong indication, that their client is telling the truth.

Of course, Spain's CGI and judicial bodies were not wholly transparent. Their RFFI responses were littered with attempts to obfuscate critical facts, such as Judge Garzon's assurance in 2001 that I would be a "protected witness". Spain denied that I was ever a protected witness. Nonetheless, my lawyers were confident that we could now prove my status as a betrayed informant or asset.

In an early statement, George told the media that I had been "sold down the river" by Spain. It was a hard-hitting phrase, yet it summed up my case beautifully.

Mark, George and Keith spent months going through my documentation, sieving out unnecessary facts and honing our legal argument so that two decades' worth of material could be distilled into a three-day extradition hearing. It was an impressive feat.

Mark Summers co-ordinated our legal affairs, but George and Keith did the leg work. They were an eclectic trio. Different characters, yet they dovetailed perfectly. Unlike Keith and George, Mark Summers sometimes presented as cold and dispassionate. But that was his approach. He saw all the angles, from all sides, so that he could second-guess what his opponents would do. And Mark drew on his extraordinary knowledge of case law to dismantle opposition arguments.

To achieve that, Mark purposefully created critical distance between himself and me. During an early meeting, my QC assessed the materials before him, leant forward in his chair and looked me directly in the eyes.

"We are making good progress, Paul," he said. "But there is one question I must ask. You are an intelligent man. If you were innocent of the crimes you went to prison for in 2008, why did you plead guilty?"

My QC was testing me with the kind of query a judge would ask. But I was ready.

"It's simple," I said. "Without my covert recordings, which unbeknown to me were sitting inside the offices of Huzla Rawat my former junior counsel, I could not prove that I was monitoring the two frauds for the CGI.

"My former legal team could not make that argument because somebody had misplaced the recordings. They did not believe that evidence existed. In those circumstances, my barrister and solicitor advised me to plead guilty or face a longer prison sentence."

Mark sat still for several seconds, never breaking eye contact. After a while, he began to nod to himself. Then towards me.

"That's it, isn't it? The evidence boils down to those recordings. They prove contact with Spain's police-intelligence service," Mark said. "So, when Spanish officials say they have no evidence of your relationship with them, that can be disproved. They are lying, and we will say so in court."

My QC smiled. Cold, rational analysis was his greatest strength. Mark asked difficult questions without fear or favour – even putting his own clients on the spot.

Whenever I felt down about the looming extradition case, I would reflect on my discussions with Mark, George and Keith and remind myself that I had the country's best legal minds in my corner. For the first time in years, I emerged from legal meetings feeling more upbeat than when they began. That contrasted starkly with 2008 when I had little choice but to plead guilty.

* * *

Between them, Mark, George and Keith produced a compelling legal argument against my extradition. My legal team challenged every central claim made by Madrid's criminal court with persuasive evidence and case law.

But throughout the build-up to my trial, all three lawyers warned that while they were confident we would ultimately win, we might lose when the case was first heard at magistrates level.

Their reasoning was simple. We had a strong argument that Judge Garzon's betrayal in Spain, and that Madrid's subsequent decade-long delay in proceeding with a case against Mohamed Derbah, constituted an abuse of process. But what Spain had in its favour, my lawyers advised, was the inherent strength of the EAW. I learned that lower court judges tended to lean on such reciprocal arrangements as the backbone of Britain's extradition arrangements. Court of Appeal judges were often more critical of such rubber-stamping.

That is not to say that Mark, George and Keith did not plan to win at the magistrates' court. They prepared their argument for the lower court as meticulously as they would any high-profile case at the Court of Appeal or Supreme Court. Indeed, all three lawyers pointed out that it was imperative to make the most robust case possible at Westminster because we'd be unable to introduce fresh evidence to the Court of Appeal.

Mention of higher courts so early in proceedings would have made me nervous had I not trusted my legal team. But I did, even with what remained of my life.

* * *

Of course, the great unknown was how a judge would respond to Spain's extradition request.

At Westminster Magistrates Court, my case was handed to the deputy chief magistrate for England and Wales, Tan Ikram: one of the most senior figures operating across the lower courts.

Judge Ikram had an impressively unconventional background for a beak. Born to working-class Pakistani parents in 1966 and educated at Wolverhampton Polytechnic, he was called to the Bar – meaning he could practice as a barrister – in 1990.

He was appointed deputy district judge in 2003, became a district judge in 2009 and even presided over legal cases inside the Sovereign Base Areas of Akrotiri and Dhekelia: two tiny areas of British sovereign territory on Cyprus. Akrotiri and Dhekelia are home to British military bases and, combined, represent one of the UK's lesser-known overseas territories.

Cyprus is also home to a vibrant, if sometimes insalubrious, offshore finance industry dominated by the tidal wave of money leaving eastern Europe since the break-up of the Soviet Union. Trust me to stumble into a British judge who sometimes worked on an offshore territory!

Judge Ikram was experienced and trusted to manage complex cases, as well as volume. He made headlines following the London riots of 2011, when he heard up to 60 cases a day linked to five days of violence, looting and damage.

* * *

My legal team opted to fight Spain's extradition request on ten grounds, with four likely to become the key battleground in court:

- It was an abuse of process
- The EAW did not satisfactorily outline my alleged crimes
- Neither did it explain the maximum punishment I faced
- Finally, Spain had gathered my evidence without offering me the right to silence

Explaining the 'abuse of process' claim, Mark Summers QC's final submission stated: 'The defence's over-riding case is that this is a bad faith prosecution and extradition. It is designed to manipulate a prosecution witness [and] undercover state agent into giving evidence following a breakdown in his relationship with the police – in order to continue a case against co-accused [Derbah]. The judge that orchestrated it has himself been disbarred for dishonesty."

If I could have summed up the last sixteen years of my life, the period since CGI officers turned on me, I could not have chosen a better or more succinct paragraph. Mark's submission asserted that Spain could not be trusted with this extradition because Madrid's judicial authorities were hell-bent on betraying their crucial witness. My barrister argued that the potential corruption inherent in Spain's action was highlighted by the fact that the judge who betrayed me had since been disbarred for unrelated corruption linked to his evidence-gathering methods.

Mark's final submission then contested Spain's claim that I was part of Derbah's alleged violent mafia. The EAW, it stated, 'asserts the commission of a) threats and coercion and b) perverting the course of justice.

'Yet [our] Request For Further Information positively asserts that the defendant "does not take part in the crimes of threat and extortion perpetrated by the rest of the co-accused".'

When my lawyers challenged Spain's description of me as some sort of hoodlum, Madrid's judicial authority performed a swift U-turn and confirmed I had absolutely nothing to do with alleged threats or violence. Yet, that is not what Spain's EAW stated. It was almost as though Spain was trying to deceive a UK judge into rubber-stamping a flawed arrest warrant.

Mark Summers QC was busy picking huge holes in Spain's confused and misleading argument. He also attacked the EAW for failing to provide sufficient evidence of the offences I'd allegedly committed – for example, the value of supposed frauds and the absence of any named victims.

But Spain's bigger abuse, my lawyers claimed, was that of Article 6 of the European Convention on Human Rights (ECHR). Under Article 6, European citizens enjoy the right to silence when interviewed by the police or investigators. Of course, I'd provided detailed evidence of Mohamed Derbah's financial activities to the CGI and Judge Garzon in a voluntary capacity as a potential prosecution witness. It was not until after Spain's 2007 betrayal that I was treated as a suspect, although that is not what Spain now claimed.

But as Article 6 states, if you are a suspect in a European case, you have the right to remain silent when interviewed. So if Spain was now insisting that I was a suspect all along – then the likes of Fernando, Enrique and Garzon had a legal duty to inform me of that in 2001.

Mark Summers QC argued: "The case in Spain is founded on Mr Blanchard's statements given as a prosecution witness and without notice of his Article 6 rights to silence [or] non-incrimination," my legal submission stated. "Spain's attempt to place reliance on those statements now is a very serious (and deliberate) substantive and procedural violation of Article 6, and the resulting trial prejudice caused to Mr Blanchard is irremediable."

This was not an extradition request made by a rational, evidence-based judicial authority committed to upholding fundamental human rights. This was the behaviour of an organisation with a barely concealed agenda. A vendetta.

I was delighted with my lawyers' work. From thousands of complex documents, audios and witness statements, they had produced a concise, cogent and hard-hitting argument against extradition. In my view, their argument was irrefutable – although there remained a chance Judge Ikram would see it differently.

And that's where our star witnesses came in.

* * *

It's never enough simply to stand in court and argue your case through your barrister. Any high-performing defence requires strong, independent and corroborative witnesses. And despite almost two decades that had passed since I first approached the CGI and Garzon, I was still in touch with people who were prepared to attend court and provide first-hand accounts of what really happened on Tenerife between 1999 and 2007.

As my trial at Westminster Magistrates neared, Keith, George and Mark narrowed down the list of defence witnesses best-placed to corroborate the facts.

In an ideal world, I would have demanded that the two CGI agents, Fernando and Enrique, should answers questions under oath. But after early discussions, both Mark and George decided not to call anybody from the prosecution side to give evidence. It is always a tricky decision: on the one hand, there exists the possibility that, if forced to attend a UK court, the officers would have to acknowledge my role as an intelligence asset and explain the decision to prosecute me.

But on the other hand, Fernando and Enrique could become hostile witnesses and seize an opportunity to present the worst-case scenario for me – however disputed.

As it turned out, the decision was taken out of our hands. Spain's pre-trial court submissions revealed the two agents were available to give evidence. Yet Spain barely contested the fine details of my official court statement – beyond rejecting claims that I was Garzon's protected witness and asserting that I was the financial architect of Derbah's alleged mafia.

Spain's legal strategy was clear: say as little as possible in response to my evidence and rely on the strength of the EAW to try to extradite me. With so little of my evidence likely to be contested in the UK, my lawyers felt there was no need to call potentially hostile witnesses.

That left just four likely defence witnesses: my former PA Sarah Hill, my Spanish lawyer Vidal Merchan, an independent Spanish legal expert in Professor Jaime Campaner and me.

Everything was now in place for the extradition trial.

* * *

I speak from unfortunate and regretful experiences, but the days before court trials are always difficult. While I knew I was innocent of any crime on Tenerife, I also knew that criminal justice systems, and judges, are imperfect. Mistakes get made when courts reach verdicts in complex cases.

So despite having complete confidence in my legal team, the days before my extradition trial served as a stark reminder of what happened to me in 1992 and 2008.

I tried not to show it in front of Gill, but I could not help but feel nervous. Here I was, an ageing entrepreneur in his eighth decade, wondering whether I'd get to enjoy my later years with my wife, children and grandchildren – or spend them behind bars in an unforgiving Spanish prison.

CHAPTER SEVENTEEN
Trial & Error

London, 3 December 2019. My three-day extradition trial had finally arrived.

In the final weeks before the big day, my legal team ensured I was as well-prepared for court as possible. I knew every key date, statement and fact. In my calmer moments, that made me confident we'd win. We had also considered every tricky question that the judge or CPS might ask while I was under oath. I had an answer for everything and knew that I did not need to resort to committing perjury or lying in court. But I would be a liar if I reported that I didn't question why my lawyers were so confident during the build-up to the trial.

Separately, Keith, George and Mark had all told me: "You're not going to Spain, Paul." But as my lawyers knew, I'd already been the victim of a miscarriage of justice.

My nervousness was perfectly normal, I reminded myself just a few days before the trial: Mark, George and Keith are not the men who must stand in the witness box! I just hoped that, when the day of the trial came, I would stay calm.

The early morning of Tuesday 3 December was surprisingly bright and mild when I awoke inside my hotel room. Paul Jnr had taken time off work to attend the trial, but Gill and Sarah stayed in Yorkshire. Both revealed they would be too nervous sitting in the courtroom, and neither wanted to make me feel uncomfortable.

Thankfully, I'd slept well and awoken with a clear head and ready for battle.

From the window seat of a café over a coffee-laden breakfast opposite Marylebone Station, I witnessed London awaken from its nightly slumber. I've never wanted to live in the capital, but it's an awe-inspiring sight watching a metropolis of nine million people burst to life during rush hour: wave after wave of workers emerging from every nook and cranny until, just after 9am, with everybody busy in their offices, many streets fall quiet again. Only once did I consider whether I would be around to witness the spectacular show again any time soon.

* * *

"Here's the condemned man. Any special requests for your last meal, sir?"

Paul Jnr's dark humour knew few limits. On rare occasions, it irked me that my son made light of serious situations, but I knew it was his way of dealing with stress. Today, I appreciated his barrage of jokes. I greeted my son, and we took seats in a quiet corner of Westminster Magistrates' reception area.

"Everybody sends their best wishes, Dad," Paul Jnr said, glancing at his smartphone. "To the prosecution."

I chuckled.

"If it goes badly today, I just want you to know that the getaway car is waiting out the back. For me. You're travelling to Spain in a prison van."

Relentless. But typical, so strangely reassuring.

A few moments of silence passed, and I looked my son in the eye a little nervously.

"You're going to win this case, dad. Stay confident," Paul Jnr lent forward and smiled. My son had read the legal briefings, of course. Behind his joker's mask was a hard-working, intelligent, loyal soul who didn't miss a trick.

On that morning, he also had a knack for calming me down.

* * *

Those present in Courtroom Four stood to greet Judge Ikram as he took his seat.

My legal team sat to the left of the judge as we looked at him, the CPS team to the right. I glanced towards the benches behind the CPS personnel and noticed a scruffy-looking Mediterranean man in an ill-fitting suit, which involved far too much corduroy, who must have been part of the Spanish entourage. Next to the mystery Spaniard sat a younger, pristinely attired woman with long dark hair pinned back in full 'courtroom battle' mode. She looked more like a character from a slick American legal drama and appeared to be part of Spain's delegation. She was busy taking notes.

At the back of the courtroom sat Paul Jnr and several journalists – including Jon Austin, crime editor at *The Sunday Express*. Word of my trial had reached Fleet Street, after all.

Daniel Sternberg introduced himself as the barrister acting for the CPS on behalf of the judicial authority in Spain.

Sternberg carried an air of confidence and authority not dissimilar to that of my QC, Mark Summers. Silver-tongued and assiduous, the prosecutor was well-briefed and showed within minutes that he knew the case files. I had a superb QC, but I remember thinking that, in other circumstances, Sternberg was somebody I'd want onside. It was not a good early sign: I'd hoped for a disorganised fool as an opponent. No such luck.

At an early stage, Mark Summers QC described to Judge Ikram the 'shaky foundations' on which he believed the EAW had been based – and how he intended to prove it.

I took to the stand at 11.01am.

* * *

My two evidence sessions, either side of the lunch break, seemed to pass quickly. But I never once felt flustered or unable to answer questions from Summers or Sternberg.

In the morning, Mark Summers QC walked Judge Ikram through the case. The judge appeared engaged with the material, but his habit of nodding in response to my QC, rather than speaking, sometimes left me wondering whether he was taking it all in.

Summers was an extraordinary court performer. He effortlessly navigated my complex relationship with Spain's authorities and built what I believed was an unanswerable case for me having been made an intelligence asset and protected witness by Judge Garzon in 2001.

My QC also presented compelling evidence that Spain's betrayal in 2007 left me with no option but to plead guilty to UK fraud charges, and challenged Spain's retrospective claim that I had been a suspect in the Derbah investigation all along.

At one stage, Summers asked a beautiful but straightforward question: "If you had been told that you were being treated as a suspect from the start, how would you have responded?"

"I wouldn't have bothered with any of it," I said, tripping over my words for the first time since taking the stand.

Immediately, Summers clarifies my response. "You would have asked for your right to a lawyer or the right to stay silent?"

"Yes," I confirmed. "Absolutely."

Summers had effortlessly introduced the idea that even Spain's hastily revised version of events would be exposed as a string of lies. Out of the corner of my eye, I saw Jon Austin send a firm stare towards the Spanish contingent, who awkwardly looked at their feet.

* * *

As expected, my afternoon evidence session was more challenging. Daniel Sternberg proved to be a forensic and resilient cross-examiner. He presented a case on behalf of Spain which, at the very least, followed some logic.

Sternberg tried to dismiss my lawyers' claim that the EAW represented an abuse of process and violation of my rights, argued that I would receive a fair trial if charged in Spain, and suggested that my evidence be heard by a Spanish jury.

As expected, Sternberg also argued the EAW was a powerful piece of legislation that, in many cases, compelled extradition. The critical decision Judge Ikram had to make, he argued, was whether the application to extradite had been completed correctly. To my mind, this translated as: "Has Spain filled out the form correctly, Judge? If so, throw him on a plane to Madrid and the tougher decisions will be somebody else's problem."

As a British citizen, it concerned me that the CPS paid little attention to my claim that I would not receive a fair trial in Madrid.

But Sternberg did not focus exclusively on EAW bureaucracy. During cross-examination, he also questioned my version of events on Tenerife and the Spanish mainland. For example, he raised Spain's ludicrous claim that the CGI had no record of phone calls and meetings between myself, Munoz and Esteban.

Immediately, I recalled Fernando's warning at our final meeting: that the CGI would deny its relationship with me.

"Indeed, Spanish police assert that they have no record of the calls you allegedly made," Sternberg said, staring at me directly.

For a split second, the prosecutor's calculated act worked. For the first time since I'd taken the stand, I felt irrationally nervous. I guess it is a natural response when a well-drilled barrister cross-examines you in court.

I bit my tongue for a few seconds, resisting the temptation to respond angrily. And then I remembered one of my favourite quotes from a historical courtroom exchange.

"Well," I replied. "They would say that, wouldn't they?"

The courtroom fell silent for a split second before wry smiles spread across faces. From the back of the court, I heard a journalist chuckle. I glanced at Judge Ikram and then back at Sternberg, both serious professionals struggling to hold back grins.

Of course, the phrase I'd used was synonymous with a vast political scandal linked to the courthouse in which we were sat: the Profumo affair.

In 1961, John Profumo, the married secretary of state for war in Harold Macmillan's government, began an affair with a beautiful 19-year-old 'showgirl' and suspected prostitute, Christine Keeler. It later emerged that Keeler was simultaneously involved in a sexual relationship with a senior Soviet naval officer based in London during the Cold War – sparking national security concerns over potential 'pillow talk'.

The gossip-loving British press and public were obsessed with the case.

Initially, Profumo denied his affair in the House of Commons. But he later resigned after it emerged he had misled Parliament. The scandal intensified when it emerged other members of the British establishment had affairs with women linked to Keeler's alleged 'pimp': the well-connected osteopath Stephen Ward.

Following the scandal, Britain sought to prosecute Ward for living off the immoral earnings of Keeler and her close friend – the glamorous blonde 'showgirl' Mandy Rice-Davies. Ward was initially charged at the old Marylebone Magistrates, which later became Westminster Magistrates Court.

During cross-examination at Ward's trial in 1963, 18-year-old Rice-Davies caused an uproar when she delivered her famous retort. Told by the prosecution that Lord Astor, another Conservative politician, denied he'd had an affair with her, Rice-Davies giggled and quipped: "Well, he would, wouldn't he?"

Rice-Davies' line is misquoted so often that it is now more commonly cited as: "Well, he would say that, wouldn't he?" But her retort is now immortalised as meaning a denial somebody feels compelled to issue despite solid evidence against them.

* * *

Laughter momentarily eased the tension in Courtroom Four. Even Sternberg took a step back and recomposed himself. I think I made my point: my prosecution team held a mountain of evidence about my lengthy and secretive relationship with the CGI.

By the end of the day, I had a begrudging respect for Daniel Sternberg: a talented barrister who, in my view, happened to be on the wrong side. But

I also knew that my legal team had to disprove Spain's argument, which meant corroborating my evidence through witnesses.

* * *

Vidal Merchan was an intelligent, hard-working and fastidious criminal lawyer from Madrid. Despite language difficulties – Vidal spoke little English and I spoke only basic Spanish – we got on from the day we met. But here's an often-overlooked point in this sorry tale: Vidal was not my choice of legal representative in Spain.

The CGI, via Madrid's College of Lawyers, recommended Vidal to me when I approached the police about Mohamed Derbah in 2001.

CGI agents knew that, under Spanish law, I required legal representation and a translator when providing official statements as a potential prosecution witness. So with no indication of the CGI's betrayal to come, it was a relief to have Vidal appointed. At the time, I believed Vidal's role would be purely administrative – effectively ensuring the correct procedures for giving basic statements. How wrong I was.

Sarah Hill often referred to us as 'the *Odd Couple*'. Like Walter Matthau and Jack Lemmon, Vidal and I came from different backgrounds. Yet, we respected each other and grew to become friends.

As somebody who spoke fluent English and Spanish, Sarah translated during my stilted discussions with Vidal. She also meticulously translated transcripts of calls she made to Vidal and scores of letters and faxes sent between offices in Madrid, Tenerife, York and southern Spain. When the three of us were together, Sarah often repeated word-for-word, everything that Vidal said to me and vice-versa. It would take hours to hold what would otherwise have been a thirty-minute discussion. But Sarah and Vidal had the patience of saints.

The 'Odd Couple' arrangement worked, primarily because Vidal's legal advice was masterfully clear – if not always concise. He was extremely fussy, even when making basic legal points, and the potential for confusion between us meant he spent hours repeating himself and ensuring that I understood everything that was going on.

But Vidal's penchant for detail sometimes rubbed people up the wrong way. So it was with Judge Ikram.

Problems started shortly after Vidal was sworn in as a witness on day two of my trial.

Vidal had flown to the UK from Madrid late the previous evening and, due to a delay, arrived at his hotel in the early hours of the morning he gave evidence. I had been unable to meet Vidal at Gatwick Airport – my lawyers advised me not to speak to other witnesses until after they had given evidence. So I was unaware that Vidal had barely slept before entered the witness box.

When asked to take the witness stand, Vidal slowly raised himself and shuffled cautiously into place. He was several years older than when I last saw him, and age was beginning to take a slight toll. Vidal appeared smaller and a little frailer than I remembered.

For a brief moment, a sense of regret washed over me and I wondered whether it had been a good idea to call my now-retired Spanish lawyer as a witness.

Vidal was introduced to the court-appointed translator, a short and robust-looking woman with reddish-brown hair. But there was a problem. While the translator sat within a reasonable distance of Vidal, they sometimes appeared unable to hear each other. Initially, I thought the problem was Vidal's hearing. But after a few moments, I realised that the translator was struggling with the courtroom acoustics. She began to raise her voice, without shouting, to communicate Judge Ikram's questions.

When he responded, Vidal immediately allayed any fears about his frailty. Mentally speaking, he was still as sharp as a tack. His familiar scholarly approach was immediately apparent. But that merely created what became the day's biggest problem: Vidal's obsession with detail.

Conscious of the need to adhere to a tight schedule, Judge Ikram was in no mood to receive long-winded translated replies. The judge tried to avoid simply repeating the superb detail in Vidal's official witness statement, which supported my version of events in Spain. Instead, Judge Ikram attempted to focus on essential points of dispute.

But Vidal's orderly mind, and detailed approach, meant he kept trying to explain the differences between Spanish and UK law – and why they were so crucial to my case.

One of the most stilted and excruciating evidence sessions the famous Westminster courthouse has hosted played out amid farcical scenes. The translator tried hard to communicate as concisely as possible. But the two men of law were, on this day, taking very different approaches.

Judge Ikram demanded swift responses. But Vidal repeatedly explained more than was necessary and his answers were summarised, sometimes badly, by the interpreter. Seeking clarity over critical issues, Vidal then began to ask questions relayed back to the judge.

Irked by the fact he was not receiving swift answers, Judge Ikram grew impatient with Vidal and the translator.

Vidal attempted to explain his view that the CGI and Judge Garzon granted me "protected witness" status in 2001 – and that I was not treated as a suspect until after I had fallen out with them years later. Remember, this was my police-appointed lawyer giving evidence: not some patsy I had cherry-picked.

Judge Ikram received Vidal's evidence, but his patience gradually eroded. At one point, the judge spoke candidly to the interpreter: "Could you ask the witness for just the basic facts?" On another occasion, he was sharper: "Could we hurry this along? The question I'm asking is straightforward..."

Thankfully, Mark Summers QC stepped-in to help conclude the evidence session shortly after Vidal confirmed that the Spanish High Court had quashed Judge Garzon's 2007 indictment in 2009 – and that he made approximately fifty (count them!) trips to Madrid's courts while trying to get Spain to confirm my status as an asset before my UK fraud convictions.

It was undoubtedly an eventful session, but Judge Ikram looked unimpressed.

I felt for Vidal. He had made a considerable effort to come to the UK on my behalf, only to be frustrated by language barriers. Sure, Vidal liked to spend time clarifying the finer points of Spanish law – that's why he was such a good solicitor. And the finer points of Spanish law, such as the absence of a valid lawyer or interpreter when I signed key documents for CGI agents or Judge Garzon, were crucial to my case. For these reasons, I felt sure Judge Ikram would have shown more patience if he and Vidal had communicated in the same language. Likewise, I'm sure Vidal would have been a little more responsive to Judge Ikram's demands!

On completing his testimony, Vidal left the witness box and approached me with his hand outstretched. "Paul, you will be OK. They have broken the law at every turn," he said in Spanish.

I smiled and shook his hand. "I know they have Vidal. Thank you so much for coming. I really appreciate it. Please give my best regards to your family."

Later that day, I managed to catch up with Vidal in the lobby of his hotel before he made his way back to Gatwick. During our chat, my Spanish solicitor's warmth and humanity shone through as it always did. His was a brief and spectacular visit, but I was unsure how the judge would view it.

* * *

"That was an absolute shitshow. It felt like a dark comedy."

"I've seen worse. Just be grateful the interpreter wasn't a Hindu trying to speak Punjabi. That often ends in dialectal confusion and an unsafe verdict!"

I overheard two journalists joking as we gathered in the courtroom reception after Vidal's evidence.

"Was it that bad? What did you think?" I asked a friend who had witnessed the exchange.

"Vidal was fine," my friend replied, trying to keep my spirits up. "He likes detail. Your lawyers took a detailed statement from him which the judge will read before he makes his decision."

He was right: Vidal's official statement was a corker.

* * *

One of Vidal's statements noted that, on the day Vidal and I first met at the Spanish Police HQ in Madrid, I "was not under arrest" and had provided information against Mohamed Derbah as "an accuser".

The same statement explains that the following day, when I was asked by Munoz and Esteban to meet Judge Garzon at his chambers, my lawyer was not present. "I was not notified by the police or the court as I believe I should have been, But this really confirms the fact that my client is a prosecution witness," Vidal explained.

My police-appointed lawyer also stated that, in his view, I was a CGI asset or informant who later fell out with my handlers, revealed my concerns that I'd been abandoned by Spain's police and outlined fears that I could be targeted by Derbah's men. It also revealed details of the July 2004 meeting with Spain's director-general of police, Jesus Nieto Rodenas, which Vidal attended when we tried to patch things up with the police – and Vidal's later battle with the Spanish High Court, which ended in him overturning Garzon's original indictment.

Vidal's memory and knowledge of my case were immense. And it was embarrassing for the CGI because they had chosen him for me.

* * *

Next on the witness stand, albeit giving evidence remotely from Spain, was Professor Jaime Campaner: an independent Spanish legal expert I had contacted to provide an authoritative view of the alleged evidence against me.

Jaime runs a law firm called Campaner Law, which specialises in white-collar crime – and his CV showed significant experience in dealing with complex and high-profile money laundering cases. Indeed, his legal knowledge is held in such high regard across Spain that he also tutors training judges and prosecutors.

When I stumbled across Jaime's details online one evening, his profile read: "He has deep experience in extradition cases and preparing legal opinions before international courts on extradition and improperly obtained evidence."

Just what my legal team needed to complement evidence provided by Vidal.

Dr Campaner has been described by Vanity Fair magazine as "meticulous, disciplined, practical and cool-headed". Over the phone, he was precisely that. Over several weeks, Dr Campaner examined the entire case in Spain – including documents lodged with Madrid's courts.

My UK-based legal team had long known what Dr Campaner had concluded when my extradition hearing came around.

* * *

Dr Campaner's courtroom evidence was based on a report he submitted to my lawyers in May 2019. It could not have been any clearer about Spain's case.

In the second paragraph, Dr Campaner stated: "The evidence given by Mr Blanchard before the investigating judge Number 5 of the High National Court [Judge Garzon] was improperly obtained.

"Instead of playing the role of guarantor of fundamental freedoms, the judge behaved like an inquisitor. In my opinion...there is an abuse of process and it is not admissible under Spanish law to justify the charges against Mr Blanchard using the evidence that he improperly gave in the course of the judge's unlawful action."

Thump!

Dr Campaner had driven a bus through Spain's legal argument and Judge Garzon's "unlawful" behaviour with one scathing paragraph.

What's more, Campaner's review confirmed something that I'd been told previously but which had never been evidenced: the CGI had tapped Mohamed Derbah's phones for months before I approached their agents. Consequently, the CGI had overheard telephone conversations among Derbah's entourage in which my name was mentioned. What's important about that, I discovered through Campaner's report, was that the CGI had secretly pulled my financial records before I had even met with its agents – and one police report even described me as a 'suspect' purely because of my relationship with Derbah.

Therefore, in Campaner's view, I *was* officially a suspect before I walked into the CGI's offices. Even if CGI agents had no intention of treating me like one. Under Spanish law, Campaner said, I should have been informed of my 'suspect' status from day one. I was not.

Spain's police and judiciary had been hoist by their own petard. Madrid's argument since Judge Garzon's betrayal in 2007 has been that when I first provided statements to the CGI in 2001, I incriminated myself and that, ever since those statements, I had been a suspected member of the alleged Tenerife mafia. Of course, I know that to be untrue.

But Dr Campaner's report showed that I was a suspect even *before* I met CGI agents – in which case Judge Garzon had potentially acted illegally when taking my evidence.

According to Professor Campaner, if I had been a suspect from 2001 onwards, I should have been told immediately and been advised that I had the right to remain silent. Instead, I waited six years to discover Spain's retrospective claim that I had been a suspect all along. During that time, I handed the CGI and Garzon reams of information as an intelligence asset: having been told I was a protected witness.

In Campaner's opinion, Spain's case was undermined by Judge Garzon's illegal evidence-gathering.

Spain's police and judicial bodies were caught in a web of their own lies. According to Professor Campaner, even if the UK extradited me to Madrid, my statements in the Derbah case were most likely inadmissible in any Spanish court because they had been obtained illegally.

You couldn't make it up.

In court at Westminster on 4 December 2019, Dr Campaner talked Mark Summers QC and Judge Ikram through his legal opinion. "The evidence is contaminated. There is no way to turn back the clock," he concluded.

These were dramatic revelations.

* * *

Sarah Hill was my former PA on Tenerife who became a close friend. Bright and well-organised, Sarah also became my eyes and ears on the island when I was away on business.

And she made a superb court witness. Sarah's fluent Spanish and ability to quickly translate documents and notes meant I shared almost everything with her. She had dealt with my clients, including Mohamed Derbah, as well as the police, CGI agents, my lawyers: almost everybody who contacted Goldcrest Hispania for several years.

When Sarah flew into London to give her court evidence, my lawyers were initially concerned that she might be overwhelmed. Sarah's flight into Gatwick had also landed late one evening and, the morning after she arrived, my lawyers reported that she seemed tired and nervous. Out of concern for Sarah's welfare, Keith questioned whether it was wise to put her on the witness stand. George and Mark said she'd be fine after a good rest.

Keith need not have worried.

On the morning of 5 December 2019, Sarah entered the witness box refreshed after two nights of solid sleep – and blew us away. She was the perfect corroborative witness: clear, concise and well-informed about her past statements. She left the court in no doubt about what happened on Tenerife.

Sarah explained that she'd been my personal assistant between 1999 and 2007, and how my relationship with Mohamed Derbah had evolved from establishing businesses as a freelance offshore consultant through a period of friendship to one of deep suspicion about his commercial activities.

Referring to what she now knows about my former client, Sarah explained: "I would describe him [Derbah] as mafia. He is infamous on the island."

Sarah also described the shocking moment in 2001 when we realised the scope of Mohamed's influence on Tenerife. After I had raised suspicions about Derbah's holiday pack businesses, she confirmed, a national police officer warned me: "If I were you, I would leave the island now."

But the most important part of Sarah's evidence was that she corroborated information about my relationships with CGI agents Munoz and Esteban, as well as Judge Garzon and other senior Spaniards. Sarah had met, spoken or communicated with all of them. For the first time, I had a corroborative witness in a British court telling the judge about my interactions with Spain's intelligence services and judiciary.

She described how I'd been recruited as an informant or asset and her belief that Garzon had provided me with protected witness status. Quite literally: referring to the period after local police warned me to leave Tenerife, when I returned to the island to complete my company accounts, Sarah told Judge Ikram: "When Mr Blanchard came, two policemen were with us. Plainclothes armed national policemen."

To confirm my role as Spain's offshore asset, Sarah also detailed many occasions on which she translated reports and documents for the CGI, Judge Garzon's office and – after my fall out with both – material from meetings with Spain's sub director-general of police, Nieto. She also explained how she translated Vidal's messages, including those sent when Vidal met with district attorney Molina, who was prosecuting the Derbah case.

Sarah confirmed Vidal had met with Molina on 21 July 2004 and that the district attorney warned me 'lie low' while he put together his case against Derbah: or "he [Blanchard] could end up looking up at the sky from his own grave".

At that same meeting, Sarah told the court, Molina said I should consider myself a protected witness.

Finally, a British court had heard from somebody else what actually happened on Tenerife and in Spain. Relief washed over me. The truth had emerged.

For the avoidance of doubt, Mark Summers QC asked Sarah: "Were you acting out a delusion that you were police informants?"

"No," came Sarah's instant reply. "This is real, and it is still very real."

* * *

Sarah Hill had again shown that she is a friend, colleague and professional. More than that, she'd shown bravery and a commitment to the truth that many people in her position would eschew when asked to give evidence against alleged mobsters.

When she took the stand in Westminster, Sarah still lived on Tenerife. While out socialising, she would sometimes see Mohamed Derbah's entourage, including his brothers. It took a great deal of courage for Sarah to stand in the witness box and describe my former client as "mafia" – even if she was merely repeating a term first used by the Spanish police. But Sarah did it because she cared. She spoke truth unto power despite the risks involved, and for that I will be eternally grateful.

* * *

It would be remiss and unbalanced of me to ignore the evidence provided by Spain's judicial authority.

Even though Spain's evidence had been undermined by defence witnesses, Madrid's final submission was sufficiently logical to make my lawyers wonder whether an overworked judge might see some merit in it. Until we read the fine details.

Spain's opening paragraph still insisted only that Madrid's court wanted to extradite me "for an offence of participation in a criminal organisation, punishable on conviction in Spain with up to fifteen years of imprisonment".

A more detailed explanation of the alleged offence was still missing. Instead, Spain's final submission claimed that I had 'accepted helping Derbah structure businesses' under cross-examination.

Of course I had! For a short period, I was Mohamed Derbah's offshore financial adviser and, whether Spain liked it or not, that is not a crime. The only way that relationship could have been criminal would have been for me to have had prior or ongoing knowledge of Derbah's alleged frauds – or to have encouraged, purposefully facilitated or been complicit in the alleged crimes.

Spain's final submission even acknowledged that I spoke voluntarily to the CGI in 2001. Referring to my meeting with Judge Garzon on 20 July 2001, it also acknowledged my willingness to "give evidence as a prosecution witness".

But the judicial authority argued that I knew I'd "not been granted the status of protected witness at any time". Laughably, the submission attempted to prove Spain's point by adding: "He knew that his application to be made a protected witness had been refused by Judge Garzon on 20 December 2006."

Not only was this untrue, but it failed to address a rather obvious question: if Spain was telling the truth, why did the judicial authority claim Garzon made his only decision about my witness status in 2006 – five years after I first met him and the CGI? Any reasonable person would surely ask what my status was between 2001 and 2006? Funnily enough, Spain's final submission did not address that.

The truth is that the CGI and Garzon stated I was a protected witness in 2001.

Desperate for a more robust line than 'Blanchard did some consultancy work for Derbah', Spain then pointed to my 2008 guilty pleas in the UK and the fact that I'd not officially appealed those convictions. It was an attempt to convince the court I was a fraudster simply by pointing to a contentious past conviction. I was fuming. Spain's refusal to acknowledge my status as an informant was a key reason why, in the absence of my audio recordings as proof, I pleaded guilty in 2008!

Spain's submission ended with what prosecutors believed would be their trump card. Officials claimed I could "raise co-operation with the authorities if tried in Spain" and "ask for improperly gathered evidence to be annulled if he is tried in Spain".

In other words, my legal team's claim that I would not receive a fair trial in Madrid would be something prosecutors in Spain could consider if Britain just extradited me anyway!

Given the volume of lies, deceits and misdirections in Spain's extradition application, the corruption exhibited by Garzon while in office and the betrayal by my Spanish handlers, there was no way on Earth I would receive a fair trial in Madrid.

But it was a clever sign-off. Spain has been considered a close ally of Britain since it ditched Franco's dictatorship and embraced the liberal democracy synonymous with the EU. In most instances, a British judge would feel confident that, were he to extradite somebody to an EU member state, the recipient country would uphold the Europe-wide legal rights of that individual – including the right to a fair trial. So it was a sign-off that pulled at Judge Ikram's heartstrings: "Don't worry: Spain is just like Britain, and we will treat him fairly."

I was unsure which way Judge Ikram would lean after he considered these points.

* * *

On the afternoon of 5 December 2019, Judge Ikram adjourned court proceedings until February 2020. By that date, he warned, both sides must have filed their closing submissions. In the meantime, the judge would consider the relevant case law.

While Spain could rely on the general power of the EAW to support its extradition application, I felt satisfied that my legal team and witnesses had presented a strong defence. Judge Ikram's adjournment meant a further delay, but I didn't mind: the festive season was close, and Gill and I had planned a busy Christmas and New Year.

"You deserve a good Christmas, Dad," Paul Jnr said over a coffee after the final day of evidence. "Besides, it might be your last Christmas in the UK!"

My son winked. I'd been trying to put that fact to the back of my mind.

* * *

5 February 2020.

Inside Courtroom Four at Westminster Magistrates Court, Mark Summers QC was in full flow.

"Lies, lies, lies!"

My barrister repeated the word with uncharacteristic passion as he looked up at Judge Ikram. Summers was busy deconstructing Spain's hastily amended closing submission.

My lawyers focused much of their final argument on two points: the glaring defects in Spain's EAW application and the fact that the Spanish judicial authority continued to deceive the British courts over my relationship with CGI officers and former judge Baltazar Garzon.

Despite the mountain of evidence provided by witnesses *and* the audios presented in court, Spain continued to downplay my relationship with the CGI. Even at this late stage, Summers wanted to ensure that Judge Ikram was in no doubt.

Referring to Spain's RFFI responses, Summers described as "outright lies" Spain's claims that there were no records of my contact with CGI officials and that I was responsible for delays to the Derbah investigation since leaving prison in 2010.

"Lies, lies, lies! There isn't a single truthful thing in that first page [of RFFI evidence]," Summers told the judge.

"They're even lying now about how they lied back then," he added, referring to Spain's explanation for how I came to be a suspect and not Garzon's protected witness.

Mark's slow build-up to righteous anger was masterful. His approach was intellectually forensic and linguistically scathing of our opponents. UK lawyers often claim the great strength of UK courts is that, unlike in the United States, hearings are not recorded – so there's less temptation for lawyers to 'perform' like they're in a TV show.

I'll have none of it.

Mark Summers QC was a courtroom performer. Perhaps not in the American sense of the term, but certainly in his approach to dismissing opposition arguments. He loved nothing more than showing the courtroom that, while the judge was in charge of proceedings – and Mark was always impeccably polite towards Judge Ikram and Daniel Sternberg – he knew extradition law. Every word of Mark's argument mattered. Each description of the evidence, every case law citation was a laser-like verbal smart bomb aimed at destroying the prosecution. And he rarely missed.

Turning his attention to what Summers considered the "defective" bureaucracy behind Spain's EAW, he pointed out that the warrant failed to clarify the number of alleged offences for which my extradition was sought, as well as the maximum sentence that I stood to receive if extradited.

Spain's EAW document was confused and contradictory. One section stated that I had allegedly committed "one" ongoing offence of fraud. At the same time, another claimed the number of alleged crimes was five or six – including membership of a criminal organisation, money laundering, threats of violence and credit card forgery.

None of it made sense.

At first glance, such bureaucratic details appear less important than the question of whether an individual is sought for an alleged crime. But, as Summers pointed out using existing EAW case law, similar inaccuracies in past cases led judges to deny extradition requests. Under European law, it is not acceptable for the requesting state to produce vague and ill-defined grounds for somebody's extradition. UK judges required detailed descriptions of alleged offences, in case they were so unimportant or politically motivated as to be irrelevant.

Extradition judges must also know the likely maximum sentence facing an accused. These details are crucial because some states, including Spain, do not impose custodial sentences for minor offences. Other states impose disproportionately hefty custodial tariffs on crimes considered elsewhere as unworthy of long prison stints.

So a British judge, for example, usually seeks evidence that the maximum sentence facing a requested person is proportionate to the alleged crimes outlined in a EAW.

And on that point, Summers felt sure that Spain's warrant was appallingly vague and ill-conceived.

When Daniel Sternberg stood to give his final statement, he argued that case law suggested my extradition to Spain was inevitable. Summers quickly challenged the claim, pointing to multiple high-profile cases where judges had good reasons not to deport individuals. 'Mr Extradition's' knowledge was extraordinary.

Turning to Judge Ikram but still addressing Sternberg's claim, Summers signed off with another killer line: "If the court thinks that, well, good luck with that: we'll see you at the Court of Appeal."

And with that, my QC smiled politely and nodded towards Judge Ikram and Daniel Sternberg. Both men reciprocated. It was a quintessentially British way of courtroom adversaries and judges showing respect to each other.

Extradition court proceedings were over. But would my lawyers' exceptional work be enough? Judge Ikram earmarked his verdict for 4 March 2020.

* * *

Outside the courtroom, my legal team gathered for a debrief.

George and Keith looked happy but were taking nothing for granted. Keith articulated what we were all thinking. "He's unbelievable, Mark, isn't he?"

George nodded and smiled. "He's like that every time. 'Good luck with that: we'll see you at the Court of Appeal!' I loved it."

I thanked my solicitor and junior barrister for the umpteenth time. Summers had stolen the show, but their hard work put my QC in that position.

When Summers appeared from inside the courtroom, he wandered over, looking unusually relaxed.

"That was incredible, Mark," I said. "Thank you for everything."

"You're welcome, Paul," Mark replied. "These hearings are always easier when we have strong evidence to work with. And we had plenty. Now we have to wait and see what the judge decides. You never can tell what will happen next."

My QC's final words proved fatefully accurate.

* * *

Within three weeks of the final court hearing, prime minister Boris Johnson was forced to announce the first UK-wide 'lockdown' to tackle the most deadly and virulent threat to the world's health for more than a century.

Coronavirus, and its related disease Covid-19, had arrived in the UK with such ferocity that the formidable National Health Service (NHS) was almost overwhelmed by a tsunami of hospital admissions, sickness and deaths. A month later, most emergency services were close to breaking point.

It felt like the world had stopped turning. Like many countries around the world, the UK ground to a halt. The entire population was ordered to stay at home for all but the most essential activities, often conducted while wearing protective masks. 'Social distancing' was introduced to slow the spread of the virus. People stopped hugging, touching or shaking hands often left red-raw from scrubbing or disinfecting with ubiquitous hand gels. Businesses shut their doors, schools closed, courts postponed their hearings and roads emptied. Barely a soul walked city streets, which fell into a silence punctuated only by the dreaded sound of ambulance sirens.

Swathes of intrusive but essential measures designed to save lives were introduced, sometimes through emergency legislation forced upon governments borrowing and spending unimaginable sums to support businesses that had stopped trading. Despite these unprecedented mitigating policies, the economic impact was catastrophic. The UK's economy shrunk by ten per cent within months: the worst financial collapse in the state's history.

Life became necessarily monotonous and bleak for millions of people holed up inside their homes. Those over seventy years old were deemed at the highest risk, and my underlying heart condition meant I was especially vulnerable. Like millions of older folk, I found myself 'shielding' – which meant no direct contact with friends or family outside our household while the global race to develop life-saving vaccines began.

My mind was elsewhere by the time I received notification that Judge Ikram's extradition decision had been delayed by court closures. It takes a significant event to distract a man from an impending legal decision that could end with his imprisonment. But the near-existential threat posed by Covid-19 managed just that.

Mark Summers was right: you can never tell what will happen next.

* * *

May 2020.

As Gill and I wandered along the quiet public footpath next to Fulford Golf Course, I heard the bark of a playful dog behind us. Following reports that animals could carry Coronavirus on their fur, the unpredictable movements of man's best friend had become the scourge of locals taking their daily dose of government-approved exercise.

I had felt too couped up while shielding and endured some violent headaches. So I'd begun to venture out for short walks, albeit carefully.

Staying at least two meters away from the few tense-looking folk who wandered past was easy. But the logistics involved in avoiding an excitable, slobbering hound suddenly felt comparable to that of a military deployment. Some walkers perceived the experience as a potentially deadly encounter and would jump out of their skin at the sight of a tiny terrier.

On this occasion, though, an enthusiastic spaniel simply scampered past.

Gill and I looked at each other and laughed, embarrassed by our hyper-alert state. Panicked mindsets had become the norm. Lockdown had already been a torrid experience.

In April, I had been knocked sideways by the devastating news that my great friend and former Cheavours bandmate, Alex Bladen-Hill, died after contracting Covid-19. I'm a tough, old-fashioned Yorkshireman and ex-jailbird. But I don't mind admitting that I almost cried when I found out. Alex had been such a loyal friend, and we had only recently reconnected after losing touch. I cherished every moment I spent with Alex and his wonderful, warm family. I'll miss him dearly.

Alex's death was a sharp reminder of man's mortality and refocused my mind on the extradition battle. My close friend had died having lived life to the full: so I was damned if I was going to spend the rest of my life as an innocent man behind bars once again.

Mind back on the legal case, I planned for every eventuality. If we lost at Westminster, my legal team's Court of Appeal case would need to refocus on evidence provided by Sarah Hill and Jaime Campaner.

Vidal, too.

* * *

"I'm sorry, Paul. He was such a lovely man. It's just so sad."

Sarah Hill struggled to hold back tears as she spoke.

It was late May, and Judge Ikram's verdict was due within weeks. The previous day, I'd called Sarah to ask whether she could assist my legal team ahead of any Court of Appeal hearing. I was delighted when she said yes. Then I asked for a favour: could Sarah call Vidal and ask him the same question? My Spanish was rusty and Sarah, fluent, would make a far more eloquent request.

My phone rang late the following evening.

"Paul, it's Sarah," she sniffed. "I've got some terrible news. Vidal has passed. I think it was the virus."

My heart sank. Vidal Merchan, my fearless lawyer in Madrid who stood in front of corrupt judges and powerful policemen to proclaim my innocence, had died. It was a second devastating blow in a matter of days.

Vidal was a man of enormous integrity and admirable honesty – a lawyer never compromised by corruption or cowed by reputation. He was ferocious in pursuit of legal truths, yet a kind-hearted family man to his core. And now he was gone. He had left behind a loving wife and two children. Their heartbreak would be unmeasurable.

After the call from Sarah, I sat back in an armchair and closed my eyes. A few short months ago, after he'd given court evidence in London, Vidal and I had gossiped and joked like old schoolfriends. His star had shone brightly. It always will.

* * *

As I shaved on the morning of 29 June 2020, I stared intensely at the man in the mirror.

It had been twenty-one years since I'd met Mohamed Derbah. Fourteen years since Judge Garzon added me to an indictment designed to prosecute an alleged mafia of which I had never been a member.

I had aged visibly since – the result of prison and ill-health brought about by this case. I'd been honest with everybody throughout the period. Yet later that day, I would discover whether I would be extradited to Spain to face a ludicrous and potentially illegal prosecution.

With Coronavirus still preventing most defendants and lawyers from entering courts, Judge Ikram ordered his verdict be delivered via a remote hearing.

I'd like to report that I was not nervous.

Deep down, I was confident that my legal team would ultimately win the case. But they had warned me that we might lose the initial magistrates' court battle, so a few nerves had crept in. I knew that even if Judge Ikram ruled in favour of extradition, I would not be immediately thrown onto a plane. Instead, Mark Summers QC would submit our grounds of appeal and we'd all head for the Royal Courts of Justice.

That meant there were no tears or histrionics within my family as Judge Ikram's verdict drew close. Gill shared my nervousness but understood that we were playing the long game. From their lockdown bunkers in Yorkshire and the Midlands, Sarah and Paul Jnr had been as supportive and loving as ever.

I finished shaving.

The morning of the verdict was strangely unspectacular. I had a quick chat with Keith and George, who were due to listen in. But my lawyers were so clued-up on how to handle matters, regardless of the verdict, that I spent the rest of my time sipping tea and watching the clock tick towards 2pm.

* * *

Perhaps I should have been more concerned.

At 2pm, I entered the password for my online hearing and proceedings began.

We quickly learned that Judge Ikram would not conduct the hearing. Instead, his written verdict was delivered by district judge Michael Snow, and the stand-in was in no mood to hang around.

Copies of the judgment would be sent by email to my legal team, Snow stated in a perfunctory manner.

"So I'll cut to the chase, Mr Blanchard," he said. "The Judge has rejected your defence and ordered your surrender to Spain under Section 21(a) 5 of the Extradition Act 2003.

"You have seven days in which to appeal this decision. If you do not appeal, you will be surrendered to Spain. Your bail conditions will apply as before..."

The district judge continued to read out the formal details, but I stopped hearing his words. My ears felt like they had filled with blood. I was shocked at Judge Ikram's decision and the blasé and officious manner in which it was delivered.

I was asked if I understood the verdict, but little else. I wanted to interject as the judge droned on. I wanted to ask: "Have you lost your marbles?"

Questions swarmed in my mind. Judge Ikram was diligent, professional and bright. But I couldn't stop myself from wondering – had he listened to the recordings which explained my relationship with Spain's CGI agents? Had he reviewed the hundreds of pages of evidence I'd provided about my co-operation with Spanish police, intelligence and judicial figures? Had he heard the late Vidal Mechan tell the court that Judge Garzon, later disbarred for corruption, had led us all to believe I was a 'protected witness'? Had he fully considered the glaring errors in Spain's EAW application?

I stayed calm enough to get through the remainder of the hearing and hang up. But as soon as the phone went down, I yelled out.

"Fucking hell! Did they listen to anything?"

Gill and Sarah, sat across the room, stirred. My wife threw a comforting arm around me. "You'll appeal. It's OK. You're going to appeal, Paul," she said calmly. But I could see from the expressions on the faces of my wife and daughter that they were shocked.

I'd been briefed by my lawyers that we might lose at Westminster, and to remember that an extradition judgment is not a criminal judgment. But the verdict still hurt. Just moments ago, I had been one evidence-based decision away from being free to live the rest of my life in peace. Instead, I was now going to have to go the 'long route' around the courts. Possibly in Spain.

It did not seem fair. The Court of Appeal beckoned.

CHAPTER EIGHTEEN

D-Day

My lawyers had several days in which to submit a notice of appeal against Judge Ikram's decision. But they had been so conscious of the risk that the lower court would find in Spain's favour that most of our documents were ready within hours.

After the appeal was filed, it was just a case of waiting. And waiting.

The Coronavirus pandemic had spread across the globe with such deadly ferocity that the UK was preparing itself for a likely 'second wave' when Judge Ikram delivered his verdict. UK hospital admissions had begun to fall in the summer of 2020 as the combination of emergency lockdown measures, business and school closures, and summer heat contributed to a decline in virus cases from a horrific early peak. But few experts were duped into thinking that the pandemic was over, least of all leading virologists.

While public health officials scrambled to advise governments on managing successive waves of a pandemic, elite research institutions and pharmaceutical companies continued their painstaking work on life-saving vaccines. But the world was still months away from a breakthrough, so life in our Covid bubble continued.

Back in Yorkshire, I had the unedifying experience of observing Covid-related bail arrangements. While most 'at risk' folk continued to shield or limit their social interaction, I still had to wander up to York Police Station to report to the same bored-looking civilian police staff on Mondays and Fridays.

I got to know the staffers well. They were friendly and, after a time, we began to joke about my regular 'pilgrimage'. Initially, I'd enter the police station wearing a protective mask and briefly remove it to confirm my identity.

At an early stage, two of the civilian staff realised that I lived next door to North Yorkshire Police's chief constable, Lisa Winward.

"Maybe just pop next door and get the chief constable to sign your forms, Paul," one joked. "It would save us a job. Although I'm not sure the chief will be keen on more paperwork: she's trying to reduce the burden!"

I laughed. "But if I did that, I'd have no station gossip to share with your boss next time I see her," I replied jokingly.

Several weeks later, a senior official must have worried that too many people on bail were removing their facemasks inside the station. So a new system of Covid-related identification was introduced.

This involved me walking up to the police station door, maskless, before giving a 'thumbs up' to the staffers who stood directly behind the security glass with their bail list. It was a necessary measure, but it all looked comical. After a while, the civvies and I started to have fun with the new regime. They often struggled to keep a straight face at the sight of me exaggeratedly strolling towards them, back straight and knees slightly bent like Charlie Chaplin, while holding my thumbs aloft and grinning.

Staff would then sign the bail book for me. Often, they'd pretend not to hear anything I said from behind the glass – exacting revenge for my shoddy comic performances. It was good-natured fun and took my mind off the fact that my court worries were not over.

★ ★ ★

The Court of Appeal exists to review decisions taken by judges in England and Wales. It is the accountability mechanism through which expert and independent judges – some of the finest minds in the profession – assess whether the original judge came to the correct verdict.

Before a full Court of Appeal hearing can proceed, an independent judge must first determine that the contested verdict merits review.

In my case, the Court of Appeal was asked to review Judge Ikram's decision-making based on the evidence that was presented to him – rather than any fresh evidence.

As Keith Wood said at an early stage: "What we must do is show that Judge Ikram was entirely wrong to approve the extradition request given what was in front of him."

This brings us to Judge Ikram's verdict.

★ ★ ★

My lawyers asked Judge Ikram to consider dismissing the EAW on nine grounds, with four of them central to our argument.

Firstly, my lawyers argued the legal requirements for issuing an EAW were not met because Spain's application contained details of at least four alleged crimes for which my arrest was not sought. Remember, Spain's disorganised EAW initially referred to one alleged offence of fraud, before inexplicably going on to infer I had committed five or six crimes: including 'participation in a criminal organisation', 'swindling' and 'counterfeiting of currency'. I knew that none of Spain's claims was accurate. Still, extradition law requires judicial authorities to stipulate exactly how many crimes a requested person is sought for. My lawyers argued the 2018 EAW cleverly referred to crimes allegedly committed by other members of the Tenerife mafia, to make it appear there was a greater weight of evidence against me.

Judge Ikram took the view that Spain's EAW was clear on this point and valid.

He concluded: "I find that the warrant clearly states that the Requested Person is wanted for a single offence as defined under Spanish law as per box C of the EAW, 'a continuous crime of fraud'..."

Secondly, Judge Ikram dismissed my lawyers' assertion that the EAW lacked clarity about the maximum sentence facing me if extradited. Spain's EAW stated that I faced up to fifteen years in prison. But the document was unclear on whether that related to Spain's initial allegation that I had committed one offence; whether it described Spain's later reference to six crimes; or whether the maximum sentence was based on some combination of between one and six offences.

Spain's document was an incomprehensible mess. It was the firm view of my lawyers that the RFFI process only served to further muddy the waters.

But once again, Judge Ikram backed Spain. "The Requested Person faces the one allegation which carries a maximum 15-year sentence. I am satisfied that the other maximum sentences that are referred to are not in relation to the matter the Requested Person faces. They are irrelevant in the context of this case," he concluded.

But if they were "irrelevant" to my case, then why had Spain listed so many alternatives in *my* EAW and supporting documents?

As my legal team read through Judge Ikram's official verdict, glaring points of dispute emerged.

Thirdly, my lawyers argued that, given the betrayal I suffered at the hands of the CGI and Judge Garzon, including deceit over whether I had been a suspect from the moment I met them in 2001, I stood little chance of receiving a fair trial in Spain. Under Article 6 of the European Convention on Human Rights (ECHR), signed by the UK and Spain, every European citizen has a right to a fair trial. This includes the expectation that cases are heard by an 'independent' and 'impartial' tribunal.

According to my lawyers, Judge Garzon's U-turn in 2007, when he indicted me despite having treated me as a protected witness for six years, was a glaring example of how Spain had breached my Article 6 rights.

Based on Professor Campaner's assessment of Spanish law and documentation, our argument was that if Spanish authorities genuinely considered me a suspect from the day I met Munoz and Esteban, then I had been denied critical rights from that very moment: because they had not informed me that I was a suspect and allowed me the right to remain silent. Neither the CGI nor Garzon had treated me as a suspect in 2001, of course. But they were committed to that lie after Garzon's 2007 *volte-face*.

"A key part of the Requested Person's argument is that in being treated a witness, he has been denied the safeguards that must be afforded to a person who was a suspect or should have been treated as a suspect," Judge Ikram noted.

"I have considered carefully the report of Dr Jaime Campaner. He eloquently argues whether the Requested Person should have been treated as a suspect, rather than as witness and the conduct of Judge Garzon. He, however, also gives evidence that the Requested Person will have an opportunity to have a lawyer at trial, give evidence and challenge the admissibility of any evidence unlawfully obtained.

"I find, ultimately, that whether the Requested Person should have been treated as a suspect or defendant with the rights of a suspect (right of silence, access to legal advice etc.), can only be determined by the trial court after testing of the evidence.

"Similarly, whether any evidence secured is admissible against him, is also, in my judgment, a matter for the trial court. I can properly assume that the Requested Person will receive a fair trial in Spain. He will be entitled to argue all the points he makes here at his trial. He can appeal as he has done previously. He will get a fair hearing on appeal in the Spanish legal system."

In other words, my argument that I would not get a fair trial in Spain could only be tested by me being extradited, going on trial in Madrid and launching an appeal in Spain if I did not receive a fair trial!

For me, it was an extraordinary verdict that highlighted a glaring weakness in the modern judicial system: judges, barristers and solicitors are so intrinsically tied to 'legal logic' that common sense can get cast aside. The argument that a UK court could only test whether I would receive a fair trial in Spain by sending me to Spain ignored the catastrophic impact of one of two potential outcomes: that any prosecution in Spain would not be fair. In those circumstances, I'd be sent to a Spanish prison and face the daunting prospect of trying to prove a miscarriage of justice from inside the very country that had illegally imprisoned me!

Judge Ikram's verdict followed a logic. But in my opinion, it failed any common sense test. It was almost as if Judge Ikram seemed content for me to be used as a legal lab experiment: "Let's see whether this fella actually does receive a fair trial in Spain. If he does not, he can pick up the pieces of his shattered life afterwards."

Fourth and finally, Judge Ikram was asked to consider whether, all evidence considered, Spain's extradition request was an 'abuse of process'. My legal team effectively invited the judge to review whether Spain had acted in bad faith in pursuing a prosecution against me.

Again, this in part boiled down to Judge Ikram's view of whether I had been a protected witness before Judge Garzon decided to indict me in 2007.

Incredibly, despite the detailed witness evidence provided by Vidal and Sarah Hill, and the many documents my lawyers submitted, including my discussions with CGI agents, Judge Ikram ruled that I was not a protected witness. Moreover, the UK judge appeared uncomfortable with the idea that Judge Garzon was corrupt – despite the undeniable evidence that Garzon was later found guilty of, and disbarred for, obtaining evidence illegally.

To get to his position, Judge Ikram again defaulted to the idea that I could make my argument about whether the CGI and Garzon obtained my evidence illegally – and therefore question the admissibility of evidence – in Spain. The judge's default position was that there was no proof that Spain had lied in correspondence with his court and that I had nothing to fear about going to Spain.

"I find no evidence of bad faith on the part of the Spanish Judicial Authority," Judge Ikram observed. "It is common ground that the Requested Person came forward voluntarily to give information and co-operated with the Spanish police. Why he did that might be a matter to be determined by the Spanish trial court. There came a time when his status was changed from a witness to a suspect. Such a change of position is known here and not, in itself, evidence of bad faith.

"I do not find that he was a protected witness. Further information states that he did not have this status. Whether he should have been treated as witness or suspect or defendant is a matter for the trial court. The means by which evidence was obtained and its admissibility is a matter that can only properly be determined by the trial court.

"I find no abuse of the court process."

Rough justice? Mark Summers QC had already warned Spain that the battle was far from over.

"We'll see you in the High Court," he told the Spanish at Westminster. And so it was.

* * *

Despite being one step closer to a prison cell in Spain, I felt surprisingly relaxed about having to go to the Royal Courts of Justice, which hears extradition appeals, to win my case.

But I'd be a liar if I claimed I did not have low moments after the Westminster defeat. There were occasions when I found myself sitting at home while Gill was out, or lying awake at night, catastrophising the final outcome. Professor Campaner had already informed me that, if I was extradited, the likelihood of being held on remand in Spain was low due to my age. So I knew that I stood a good chance of being bailed and ordered to remain in Spain, even if I was shoved onto a Madrid-bound plane.

Nonetheless, that did not eliminate all thoughts of what a Spanish prison cell looks like. I'd read a lot about Alcala Meco Prison on the outskirts of Madrid, where Mohamed Derbah had been remanded years ago, and it sounded horrendous. According to Spain's EAW application, I faced up to fifteen years inside if found guilty. Believe me, even as an innocent man, that plays on your mind: usually around 2am!

Professor Campaner had also agreed to represent me in Spain if I was extradited. His potential appointment was a no-brainer: he knew the case well and had concluded that my evidence was inadmissible. In fact, he'd concluded that the Spanish police and Judge Garzon had likely acted illegally. "I'm very confident that we'd get the case against you kicked out of Spain's courts before any trial, Paul," Professor Campaner explained over the phone one evening.

He oozed confidence and authority without ever sounding arrogant. I knew he'd be an exceptional backup plan.

But Mark, George and Keith always believed they stood a good chance of winning my case at the Court of Appeal, and acted quickly to reassure me after the loss at Westminster.

* * *

After my appeal papers were lodged, weeks of further Covid-related delays turned to months. The pandemic had not only left a trail of health-related devastation: its associated lockdowns and changed working practices meant most UK public bodies experienced huge backlogs.

The courts were no exception. Few staff could work from court buildings, which were often closed to the public. Jury trials were cancelled because of emergency rules over social distancing, leaving courtrooms empty and stressed-out lawyers able only to complete pre-hearing paperwork. Many older judges with health conditions were also forced to shield themselves at home. At the same time, any court staff who contracted Coronavirus had to self-isolate.

The backlog of unheard crown court trials alone reached 57,000 across England and Wales by mid-2021, with many defendants, victims and witnesses expected to wait up to four years from the date of their alleged offences.

Magistrates, High Court, Court of Appeal and Supreme Court cases were also severely disrupted. Thankfully, my appeal case was of a non-criminal nature and no jury was required. That meant the likely delay was shorter.

The death toll associated with Covid-19 globally continued to soar as more transmissible mutations of the virus emerged, with developing states among the hardest hit. What the world needed was vaccines: and several were developed, tested and rolled out astonishingly quickly.

Before Covid-19, no infectious disease vaccine had been produced in less than a few years. But states worldwide invested massively in research and testing programmes, often based on existing vaccines for coronaviruses found in animals.

As late as February 2020, the World Health Organisation said it did not expect an effective Covid-19 vaccine to be available for at least 18 months. Yet on 2 December 2020, the UK became the first western state to approve a vaccine developed by Pfizer-BioNTech. Others soon followed, and the more significant challenge became scaling up production and getting the life-saving liquids into the arms of desperate populations.

Unfortunately, it was all too late for the UK to prevent a huge 'second wave' of deaths in the winter of 2020/21. Early in January, Gill and I again found ourselves holed up in our apartment after the government announced a further lockdown designed to save lives.

However, boosted by restrictions on population movements and socialising, states wealthy and fortunate enough to have early access to Covid-19 vaccines gradually began to win the battle against virus-related deaths. By late Spring 2021, talk turned to how the UK would carefully re-open during the remainder of the pandemic.

Life gradually began to return to 'normal'.

In late spring, Keith Wood received confirmation that the Court of Appeal would proceed with the case as a 'rolled up' hearing lasting just one day. 'Rolled up' meant my application to appeal, and the appeal itself, would be heard together. Often, a single judge decides whether an application to appeal has merit and two or more judges later hear the actual appeal. But with the courts facing huge backlogs, a decision was taken to hear my entire case in one sitting.

Again, my lawyers had submitted a whopping nine grounds of appeal against Judge Ikram's verdict – including the same four we believed were central to the magistrates' court hearings. Initially, I wondered whether my legal team had overcooked our application. But Connor, the journalist, soon put me straight.

"They should throw everything, including the kitchen sink, at your appeal, Paul," the hack said. "This is your last chance to win in the UK. But it also happens to be your best chance. Your lawyers have been preparing for this.

"No offence meant to Judge Ikram, but Court of Appeal judges are generally better informed than time-poor magistrates. More than one judge will review the evidence and they are meticulous at assessing case law."

I already felt reassured by what I'd heard, but Connor signed off with a motivational flourish.

"Besides, Mark Summers has an excellent record at the Court of Appeal. He worked the Julian Assange case, remember?"

It was true. In January 2021, Mark Summers QC was part of the legal team which, at the Court of Appeal, ensured Wikileaks founder Assange was not extradited to the US to face espionage charges.

Assange's defence team successfully argued that, due to his deteriorating mental health, there was a serious risk the Wikileaks founder would commit suicide if taken to the US – despite Washington's unproven allegations that he'd endangered intelligence assets' lives when he published classified information.

As a former intelligence asset who'd reluctantly made my role public, I had some sympathy for Washington's argument. But there seemed little doubt that Assange was not fit to be extradited.

With Mark Summers QC as lead counsel, I knew my future remained in expert hands. It was time to focus on the key grounds of appeal.

★ ★ ★

Firstly, my lawyers revisited the idea that Spain's attempt to prosecute me represented an 'abuse of process' and 'bad faith'. This was based on our contention that Spain had manipulated its case against Mohamed Derbah, so that a prosecution witness and undercover state agent (me) was forced to give evidence against the alleged mafia boss – and that the judge who contrived the situation, Garzon, had since been disbarred.

The following five grounds of appeal, numbered two to six on Court of Appeal documents, argued that Judge Ikram had overlooked significant inaccuracies in Spain's EAW application. These included claims that Spain had failed to provide sufficient details about my alleged crimes and no logical explanation for the length of sentence I faced.

This section of the appeal also argued Judge Ikram ordered my extradition for alleged crimes listed in the EAW that the Spanish confirmed (through the RFFI process) I was not wanted for.

Another appeal point asserted that I had been denied my fundamental human rights when Garzon and the CGI effectively treated me as a suspect in 2001, including my right to remain silent.

Keith, George and Mark had worked tirelessly to ensure the challenges to Judge Ikram's verdict were supported by significant evidence – statements, witnesses, audio transcripts and more – that had been available to the magistrates court.

It just remained to hear what two expert judges thought.

On 19 May 2021, I travelled to London by train and checked in to my usual Marylebone hotel. Gill and Sarah chose not to join me due to strict anti-Covid measures limiting the number of people who could attend court. Besides, I knew I would be travelling home to York the following day: I had already been made aware that the Court of Appeal would reserve its judgment.

The following morning, I showered, shaved, changed into a smart suit, arranged to meet Paul Jnr and hailed a London taxi to the Royal Courts of Justice. I'd made so many visits to courthouses throughout my life, and had so many false dawns, that it wasn't until I slumped into the back of the cab that it occurred to me:

Today was *the* big day. What the court heard today would decide whether I would be ordered to Spain.

* * *

Lord Justice Singh is regarded as one of the finest legal minds in Europe. He was part of an elite team of barristers who established the influential Matrix Chambers in 2000, specialising in human rights cases with an international dimension. Other founder members of Matrix included Cherie Booth, wife of the then-UK prime minister Tony Blair, and future director of public prosecutions and peer Ken Macdonald.

Rabinder Singh grew up in a working-class area of Bristol before obtaining a double-first in law at Cambridge. He was called to the bar in 1989 and swiftly established an interest in cases involving the abuse of power. Given my past as an offshore finance consultant who specialised in minimising clients' tax liabilities, readers might find it ironic that Lord Justice Singh also acted as junior counsel to the Inland Revenue early in his career!

In 2011, Singh was appointed as a high court judge. He became the first non-white judge to sit at the Court of Appeal when elevated in 2017 and has since reviewed many high-profile cases, including a controversial challenge to the UK's hastily implement anti-Coronavirus measures in 2020.

Lord Justice Singh is a man of fearsome intellect masked by an impressively patient approach to court proceedings. But nothing can quite prepare attendees for the visual impact of the judge entering his courtroom. As his surname indicates, Rabinder Singh hails from Britain's vibrant Indian Sikh community, and he long ago forsook the traditional courtroom wig in favour of a magnificent, pristine white turban framing his perfectly groomed white facial hair – including full moustache and beard.

As he entered Courtroom Three on 20 May 2021, those in attendance stood. Lord Justice Singh wore his silk robe loosely flung over his shoulders. The combination of swirling gown, striking turban and bold whiskers made an imposing sight.

From alongside me, I heard the only journalist in court break the silence. "Now *that* is a look that says: 'I'm in charge'," the scribe said admiringly.

I glanced across, smiled and nodded. He was right: Lord Justice Singh was the chief judge appointed to my case.

As Lord Justice Singh took his seat, I glanced to his right and saw the second judge reviewing the case: Mrs Justice Steyn. As the daughter of a former law lord, it would be easy to dismiss Karen Steyn as somebody whose privilege presented her with the fast-track up the judicial pecking order. But such dismissive thinking belies Steyn's talent.

She was called to the bar in 1995, appointed QC in 2014 and elevated to the Queen's Bench Division of the High Court in 2019. She also had a strong background in cases involving European issues, which made her ideal for an appeal against an EAW.

With the two judges and three court clerks seated, the day's proceedings began.

* * *

It soon became clear that the court session would not be divided into 'permission to appeal' followed by 'appeal'. Instead, Lord Justice Singh and Mrs Justice Steyn would hear all of the issues and evidence together – thereby maximising the time spent exploring the key points of dispute.

Mark Summers QC and Daniel Sternberg, familiar foes, listened and nodded as the judges outlined the timetable. At an early stage, Lord Justice Singh also revealed that he would release the 'logger' – a clerk who logs official verdicts or statements – from proceedings because he was wanted elsewhere in the Royal Courts.

"I will not be making a judgment today," the judge announced.

Keith, George and Mark had forewarned me that the Court of Appeal verdict could take up to six weeks. After hearing the judge confirm he had no intention of sending me anywhere soon, I relaxed back into my seat. As much as one can 'relax' on a seemingly ancient and solid wooden bench. The Royal Courts of Justice may well be a masterpiece of Victorian gothic design, but the windowless and musty smelling courtrooms are far from comfortable.

The discomfort broke my concentration. I glanced around the room and noticed that I was closely watched by the same scruffy-looking man from the Spanish Judicial Authority who had attended court in Westminster. It's no exaggeration to say that Spaniard looked as though he'd slept in his crumpled suit every day since those hearings. His ragged appearance clashed somewhat with the sartorial elegance of the judges, barristers and solicitors – and would have made my mother wonder aloud whether he should have been the man 'in the dock'.

* * *

At an early stage, Mark Summers QC reminded the judges that Spain had barely contested the critical claims that Vidal, Sarah Hill and I had made at Westminster Magistrates: that I had approached the Spanish authorities with information on Mohamed Derbah; that I was a prosecution witness and Spanish state asset or informant for six years; that CGI officers had helped me to establish an office on the Spanish mainland and asked me to spy on other clients suspected of criminality; that several years later the Spanish authorities added me to an indictment against the alleged Tenerife mafia; and that the Spanish authorities had refused to confirm my asset status before I was jailed in 2008.

Mark presented another strong argument that Spain's attempt to prosecute me was an abuse of process and disproportionate. Drawing on Jaime Campaner's expert opinion, Summers reiterated that Spain was now wedded to its lie that I was a suspect from day one, even though neither the CGI nor Judge Garzon had confirmed this between 2001 and 2007.

My barrister asserted that, in providing evidence about the period from 2001 to 2007, Spain had provided a "palpably untruthful account of the chronology".

Summers was building up to his key point: that Spain had betrayed me in 2007 and lied to the UK courts since – meaning there was little chance of me receiving a fair trial in Madrid, as Judge Ikram had concluded.

Lord Justice Singh asked more detailed questions than Judge Ikram about the nature of my relationship with the Spanish authorities. But as Mark talked both judges through the details of my nine grounds of appeal, it quickly became apparent that Lord Justice Singh and Mrs Justice Steyn were most concerned about the content of Spain's EAW and RFFIs.

Turning his attention to Spain's wild and contradictory claims that I'd committed between one and six offences, Singh appeared angry at the huge inconsistencies and Spain's confusing explanations for them. The judge was also concerned that Spain had listed on 'my' EAW a string of offences that appeared to relate to other alleged members of the Tenerife mafia.

Summers summarised the situation perfectly: "The effect [of the EAW], is that Judge Ikram has returned Mr Blanchard for offences even Spain does not accuse him of!"

The court adjourned for lunch with my barrister having sown potent seeds of doubt in the judges' minds.

* * *

Daniel Sternberg rose to his feet and lent over his paperwork as the post-lunch session began. Keen to reinforce Judge Ikram's verdict, Sternberg attempted to dismiss concerns over the validity of Spain's arrest warrant.

"This EAW *does* include sufficient information amounting to an offence in a Category One jurisdiction..." he began. But before he could continue, Sternberg was interrupted by a stern-looking Lord Justice Singh.

"But a reasonable reader might think that there are three or four offences," the judge said. "Not one."

At this point, Mrs Justice Steyn also joined in. She asked how the CPS's stance could be consistent with Spain's most recent RFFI document, which cited three offences?

Mark Summers pointed out that Judge Ikram ordered extradition on the basis that there was a single alleged offence of fraud, whereas Sternberg suggested to the court that it was membership of a criminal organisation. None of it stacked up.

There was also a "complete mismatch", Summers said, between the alleged offences and Spain's declarations on likely length of sentence.

After three years of arguments, every lawyer in the room realised that they were still confused by Spain's warrant.

For the first time since the case began, the usually assured Sternberg looked lost for words. Here was a high-class lawyer forced to deal with glaring lies and oversights in Spain's application. I leant back on my bench, intrigued as to how the prosecutor would reply. He looked down at his paperwork and back up at the judges, stealing precious time to think: like an elite-level poker player trying to work out how to win after being dealt a two and a seven 'off suit'. But even Sternberg could offer nothing substantial in response.

I glanced across at Keith, who smiled and nodded.

At that moment, it dawned on me that from the day the EAW was issued, the most likely route to victory in court had been the inaccuracies in the extradition application forced upon the CPS by Spain's obsessive lies. Spain's case against me was fabricated. I'd committed no crime simply by moving Mohamed Derbah's money. So in their desperation to use my evidence against Derbah, Spain had variously invented one, three, four, five or six 'crimes' to try to convince the UK court of my guilt. But they'd been caught out because EAW law requires states to be precise about alleged offences.

To his credit, Sternberg made a decent fist of his remaining evidence. On Spain's behalf, the CPS argued that Professor Campaner's conclusions about the admissibility of my evidence were issues for the Spanish courts.

In his final reply before the judge's adjourned to consider their verdict, Mark Summers QC accused Judge Ikram of going "off-piste".

"The EAW is completely incoherent, suggesting one offence and listing five or six. In the end, the judges and Mr Sternberg are simply left guessing," he observed.

"The suggestion that this court should choose one of six possibilities is without merit. You might get it right. You might not," he warned. "This is a compelling ground of appeal."

And with that, the appeal proceedings were over.

Outside the courtroom, my legal team were upbeat. Nobody dared predict what the judges would conclude. Still, Keith, George and Mark felt confident Judge Ikram's extradition order would be quashed. Keith even raised the idea of starting the appeal against my 2008 convictions.

I didn't want to make assumptions. But the day's proceedings could not have gone much better.

* * *

On the train home to York that evening, I fell into a deep sleep. It's unusual for me to nod off on a train journey – I'm usually too distracted by annoying passengers – but I guess the stress of the previous few months had finally caught up with me.

You don't really pause to think about physical exhaustion when you're fighting a three-year legal battle to avoid unjust extradition and imprisonment. But on that journey home, I reminded myself that I'd done absolutely everything I could to win that battle. I'd made the odd mistake over the preceding three years, sure: but I'd fought Spain's application with everything I had. While I still did not know the final outcome, I finally felt at ease knowing that every sleepless night, every tactical discussion with lawyers, every request for documents, every hurried journey to London to collect evidence, every penny spent translating and enhancing audios for court purposes , every long phone call to family and friends, every missed social engagement and every evening spent pacing around my home refining and rehearsing my legal argument...had been worth it.

My subconscious mind must have seized its first opportunity to truly relax, because I slept like a log on the train. I awoke with a start as we pulled into York Station, had to sprint down the carriage and disembarked with just seconds to spare before the driver headed for Edinburgh!

I was home. But for how long?

June 2021 whizzed by in a whir of social activity. By early summer, most of my family had received two doses of Covid-19 vaccine and felt confident meeting up following the relaxation of government rules on social distancing.

In the developed world, vaccines were a game-changer and eased pressures on health systems. But on our TV screens, images of the virus still tearing through states such as India acted as a sharp reminder that most of the world's population remained vulnerable.

* * *

23 June 2021

I'd just put the key into the front door of my apartment, laden with groceries, when my mobile phone rang. Hurriedly, I rushed inside and answered. I heard Keith's unmistakable Yorkshire inflexion.

"It's not official yet, Paul, and the judgment can't be made public until it is formally lodged by the Court of Appeal next week. But...you've won!"

I dropped the groceries and let out an almighty roar of relief. They could probably hear me celebrating in Leeds. Or even Madrid!

* * *

"You've won on three grounds out of nine," Keith explained once I'd calmed down. "But at this stage, what we've been sent is a draft judgment. All parties will check the document for factual accuracy before the judges' verdict becomes official. But there's no escaping it: Judge Ikram's extradition ruling will be quashed."

Keith sounded as delighted as me, his soaring professional reputation buoyed by another significant success. But gradually, his tone turned more serious.

"I need to explain the judgment to you in detail, though. In theory, Spain could try again to have you extradited. It's unlikely to happen any time soon, and it may now never happen. But there are a few points in the judgment that we need to consider..."

* * *

Keith and I chatted for almost an hour.
We had won the case on three grounds:

- Spain's confusion or obfuscation over the number of alleged offences
- Judge Ikram ordering extradition for alleged crimes of which I was not accused
- Spain's lack of clarity over the length of sentence I faced

Lord Justice Singh's verdict was unequivocal. It stated: "The EAW is fundamentally incoherent and defective because it is impossible for the reasonable reader to know for what offence or offences the Applicant's extradition is requested (or even how many offences)."

The lies told by the CGI and the Spanish Judicial Authority's officials, and their scattergun approach to inventing criminal allegations against me after 2007, had finally caught up with them.

Providing more detail, Lord Justice Singh concluded: "[The EAW] purports to refer to only one offence but in fact sets out five and possibly six separate offences, namely, (i) fraud, contrary to articles 248 and 249 of the Criminal Code, (ii) money-laundering, contrary to article 301; (iii) forgery of, and fraudulent use of, credit cards, contrary to articles 386 and 389; (iv) threats and coercion, contrary to articles 169, 170 and 172; (v) perverting the course of justice, contrary to article 404; and (vi) participation in a criminal organisation.

"The Judge [Ikram] held that the "one" offence was a continuous fraud but Mr Sternberg submitted to us that it was participation in a criminal organisation. It is impossible for the reasonable reader to know for what offence or offences the Applicant is to be extradited.

"The confusion is compounded by the fact that it is impossible to work out how the maximum sentence of fifteen years specified in the EAW was calculated."

As the Court of Appeal judges pointed out, Spain's EAW variously described maximum sentences of twelve, six and five years.

"No combination of these figures results in the maximum of 15 years which was mentioned in the EAW," the Court of Appeal observed.

Referring to their verdict that Judge Ikram effectively ordered my extradition for offences Spain had not accused me of, the appeal judges stated: "Mr Summers [also] submits that the approach of the Judge [Ikram] has resulted in extradition of the Applicant being ordered in respect of offences of which he is not accused and for which extradition has not been sought. He submits that the information provided in response to requests for further information...abandoned at least three of the alleged offences which were mentioned in the EAW. I accept that submission."

Of course, the reason Spain's application was such a mess is that I'd not committed a crime on Tenerife, and there should never have been a plan for sentencing. The CGI and Judge Garzon knew it – and that's why they used me as an asset and informant for six years.

But after the CGI and Garzon betrayed me, Spain took a calculated and sinister decision to throw as much dirt at me as possible. Spanish officials got carried away with inventing offences I'd allegedly committed – resulting in claims that I'd committed any number between one and six crimes. In the end, their lies and deceits were so voluminous that even those responsible for seeking my extradition could not present them with any consistency.

I knew the truth about all of this from the day Judge Garzon added me to the indictment against Mohamed Derbah. But it had taken fourteen years to successfully highlight it in a courtroom.

There were downsides to the Court of Appeal verdict, Keith advised. Six of our nine grounds of appeal were rejected: including claims that Spain's attempt to prosecute me represented bad faith and an abuse of process, and that I'd been denied fundamental human rights if Spain's (belated) assertion that I was always a suspect was true.

The Court of Appeal ruled that these were both matters for Spanish courts to determine. I was disappointed that my lawyers' arguments did not convince the appeal judges because I felt we'd provided significant evidence of corruption.

Agonisingly, this meant that Spain could re-apply for my extradition. I knew that some people would argue I'd won the case on 'technicalities': Spain's failure to submit a complete, logical and accurate EAW.

But in reality, Spain's confused and contradictory EAW could be attributed to the mountain of lies told by its officials and their callous desperation to extradite me regardless of the truth. What was printed on the warrant was inaccurate and contrived enough. But once my lawyers requested more information, Spanish officials panicked and made up even more nonsense.

"It was fraud, Britain."

"No, it was membership of a criminal organisation."

"It was both, Britain."

"No, it was all three *plus* credit card forgery."

"Oh, plus it was threats of coercion."

"...and, I remember now, perverting the course of justice."

"Actually, can we just assume it was all of the above? Just sign the warrant, Britain, will you?"

Similarly, the appeal judges attacked Spain's inconsistencies over the likely sentence facing me. According to the EAW and RFFI documents, it was either twelve years, six years, five years or a combination of all three: twenty-six years.

"No combination of these figures results in the maximum of 15 years which was mentioned in the EAW," the Court of Appeal judges observed.

So even though, in theory, Spain could re-apply for my extradition, officials in Madrid know that they will face even more scrutiny of their past lies at any future British court hearing. Unpicking the colossal, contradictory mess created by Madrid's 2018 EAW and subsequent RFFIs will be nigh-on impossible.

No doubt some officials in Madrid will think: "We'll just re-submit the extradition application and provide simple figures for alleged crimes and sentences."

Indeed, just days after the Court of Appeal verdict, Professor Campaner obtained a letter from Daniel Sternberg to the Spanish Judicial Authority, outlining why Spain had lost and how officials in Madrid could submit a new extradition application. I don't blame Daniel Sternberg for sending the letter. That's his job, and he was merely closing his file following defeat at the Court of Appeal.

But even if Spanish officials create new documentation which, in their minds, address the flaws outlined in the Court of Appeal verdict, they face the daunting task of explaining to a British judge why their original EAW application contained so many lies they have since dropped, amended or inflated further. My legal team will contest any future extradition application during another process likely to last several years – and the evidence threshold Spain would need to exhibit in court cannot be met: because I did not commit the crimes that Spain alleges.

In addition, officials in Madrid are now aware of the expert advice on Spanish law that my legal team received from Professor Campaner. So they now know that almost *all* of the evidence I handed to the CGI and Judge Garzon between 2001 and 2007 is inadmissible in a Spanish court – and that police, intelligence and judicial figures potentially acted illegally in gathering the evidence. A potential can of worms, not to mention a media storm, awaits them in Spain.

As one UK journalist said to me in private after the Court of Appeal verdict was published: "Given the evidence now presented by appeal judges, what would be the point of Spain trying again? They'd risk further humiliation at the hands of media, lawyers and judges questioning their alleged deception."

* * *

The formal Court of Appeal judgment quashing Judge Ikram's extradition verdict was published on 30 June 2021. But, by then, I'd been celebrating quietly with my family for a week.

My success in overturning the extradition order received local and national media coverage, including the front page of my local newspaper, *The York Press*, which had previously sneered at my alleged role in a timeshare fraud. Thankfully, the paper's senior reporter spoke to me in detail after the Court of Appeal judgment and ran a positive story about my case.

On the morning *The York Press* was published, I was inside my local newsagents when none other than former Special Branch officer Andrew Blain wandered in. The front-page story was the talk of the town and, during a chat with the newsagent, I mentioned that I would appeal my 2008 convictions.

From behind me, Blain smiled and said: "Good luck." I think he meant it.

Shortly after the York Press coverage, Jon Austin, crime editor at the Sunday Express, contacted me. Jon had been following the case since the Westminster hearings, and we agreed to meet in London.

I have a lot of respect for Jon Austin. He is a rare breed among modern journalists: somebody who does the hard work of attending court, obtaining evidence and asking detailed questions before publishing material. Over coffee, Jon asked challenging questions – but gave me a fair hearing.

A week after our interview, Jon published a full-page article in the *Sunday Express* that focused on me handing the names of alleged criminals linked to Al-Qaeda and 7/7 to Europe's intelligence agencies before the London bombings in 2005.

As I explained to Jon, I've never believed that simply handing MI5 those names should have prevented incidents such as 7/7. To me, and most likely to intelligence agents, the bombers' names I handed over in late 2004 were unrecognisable. Just a couple of names among hundreds that intelligence agencies receive each month.

But I take offence to MI5's claim that the four 7/7 bombers were 'cleanskins' whose identities were entirely unknown to agents. That's not quite the case. But, intelligence agencies not being wholly transparent about information or their use of informants? That's the story of my life.

* * *

Stereotypically, a book such as this, assessing major incidents in one's life, tends to end with reflections from a wiser and older author suggesting that life is a 'journey' during which they have learned so much.

Initially, I wanted to avoid such giant clichés. But when I sat down and reflected on what I've been through – the undoubted mistakes I've made, those I've incorrectly been blamed for, the people I've met and let down, and those who have let me down – I felt compelled to jot down a few observations.

Judge Ikram initially ordered my extradition to face a potential trial in Spain. But for what, exactly?

The answer may surprise some readers: I would have stood trial for helping the victims of Mohamed Derbah's alleged fraud.

Spain has described me as an international money launderer, fraudster, member of a mafia, forger, heavy and somebody who perverted the course of justice. Yet the truth is that in July 2001, I walked through the doors of Spain's police HQ and volunteered information on potential criminality by Mohamed Derbah and his entourage. I did it to assist the customers of Mohamed's timeshare and holiday-pack businesses who reported that they'd not received the benefits they signed up for.

Earlier in this book, I described how I confronted Mohamed Derbah because I could not see his 'client accounts': bank accounts from which his businesses would make disbursements to customers. In the warm afterglow of my Court of Appeal victory, it would be easy to paint myself as some sort of knight on a white horse, riding to the rescue of such customers.

I'm not a knight on a white horse, and I won't pretend to be. I'm Paul Blanchard, a three-times convicted ex-jailbird and former furnishings magnate turned offshore corporate adviser. I hope to overturn my convictions- but I've lived an eventful life, with many ups and downs. And I've made some stupid decisions. But the one thing I will never apologise for is standing up for the vulnerable, often elderly, customers who believed they were fleeced on Tenerife.

That is why I went to the Spanish police. I did so legally and in good faith. That does not make me a criminal.

At no time after I met Mohamed Derbah did he confirm or imply he created offshore companies to defraud customers. Indeed, to be clear: Mohamed Derbah has never been found guilty of fraud or any crime related to the events and allegations described in this book.

This is not Hollywood. Sinister and cliched plotting in smoke-filled rooms rarely happens in the real world. When I set up Derbah's companies and bank accounts, I had no idea he would be accused of serious fraud: never mind arms dealing or terror links. But over time, I grew suspicious of his activities.

Yet, for the past fifteen years, I have been described as somebody who laundered money on Derbah's behalf. Spain's claim that I was part of a mafia is a million miles from the truth.

I was an independent corporate consultant. I raised invoices for the services provided to Derbah, which totalled a mere £60,000, and I declared that sum for tax purposes. Forensic accountants working for UK-based police and economic crime units scrutinised my finances during my court and POCA proceedings. They accepted that Derbah paid me just £60,000. The police also acknowledged that I had no other hidden assets. In their desperation to prosecute Derbah, Spain's officials have never once paused to think about that. Most rational folk would say that £60,000 is a paltry income for an alleged mafia accountant – and they'd be right. I can think of much easier, and legal, ways to make £60,000!

I observed my legal duty and reported suspicions about Derbah's businesses. If Spain's authorities had proved fraud or theft, well, they could have seized Derbah's assets and repaid thousands of holidaymakers.

Yet Spain's criminal justice bodies fell out with their main prosecution witness – yours truly – and then embarked on a fifteen-year mission to deceive everybody about how and why. In doing so, officials in Madrid told lie after lie until, eventually, those deceits caught up with them at the Court of Appeal.

But the true cost of Spain's deceit has been enormous.

For trying to help, I lost my business, health, friends, reputation, wealth, liberty and the best years of my life. Authors like to write about 'journeys' towards justice or redemption. Mine has been exhausting. But unlike so many victims of the alleged frauds and terrorism that I fought to expose, I have lived long enough for some sort of justice to prevail.

RELATED WEBSITES

www.secretsofamafiawhistle-blower.com

*****

www.whitevillapublishing.com

*****

Paul Blanchard Associates
International Corporate Consultants
www.paulblachard.com

*****

Twitter: The Tax Fox

*****

Instagram
mafiawhistleblower

*****

The Cheavours
www.thecheavours.com